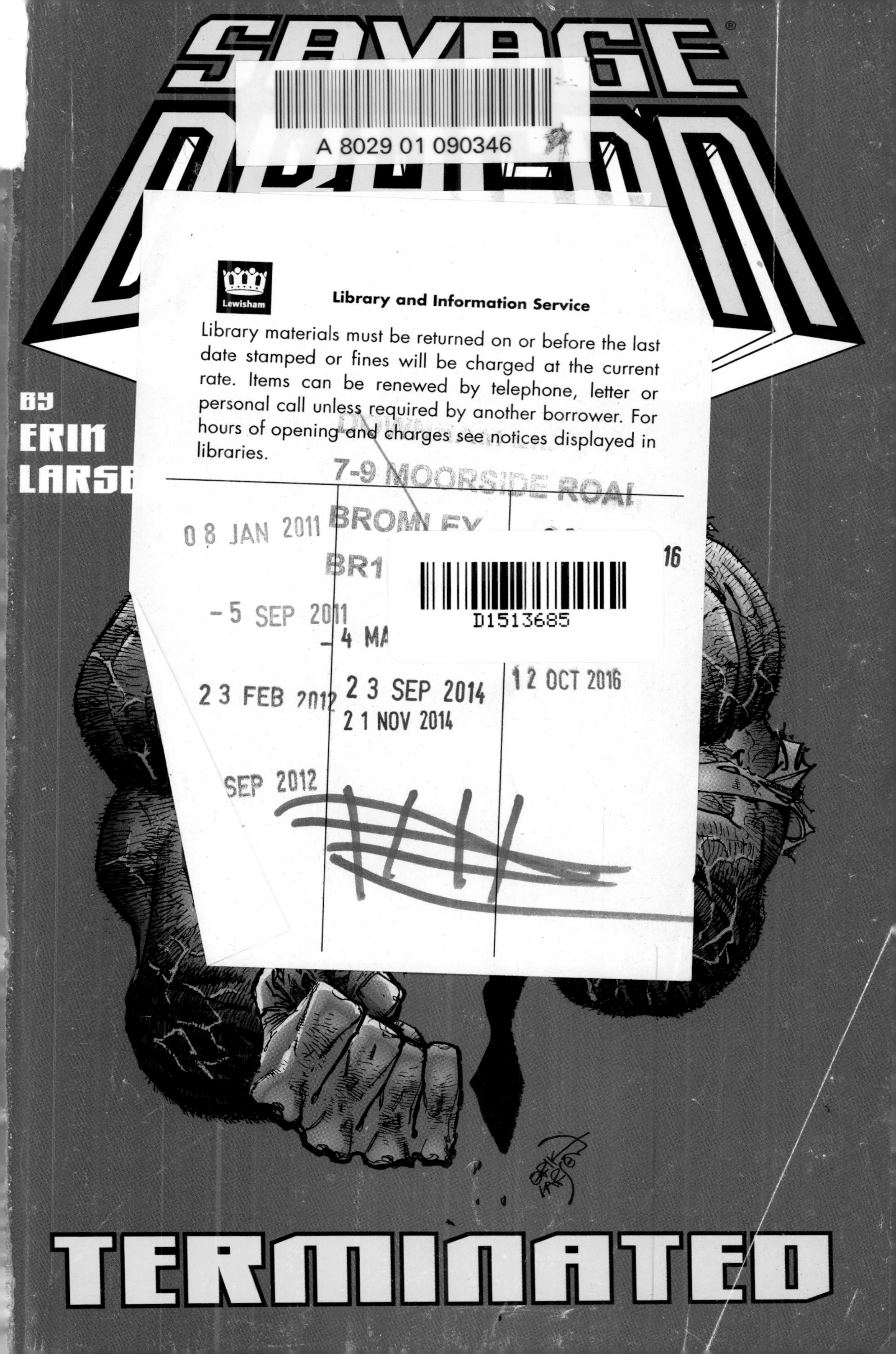
SAVAGE
BY
ERIK
LARSE
TERMINATED

SAVAGE DRAGON®

TERMINATED

ERIK LARSEN
Creator • Writer • Penciller • Inker

CHRIS ELIOPOULOS
Letterer

I.H.O.C
Colors

**REUBEN RUDE, ABEL MOUTON
ANTONIO KOHL, BILL ZINDEL
STEPHANE KRIESHOK,
LEA RUDE & JOHN ZAIA**

JOSH EICHORN
like Disco Lemonade

IMAGE COMICS

Jim Valentino	Publisher
Brent Braun	Director of Production
Eric Stephenson	Director of Marketing
Traci Hale	Controller/Foreign Licensing
Brett Evans	Art Director
Allen Hui	Web Developer
Cindie Espinoza	Accounting Assitant
Peter Mason Hauge	Traffic

SAVAGE DRAGON Vol. VIII: TERMINATED. FEBRUARY 2003. First Printing. Collecting Savage Dragon issues 34-40. Published by Image Comics office of publication 1071 N. Batavia St. Ste. A, Orange, CA 92867. Image and its logo are ® and © Image Comics, Inc. 2003. Savage Dragon and all related characters are ™ and © 2003 Erik Larsen. Mars Attacks® is a registered trademark of the Topps Company. Vanguard is copyright Erik Larsen and Gary Carlson. Hellboy is ™ and © Mike Mignola, 2003. All rights reserved.

WWW.IMAGECOMICS.COM

INTRODUCTION
BY ERIK LARSEN

I never intended the Dragon to stay a cop forever.

This may come as some kind of shock to those Savage Dragon fans that started reading the book from its inception or who watched the cartoon on the USA network, but it's the truth.

When I first conceived the Dragon as a kid, I drew a number of unpublished adventures featuring the character and he evolved over time. The last two stories that I drew were published in a fanzine called Graphic Fantasy that came out in 1982. I was 19 years old at the time.

Shortly thereafter, I moved on to working as a comic book professional. Ten years later, I left Marvel Comics and Spider-Man behind to go form Image Comics with a number of other comic book creators.

My goal from the start was to eventually get around to writing and drawing the adventures of the Dragon. THAT was the character I wanted to do more than any other! THAT was the guy whose adventures I'd chronicled for years prior to establishing a name for myself in this wacky industry.

Picking up where I left off was what I wanted to do most of all, but that presented a problem – you see, when I did Dragon stories years ago, I'd built it up to a certain point before taking an extended break. It wasn't as though I could simply reprint those stories to get readers caught up to speed – for one, they were written and drawn when I was a kid and were (by anybody's standard) pretty amateurish and for two, ALL of my unpublished comics were burned up in a fire a year before Image had formed! I couldn't print 'em if I wanted to – and I really didn't want to!

In his unpublished history, The Dragon went through numerous incarnations, was married twice and had three children, most of which were magically transformed into adults to become superheroes themselves. Starting where I left off was out of the question. To shoehorn in ALL of this as backstory that predated the new Savage Dragon adventures would be unnecessarily cumbersome and complicated and besides – it didn't make a lot of sense to begin with! I was in forth grade when I started this nonsense, after all and had the naiveté to go along with it! What I did have, however, was a character that I liked – just the way he was.

When I began Savage Dragon at Image my goal was to start from a different beginning and work toward where I'd left off. Dragon's adventures as a policeman made up the first chapter, the rest would follow.

The stories contained in this volume mark the end of Dragon's career as a law enforcement officer and prepare him for the life he would follow. Along the way, you'll be introduced to Mike Mignola's wonderful creation Hellboy and a number of characters from my own ever-expanding cast.

When I started the book, my intention was to run with Dragon being a cop for a couple years before having him move on to bigger things. As is usual, one story expanded to two and so on, until I'd done considerably more stories along these lines than I'd intended. Dragon spent nearly five years as a police officer. Fans grew comfortable with the idea and came to expect stories that were grounded in a semi-reality. Dragon fought criminals, not aliens from outer space. The stories from this book took him a step beyond the invisible boundaries that readers had set and expanded his role. Once Dragon fought giant sea Monsters and went into space, I knew he could never go back to writing parking tickets and kicking winos off park benches.

The stories here took the Dragon one step closer to my goal.

I hope you enjoy reading them as much as I enjoyed bringing them to you!

-Erik Larsen

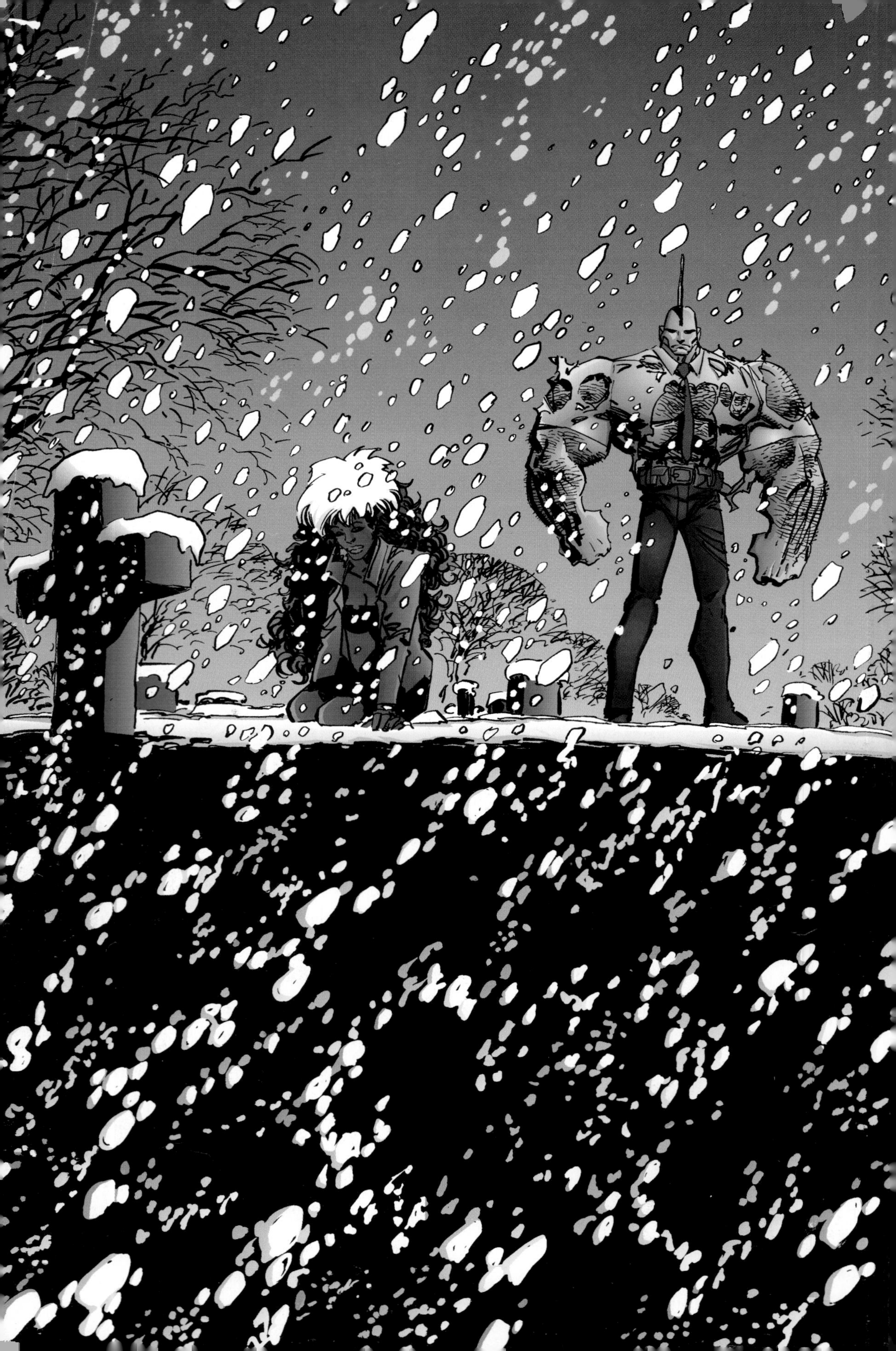

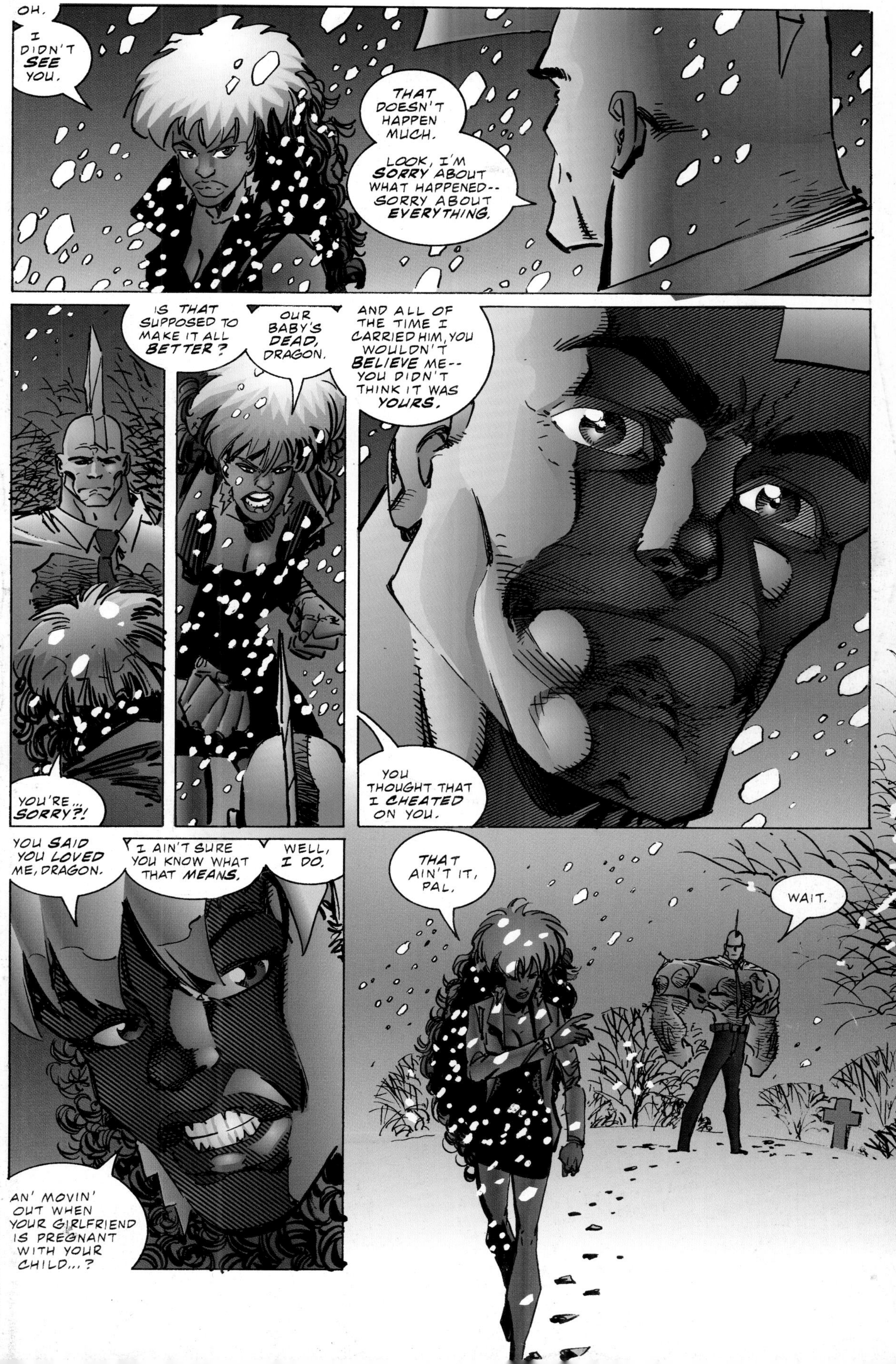
OH.
I DIDN'T SEE YOU.
THAT DOESN'T HAPPEN MUCH.
LOOK, I'M SORRY ABOUT WHAT HAPPENED-- SORRY ABOUT EVERYTHING.
YOU'RE... SORRY?!
IS THAT SUPPOSED TO MAKE IT ALL BETTER?
OUR BABY'S DEAD, DRAGON.
AND ALL OF THE TIME I CARRIED HIM, YOU WOULDN'T BELIEVE ME-- YOU DIDN'T THINK IT WAS YOURS.
YOU THOUGHT THAT I CHEATED ON YOU.
YOU SAID YOU LOVED ME, DRAGON.
I AIN'T SURE YOU KNOW WHAT THAT MEANS.
WELL, I DO.
AN' MOVIN' OUT WHEN YOUR GIRLFRIEND IS PREGNANT WITH YOUR CHILD...?
THAT AIN'T IT, PAL.
WAIT.

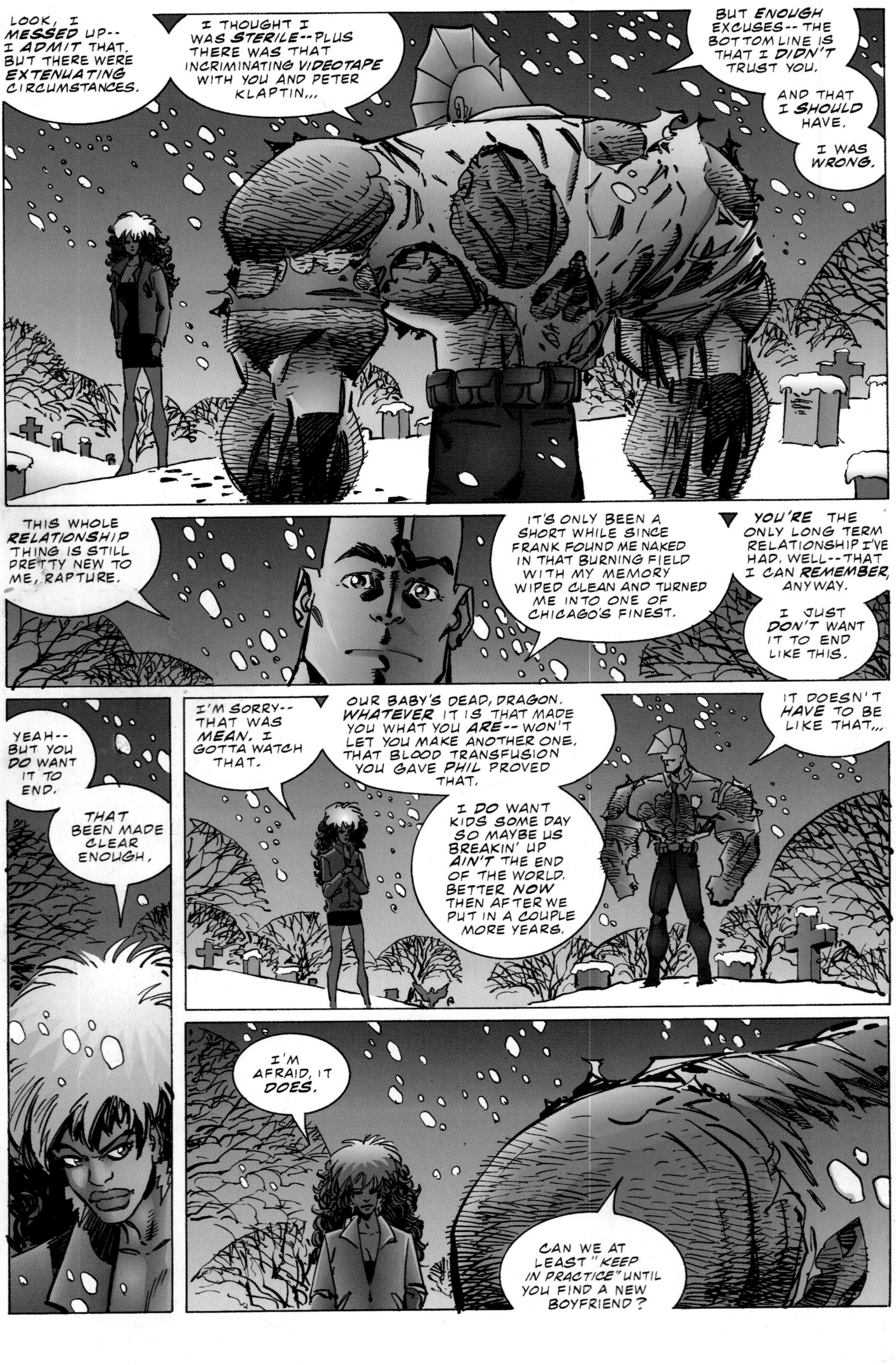
LOOK, I MESSED UP-- I ADMIT THAT. BUT THERE WERE EXTENUATING CIRCUMSTANCES.
I THOUGHT I WAS STERILE--PLUS THERE WAS THAT INCRIMINATING VIDEOTAPE WITH YOU AND PETER KLAPTIN...
BUT ENOUGH EXCUSES-- THE BOTTOM LINE IS THAT I DIDN'T TRUST YOU.
AND THAT I SHOULD HAVE.
I WAS WRONG.
THIS WHOLE RELATIONSHIP THING IS STILL PRETTY NEW TO ME, RAPTURE.
IT'S ONLY BEEN A SHORT WHILE SINCE FRANK FOUND ME NAKED IN THAT BURNING FIELD WITH MY MEMORY WIPED CLEAN AND TURNED ME INTO ONE OF CHICAGO'S FINEST.
YOU'RE THE ONLY LONG TERM RELATIONSHIP I'VE HAD. WELL--THAT I CAN REMEMBER, ANYWAY.
I JUST DON'T WANT IT TO END LIKE THIS.
YEAH-- BUT YOU DO WANT IT TO END.
THAT BEEN MADE CLEAR ENOUGH.
I'M SORRY-- THAT WAS MEAN. I GOTTA WATCH THAT.
OUR BABY'S DEAD, DRAGON. WHATEVER IT IS THAT MADE YOU WHAT YOU ARE-- WON'T LET YOU MAKE ANOTHER ONE. THAT BLOOD TRANSFUSION YOU GAVE PHIL PROVED THAT.
I DO WANT KIDS SOME DAY SO MAYBE US BREAKIN' UP AIN'T THE END OF THE WORLD. BETTER NOW THEN AFTER WE PUT IN A COUPLE MORE YEARS.
IT DOESN'T HAVE TO BE LIKE THAT...
I'M AFRAID, IT DOES.
CAN WE AT LEAST "KEEP IN PRACTICE" UNTIL YOU FIND A NEW BOYFRIEND?

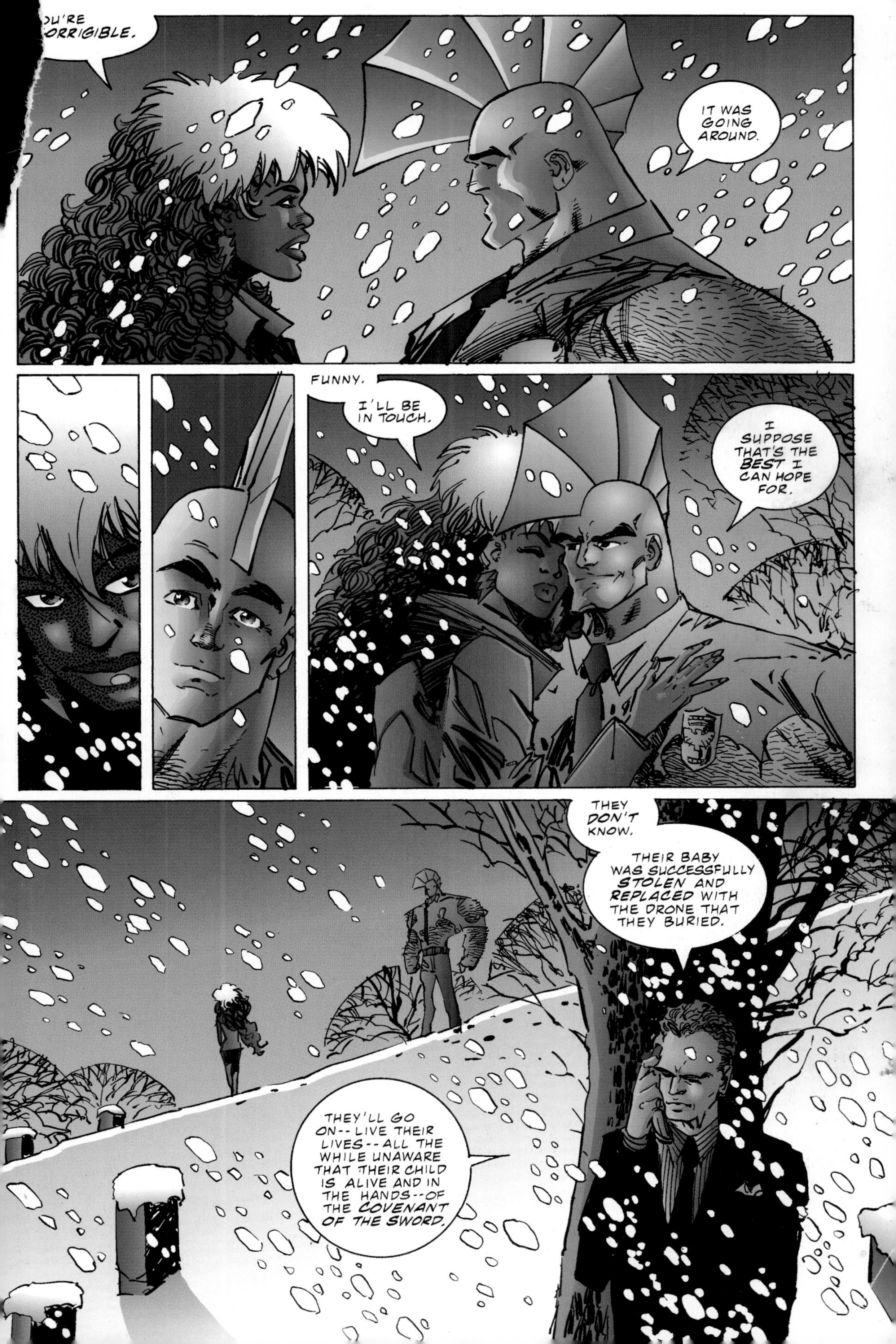
OU'RE ORRIGIBLE.
IT WAS GOING AROUND.
FUNNY.
I'LL BE IN TOUCH.
I SUPPOSE THAT'S THE BEST I CAN HOPE FOR.
THEY DON'T KNOW.
THEIR BABY WAS SUCCESSFULLY STOLEN AND REPLACED WITH THE DRONE THAT THEY BURIED.
THEY'LL GO ON-- LIVE THEIR LIVES--ALL THE WHILE UNAWARE THAT THEIR CHILD IS ALIVE AND IN THE HANDS--OF THE COVENANT OF THE SWORD.

HI.

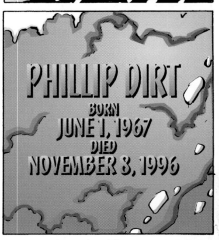

PHILLIP DIRT
BORN
JUNE 1, 1967
DIED
NOVEMBER 8, 1996

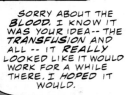

SORRY ABOUT THE *BLOOD.* I KNOW IT WAS YOUR IDEA -- THE *TRANSFUSION* AND ALL -- IT *REALLY* LOOKED LIKE IT WOULD WORK FOR A WHILE THERE, I *HOPED* IT WOULD.

ONE MORE DEATH ON MY HANDS.

MY *FIRST* GIRLFRIEND WAS SHOT DEAD IN MY APARTMENT.

THEN, THAT *CRAZY LEECH* TOOK *CONTROL* OF ME AND MADE ME GO ON A RAMPAGE -- KILLING INNOCENT PEOPLE.

NOW YOU...

...AND MY *CHILD.*

I'M LEADING *QUITE* THE CHARMED LIFE.

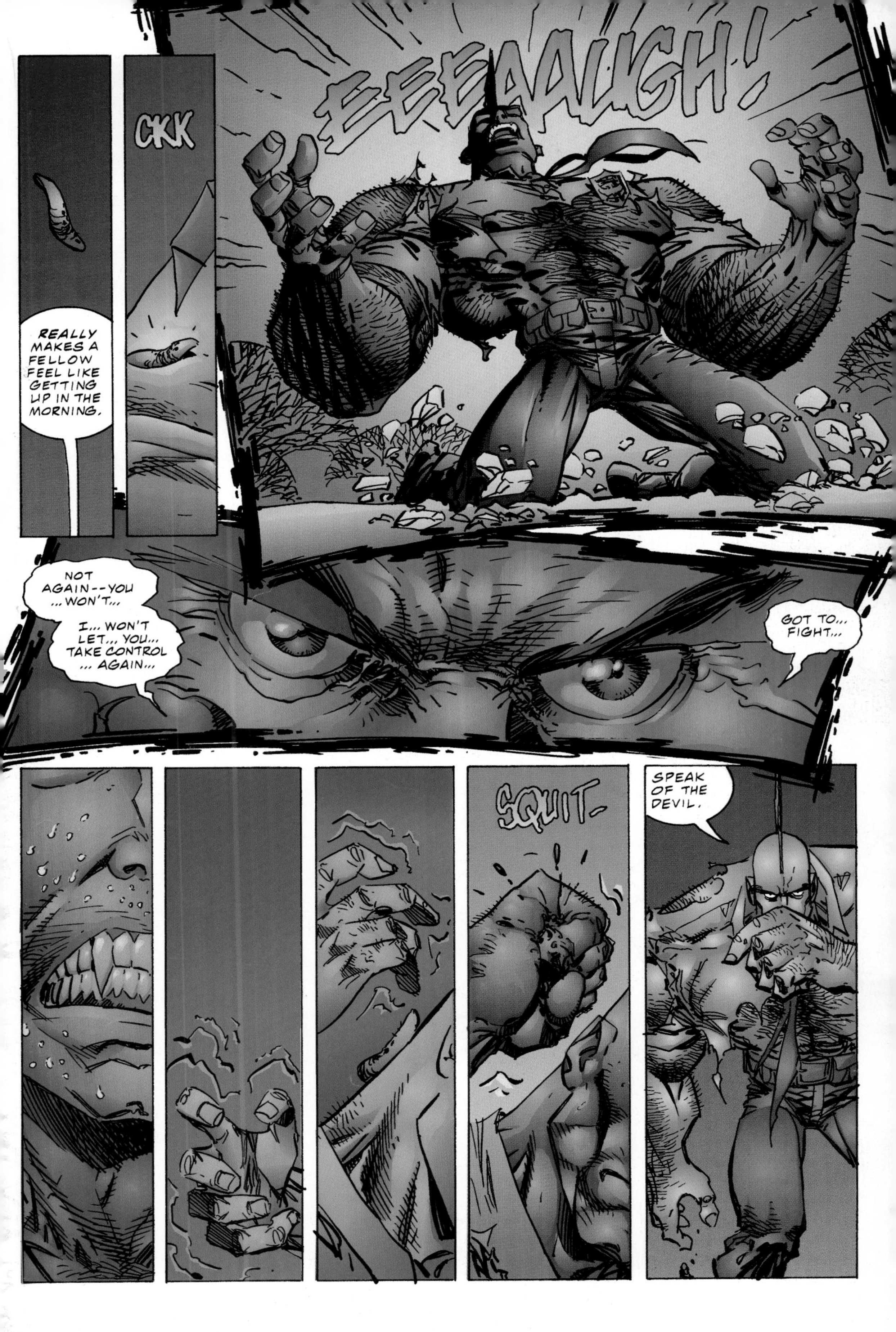

CKK
REALLY MAKES A FELLOW FEEL LIKE GETTING UP IN THE MORNING.
EEEAAUGH!
NOT AGAIN--YOU ...WON'T...
I... WON'T LET... YOU... TAKE CONTROL ... AGAIN...
GOT TO... FIGHT...
SQUIT
SPEAK OF THE DEVIL.

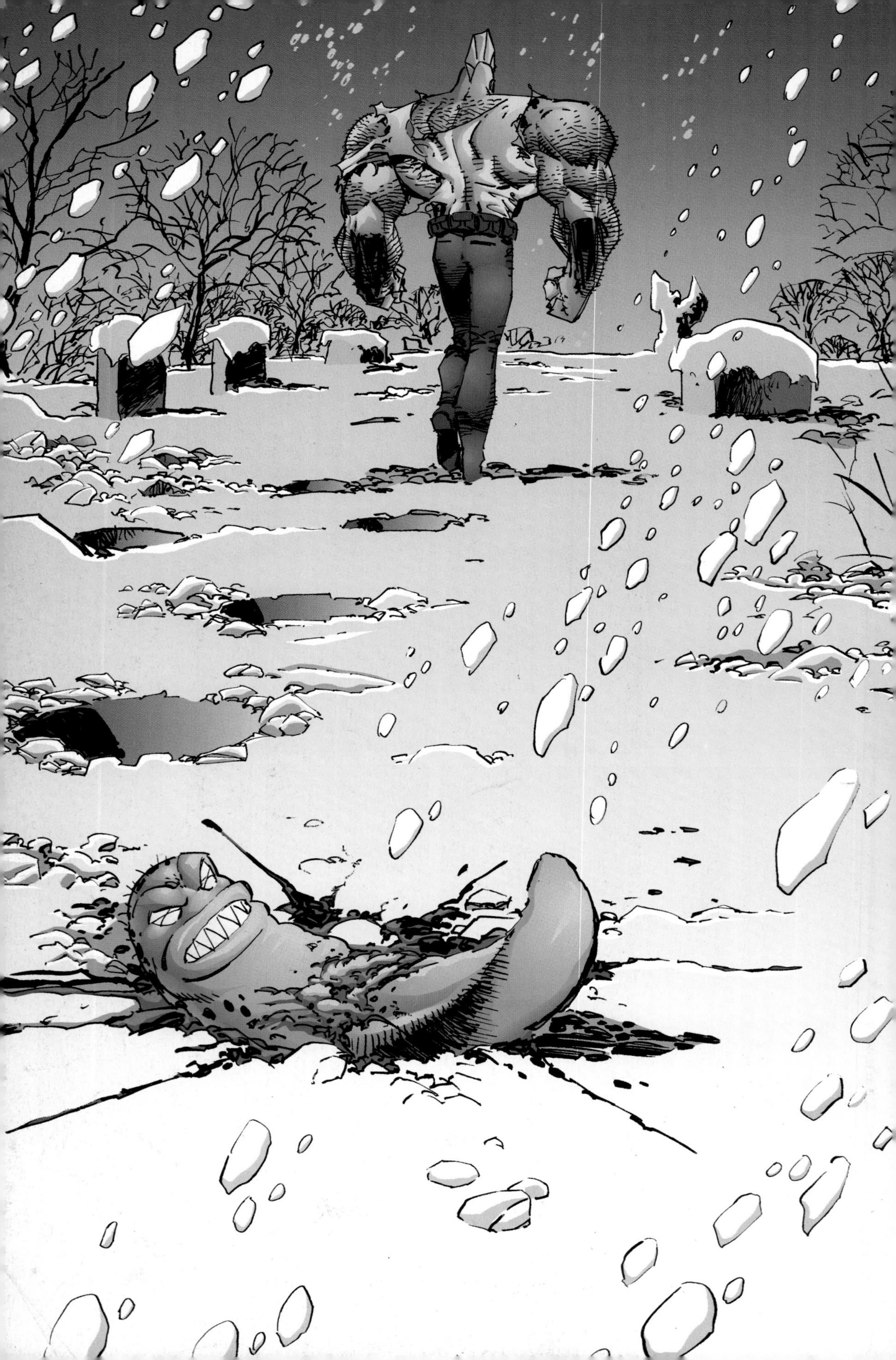

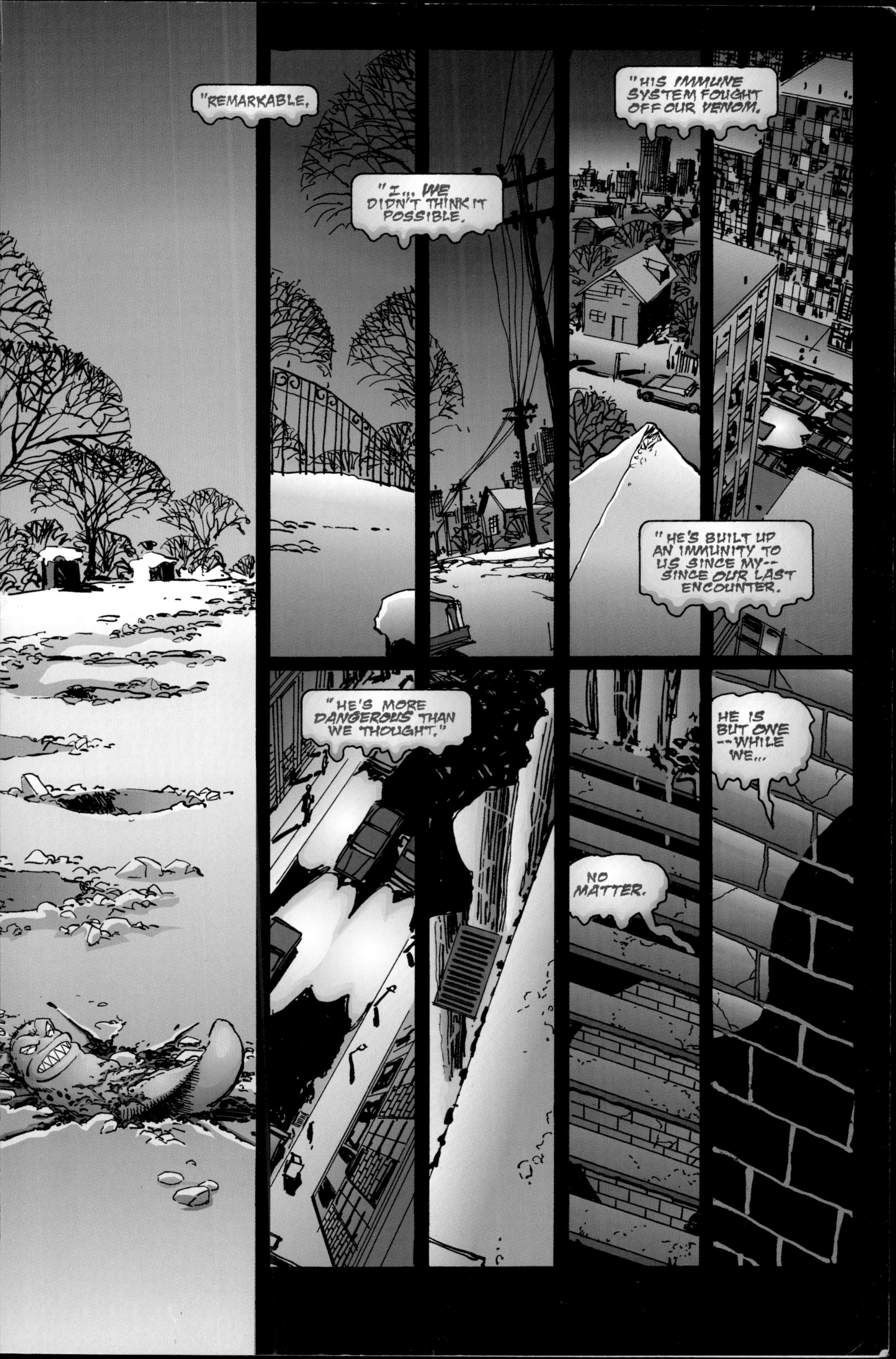
"REMARKABLE,
"I... WE DIDN'T THINK IT POSSIBLE.
"HIS IMMUNE SYSTEM FOUGHT OFF OUR VENOM.
"HE'S BUILT UP AN IMMUNITY TO US SINCE MY-- SINCE OUR LAST ENCOUNTER.
"HE'S MORE DANGEROUS THAN WE THOUGHT."
HE IS BUT ONE --WHILE WE...
NO MATTER.

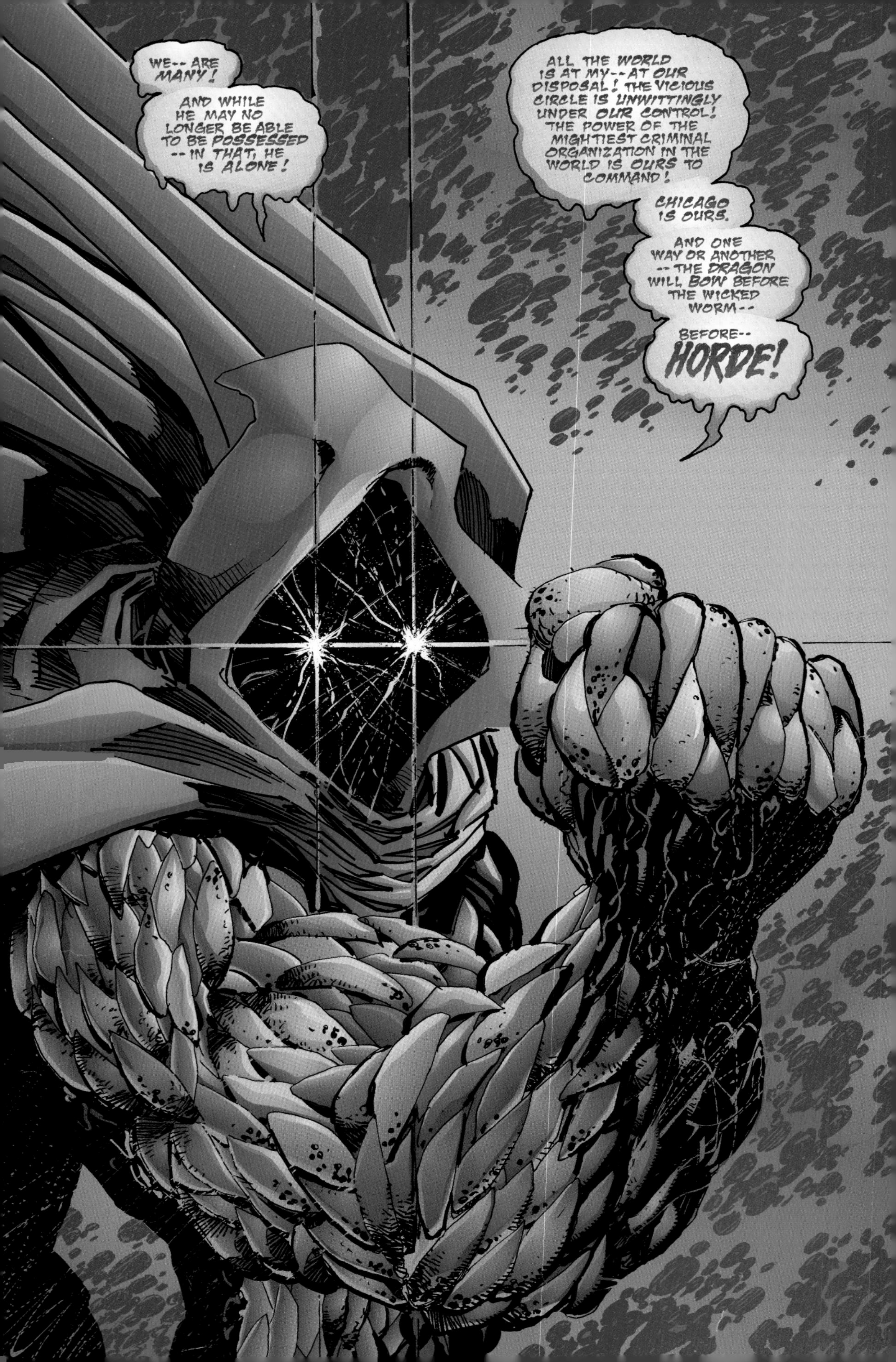
WE-- ARE MANY!
AND WHILE HE MAY NO LONGER BE ABLE TO BE POSSESSED -- IN THAT, HE IS ALONE!
ALL THE WORLD IS AT MY-- AT OUR DISPOSAL! THE VICIOUS CIRCLE IS UNWITTINGLY UNDER OUR CONTROL! THE POWER OF THE MIGHTIEST CRIMINAL ORGANIZATION IN THE WORLD IS OURS TO COMMAND!
CHICAGO IS OURS.
AND ONE WAY OR ANOTHER -- THE DRAGON WILL BOW BEFORE THE WICKED WORM--
BEFORE-- HORDE!

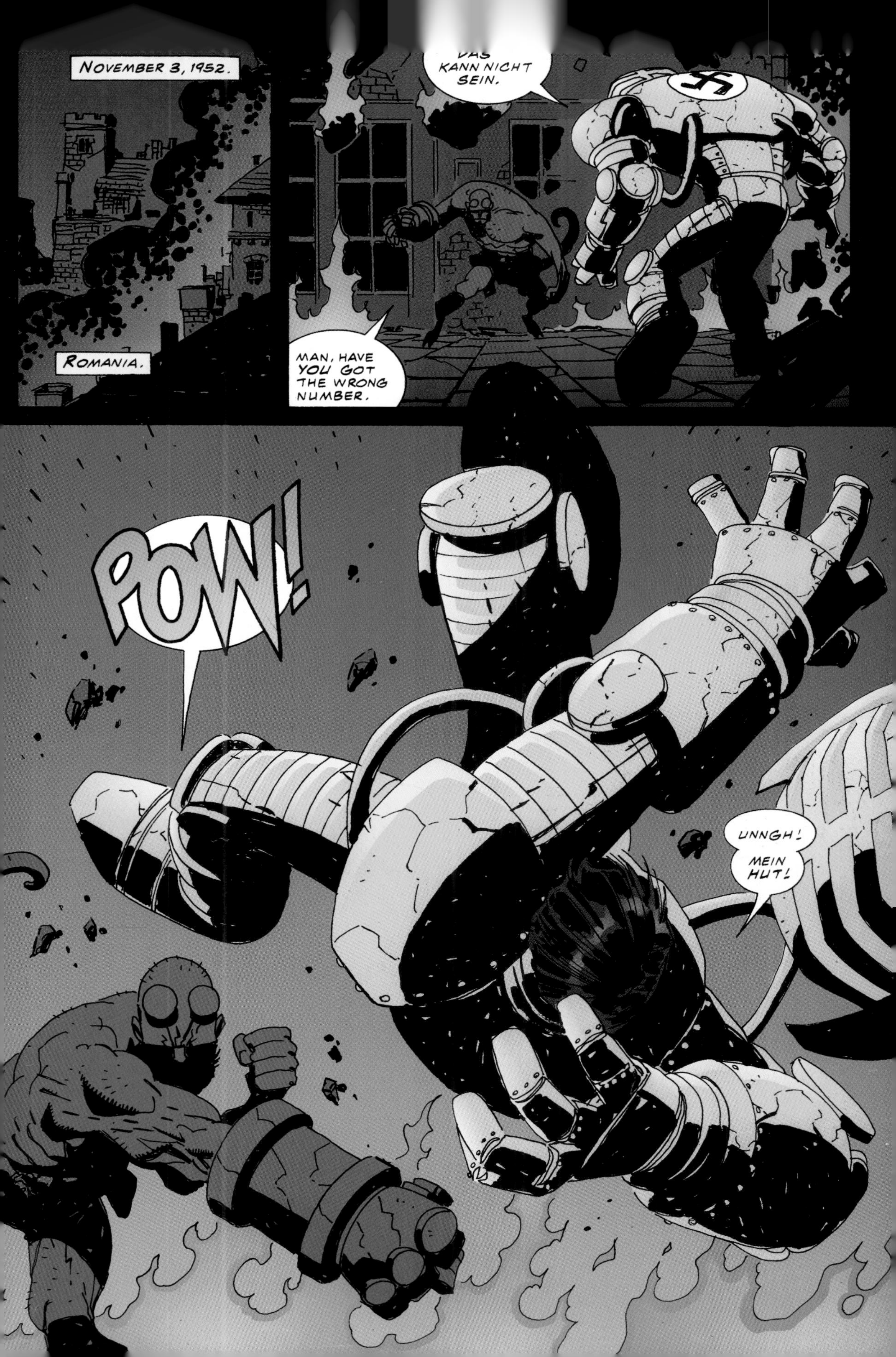
NOVEMBER 3, 1952.
ROMANIA.
DAS KANN NICHT SEIN.
MAN, HAVE YOU GOT THE WRONG NUMBER.
POW!
UNNGH!
MEIN HUT!

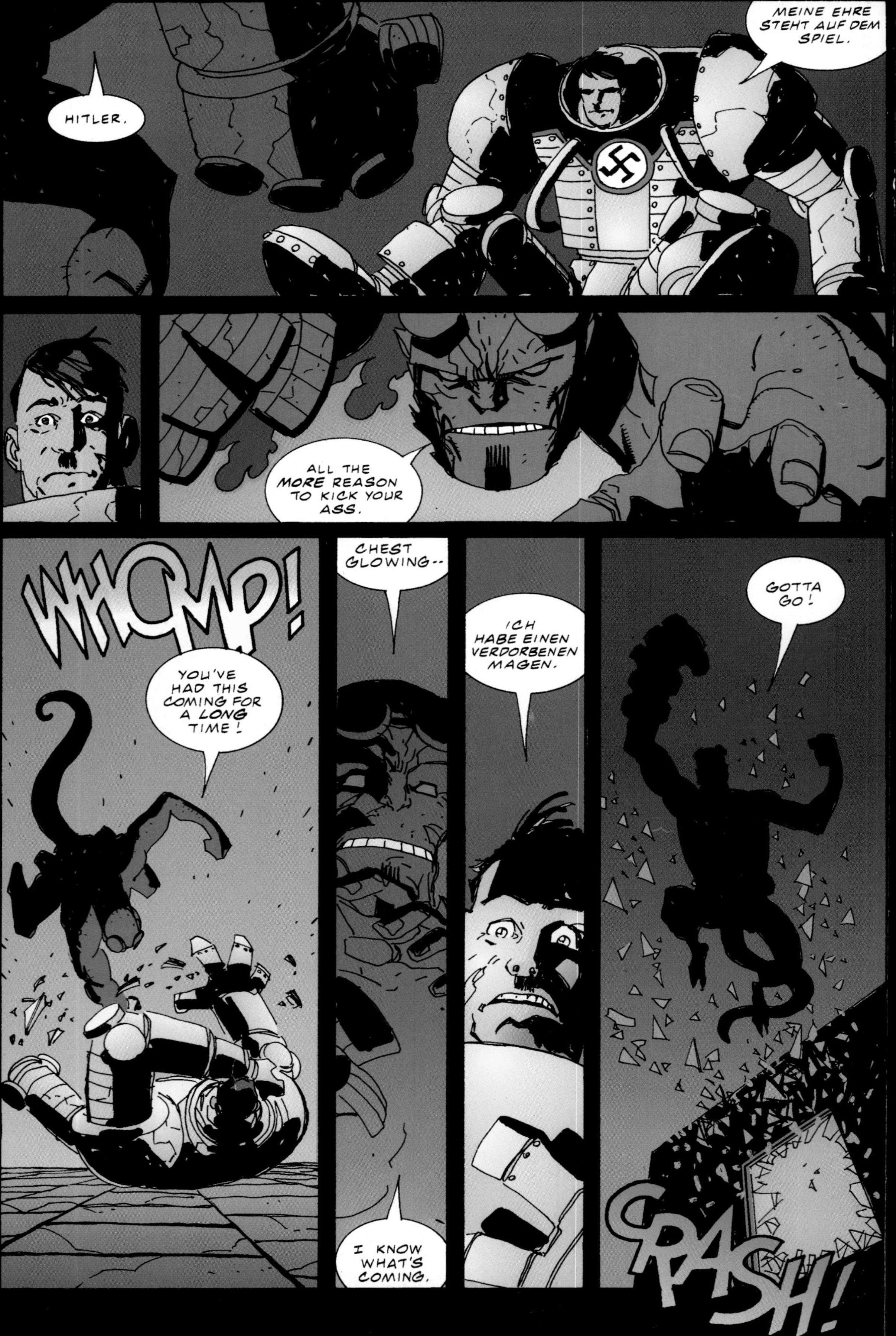
HITLER.
MEINE EHRE STEHT AUF DEM SPIEL.
ALL THE MORE REASON TO KICK YOUR ASS.
WHOMP!
YOU'VE HAD THIS COMING FOR A LONG TIME!
CHEST GLOWING--
I KNOW WHAT'S COMING.
ICH HABE EINEN VERDORBENEN MAGEN.
GOTTA GO!
CRASH!

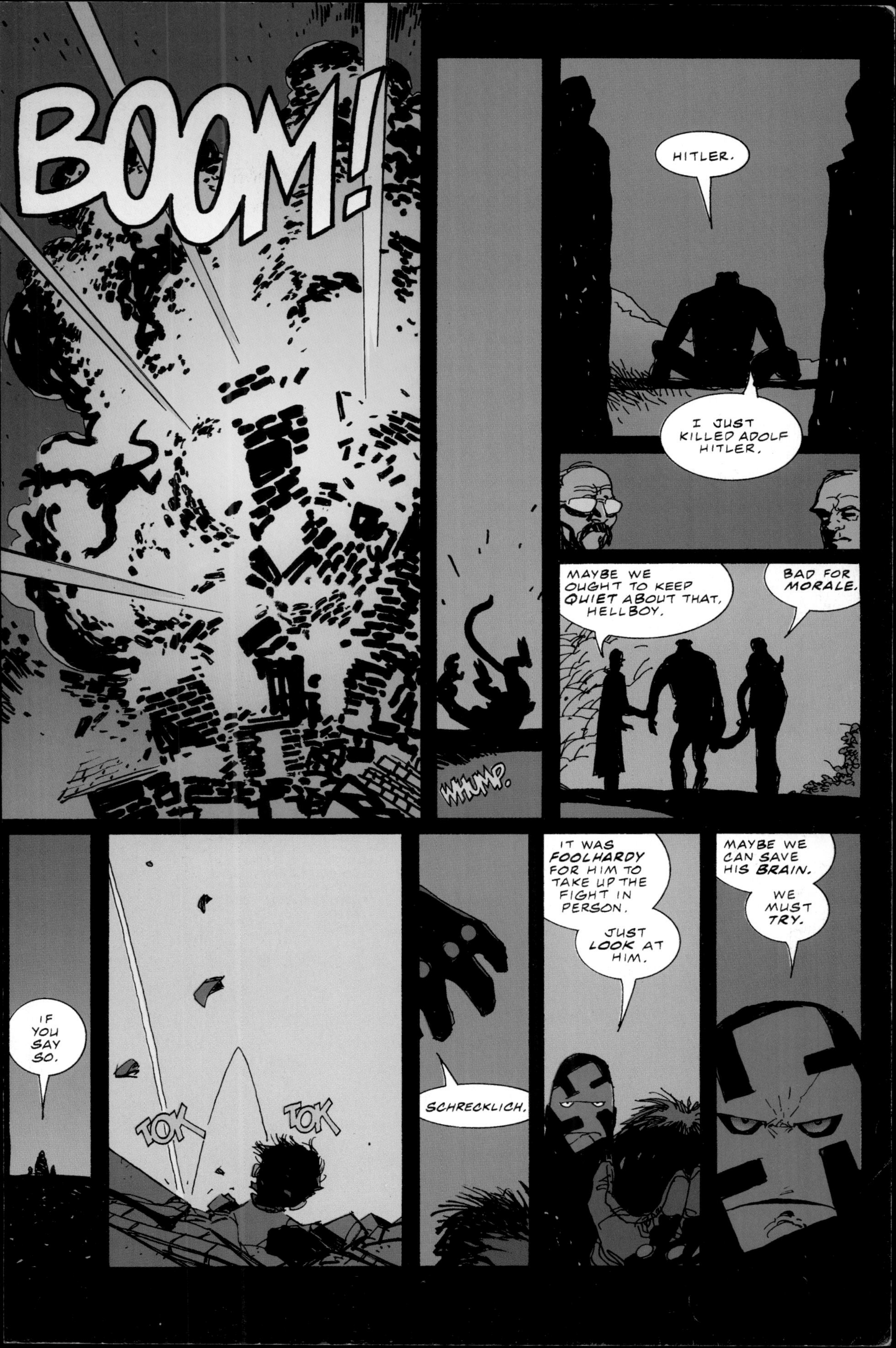
BOOM!
WHUMP.
HITLER.
I JUST KILLED ADOLF HITLER.
MAYBE WE OUGHT TO KEEP QUIET ABOUT THAT, HELLBOY.
BAD FOR MORALE.
IF YOU SAY SO.
TOK
TOK
SCHRECKLICH.
IT WAS FOOLHARDY FOR HIM TO TAKE UP THE FIGHT IN PERSON.
JUST LOOK AT HIM.
MAYBE WE CAN SAVE HIS BRAIN.
WE MUST TRY.

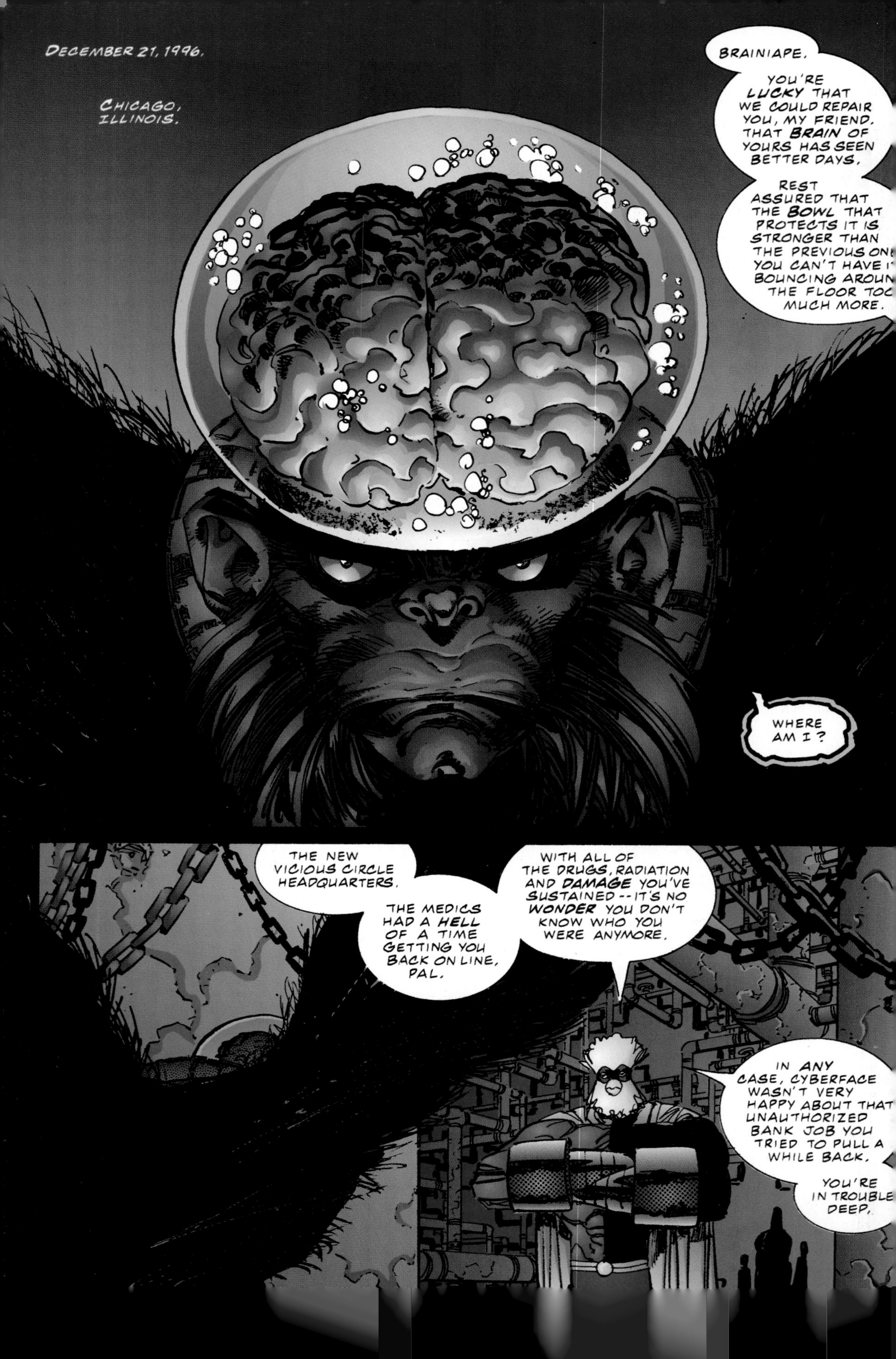
DECEMBER 21, 1996.
CHICAGO, ILLINOIS.
BRAINIAPE.
YOU'RE LUCKY THAT WE COULD REPAIR YOU, MY FRIEND. THAT BRAIN OF YOURS HAS SEEN BETTER DAYS.
REST ASSURED THAT THE BOWL THAT PROTECTS IT IS STRONGER THAN THE PREVIOUS ONE. YOU CAN'T HAVE IT BOUNCING AROUND THE FLOOR TOO MUCH MORE.
WHERE AM I?
THE NEW VICIOUS CIRCLE HEADQUARTERS.
THE MEDICS HAD A HELL OF A TIME GETTING YOU BACK ON LINE, PAL.
WITH ALL OF THE DRUGS, RADIATION AND DAMAGE YOU'VE SUSTAINED -- IT'S NO WONDER YOU DON'T KNOW WHO YOU WERE ANYMORE.
IN ANY CASE, CYBERFACE WASN'T VERY HAPPY ABOUT THAT UNAUTHORIZED BANK JOB YOU TRIED TO PULL A WHILE BACK.
YOU'RE IN TROUBLE DEEP.

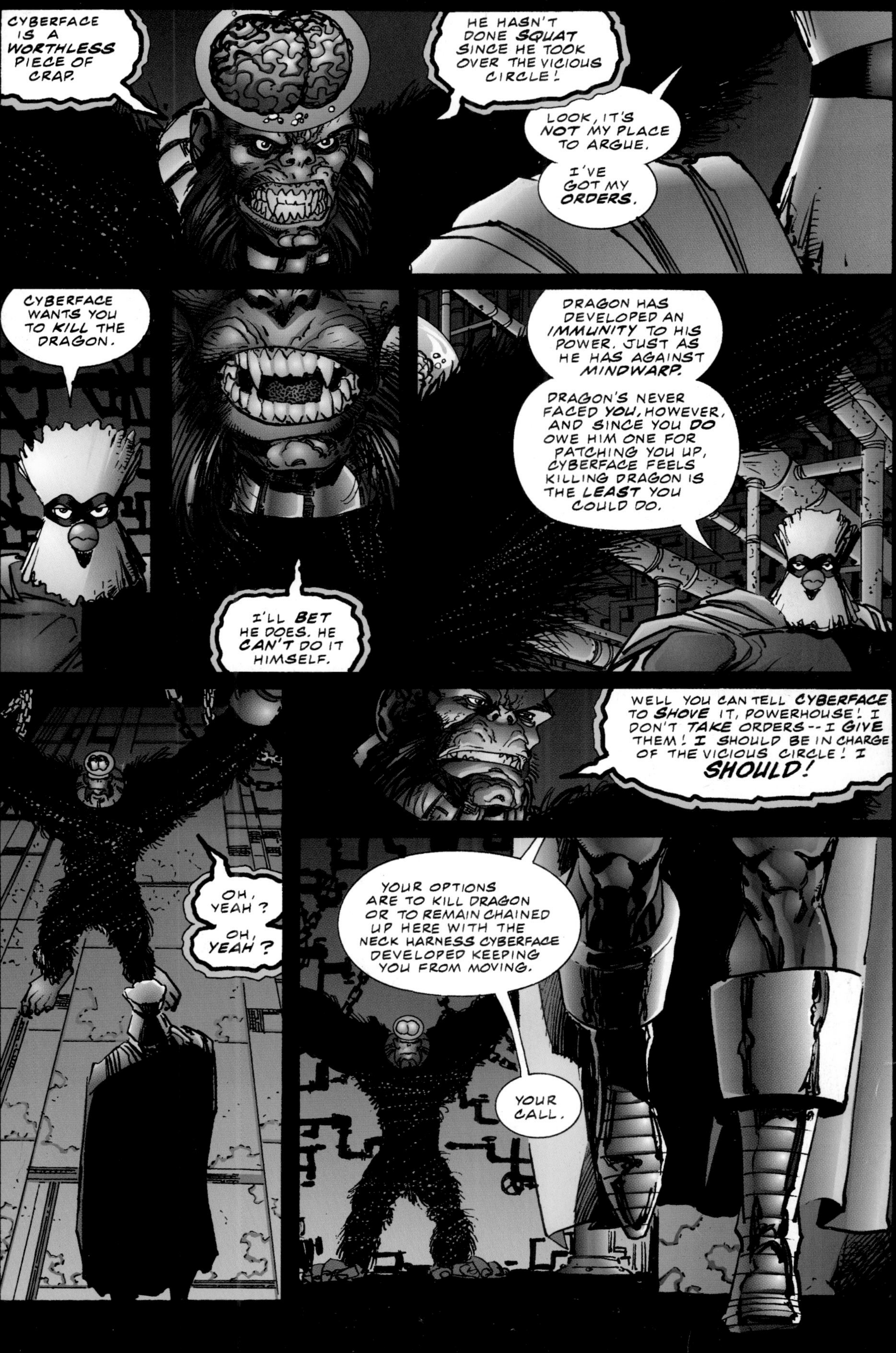
CYBERFACE IS A WORTHLESS PIECE OF CRAP.
HE HASN'T DONE SQUAT SINCE HE TOOK OVER THE VICIOUS CIRCLE!
LOOK, IT'S NOT MY PLACE TO ARGUE.
I'VE GOT MY ORDERS.
CYBERFACE WANTS YOU TO KILL THE DRAGON.
DRAGON HAS DEVELOPED AN IMMUNITY TO HIS POWER. JUST AS HE HAS AGAINST MINDWARP.
DRAGON'S NEVER FACED YOU, HOWEVER, AND SINCE YOU DO OWE HIM ONE FOR PATCHING YOU UP, CYBERFACE FEELS KILLING DRAGON IS THE LEAST YOU COULD DO.
I'LL BET HE DOES. HE CAN'T DO IT HIMSELF.
WELL YOU CAN TELL CYBERFACE TO SHOVE IT, POWERHOUSE! I DON'T TAKE ORDERS -- I GIVE THEM! I SHOULD BE IN CHARGE OF THE VICIOUS CIRCLE! I SHOULD!
OH, YEAH?
OH, YEAH?
YOUR OPTIONS ARE TO KILL DRAGON OR TO REMAIN CHAINED UP HERE WITH THE NECK HARNESS CYBERFACE DEVELOPED KEEPING YOU FROM MOVING.
YOUR CALL.

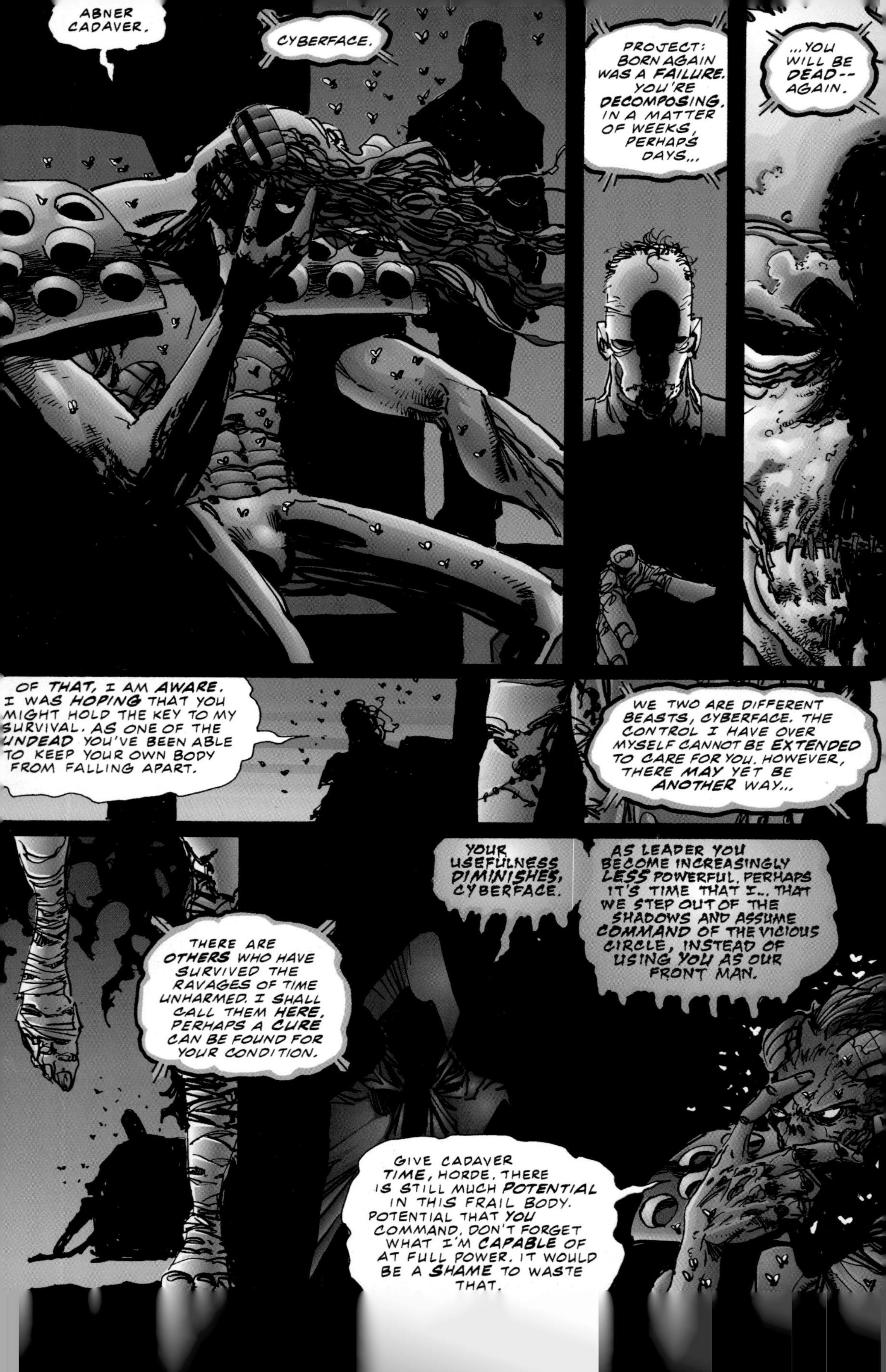
ABNER CADAVER.
CYBERFACE.
PROJECT: BORN AGAIN WAS A FAILURE. YOU'RE DECOMPOSING. IN A MATTER OF WEEKS, PERHAPS DAYS...
...YOU WILL BE DEAD--AGAIN.
OF THAT, I AM AWARE. I WAS HOPING THAT YOU MIGHT HOLD THE KEY TO MY SURVIVAL. AS ONE OF THE UNDEAD YOU'VE BEEN ABLE TO KEEP YOUR OWN BODY FROM FALLING APART.
WE TWO ARE DIFFERENT BEASTS, CYBERFACE. THE CONTROL I HAVE OVER MYSELF CANNOT BE EXTENDED TO CARE FOR YOU. HOWEVER, THERE MAY YET BE ANOTHER WAY...
THERE ARE OTHERS WHO HAVE SURVIVED THE RAVAGES OF TIME UNHARMED. I SHALL CALL THEM HERE. PERHAPS A CURE CAN BE FOUND FOR YOUR CONDITION.
YOUR USEFULNESS DIMINISHES, CYBERFACE.
AS LEADER YOU BECOME INCREASINGLY LESS POWERFUL. PERHAPS IT'S TIME THAT I... THAT WE STEP OUT OF THE SHADOWS AND ASSUME COMMAND OF THE VICIOUS CIRCLE, INSTEAD OF USING YOU AS OUR FRONT MAN.
GIVE CADAVER TIME, HORDE. THERE IS STILL MUCH POTENTIAL IN THIS FRAIL BODY. POTENTIAL THAT YOU COMMAND. DON'T FORGET WHAT I'M CAPABLE OF AT FULL POWER. IT WOULD BE A SHAME TO WASTE THAT.

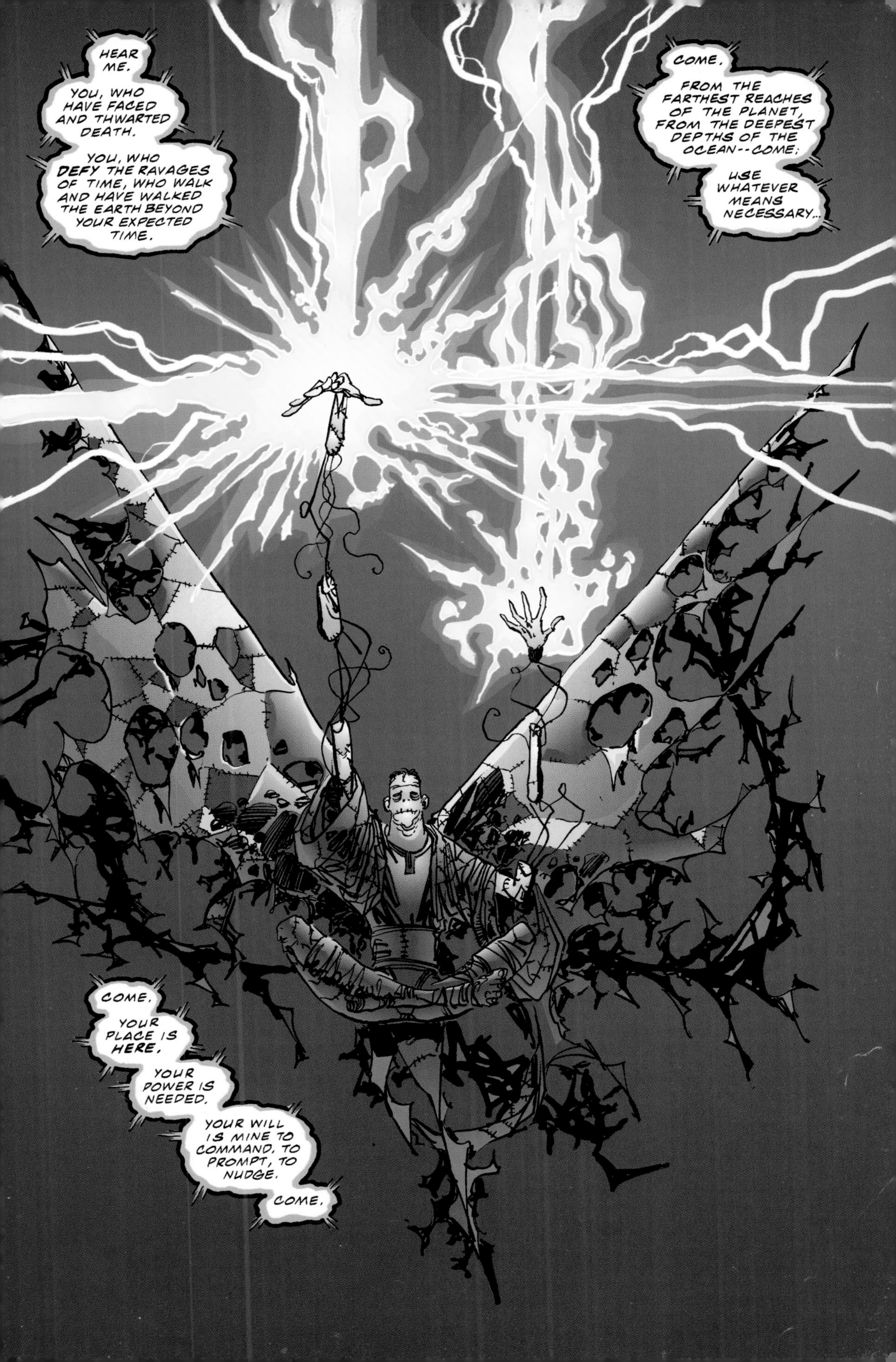
HEAR ME.
YOU, WHO HAVE FACED AND THWARTED DEATH.
YOU, WHO DEFY THE RAVAGES OF TIME, WHO WALK AND HAVE WALKED THE EARTH BEYOND YOUR EXPECTED TIME.
COME.
FROM THE FARTHEST REACHES OF THE PLANET, FROM THE DEEPEST DEPTHS OF THE OCEAN--COME;
USE WHATEVER MEANS NECESSARY...
COME.
YOUR PLACE IS HERE.
YOUR POWER IS NEEDED.
YOUR WILL IS MINE TO COMMAND, TO PROMPT, TO NUDGE.
COME.

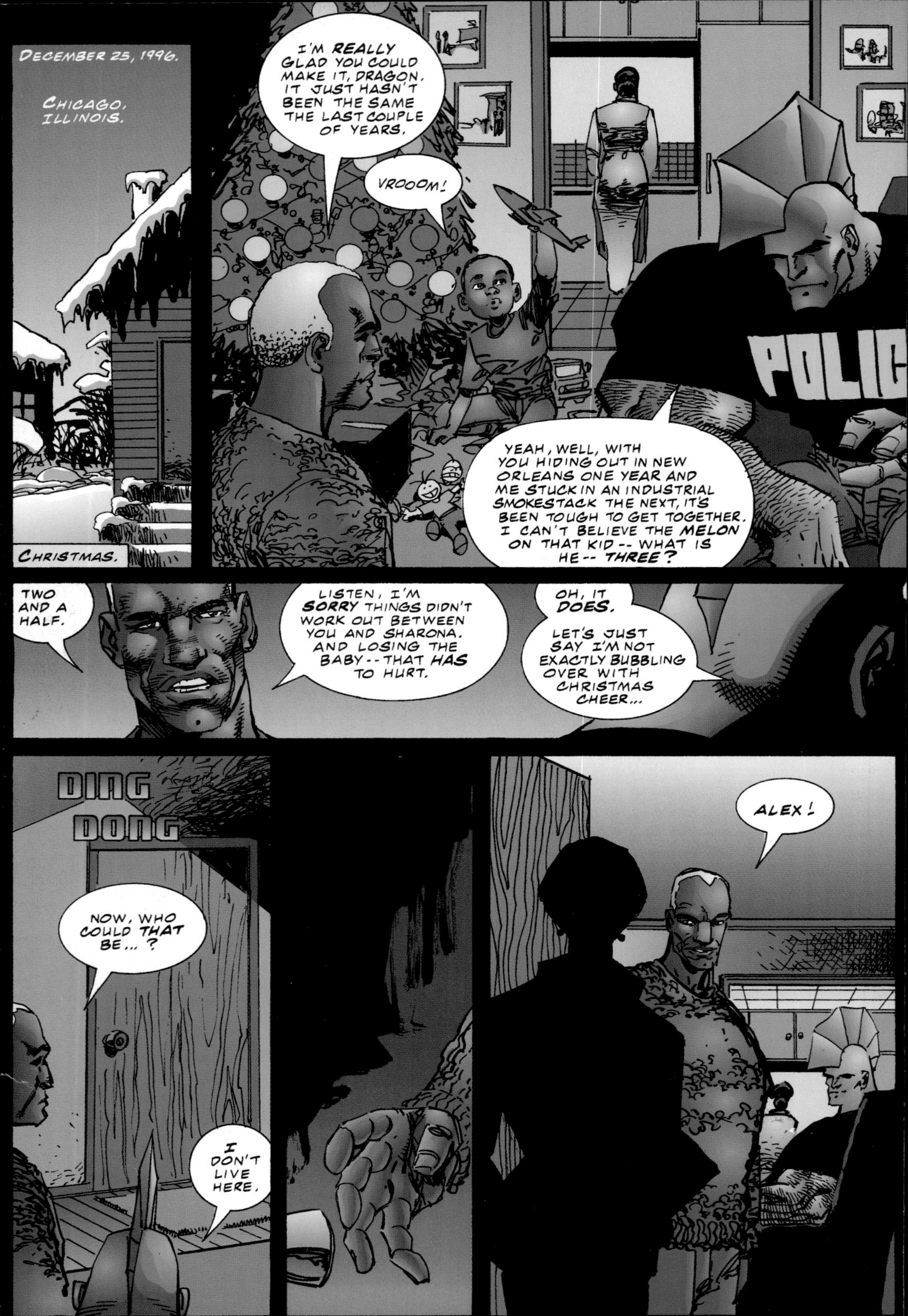
DECEMBER 25, 1996.
CHICAGO, ILLINOIS.
CHRISTMAS.
I'M REALLY GLAD YOU COULD MAKE IT, DRAGON. IT JUST HASN'T BEEN THE SAME THE LAST COUPLE OF YEARS.
VROOOM!
YEAH, WELL, WITH YOU HIDING OUT IN NEW ORLEANS ONE YEAR AND ME STUCK IN AN INDUSTRIAL SMOKESTACK THE NEXT, IT'S BEEN TOUGH TO GET TOGETHER. I CAN'T BELIEVE THE MELON ON THAT KID -- WHAT IS HE -- THREE?
POLIC
TWO AND A HALF.
LISTEN, I'M SORRY THINGS DIDN'T WORK OUT BETWEEN YOU AND SHARONA. AND LOSING THE BABY -- THAT HAS TO HURT.
OH, IT DOES.
LET'S JUST SAY I'M NOT EXACTLY BUBBLING OVER WITH CHRISTMAS CHEER...
DING DONG
NOW, WHO COULD THAT BE...?
I DON'T LIVE HERE.
ALEX!

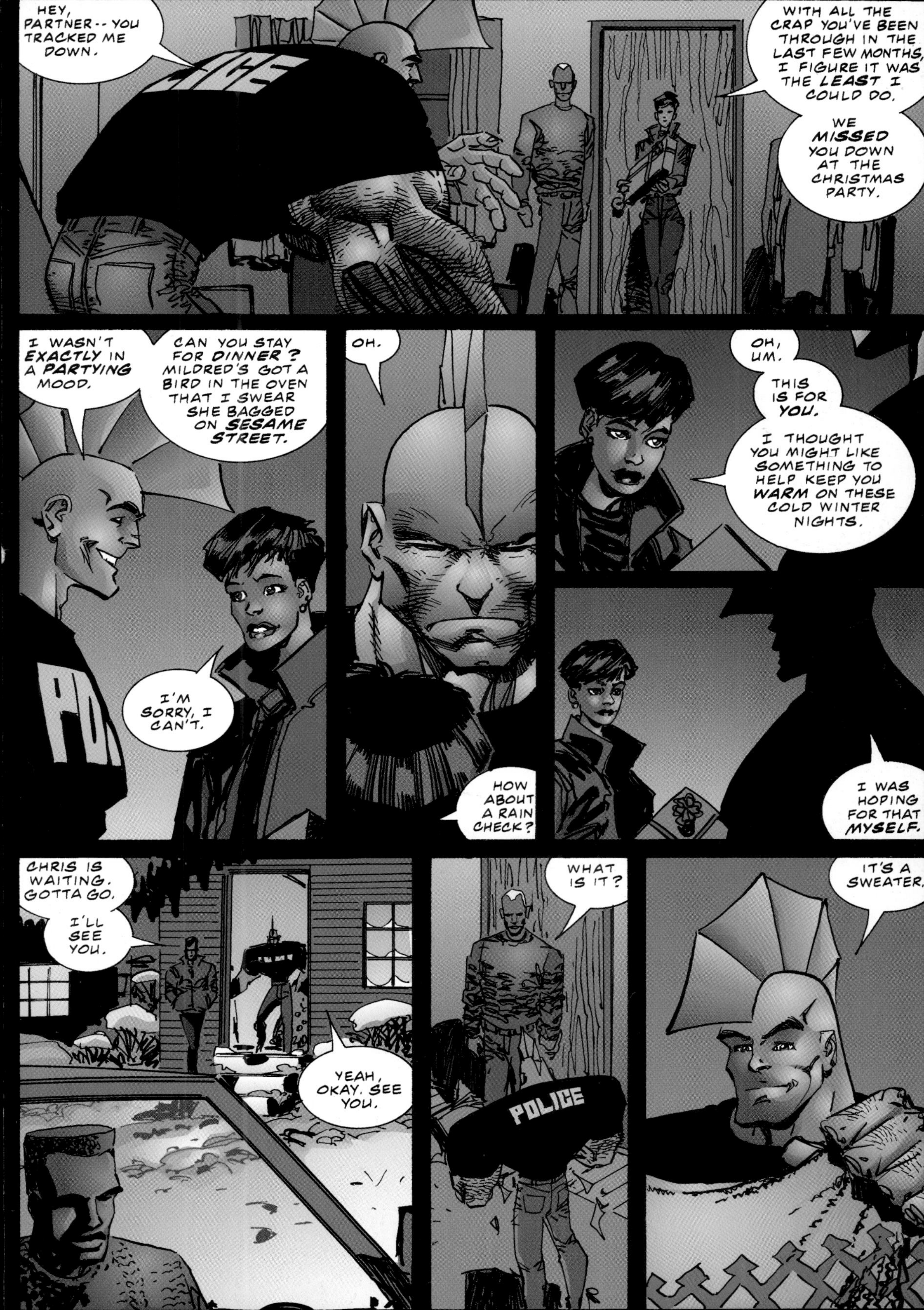
HEY, PARTNER-- YOU TRACKED ME DOWN.
WITH ALL THE CRAP YOU'VE BEEN THROUGH IN THE LAST FEW MONTHS, I FIGURE IT WAS THE LEAST I COULD DO.
WE MISSED YOU DOWN AT THE CHRISTMAS PARTY.
I WASN'T EXACTLY IN A PARTYING MOOD.
CAN YOU STAY FOR DINNER? MILDRED'S GOT A BIRD IN THE OVEN THAT I SWEAR SHE BAGGED ON SESAME STREET.
I'M SORRY, I CAN'T.
OH.
HOW ABOUT A RAIN CHECK?
OH, UM.
THIS IS FOR YOU.
I THOUGHT YOU MIGHT LIKE SOMETHING TO HELP KEEP YOU WARM ON THESE COLD WINTER NIGHTS.
I WAS HOPING FOR THAT MYSELF.
CHRIS IS WAITING. GOTTA GO.
I'LL SEE YOU.
YEAH, OKAY. SEE YOU.
WHAT IS IT?
POLICE
IT'S A SWEATER.

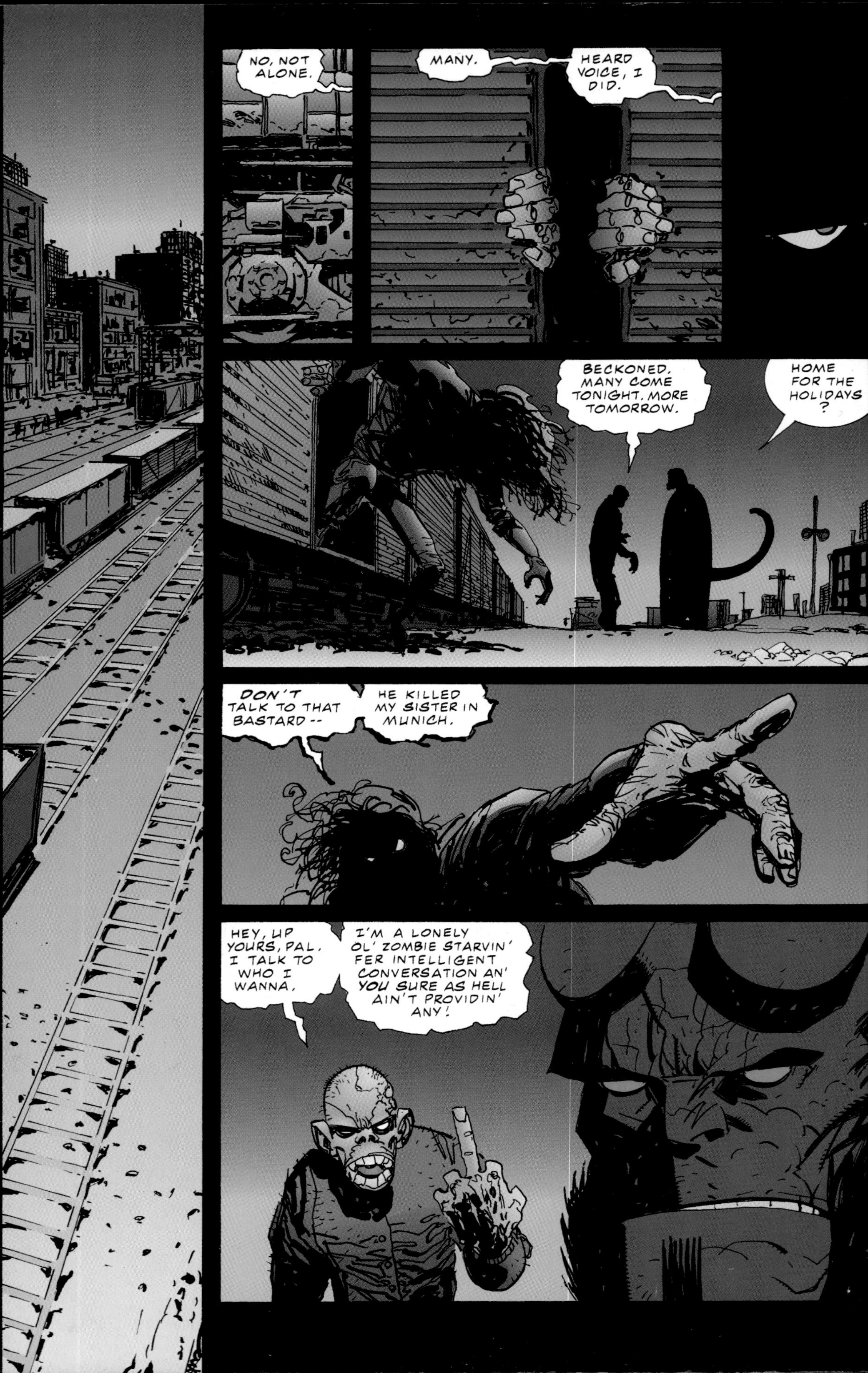
NO, NOT ALONE.
MANY.
HEARD VOICE, I DID.
BECKONED. MANY COME TONIGHT. MORE TOMORROW.
HOME FOR THE HOLIDAYS?
DON'T TALK TO THAT BASTARD --
HE KILLED MY SISTER IN MUNICH.
HEY, UP YOURS, PAL. I TALK TO WHO I WANNA.
I'M A LONELY OL' ZOMBIE STARVIN' FER INTELLIGENT CONVERSATION AN' YOU SURE AS HELL AIN'T PROVIDIN' ANY!

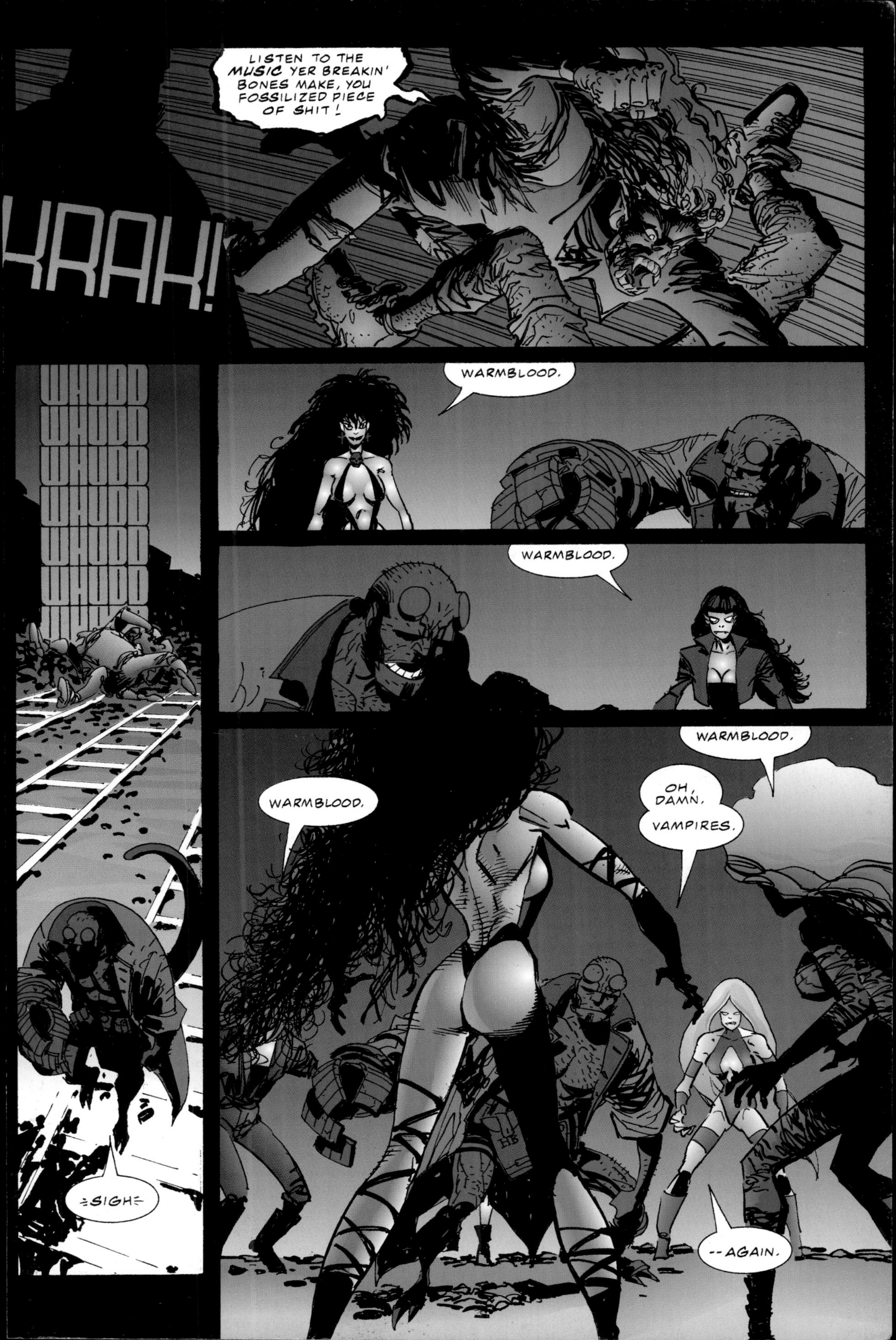
LISTEN TO THE MUSIC YER BREAKIN' BONES MAKE, YOU FOSSILIZED PIECE OF SHIT!
KRAK!
WHUDD WHUDD WHUDD WHUDD WHUDD WHUDD WHUDD
WARMBLOOD.
WARMBLOOD.
WARMBLOOD.
WARMBLOOD.
OH, DAMN.
VAMPIRES.
=SIGH=
--AGAIN.

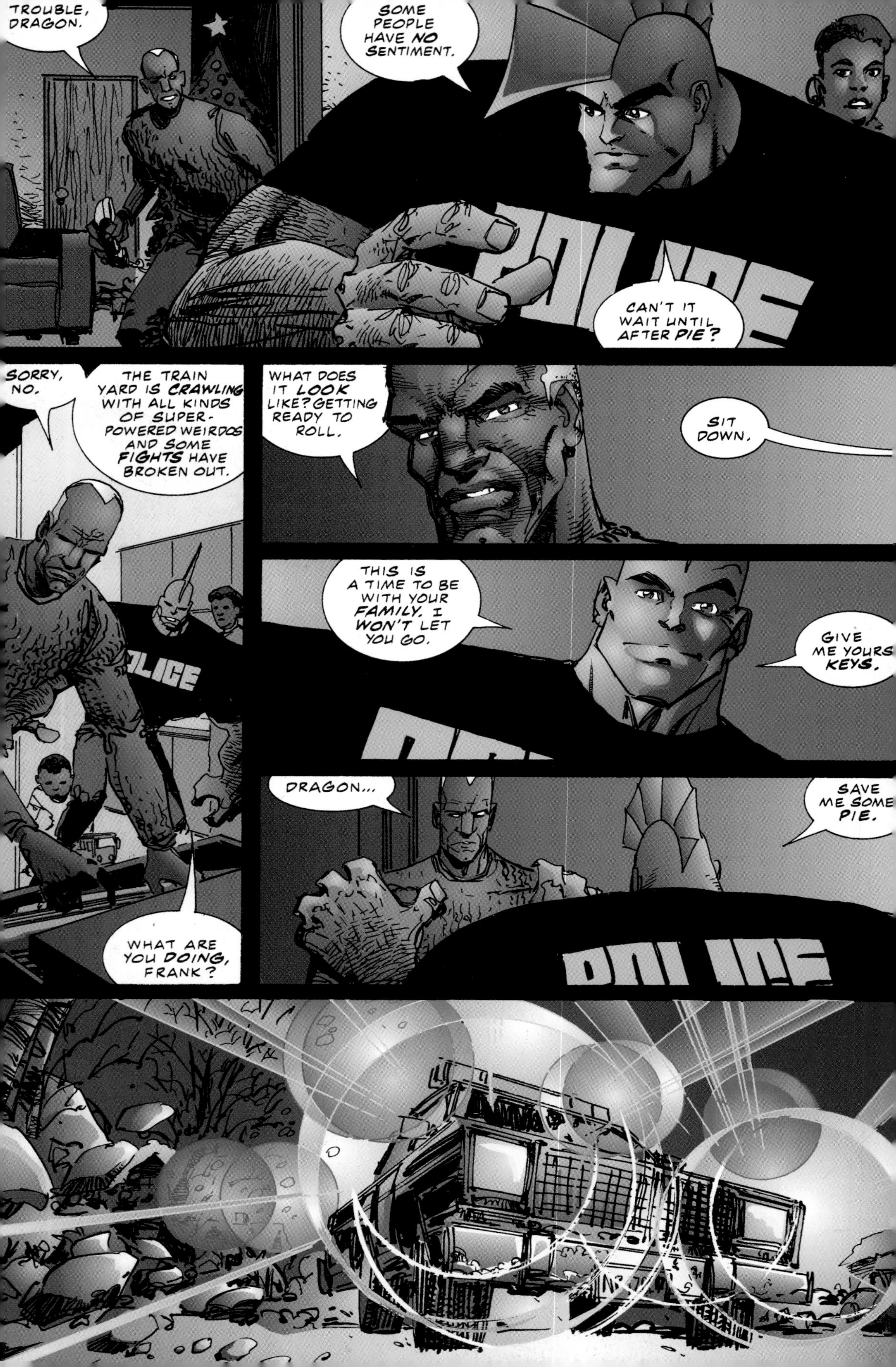
TROUBLE, DRAGON.
SOME PEOPLE HAVE NO SENTIMENT.
CAN'T IT WAIT UNTIL AFTER PIE?
SORRY, NO.
THE TRAIN YARD IS CRAWLING WITH ALL KINDS OF SUPER-POWERED WEIRDOS AND SOME FIGHTS HAVE BROKEN OUT.
WHAT ARE YOU DOING, FRANK?
WHAT DOES IT LOOK LIKE? GETTING READY TO ROLL.
SIT DOWN.
THIS IS A TIME TO BE WITH YOUR FAMILY. I WON'T LET YOU GO.
GIVE ME YOURS KEYS.
DRAGON...
SAVE ME SOME PIE.

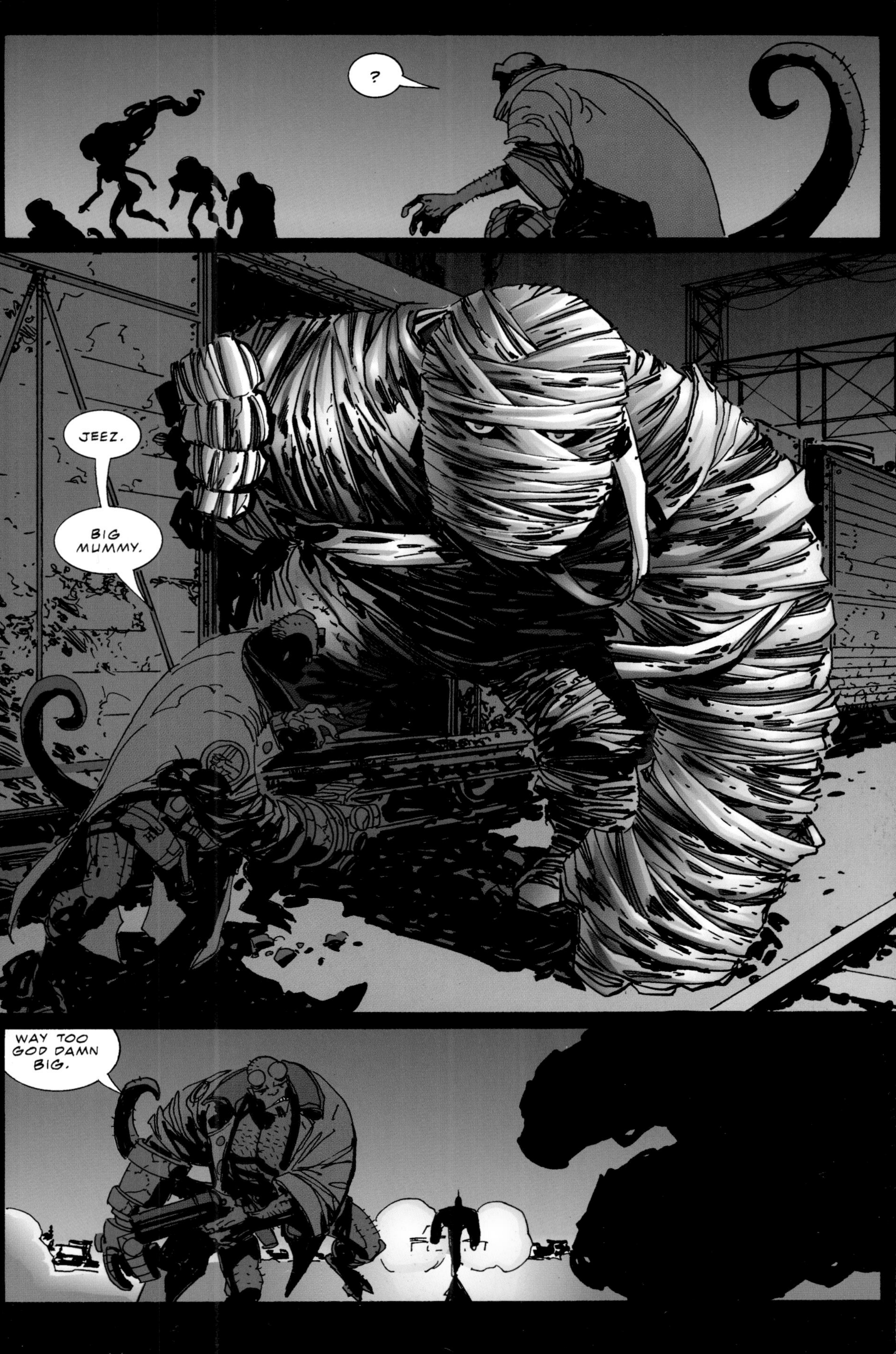
?
JEEZ.
BIG MUMMY.
WAY TOO GOD DAMN BIG.

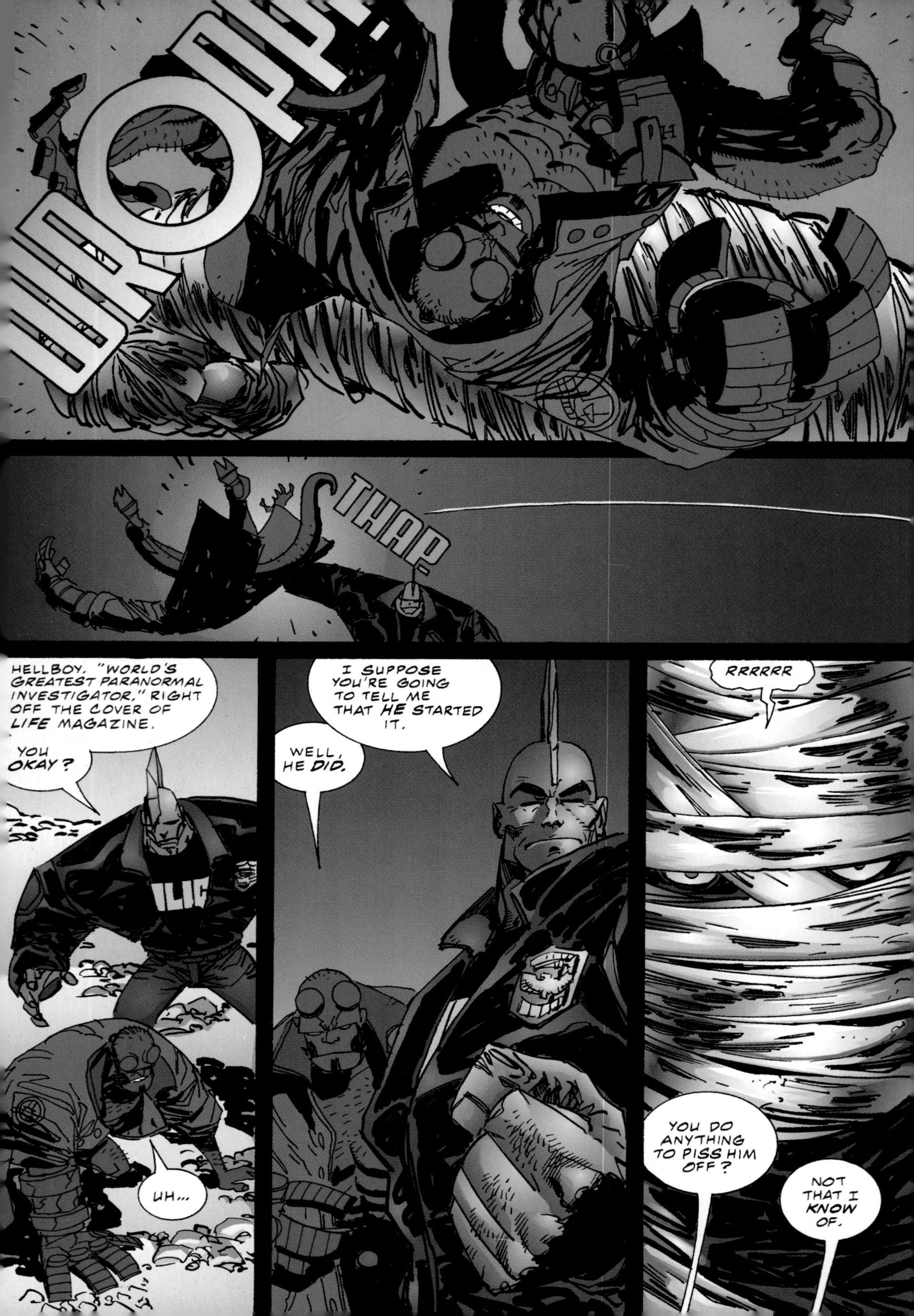

DROP
THAP
HELLBOY. "WORLD'S GREATEST PARANORMAL INVESTIGATOR," RIGHT OFF THE COVER OF LIFE MAGAZINE.
YOU OKAY?
UH...
I SUPPOSE YOU'RE GOING TO TELL ME THAT HE STARTED IT.
WELL, HE DID.
RRRRRR
YOU DO ANYTHING TO PISS HIM OFF?
NOT THAT I KNOW OF.

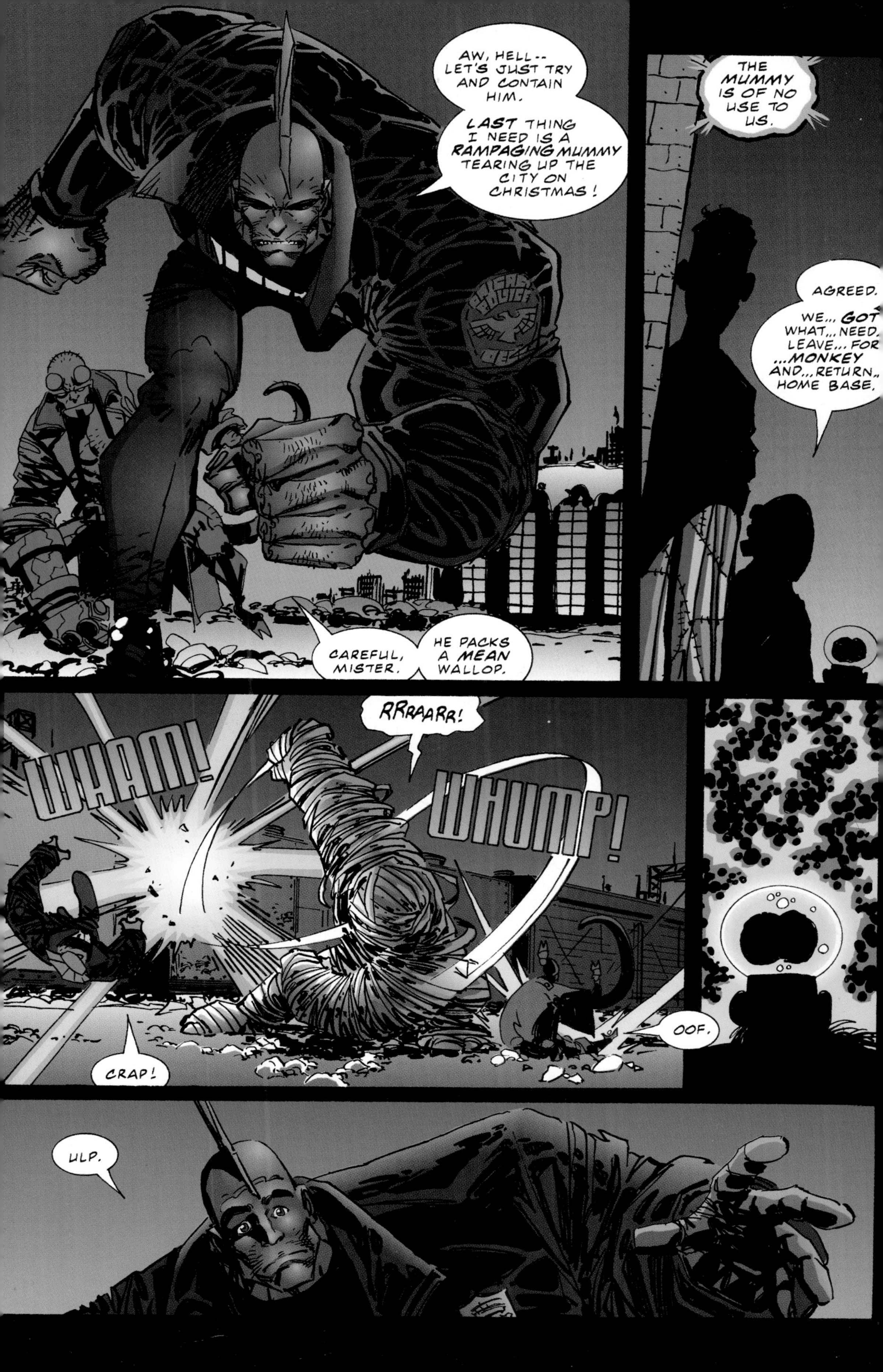
AW, HELL-- LET'S JUST TRY AND CONTAIN HIM.
LAST THING I NEED IS A RAMPAGING MUMMY TEARING UP THE CITY ON CHRISTMAS!
CAREFUL, MISTER.
HE PACKS A MEAN WALLOP.
THE MUMMY IS OF NO USE TO US.
AGREED.
WE... GOT WHAT... NEED. LEAVE... FOR ...MONKEY AND... RETURN... HOME BASE.
WHAM!
RRRAARR!
WHUMP!
CRAP!
OOF.
ULP.

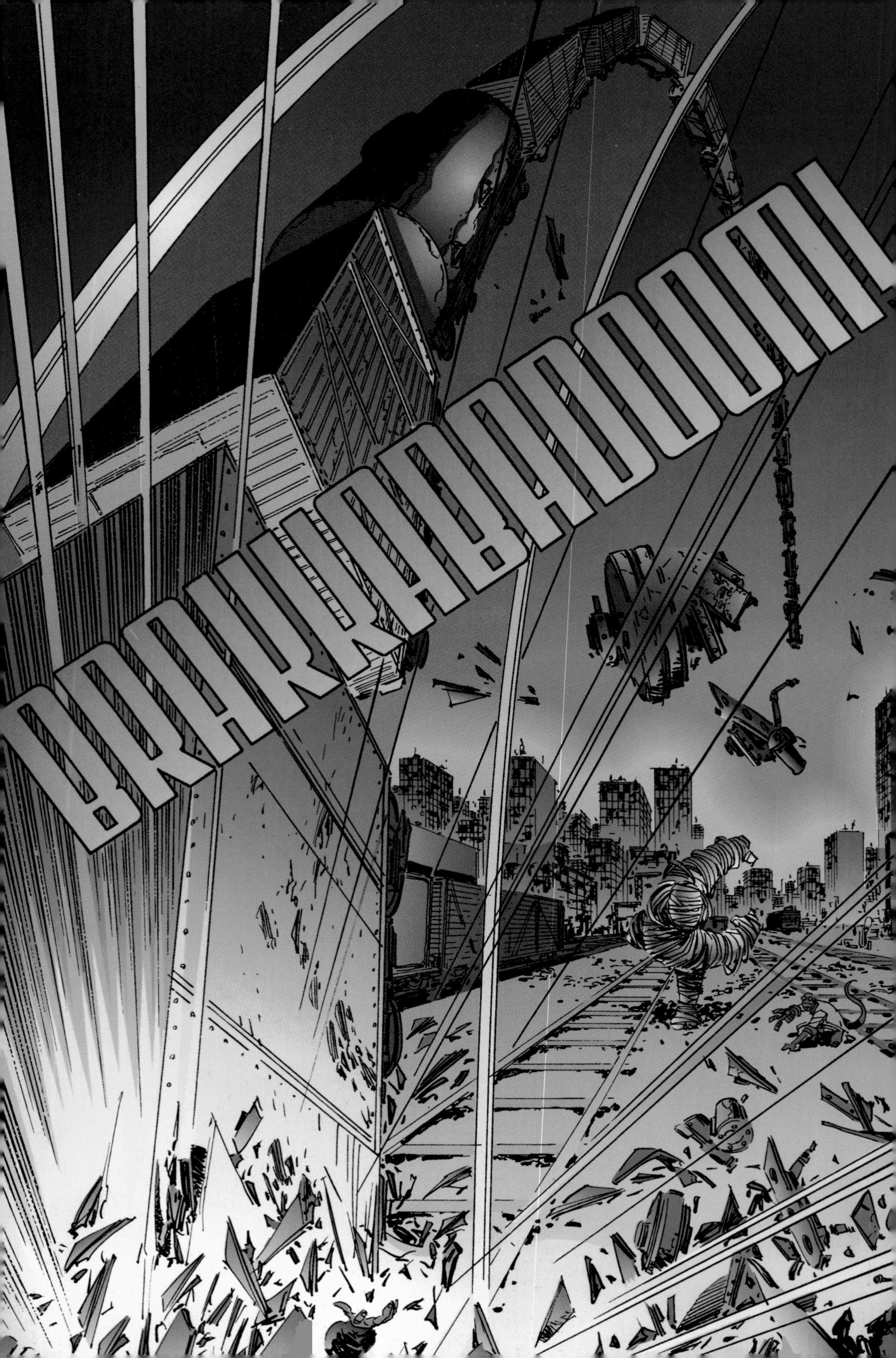
BRAKRABADOOM!

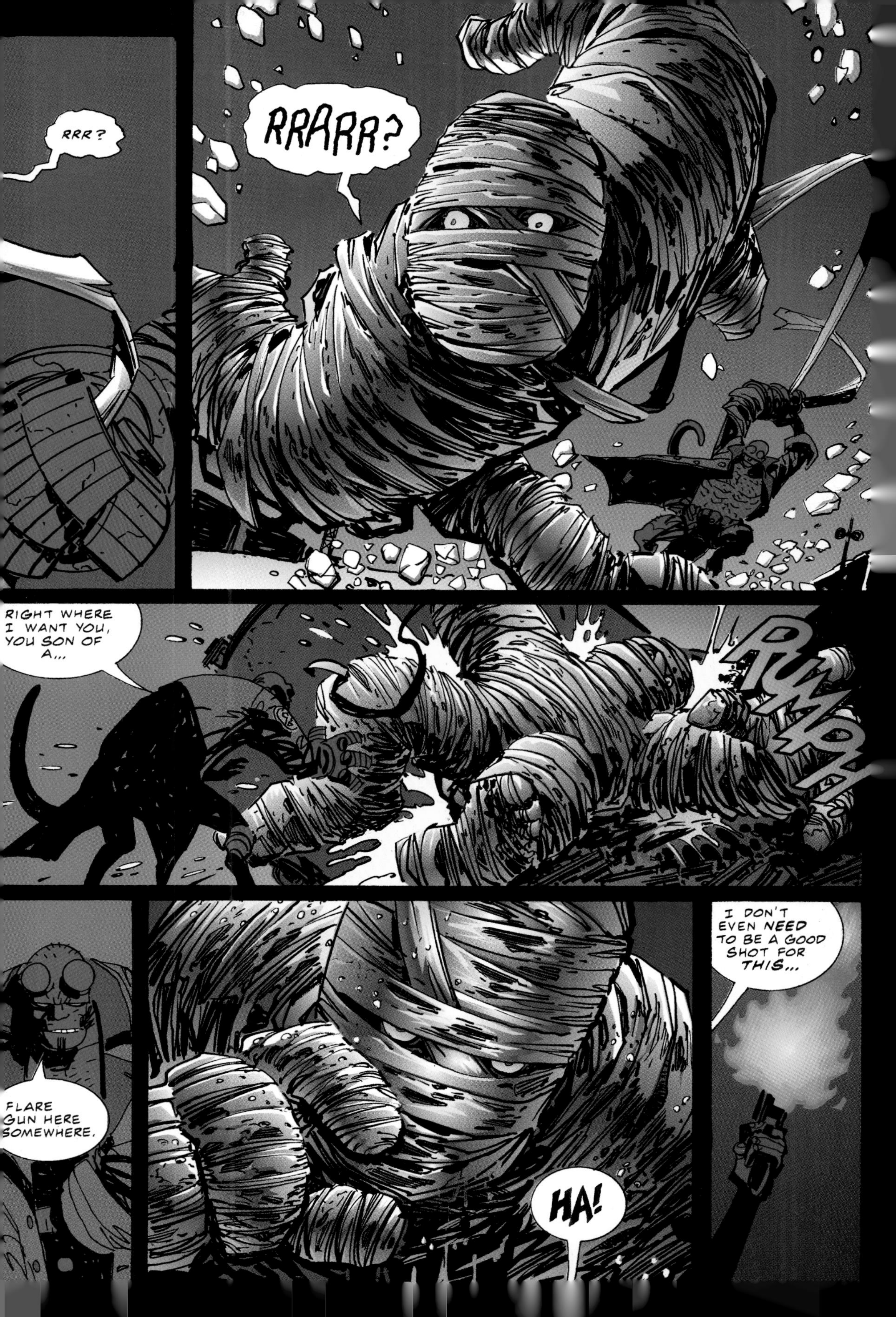
RRR?
RRARR?
RIGHT WHERE I WANT YOU, YOU SON OF A...
RUMPH
FLARE GUN HERE SOMEWHERE.
I DON'T EVEN NEED TO BE A GOOD SHOT FOR THIS...
HA!

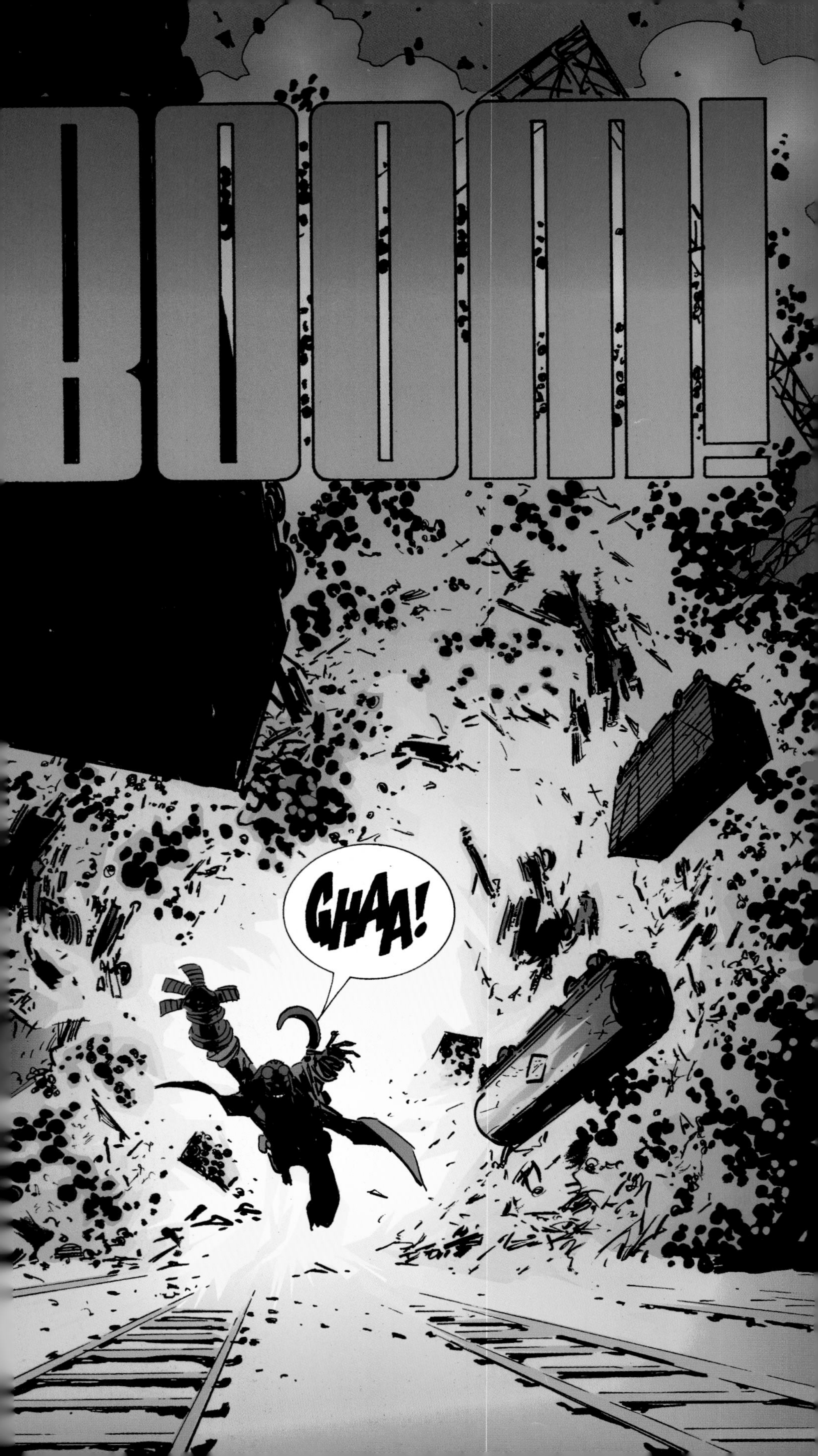
BOOM!
GHAA!

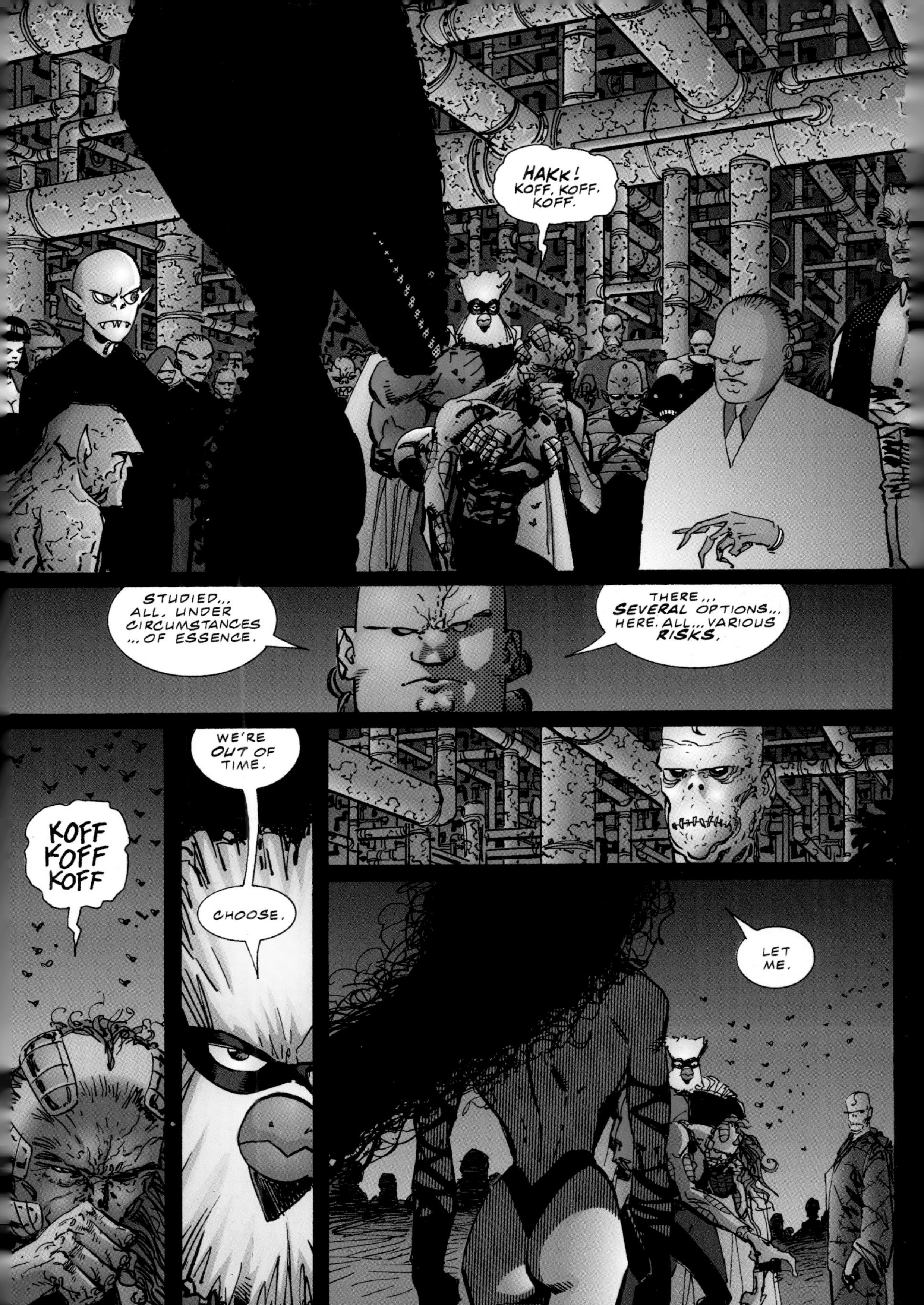
HAKK! KOFF. KOFF. KOFF.
STUDIED... ALL. UNDER CIRCUMSTANCES ...OF ESSENCE.
THERE... SEVERAL OPTIONS... HERE. ALL... VARIOUS RISKS.
KOFF KOFF KOFF
WE'RE OUT OF TIME.
CHOOSE.
LET ME.

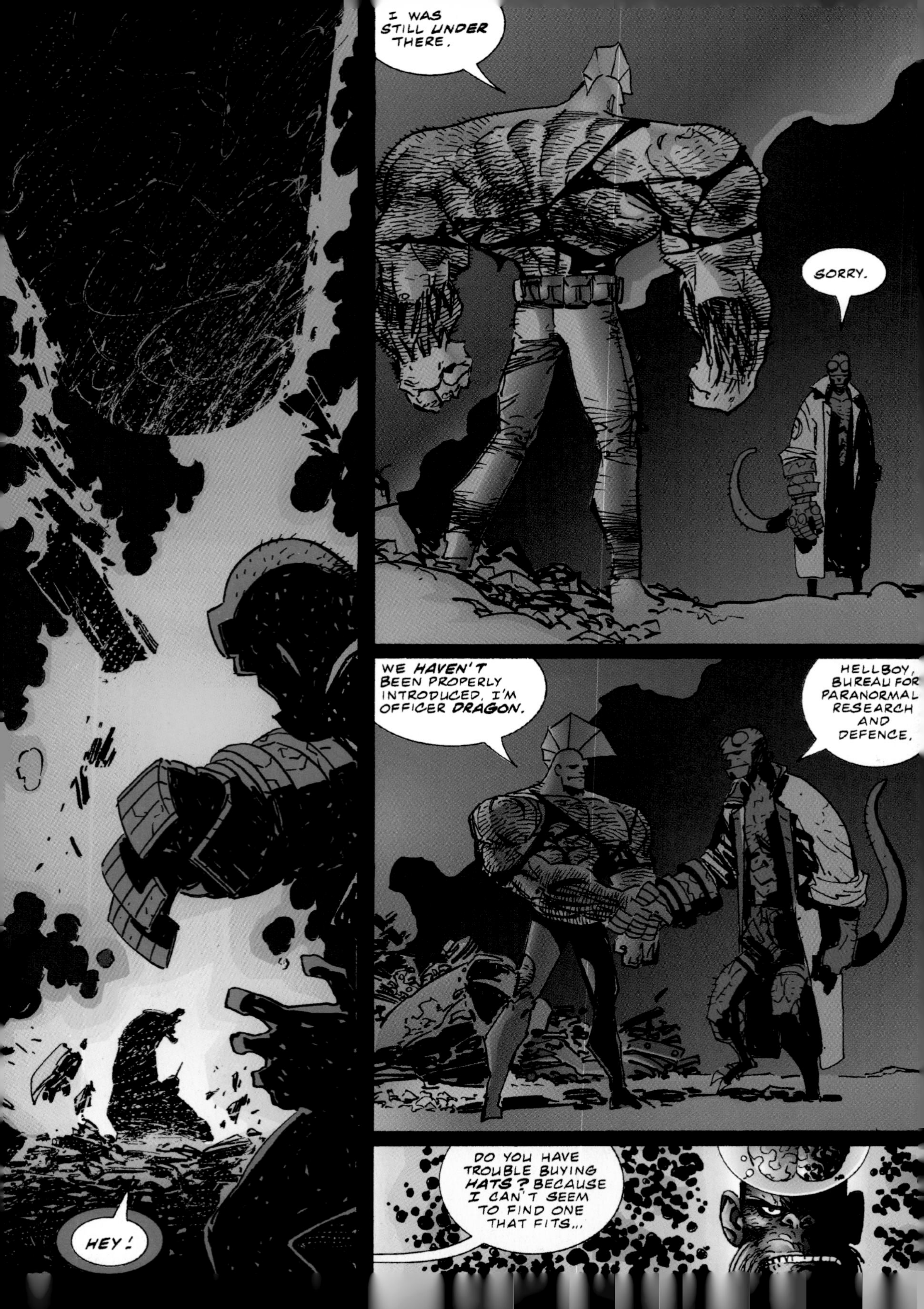
HEY!
I WAS STILL UNDER THERE.
SORRY.
WE HAVEN'T BEEN PROPERLY INTRODUCED. I'M OFFICER DRAGON.
HELLBOY, BUREAU FOR PARANORMAL RESEARCH AND DEFENCE.
DO YOU HAVE TROUBLE BUYING HATS? BECAUSE I CAN'T SEEM TO FIND ONE THAT FITS...

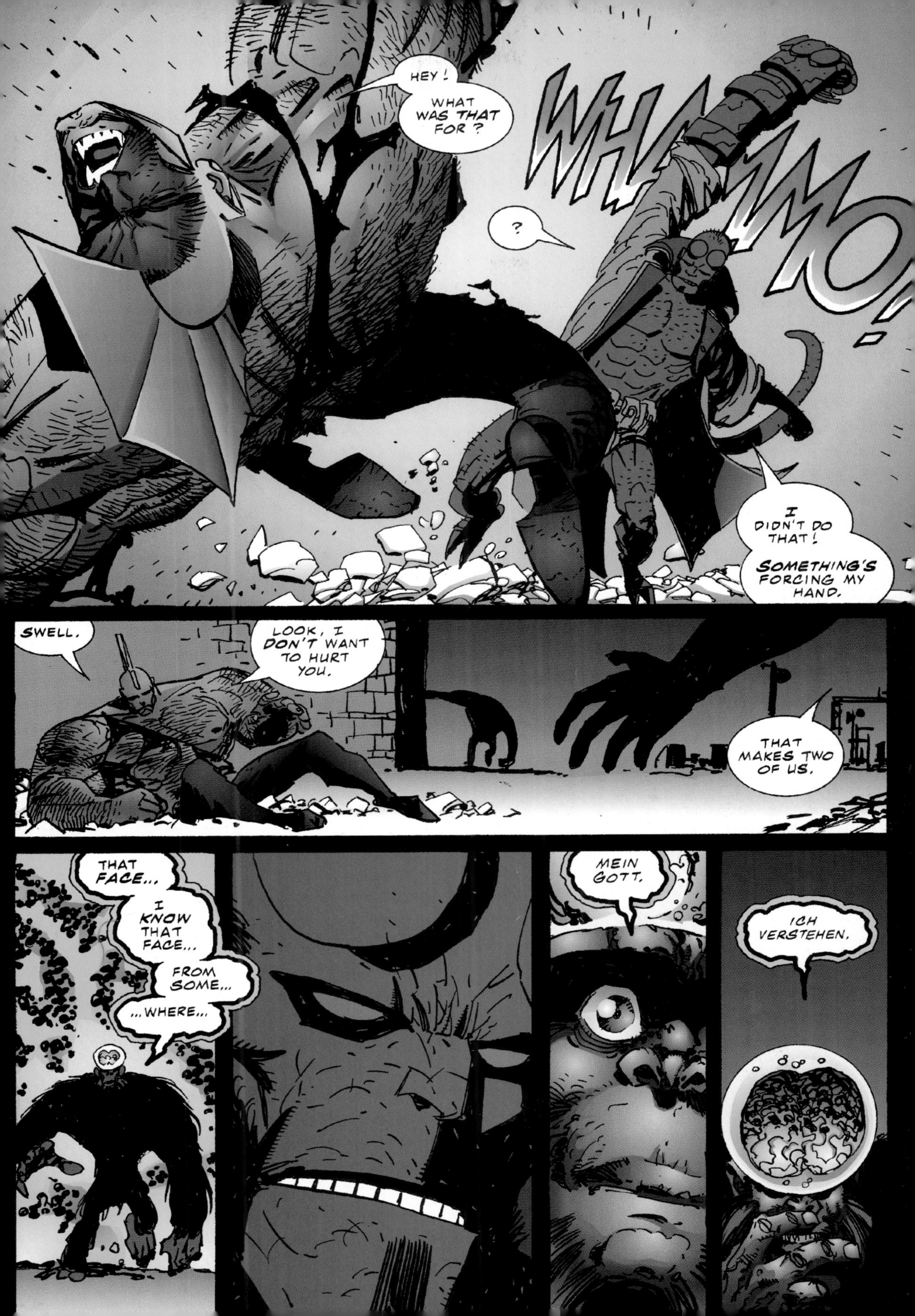
HEY!
WHAT WAS THAT FOR?
WHAMMO!
?
I DIDN'T DO THAT!
SOMETHING'S FORCING MY HAND.
SWELL.
LOOK, I DON'T WANT TO HURT YOU.
THAT MAKES TWO OF US.
THAT FACE...
I KNOW THAT FACE...
FROM SOME...
...WHERE...
MEIN GOTT.
ICH VERSTEHEN.

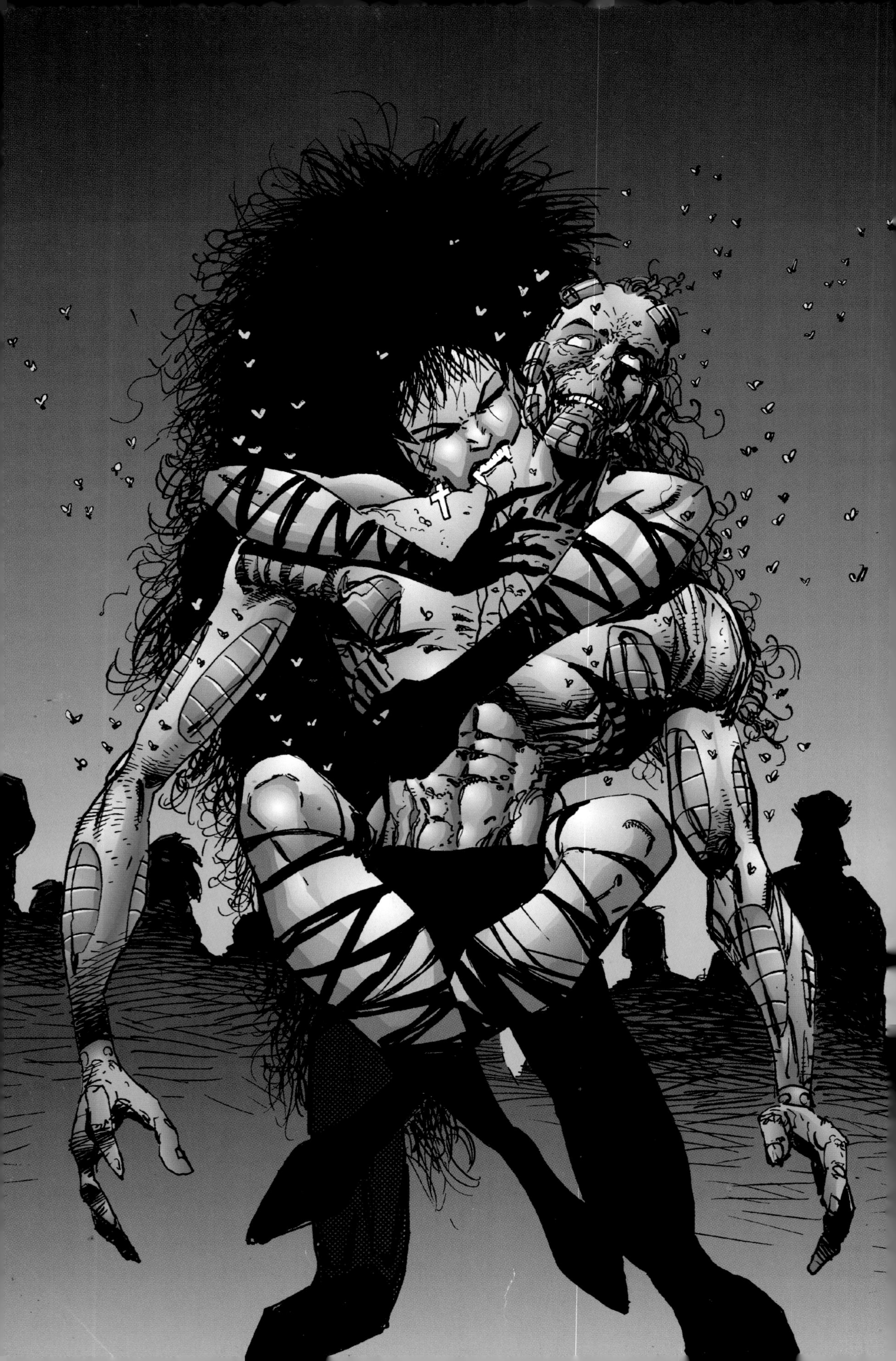

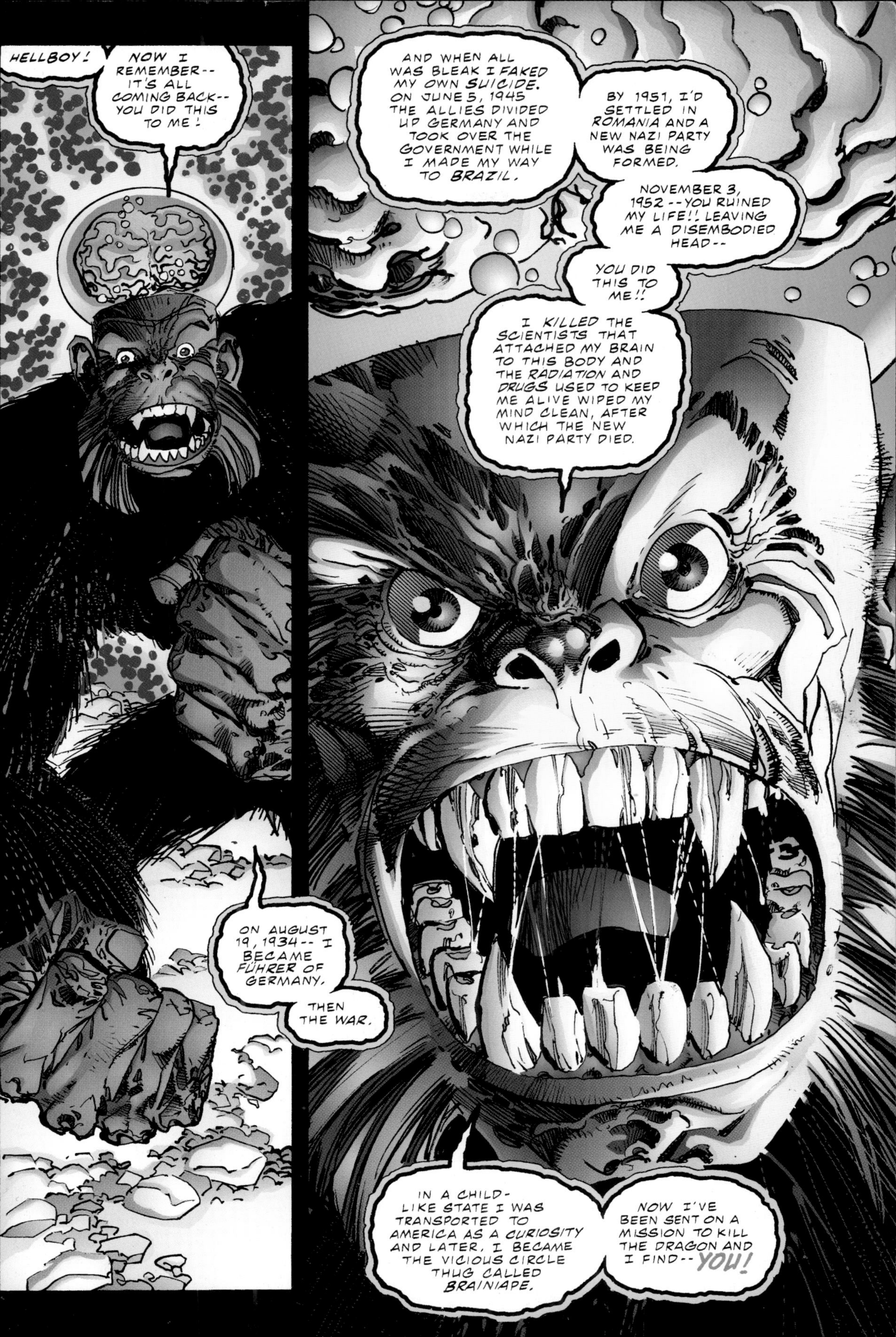
HELLBOY!
NOW I REMEMBER-- IT'S ALL COMING BACK-- YOU DID THIS TO ME!
ON AUGUST 19, 1934-- I BECAME FÜHRER OF GERMANY.
THEN THE WAR.
AND WHEN ALL WAS BLEAK I FAKED MY OWN SUICIDE. ON JUNE 5, 1945 THE ALLIES DIVIDED UP GERMANY AND TOOK OVER THE GOVERNMENT WHILE I MADE MY WAY TO BRAZIL.
BY 1951, I'D SETTLED IN ROMANIA AND A NEW NAZI PARTY WAS BEING FORMED.
NOVEMBER 3, 1952 --YOU RUINED MY LIFE!! LEAVING ME A DISEMBODIED HEAD--
YOU DID THIS TO ME!!
I KILLED THE SCIENTISTS THAT ATTACHED MY BRAIN TO THIS BODY AND THE RADIATION AND DRUGS USED TO KEEP ME ALIVE WIPED MY MIND CLEAN, AFTER WHICH THE NEW NAZI PARTY DIED.
IN A CHILD-LIKE STATE I WAS TRANSPORTED TO AMERICA AS A CURIOSITY AND LATER, I BECAME THE VICIOUS CIRCLE THUG CALLED BRAINIAPE.
NOW I'VE BEEN SENT ON A MISSION TO KILL THE DRAGON AND I FIND--YOU!

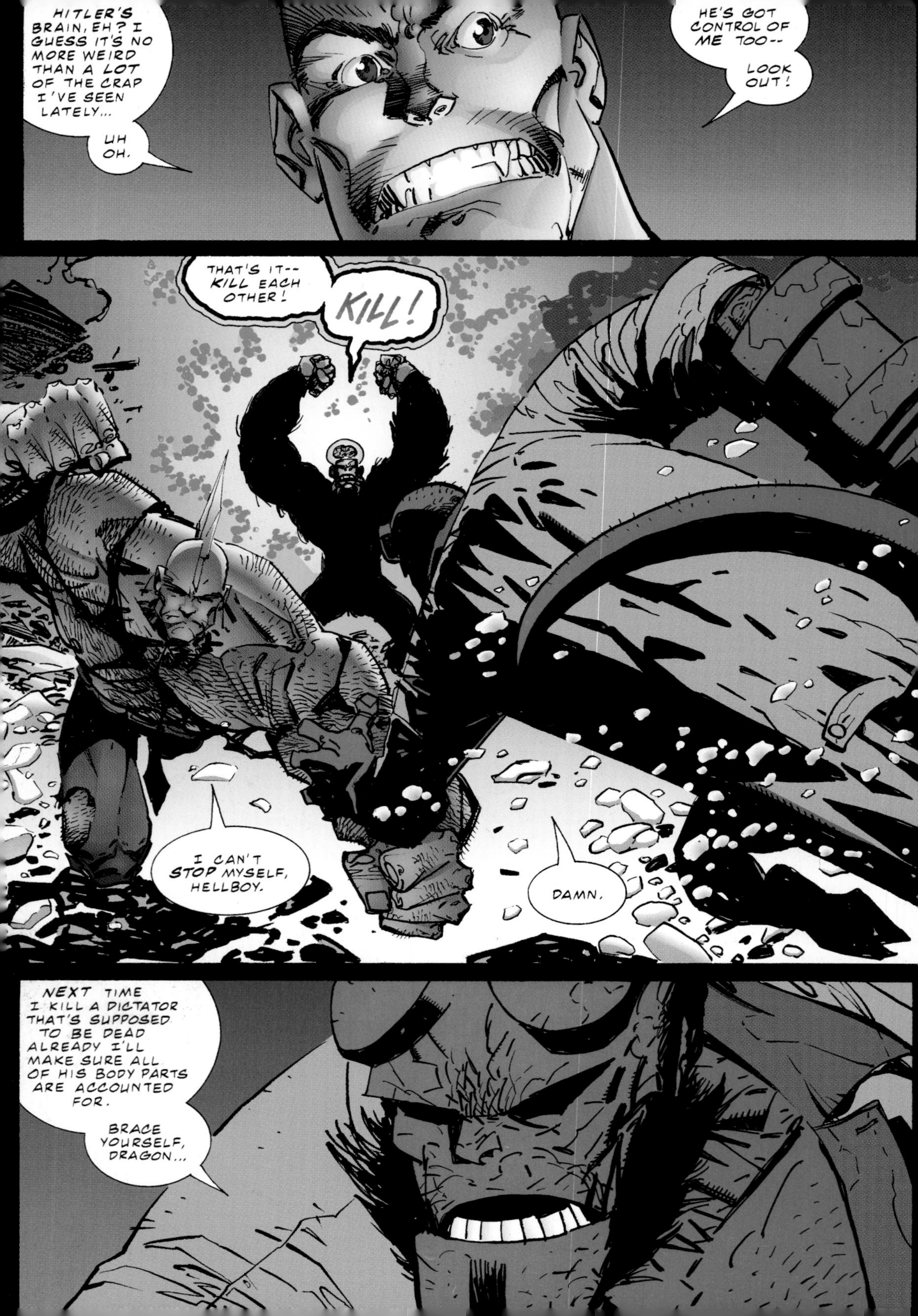
HITLER'S BRAIN, EH? I GUESS IT'S NO MORE WEIRD THAN A LOT OF THE CRAP I'VE SEEN LATELY...
UH OH.
HE'S GOT CONTROL OF ME TOO--
LOOK OUT!
THAT'S IT-- KILL EACH OTHER!
KILL!
I CAN'T STOP MYSELF, HELLBOY.
DAMN.
NEXT TIME I KILL A DICTATOR THAT'S SUPPOSED TO BE DEAD ALREADY I'LL MAKE SURE ALL OF HIS BODY PARTS ARE ACCOUNTED FOR.
BRACE YOURSELF, DRAGON...

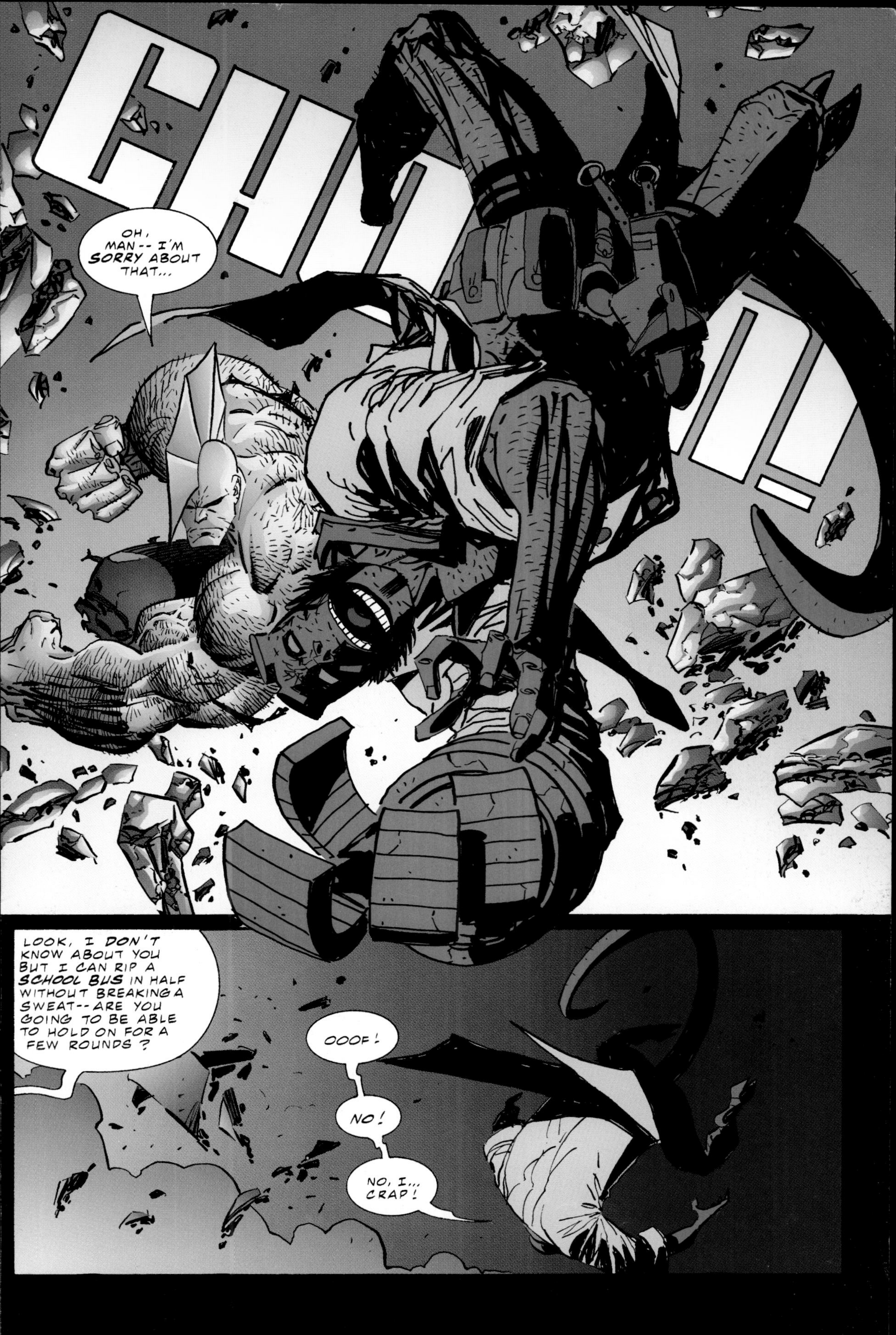
OH, MAN -- I'M SORRY ABOUT THAT...
LOOK, I DON'T KNOW ABOUT YOU BUT I CAN RIP A SCHOOL BUS IN HALF WITHOUT BREAKING A SWEAT -- ARE YOU GOING TO BE ABLE TO HOLD ON FOR A FEW ROUNDS ?
OOOF!
NO!
NO, I... CRAP!

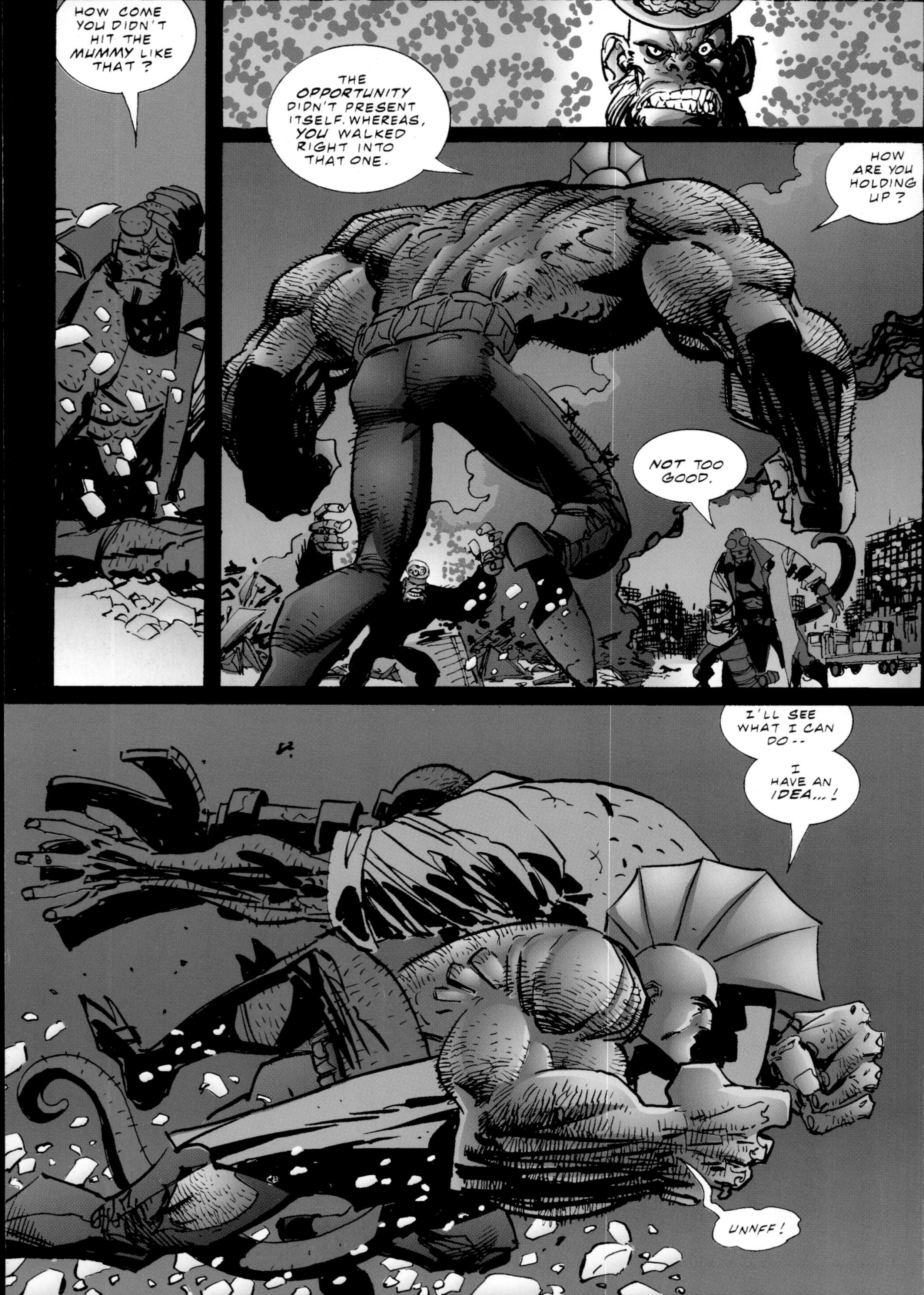
HOW COME YOU DIDN'T HIT THE MUMMY LIKE THAT ?
THE OPPORTUNITY DIDN'T PRESENT ITSELF. WHEREAS, YOU WALKED RIGHT INTO THAT ONE.
HOW ARE YOU HOLDING UP ?
NOT TOO GOOD.
I'LL SEE WHAT I CAN DO --
I HAVE AN IDEA... !
UNNFF !

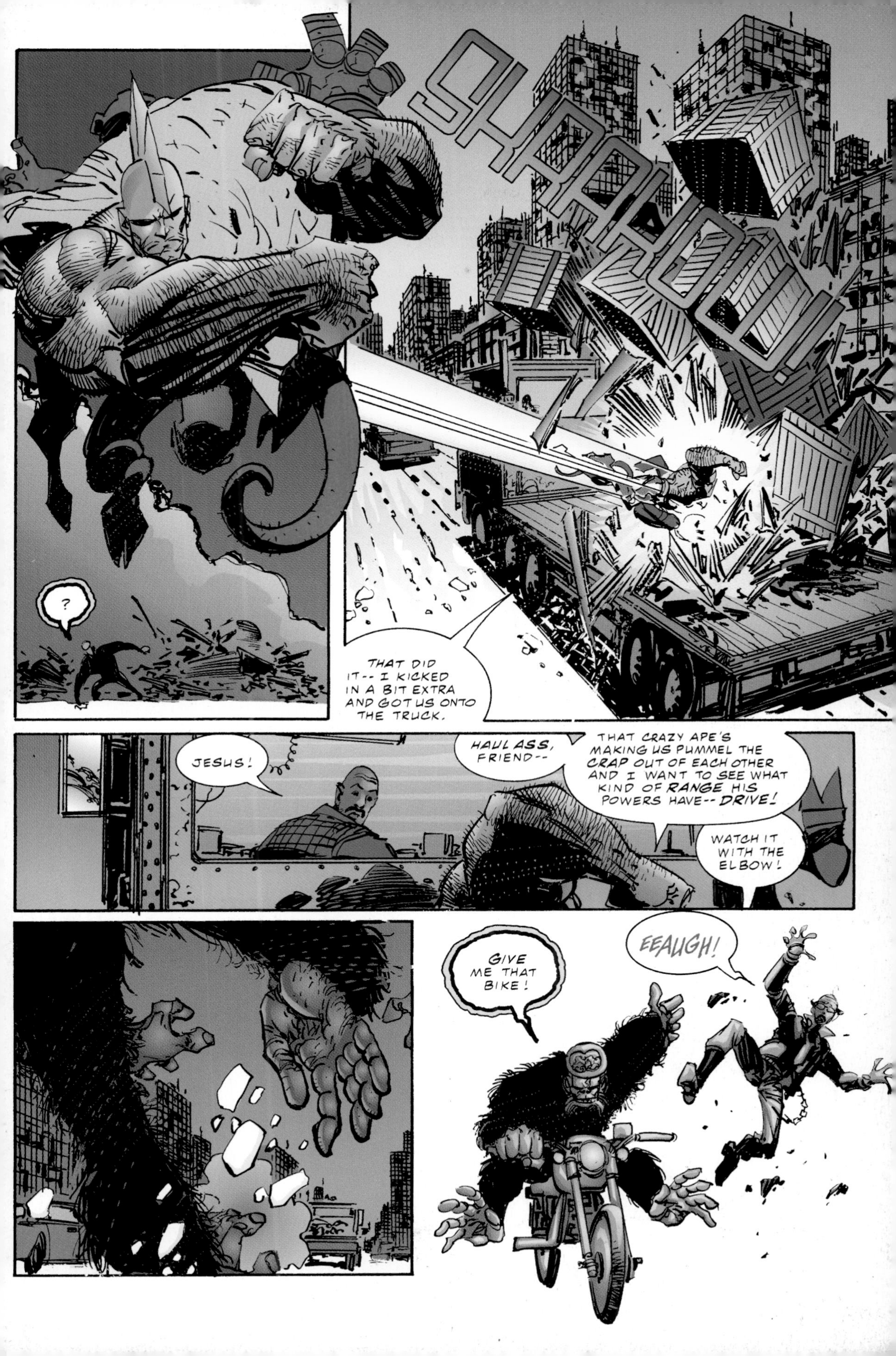

SHRAKOOM!
?
THAT DID IT-- I KICKED IN A BIT EXTRA AND GOT US ONTO THE TRUCK.
JESUS!
HAUL ASS, FRIEND--
THAT CRAZY APE'S MAKING US PUMMEL THE CRAP OUT OF EACH OTHER AND I WANT TO SEE WHAT KIND OF RANGE HIS POWERS HAVE-- DRIVE!
WATCH IT WITH THE ELBOW!
GIVE ME THAT BIKE!
EEAUGH!

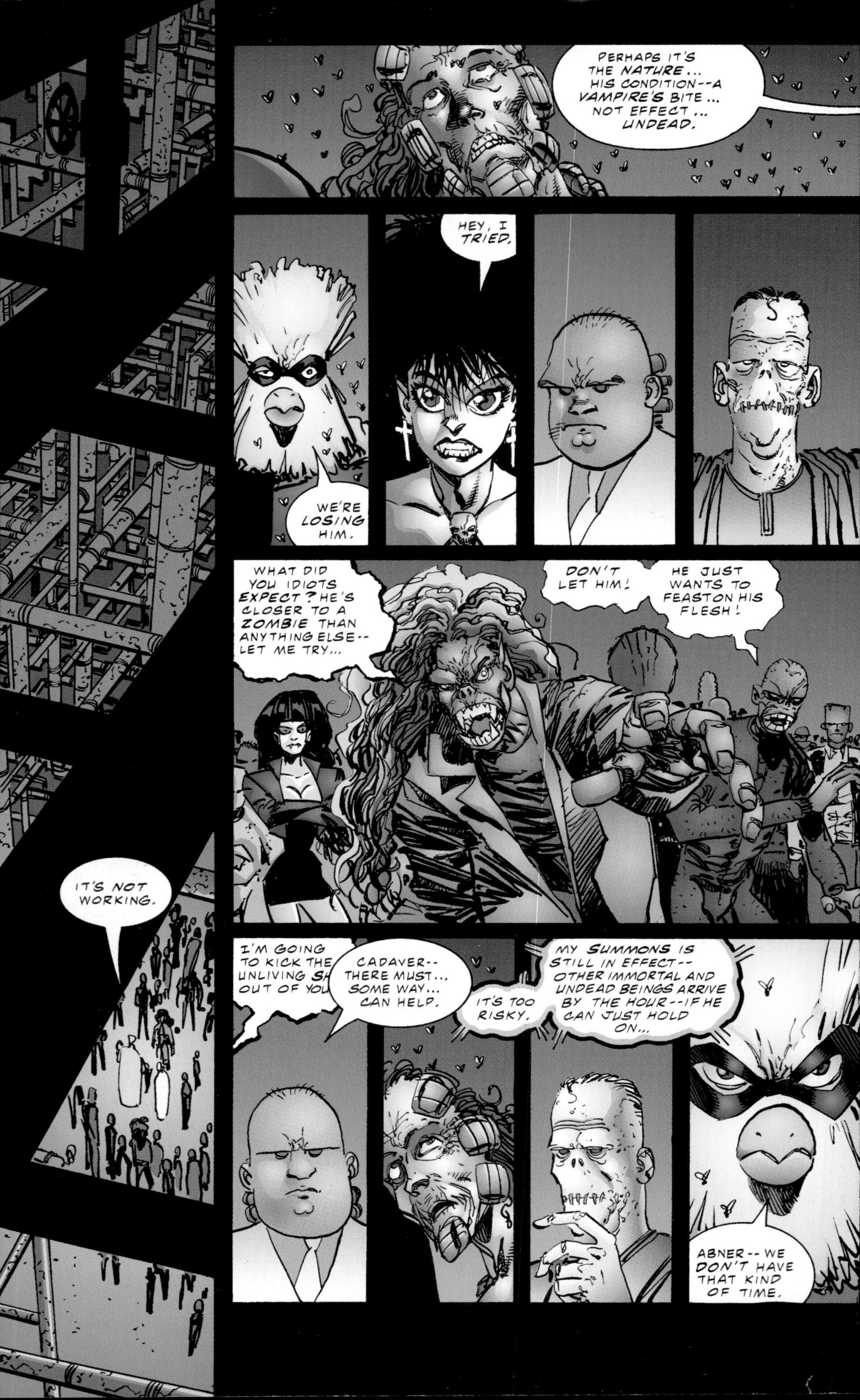

PERHAPS IT'S THE NATURE... HIS CONDITION--A VAMPIRE'S BITE... NOT EFFECT... UNDEAD.
HEY, I TRIED.
WE'RE LOSING HIM.
IT'S NOT WORKING.
WHAT DID YOU IDIOTS EXPECT? HE'S CLOSER TO A ZOMBIE THAN ANYTHING ELSE-- LET ME TRY...
DON'T LET HIM!
HE JUST WANTS TO FEASTON HIS FLESH!
I'M GOING TO KICK THE UNLIVING SH OUT OF YOU
CADAVER-- THERE MUST... SOME WAY... CAN HELP.
IT'S TOO RISKY.
MY SUMMONS IS STILL IN EFFECT-- OTHER IMMORTAL AND UNDEAD BEINGS ARRIVE BY THE HOUR--IF HE CAN JUST HOLD ON...
ABNER--WE DON'T HAVE THAT KIND OF TIME.

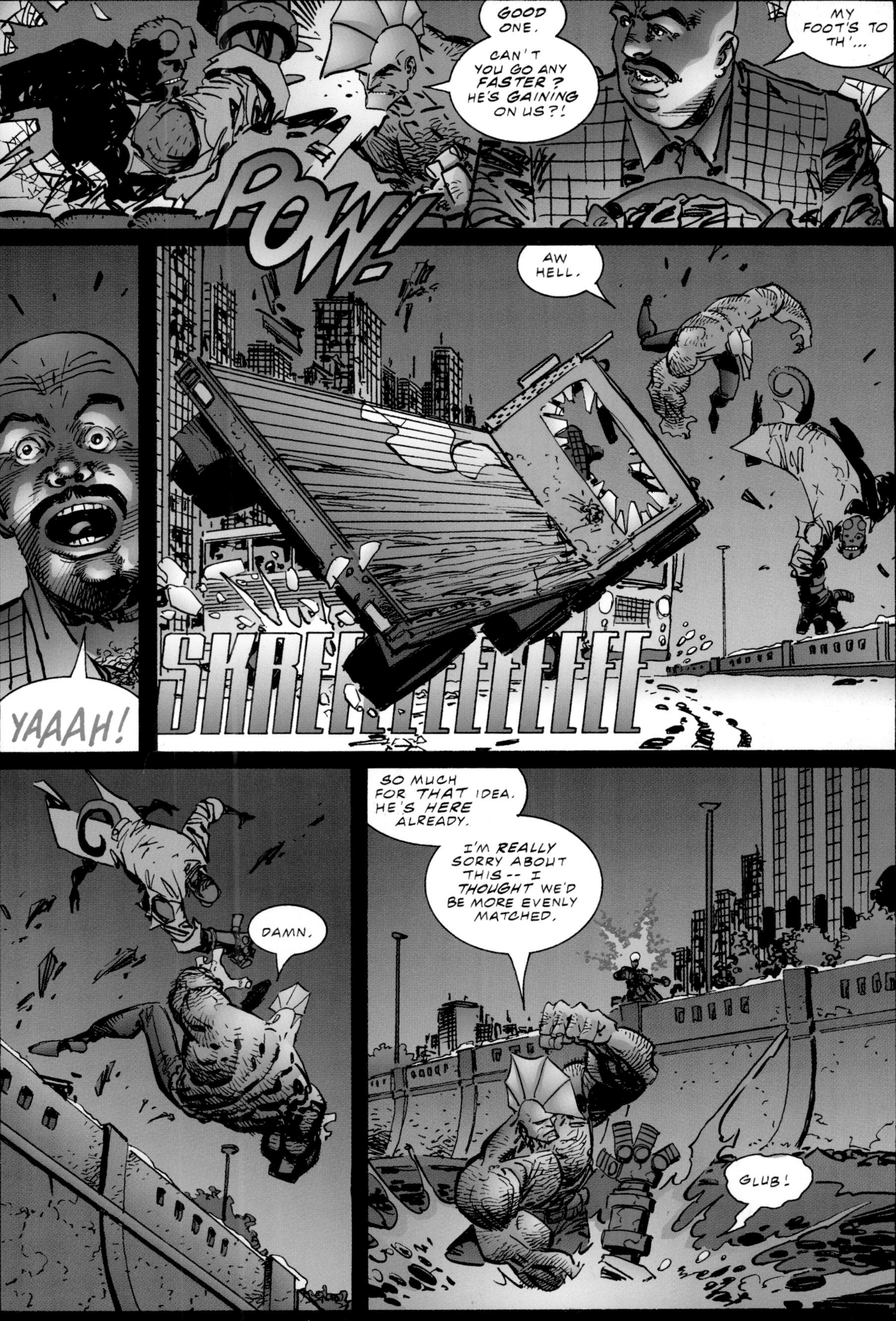
GOOD ONE.
CAN'T YOU GO ANY FASTER? HE'S GAINING ON US?!
MY FOOT'S TO TH'...
POW!
AW HELL.
SKREEEEEEEEEEE
YAAAH!
SO MUCH FOR THAT IDEA. HE'S HERE ALREADY.
I'M REALLY SORRY ABOUT THIS -- I THOUGHT WE'D BE MORE EVENLY MATCHED.
DAMN.
GLUB!

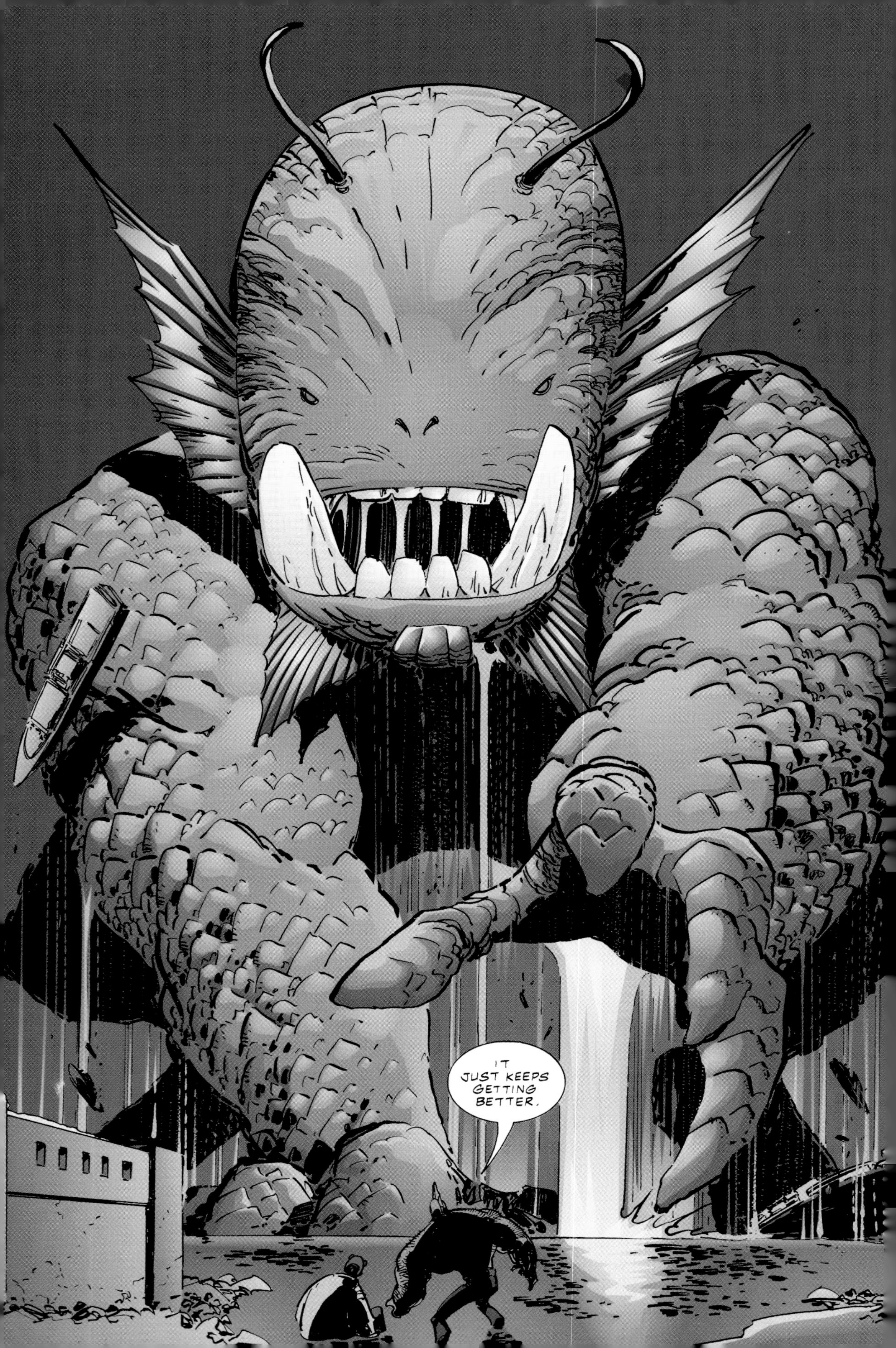
IT JUST KEEPS GETTING BETTER.

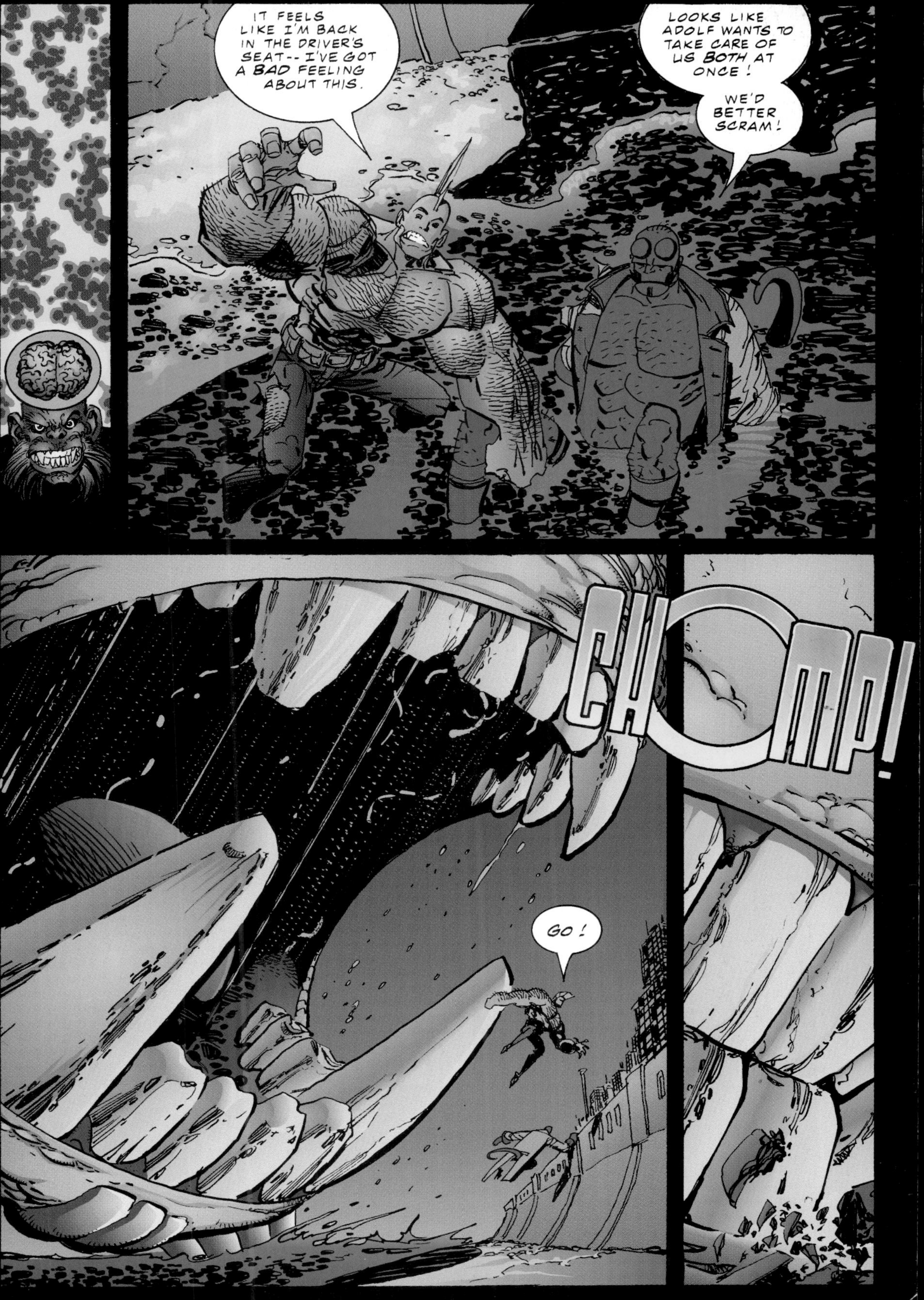

IT FEELS LIKE I'M BACK IN THE DRIVER'S SEAT-- I'VE GOT A BAD FEELING ABOUT THIS.
LOOKS LIKE ADOLF WANTS TO TAKE CARE OF US BOTH AT ONCE!
WE'D BETTER SCRAM!
CHOMP!
GO!

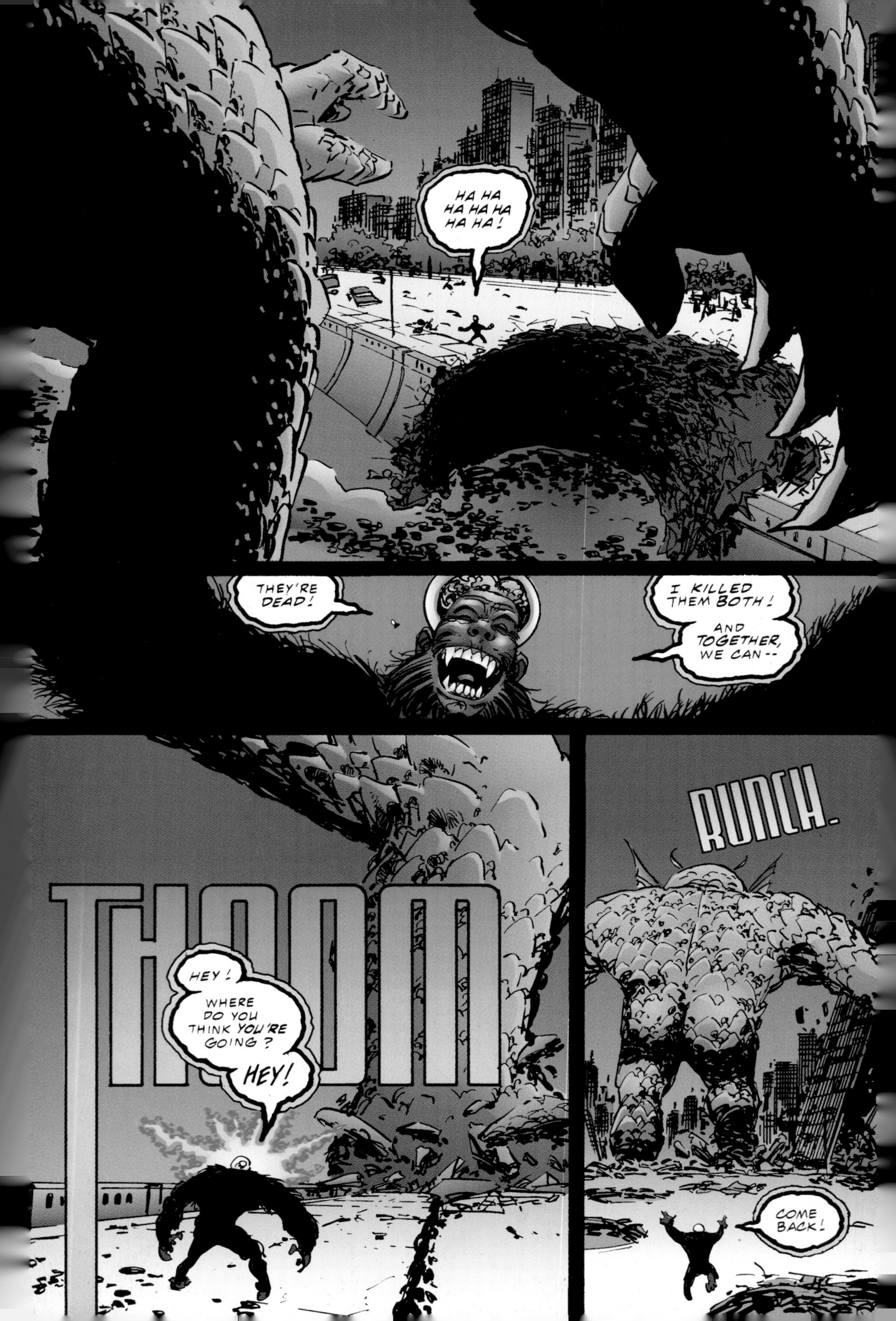
HA HA HA HA HA HA HA!
THEY'RE DEAD!
I KILLED THEM BOTH!
AND TOGETHER, WE CAN--
THOOM
HEY!
WHERE DO YOU THINK YOU'RE GOING?
HEY!
RUNCH.
COME BACK!

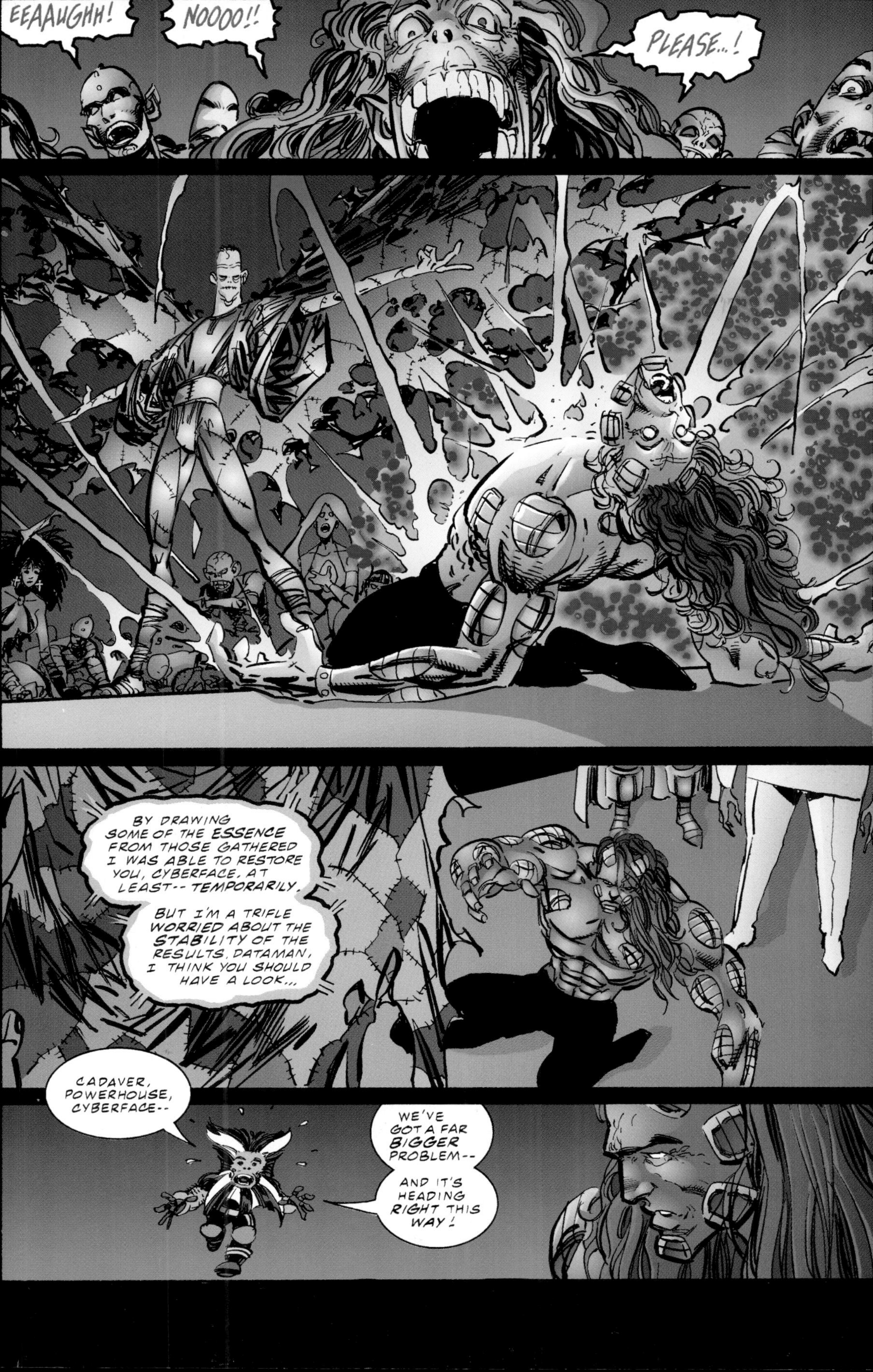
EEAAUGHH!
NOOOO!!
PLEASE...!
BY DRAWING SOME OF THE ESSENCE FROM THOSE GATHERED I WAS ABLE TO RESTORE YOU, CYBERFACE, AT LEAST-- TEMPORARILY.
BUT I'M A TRIFLE WORRIED ABOUT THE STABILITY OF THE RESULTS, DATAMAN, I THINK YOU SHOULD HAVE A LOOK...
CADAVER, POWERHOUSE, CYBERFACE--
WE'VE GOT A FAR BIGGER PROBLEM--
AND IT'S HEADING RIGHT THIS WAY!

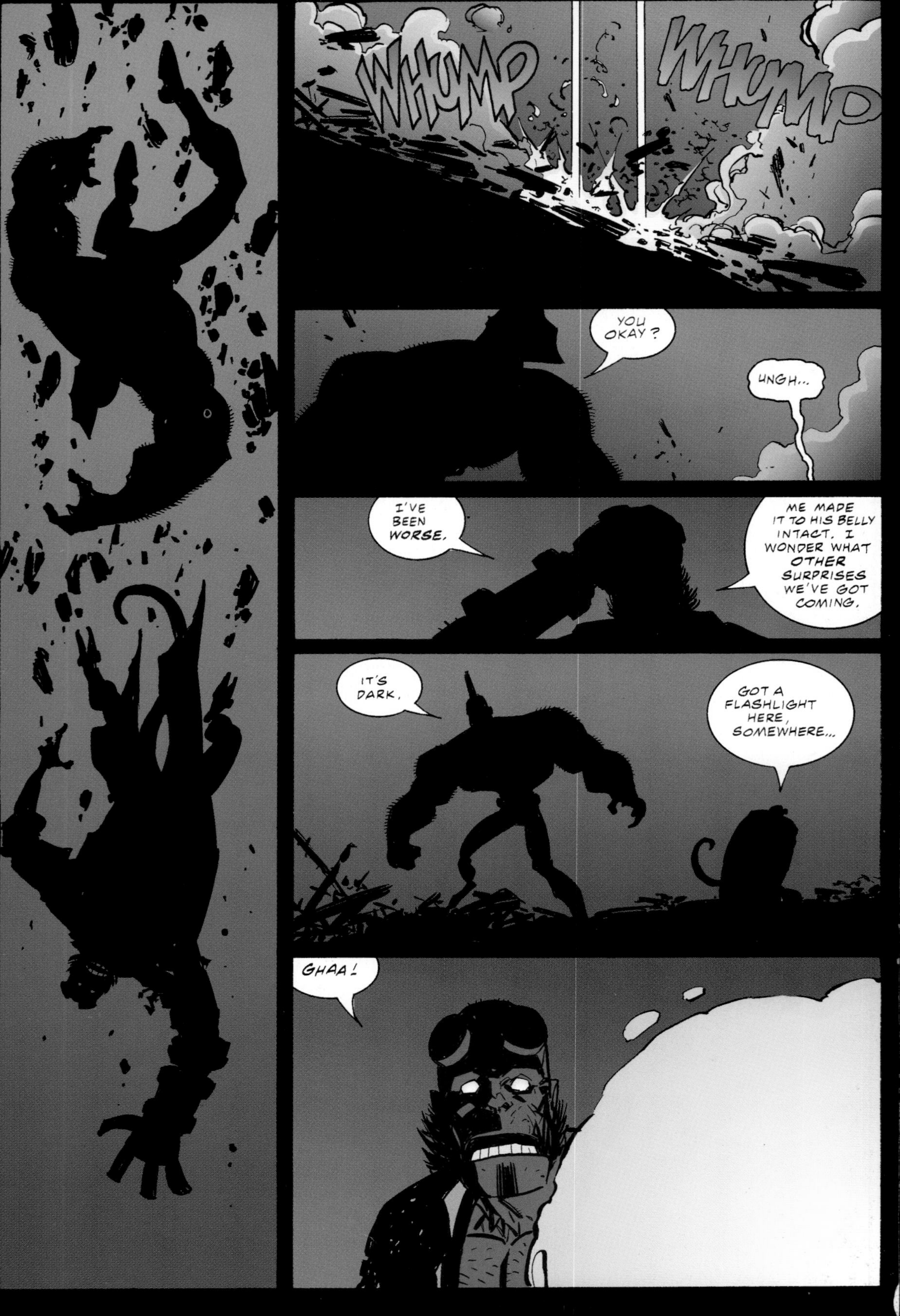
WHUMP
WHUMP
YOU OKAY?
UNGH...
I'VE BEEN WORSE.
ME MADE IT TO HIS BELLY INTACT. I WONDER WHAT OTHER SURPRISES WE'VE GOT COMING.
IT'S DARK.
GOT A FLASHLIGHT HERE, SOMEWHERE...
GHAA!

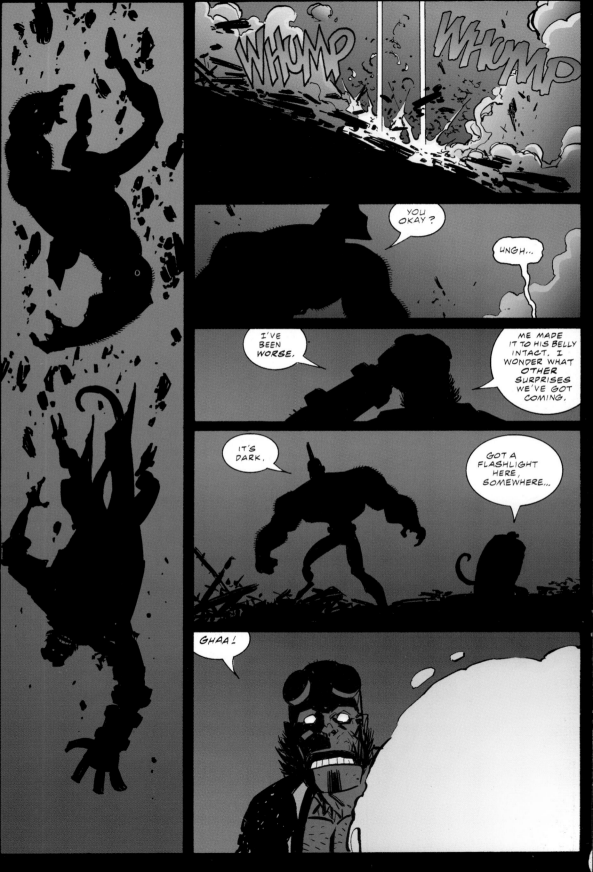

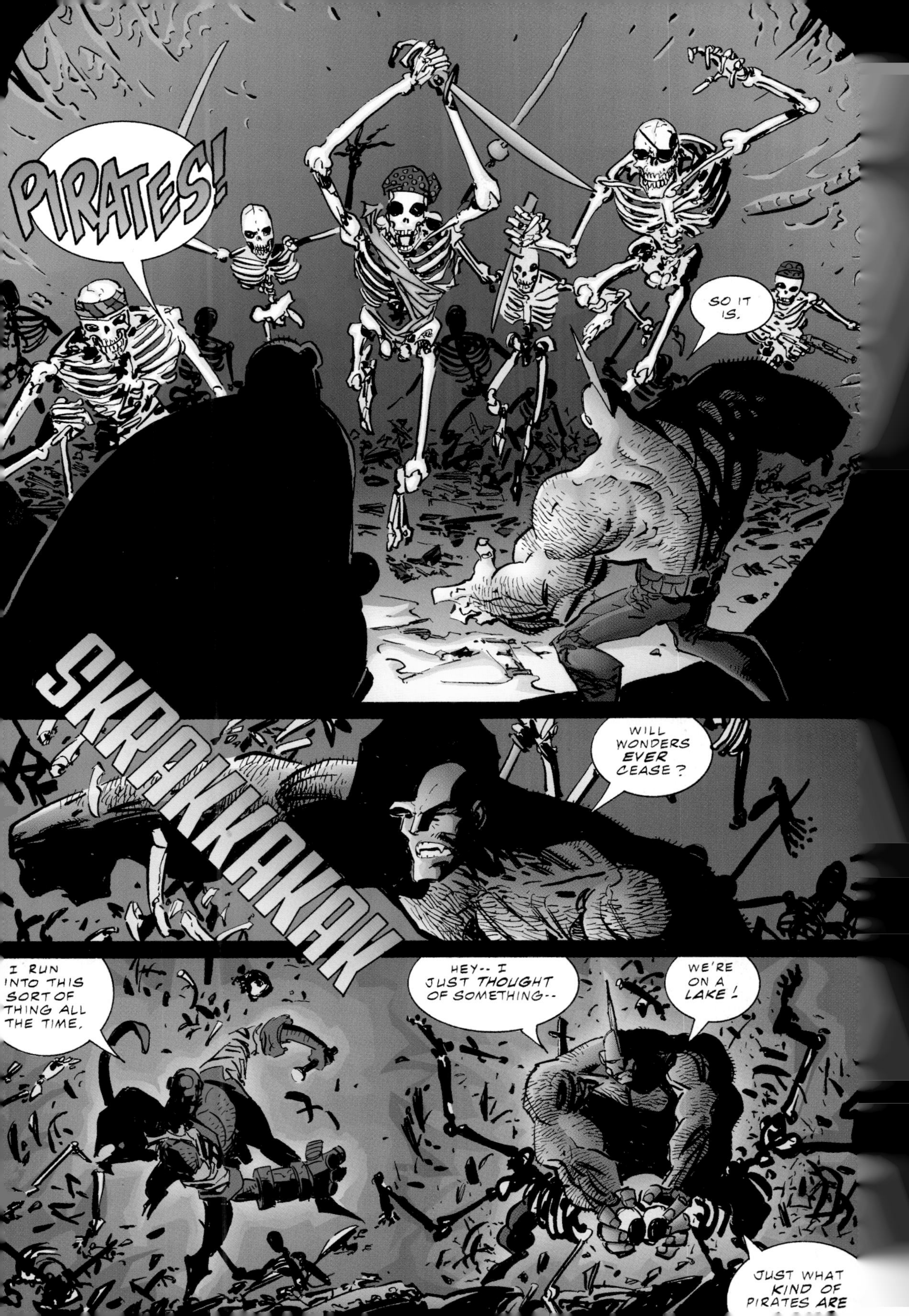

PIRATES!
SO IT IS.
SKRAKKAKAKAK
WILL WONDERS EVER CEASE?
I RUN INTO THIS SORT OF THING ALL THE TIME.
HEY-- I JUST THOUGHT OF SOMETHING--
WE'RE ON A LAKE!
JUST WHAT KIND OF PIRATES ARE

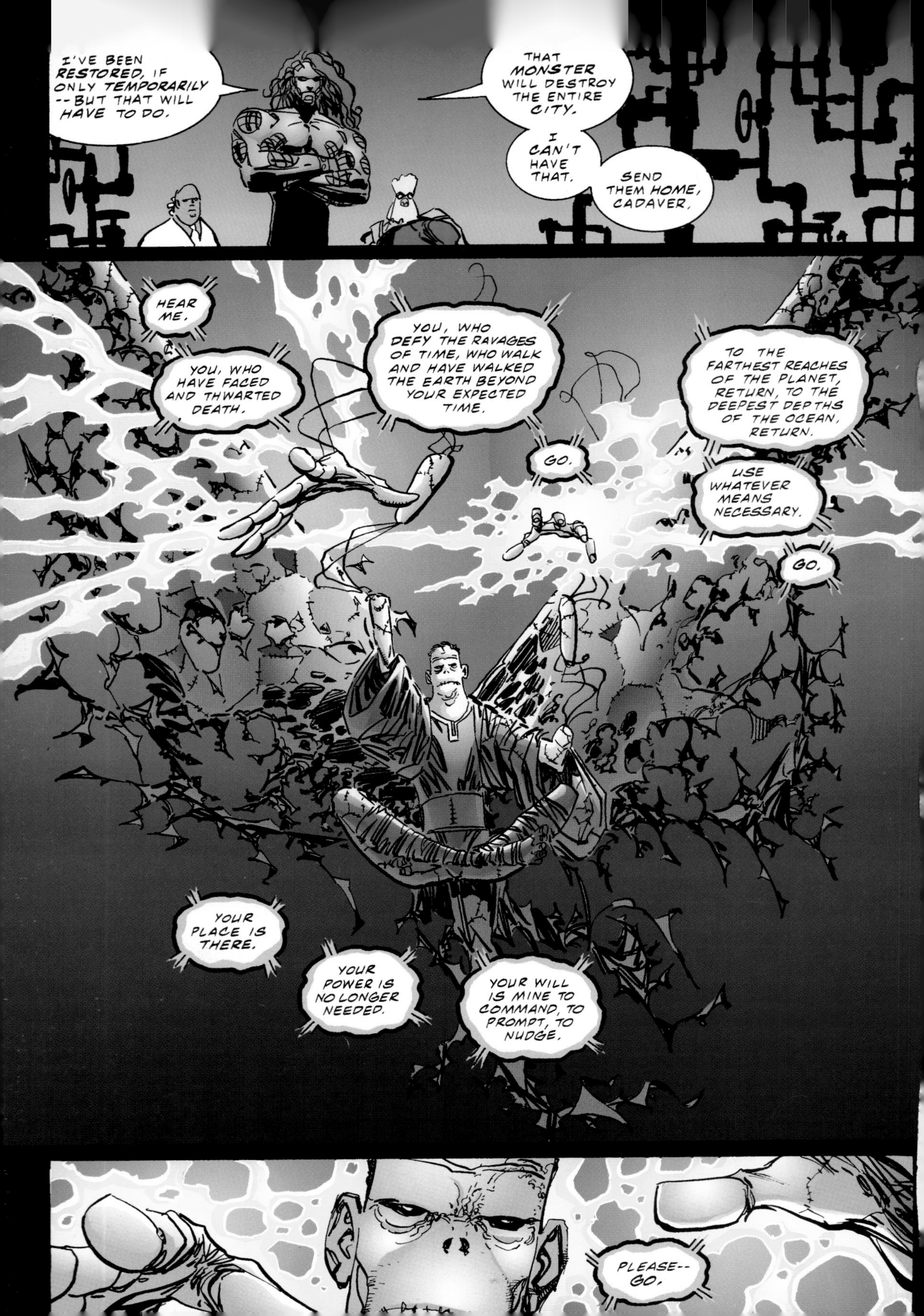
I'VE BEEN RESTORED, IF ONLY TEMPORARILY --BUT THAT WILL HAVE TO DO.
THAT MONSTER WILL DESTROY THE ENTIRE CITY.
I CAN'T HAVE THAT.
SEND THEM HOME, CADAVER.
HEAR ME.
YOU, WHO HAVE FACED AND THWARTED DEATH.
YOU, WHO DEFY THE RAVAGES OF TIME, WHO WALK AND HAVE WALKED THE EARTH BEYOND YOUR EXPECTED TIME.
GO.
TO THE FARTHEST REACHES OF THE PLANET, RETURN, TO THE DEEPEST DEPTHS OF THE OCEAN, RETURN.
USE WHATEVER MEANS NECESSARY.
GO.
YOUR PLACE IS THERE.
YOUR POWER IS NO LONGER NEEDED.
YOUR WILL IS MINE TO COMMAND, TO PROMPT, TO NUDGE.
PLEASE-- GO.

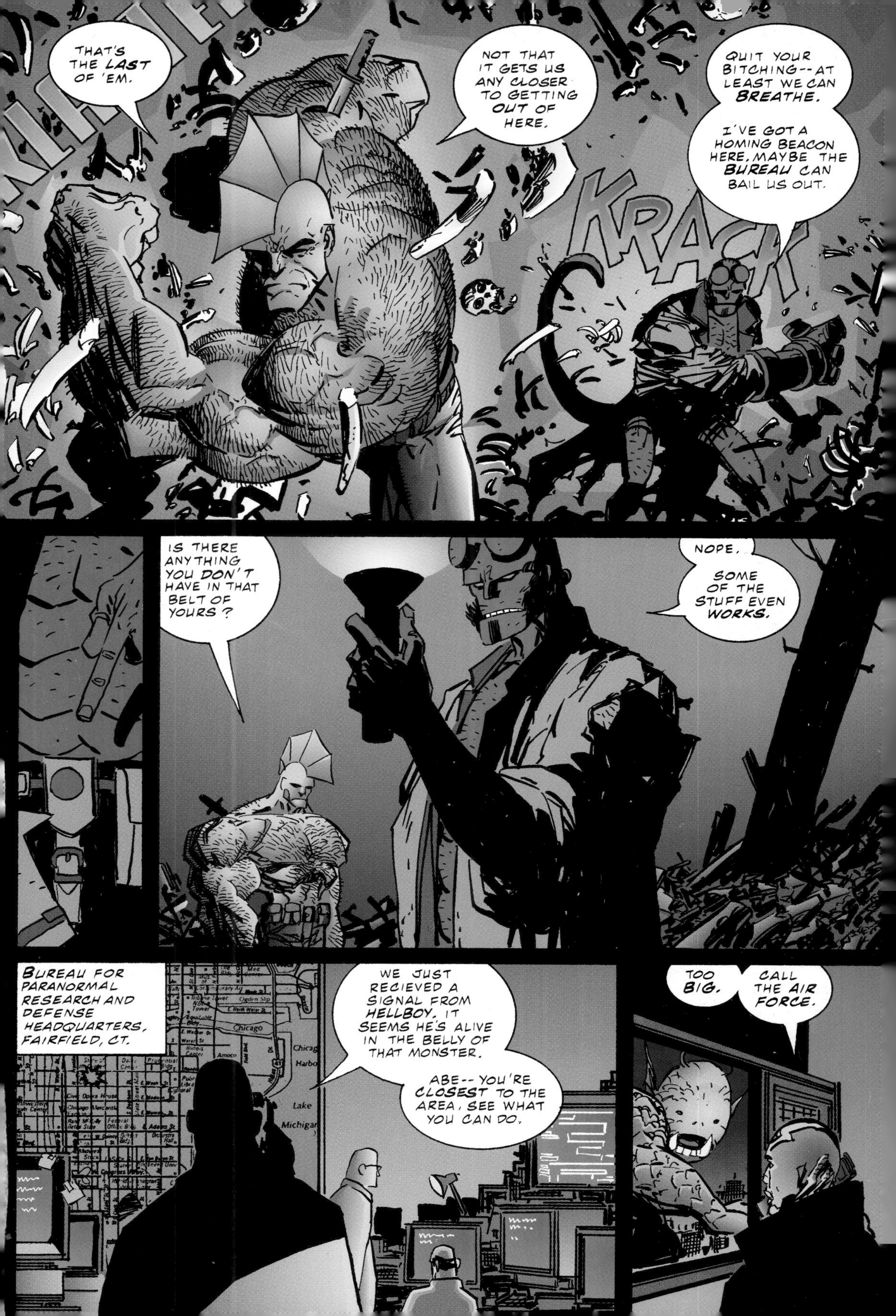
THAT'S THE LAST OF 'EM.
NOT THAT IT GETS US ANY CLOSER TO GETTING OUT OF HERE.
QUIT YOUR BITCHING--AT LEAST WE CAN BREATHE.
I'VE GOT A HOMING BEACON HERE. MAYBE THE BUREAU CAN BAIL US OUT.
KRACK
IS THERE ANYTHING YOU DON'T HAVE IN THAT BELT OF YOURS?
NOPE.
SOME OF THE STUFF EVEN WORKS.
BUREAU FOR PARANORMAL RESEARCH AND DEFENSE HEADQUARTERS, FAIRFIELD, CT.
WE JUST RECIEVED A SIGNAL FROM HELLBOY. IT SEEMS HE'S ALIVE IN THE BELLY OF THAT MONSTER.
ABE-- YOU'RE CLOSEST TO THE AREA. SEE WHAT YOU CAN DO.
TOO BIG.
CALL THE AIR FORCE.

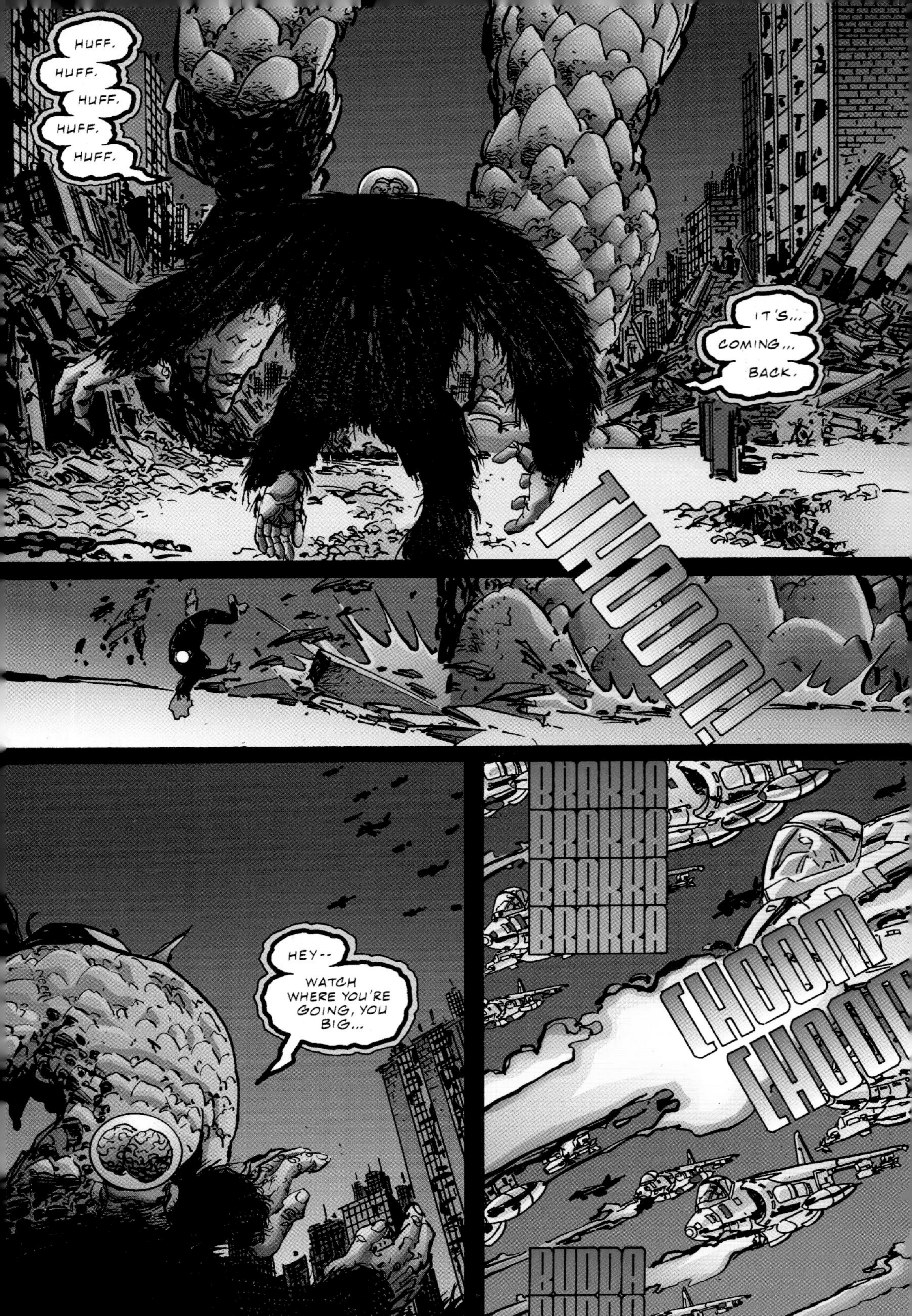
HUFF. HUFF. HUFF. HUFF. HUFF.
IT'S... COMING... BACK.
THOOM!
BRAKKA BRAKKA BRAKKA BRAKKA
HEY-- WATCH WHERE YOU'RE GOING, YOU BIG...
CHOOM
BUDDA

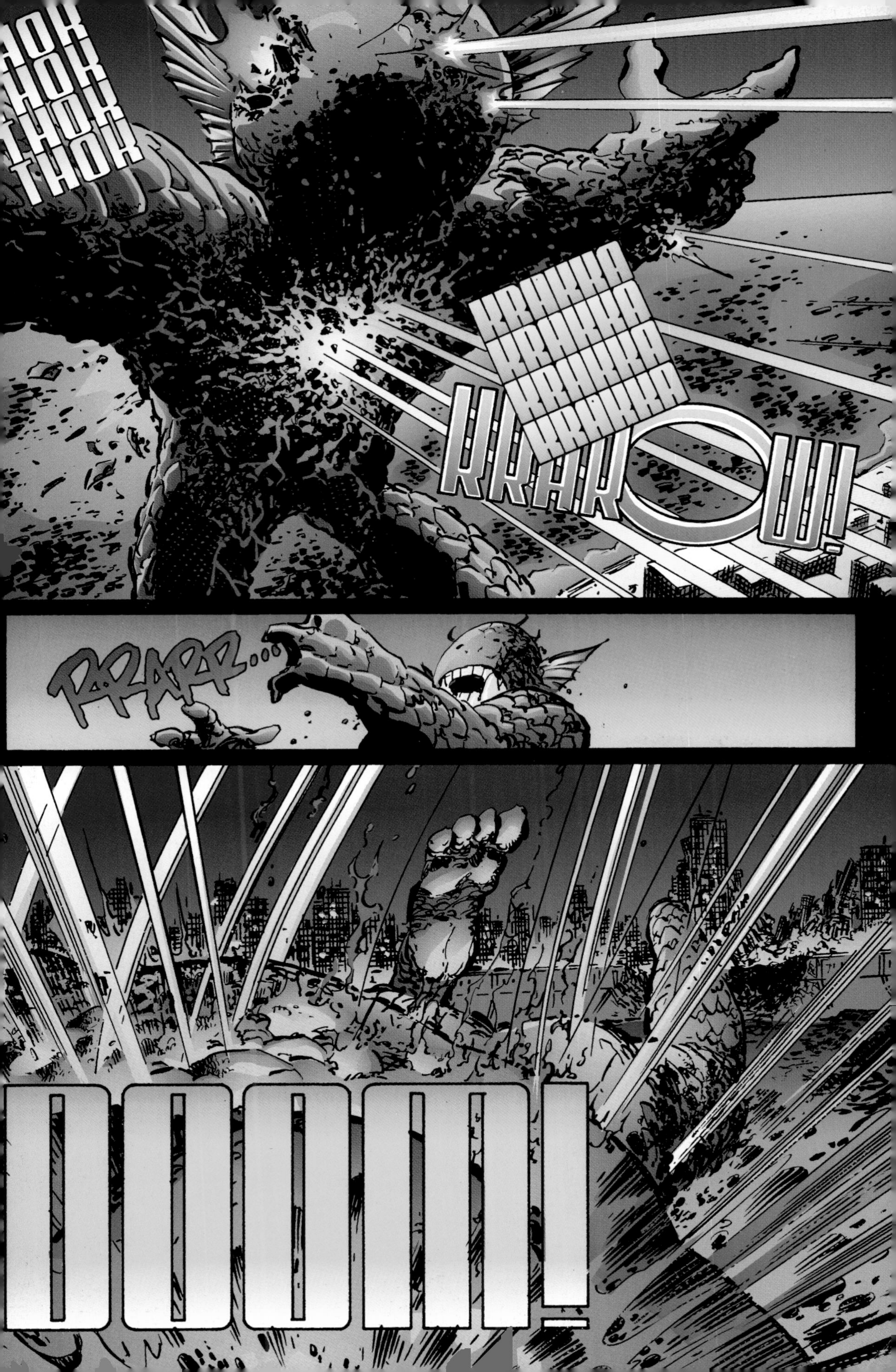
HOK
THOK
THOK
THOK
KRAKKA
KRAKKA
KRAKKA
KRAKKA
KRAKOW!
RRARR...
DOOM!

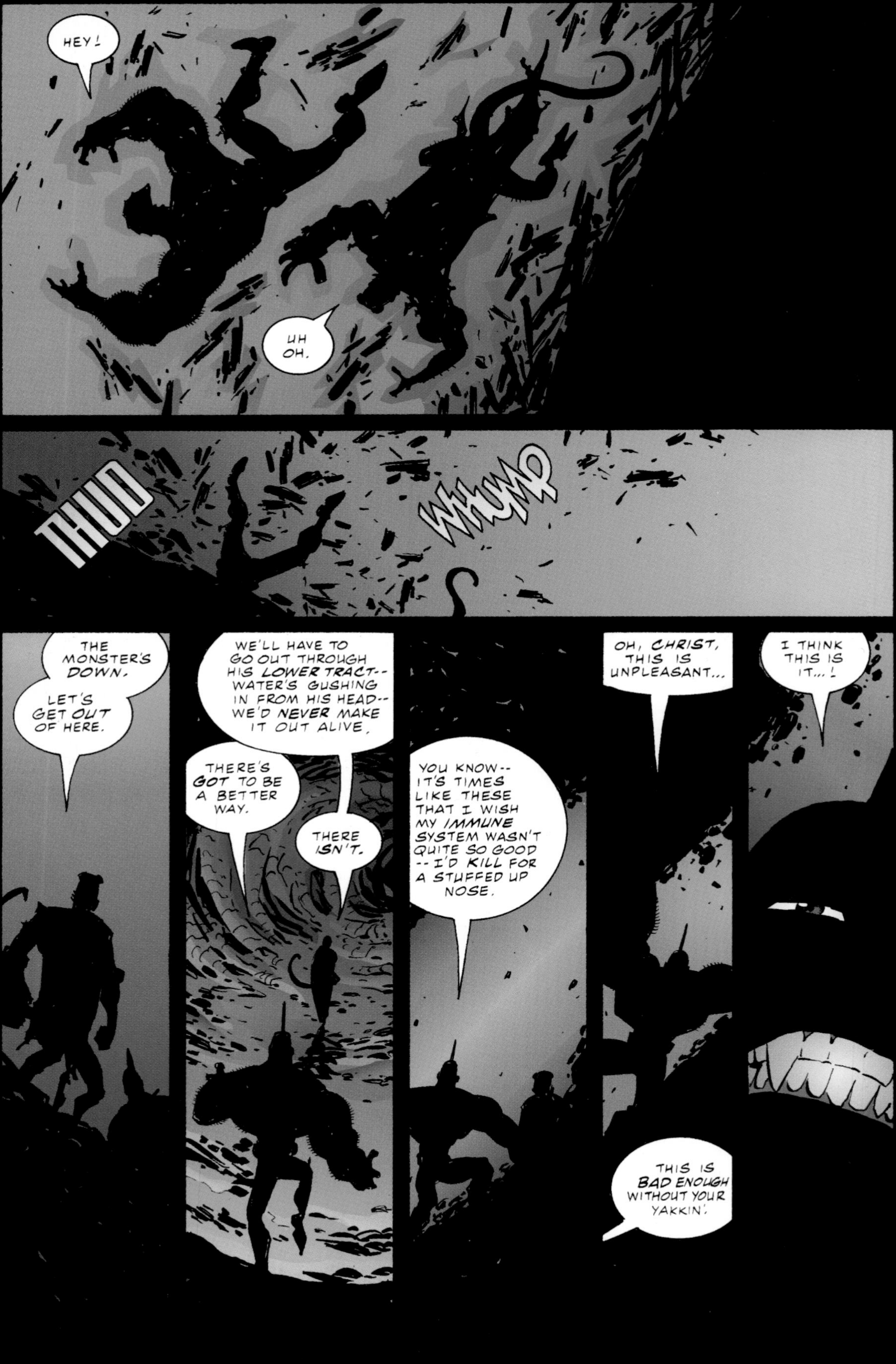
HEY!
UH OH.
THUD
WHUMP
THE MONSTER'S DOWN.
LET'S GET OUT OF HERE.
WE'LL HAVE TO GO OUT THROUGH HIS LOWER TRACT-- WATER'S GUSHING IN FROM HIS HEAD-- WE'D NEVER MAKE IT OUT ALIVE.
THERE'S GOT TO BE A BETTER WAY.
THERE ISN'T.
YOU KNOW-- IT'S TIMES LIKE THESE THAT I WISH MY IMMUNE SYSTEM WASN'T QUITE SO GOOD -- I'D KILL FOR A STUFFED UP NOSE.
OH, CHRIST, THIS IS UNPLEASANT...
THIS IS BAD ENOUGH WITHOUT YOUR YAKKIN'.
I THINK THIS IS IT...!

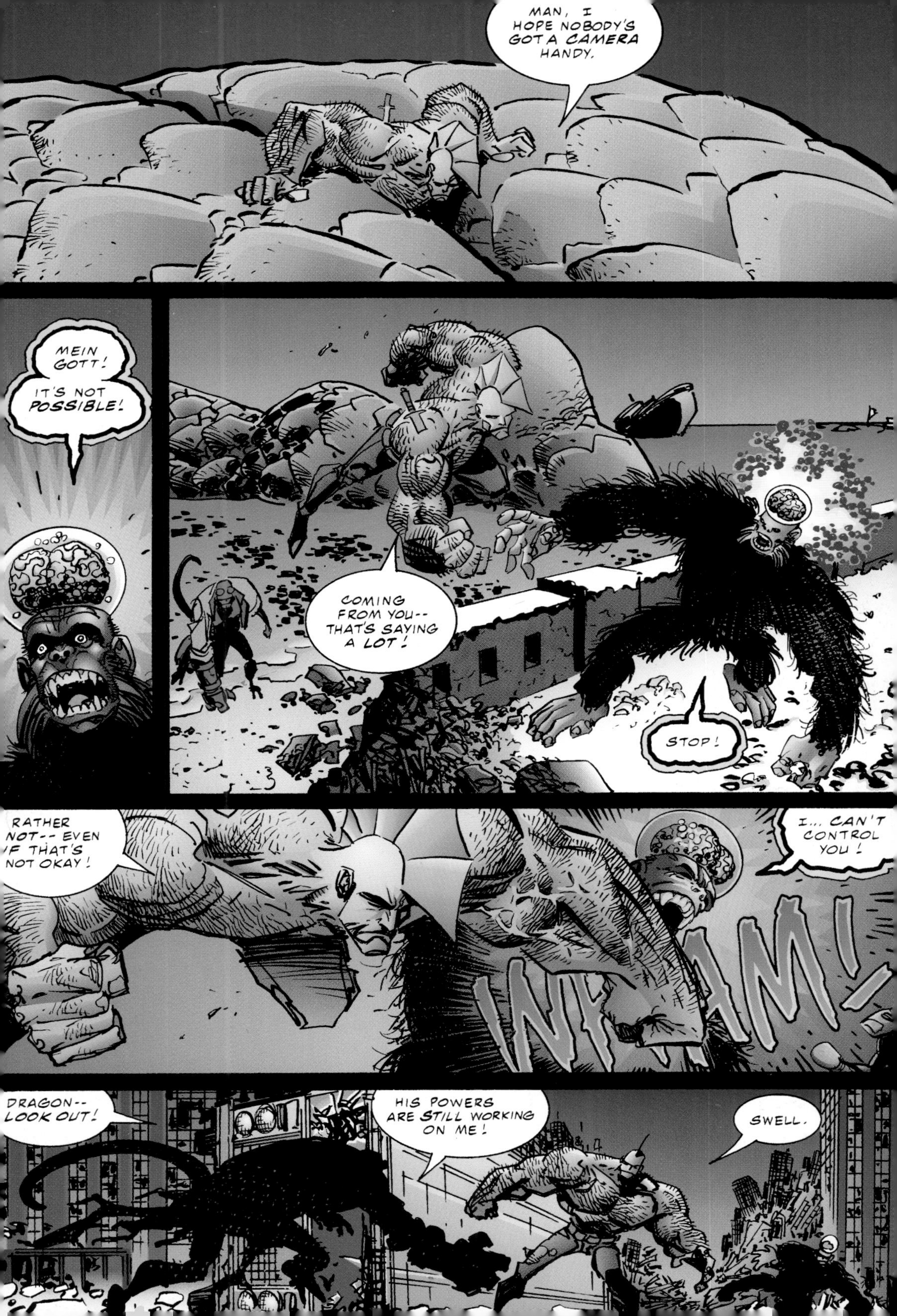
MAN, I HOPE NOBODY'S GOT A CAMERA HANDY.
MEIN GOTT!
IT'S NOT POSSIBLE!
COMING FROM YOU-- THAT'S SAYING A LOT!
STOP!
RATHER NOT-- EVEN IF THAT'S NOT OKAY!
I... CAN'T CONTROL YOU!
DRAGON-- LOOK OUT!
HIS POWERS ARE STILL WORKING ON ME!
SWELL.

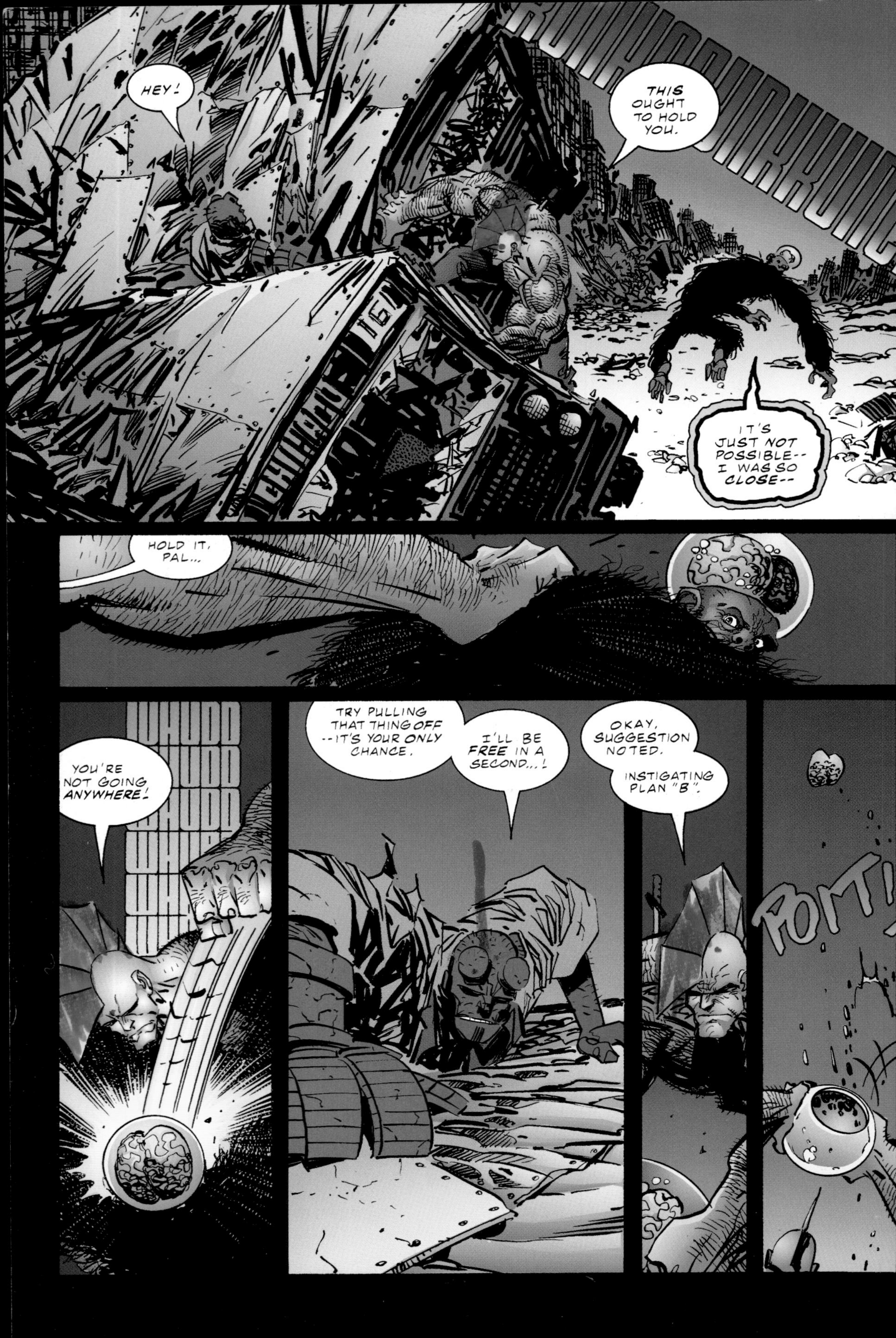
HEY!
THIS OUGHT TO HOLD YOU.
IT'S JUST NOT POSSIBLE-- I WAS SO CLOSE--
HOLD IT, PAL...
YOU'RE NOT GOING ANYWHERE!
TRY PULLING THAT THING OFF --IT'S YOUR ONLY CHANCE.
I'LL BE FREE IN A SECOND...!
OKAY, SUGGESTION NOTED.
INSTIGATING PLAN "B".

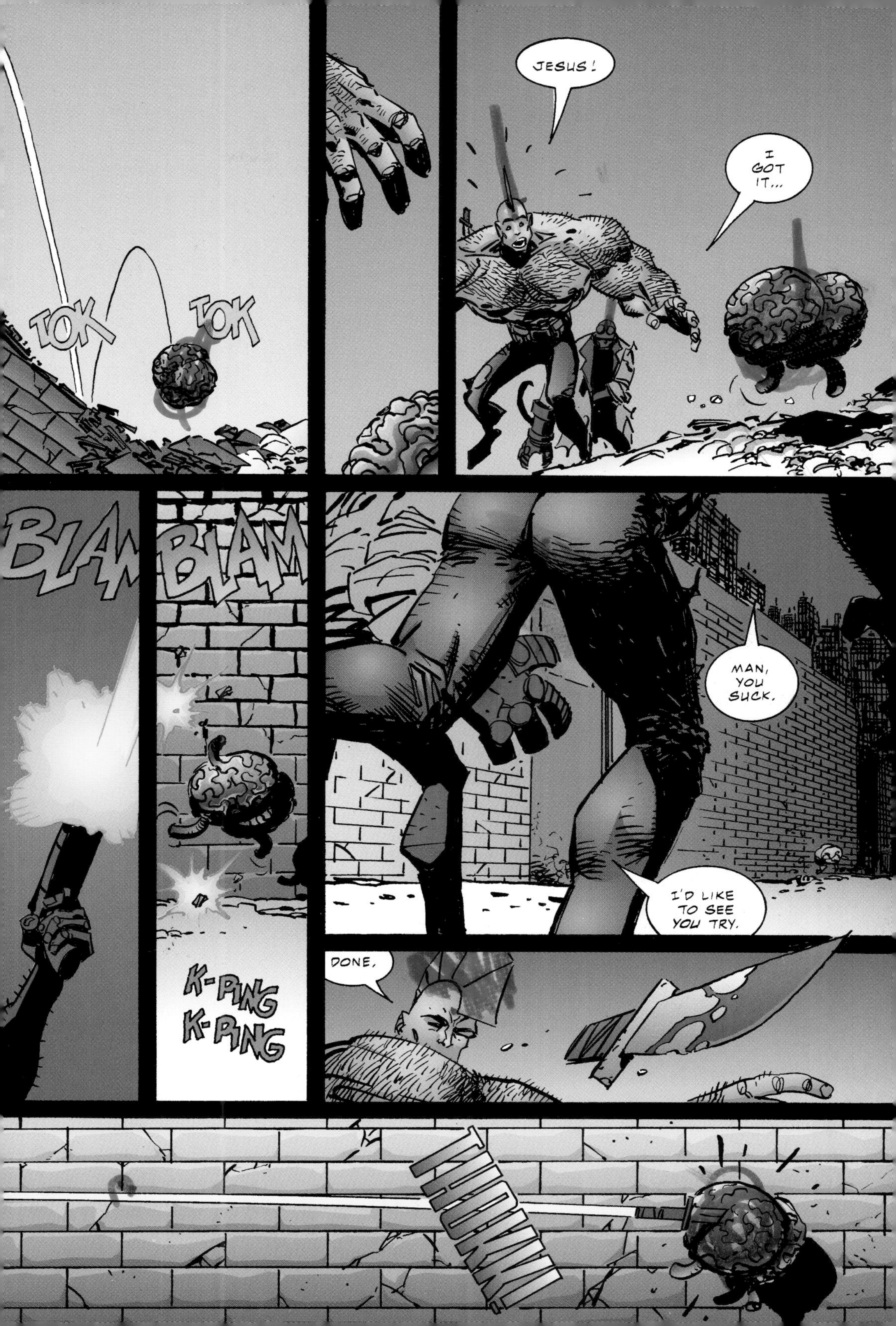
TOK
TOK
JESUS!
I GOT IT...
BLAM
BLAM
MAN, YOU SUCK.
I'D LIKE TO SEE YOU TRY.
K-PING
K-PING
DONE.
THUNK

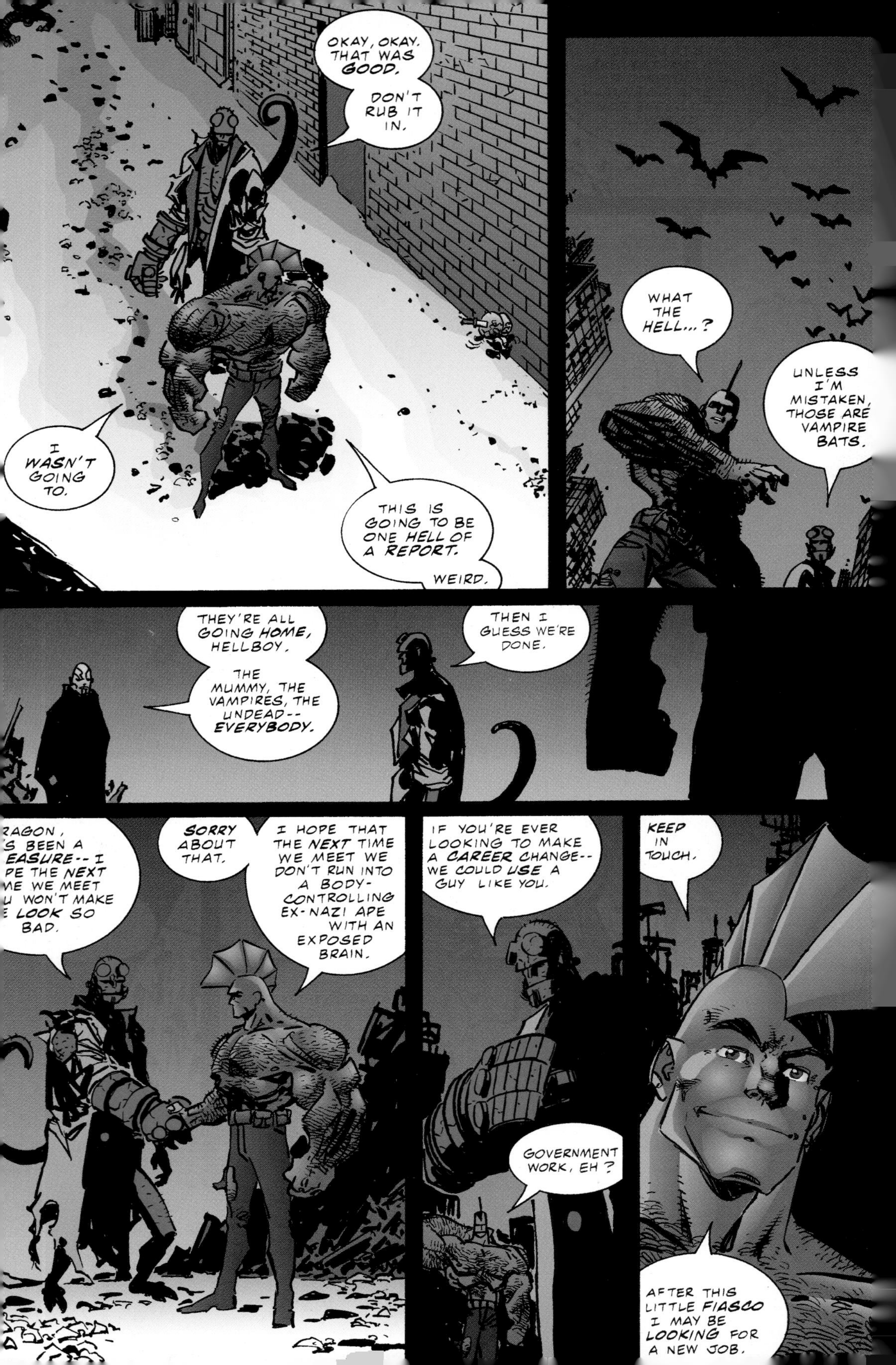

OKAY, OKAY. THAT WAS GOOD.
DON'T RUB IT IN.
I WASN'T GOING TO.
THIS IS GOING TO BE ONE HELL OF A REPORT.
WEIRD.
WHAT THE HELL...?
UNLESS I'M MISTAKEN, THOSE ARE VAMPIRE BATS.
THEY'RE ALL GOING HOME, HELLBOY.
THE MUMMY, THE VAMPIRES, THE UNDEAD-- EVERYBODY.
THEN I GUESS WE'RE DONE.
RAGON, 'S BEEN A EASURE-- I PE THE NEXT ME WE MEET U WON'T MAKE E LOOK SO BAD.
SORRY ABOUT THAT.
I HOPE THAT THE NEXT TIME WE MEET WE DON'T RUN INTO A BODY-CONTROLLING EX-NAZI APE WITH AN EXPOSED BRAIN.
IF YOU'RE EVER LOOKING TO MAKE A CAREER CHANGE-- WE COULD USE A GUY LIKE YOU.
GOVERNMENT WORK, EH?
KEEP IN TOUCH.
AFTER THIS LITTLE FIASCO I MAY BE LOOKING FOR A NEW JOB.

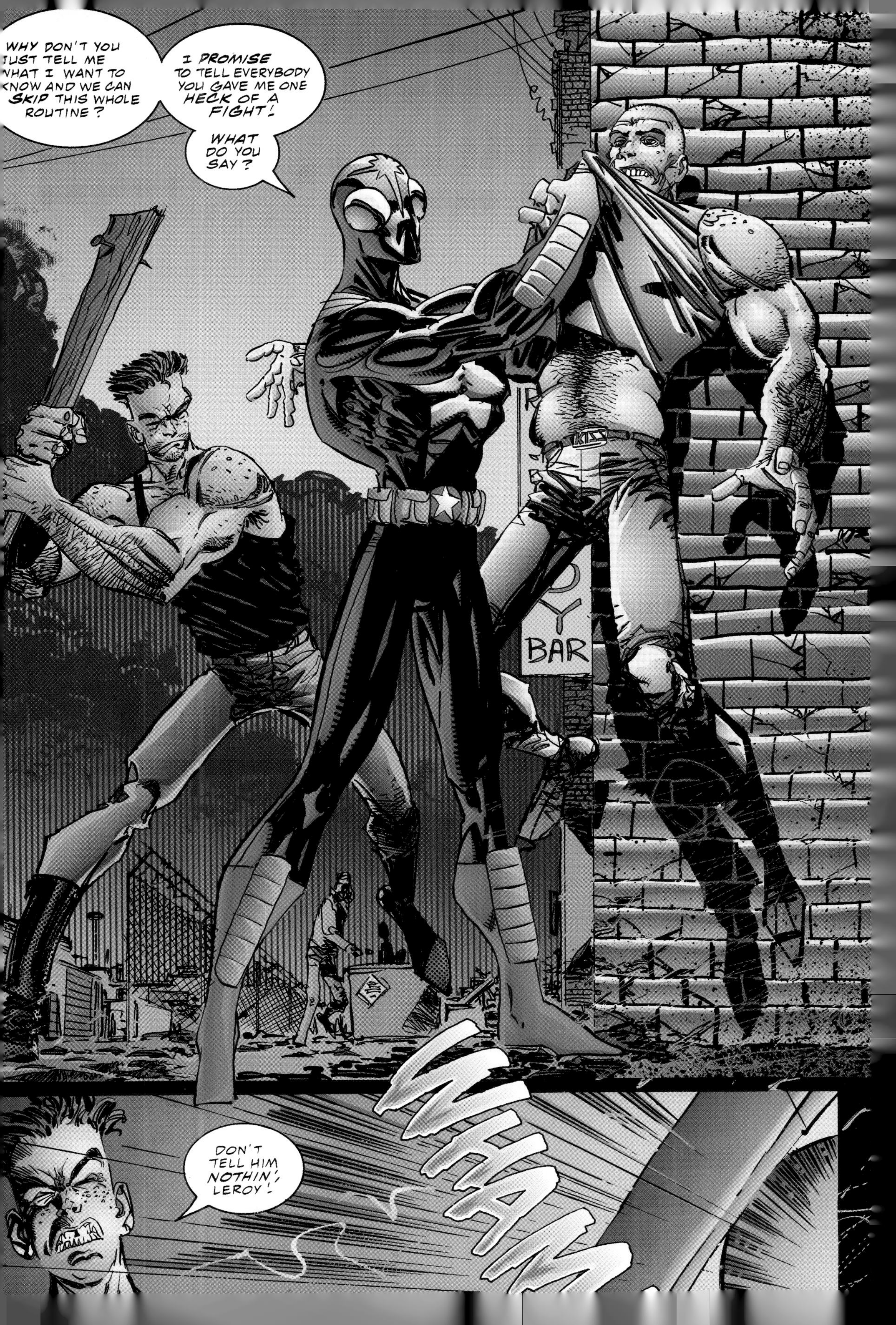
WHY DON'T YOU JUST TELL ME WHAT I WANT TO KNOW AND WE CAN SKIP THIS WHOLE ROUTINE?
I PROMISE TO TELL EVERYBODY YOU GAVE ME ONE HECK OF A FIGHT!
WHAT DO YOU SAY?
BAR
DON'T TELL HIM NOTHIN', LEROY!
WHAM

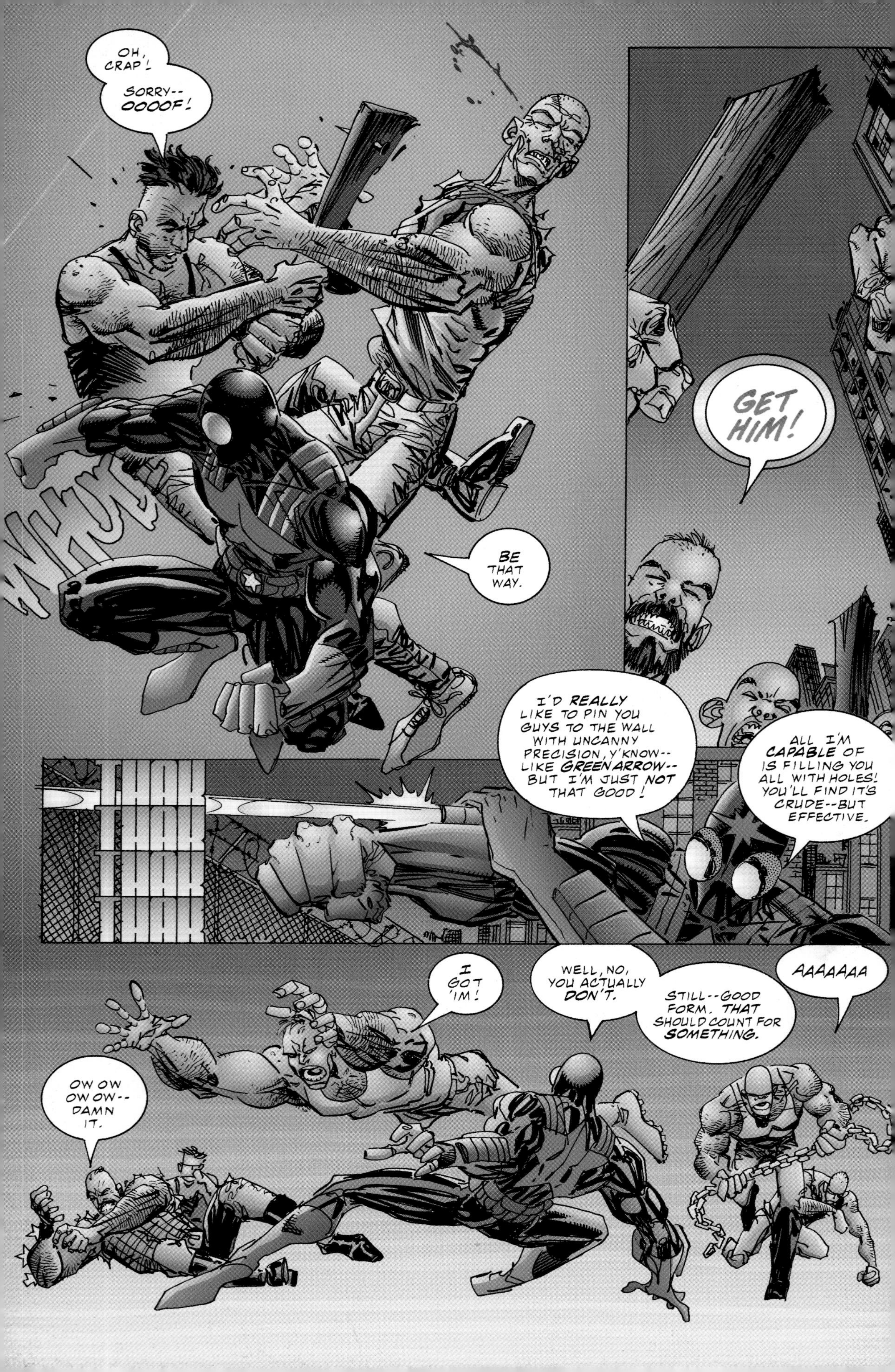

OH, CRAP!
SORRY-- OOOOF!
BE THAT WAY.
GET HIM!
I'D REALLY LIKE TO PIN YOU GUYS TO THE WALL WITH UNCANNY PRECISION, Y'KNOW-- LIKE GREEN ARROW-- BUT I'M JUST NOT THAT GOOD!
ALL I'M CAPABLE OF IS FILLING YOU ALL WITH HOLES! YOU'LL FIND IT'S CRUDE--BUT EFFECTIVE.
THAK THAK THAK THAK
I GOT 'IM!
WELL, NO, YOU ACTUALLY DON'T.
STILL--GOOD FORM. THAT SHOULD COUNT FOR SOMETHING.
AAAAAAA
OW OW OW OW-- DAMN IT.

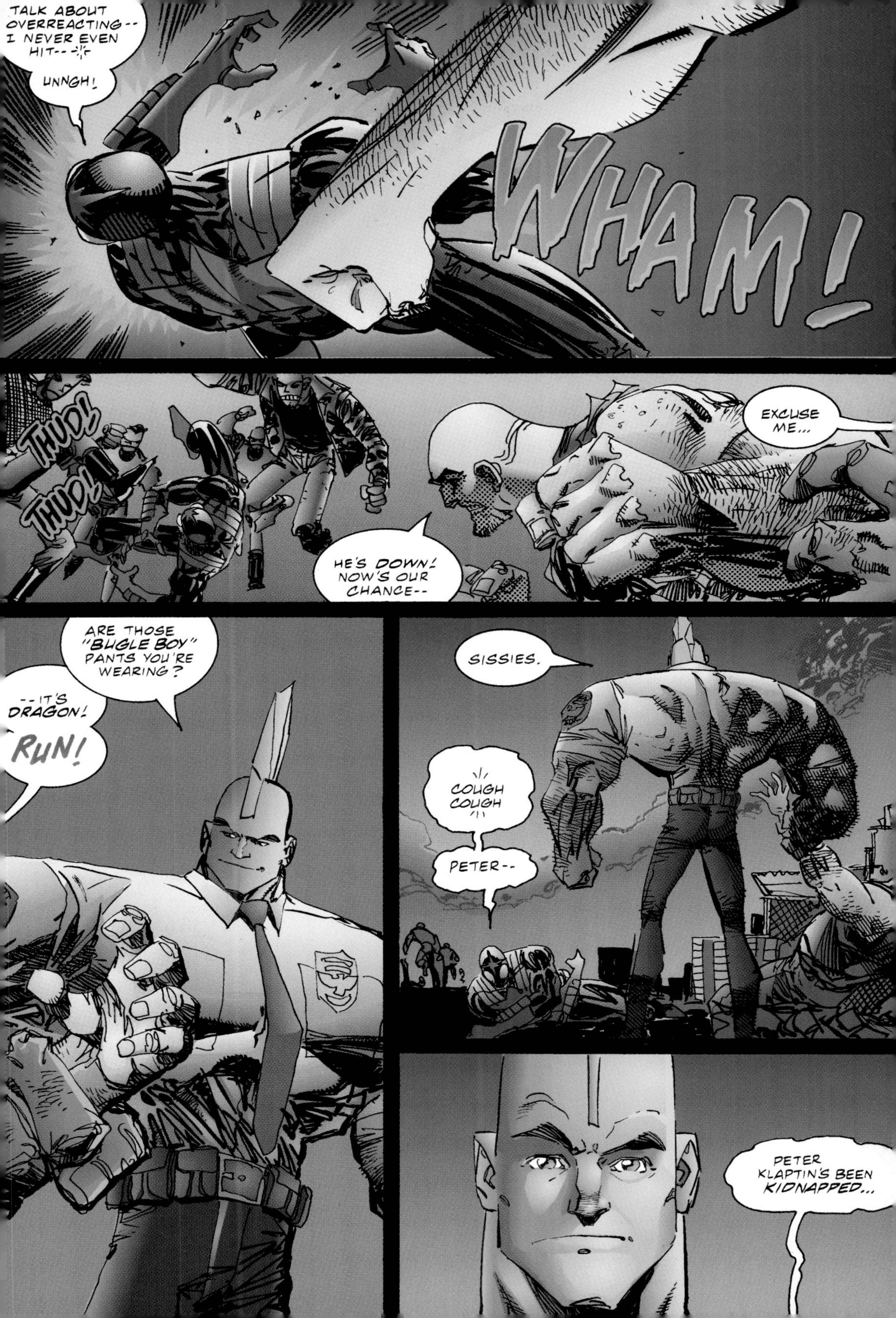
TALK ABOUT OVERREACTING-- I NEVER EVEN HIT--
UNNGH!
WHAM!
THUD!
THUD!
HE'S DOWN! NOW'S OUR CHANCE--
EXCUSE ME...
--IT'S DRAGON!
RUN!
ARE THOSE "BUGLE BOY" PANTS YOU'RE WEARING?
SISSIES.
COUGH COUGH
PETER--
PETER KLAPTIN'S BEEN KIDNAPPED...

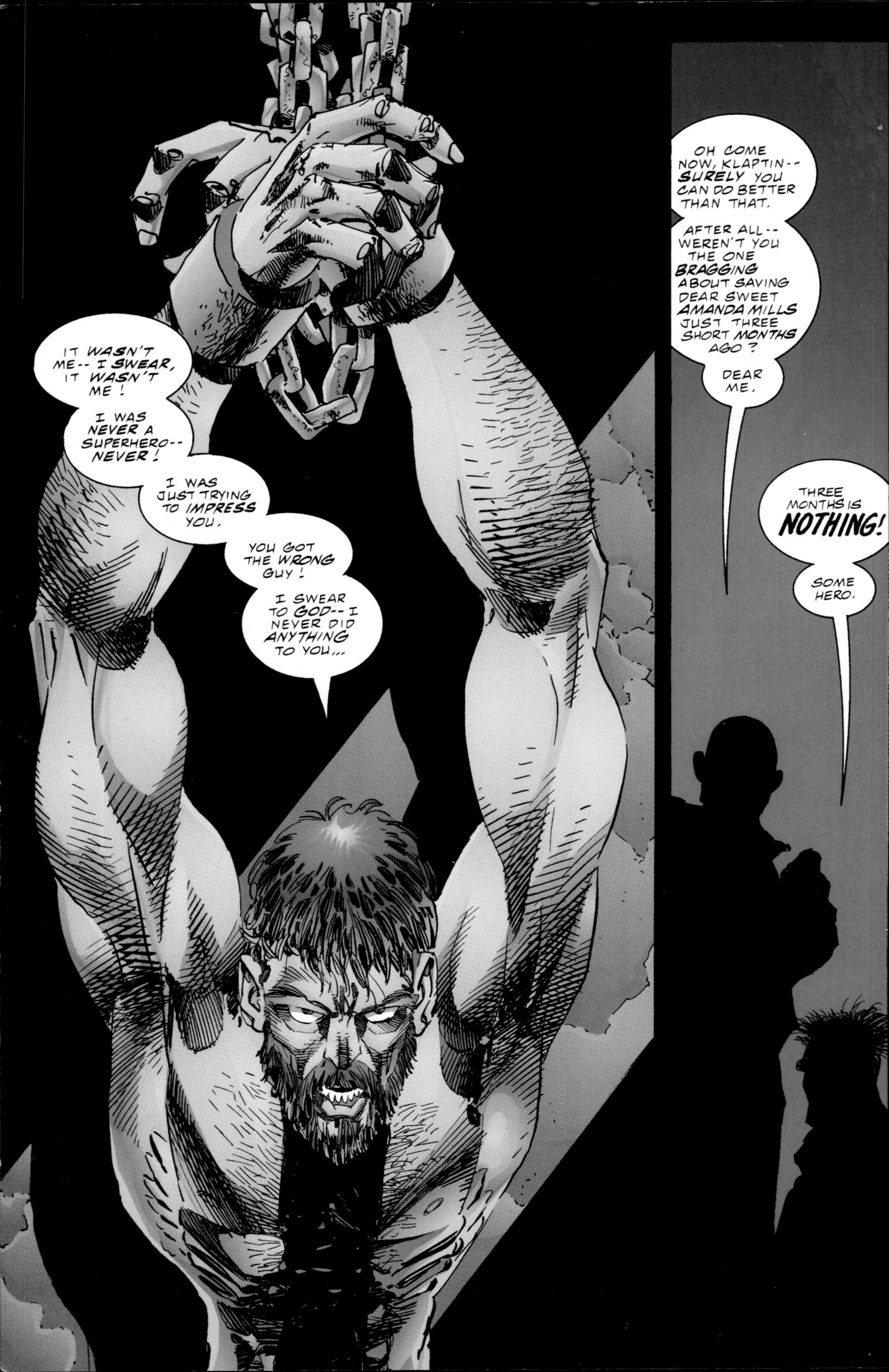
IT WASN'T ME-- I SWEAR, IT WASN'T ME!
I WAS NEVER A SUPERHERO-- NEVER!
I WAS JUST TRYING TO IMPRESS YOU.
YOU GOT THE WRONG GUY!
I SWEAR TO GOD-- I NEVER DID ANYTHING TO YOU...
OH COME NOW, KLAPTIN-- SURELY YOU CAN DO BETTER THAN THAT.
AFTER ALL-- WEREN'T YOU THE ONE BRAGGING ABOUT SAVING DEAR SWEET AMANDA MILLS JUST THREE SHORT MONTHS AGO?
DEAR ME.
THREE MONTHS IS NOTHING!
SOME HERO.

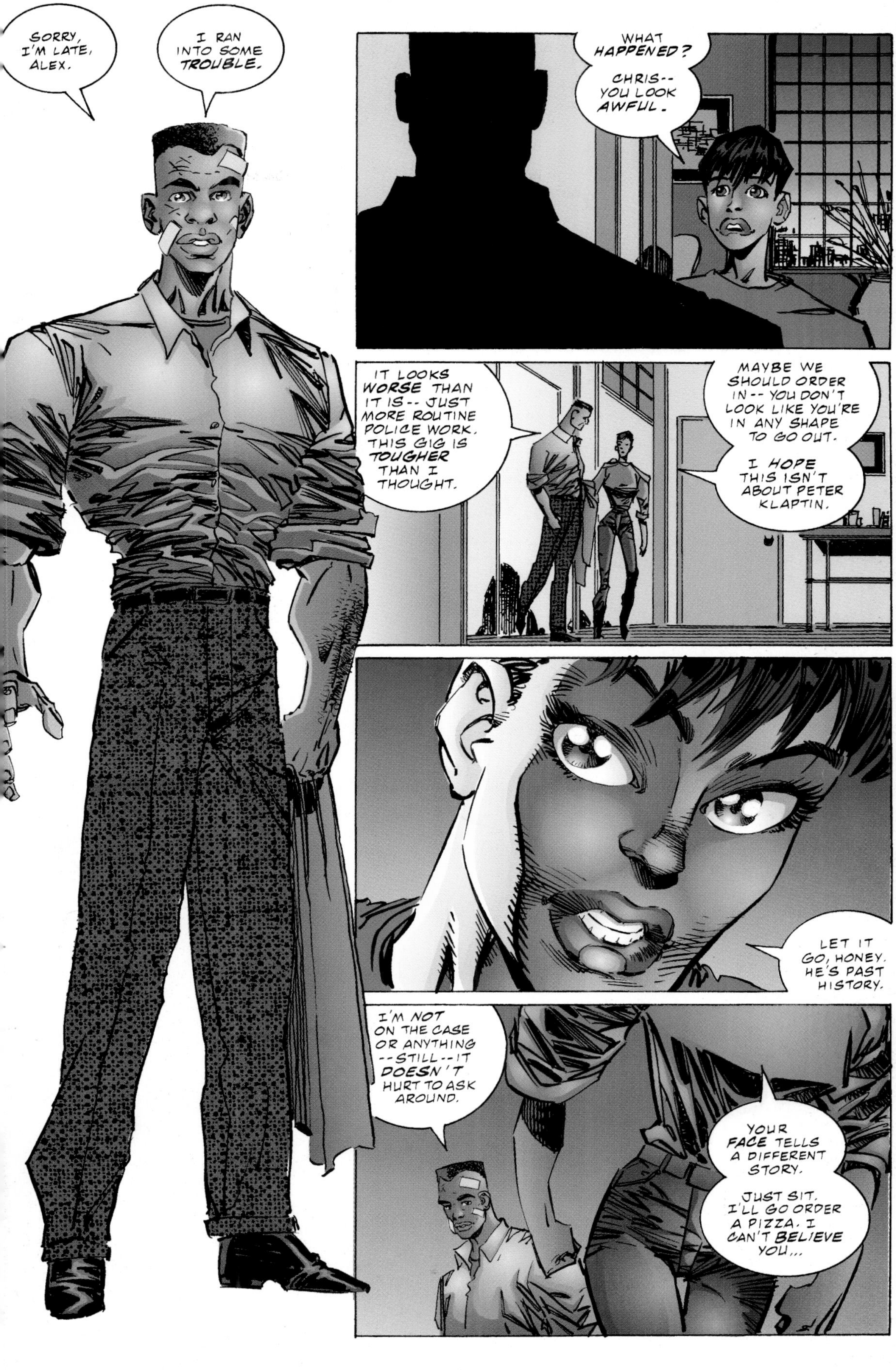
SORRY, I'M LATE, ALEX.
I RAN INTO SOME TROUBLE.
WHAT HAPPENED?
CHRIS-- YOU LOOK AWFUL.
IT LOOKS WORSE THAN IT IS-- JUST MORE ROUTINE POLICE WORK. THIS GIG IS TOUGHER THAN I THOUGHT.
MAYBE WE SHOULD ORDER IN-- YOU DON'T LOOK LIKE YOU'RE IN ANY SHAPE TO GO OUT.
I HOPE THIS ISN'T ABOUT PETER KLAPTIN.
LET IT GO, HONEY. HE'S PAST HISTORY.
I'M NOT ON THE CASE OR ANYTHING --STILL-- IT DOESN'T HURT TO ASK AROUND.
YOUR FACE TELLS A DIFFERENT STORY.
JUST SIT. I'LL GO ORDER A PIZZA. I CAN'T BELIEVE YOU...

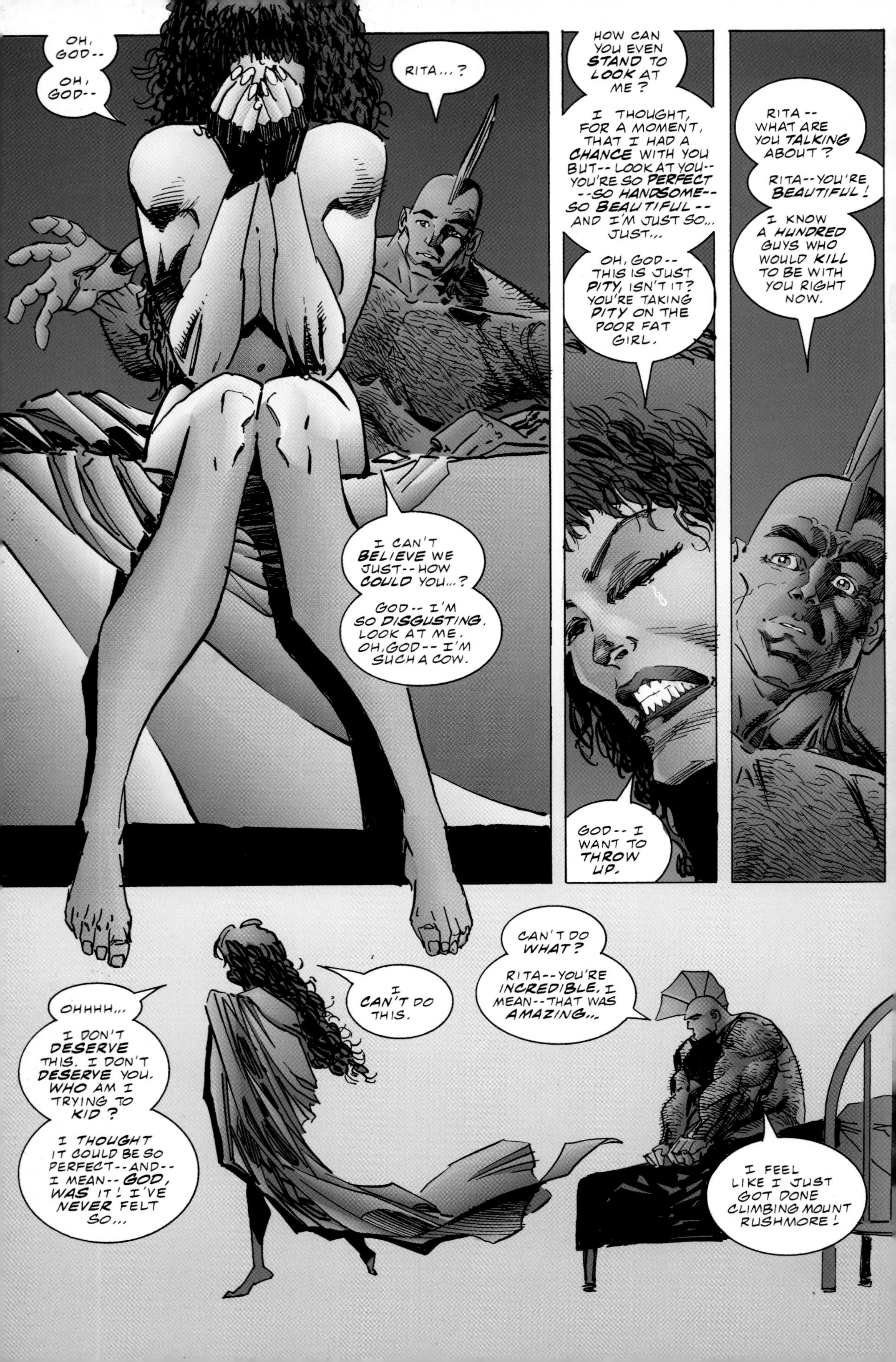

OH, GOD-- OH, GOD--
RITA...?
I CAN'T BELIEVE WE JUST--HOW COULD YOU...?
GOD--I'M SO DISGUSTING. LOOK AT ME. OH, GOD--I'M SUCH A COW.
HOW CAN YOU EVEN STAND TO LOOK AT ME?
I THOUGHT, FOR A MOMENT, THAT I HAD A CHANCE WITH YOU BUT--LOOK AT YOU--YOU'RE SO PERFECT--SO HANDSOME--SO BEAUTIFUL--AND I'M JUST SO... JUST...
OH, GOD--THIS IS JUST PITY, ISN'T IT? YOU'RE TAKING PITY ON THE POOR FAT GIRL.
GOD--I WANT TO THROW UP.
RITA--WHAT ARE YOU TALKING ABOUT?
RITA--YOU'RE BEAUTIFUL!
I KNOW A HUNDRED GUYS WHO WOULD KILL TO BE WITH YOU RIGHT NOW.
OHHHH...
I DON'T DESERVE THIS. I DON'T DESERVE YOU. WHO AM I TRYING TO KID?
I THOUGHT IT COULD BE SO PERFECT--AND--I MEAN--GOD, WAS IT! I'VE NEVER FELT SO...
I CAN'T DO THIS.
CAN'T DO WHAT?
RITA--YOU'RE INCREDIBLE. I MEAN--THAT WAS AMAZING...
I FEEL LIKE I JUST GOT DONE CLIMBING MOUNT RUSHMORE!

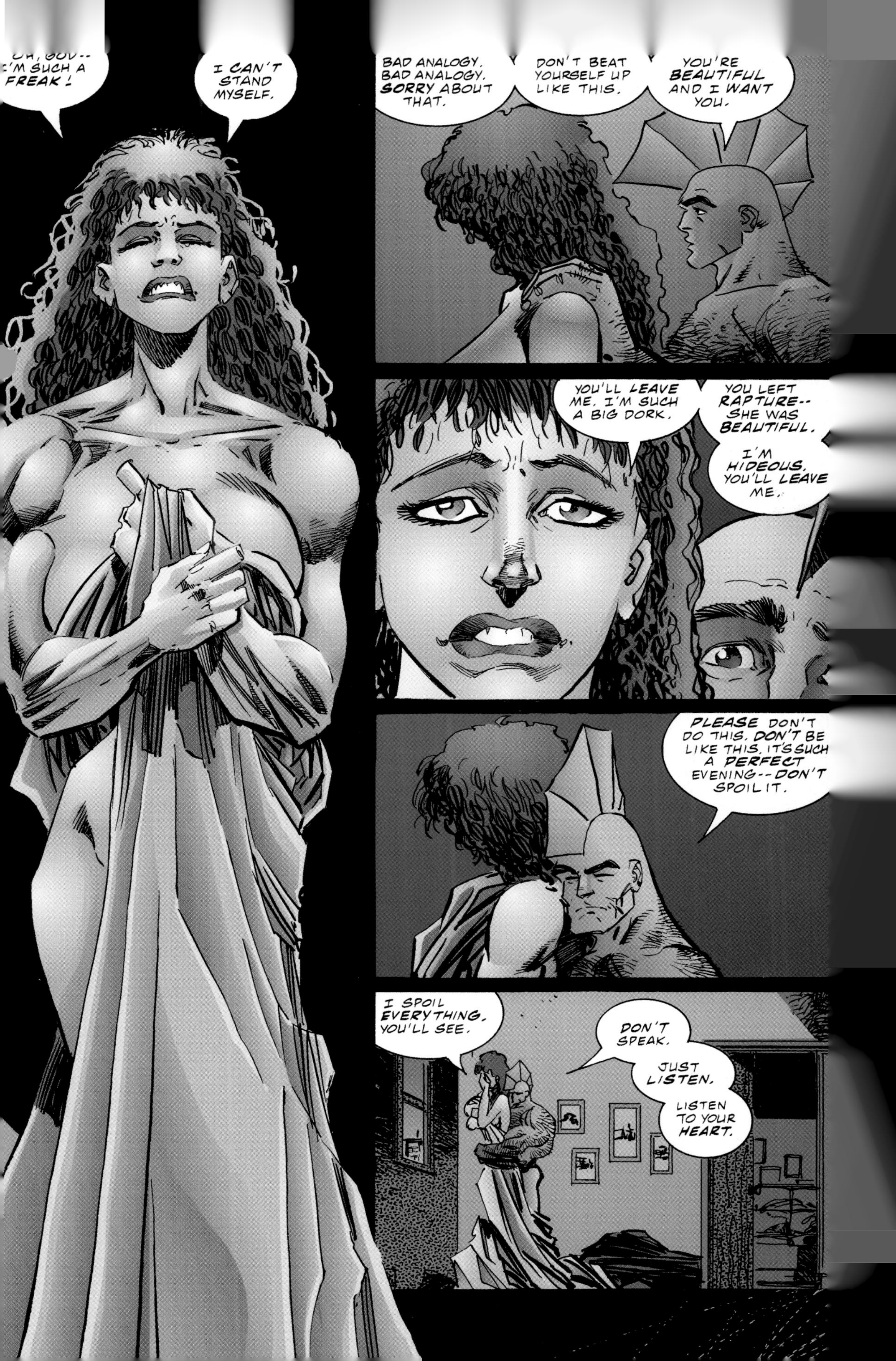
I'M SUCH A FREAK!
I CAN'T STAND MYSELF.
BAD ANALOGY. BAD ANALOGY. SORRY ABOUT THAT.
DON'T BEAT YOURSELF UP LIKE THIS.
YOU'RE BEAUTIFUL AND I WANT YOU.
YOU'LL LEAVE ME. I'M SUCH A BIG DORK.
YOU LEFT RAPTURE-- SHE WAS BEAUTIFUL.
I'M HIDEOUS. YOU'LL LEAVE ME.
PLEASE DON'T DO THIS. DON'T BE LIKE THIS. IT'S SUCH A PERFECT EVENING-- DON'T SPOIL IT.
I SPOIL EVERYTHING. YOU'LL SEE.
DON'T SPEAK.
JUST LISTEN.
LISTEN TO YOUR HEART.

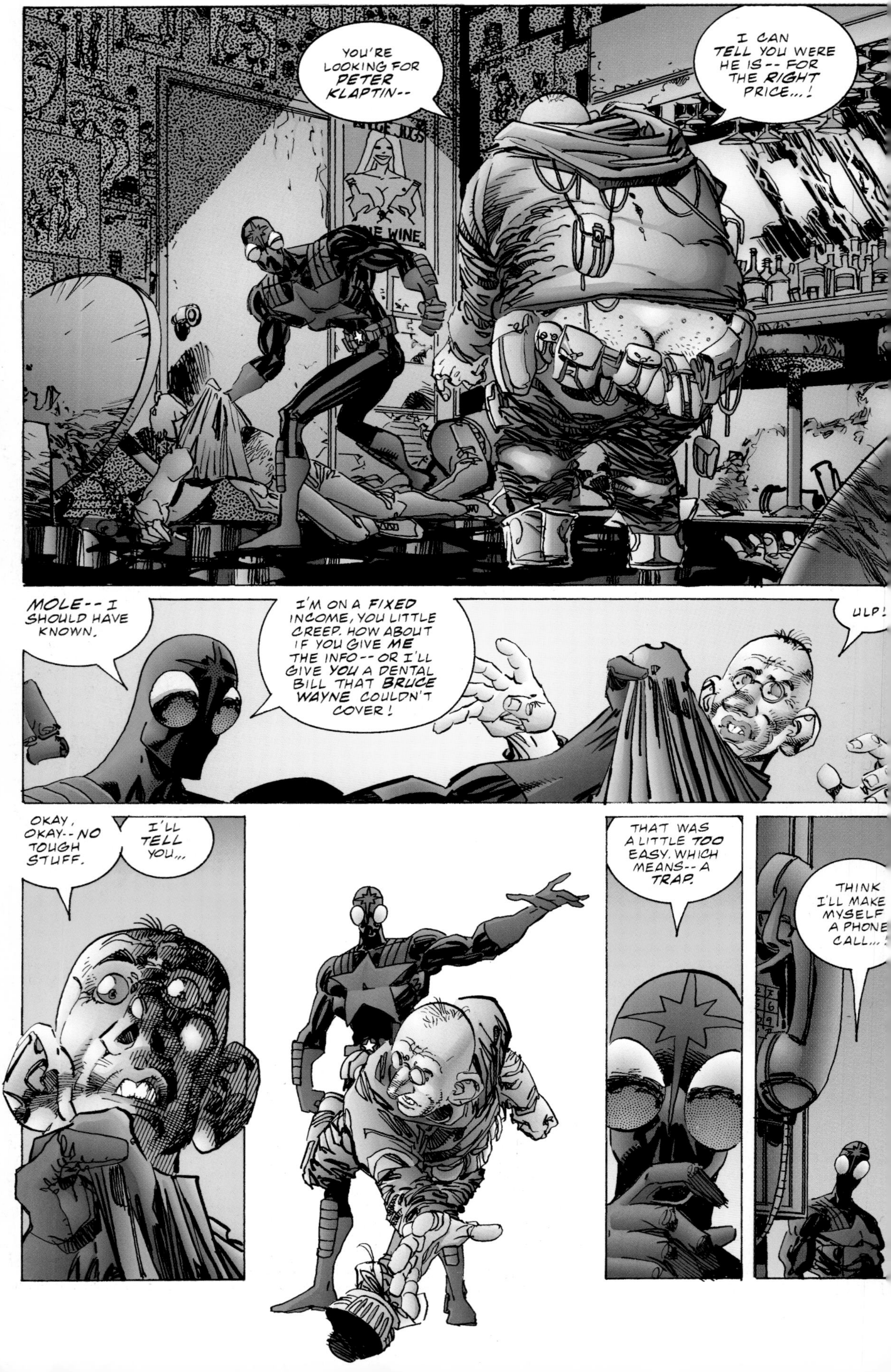
YOU'RE LOOKING FOR PETER KLAPTIN--
I CAN TELL YOU WERE HE IS -- FOR THE RIGHT PRICE...!
MOLE-- I SHOULD HAVE KNOWN.
I'M ON A FIXED INCOME, YOU LITTLE CREEP. HOW ABOUT IF YOU GIVE ME THE INFO-- OR I'LL GIVE YOU A DENTAL BILL THAT BRUCE WAYNE COULDN'T COVER!
ULP!
OKAY, OKAY-- NO TOUGH STUFF.
I'LL TELL YOU...
THAT WAS A LITTLE TOO EASY. WHICH MEANS-- A TRAP.
THINK I'LL MAKE MYSELF A PHONE CALL...!

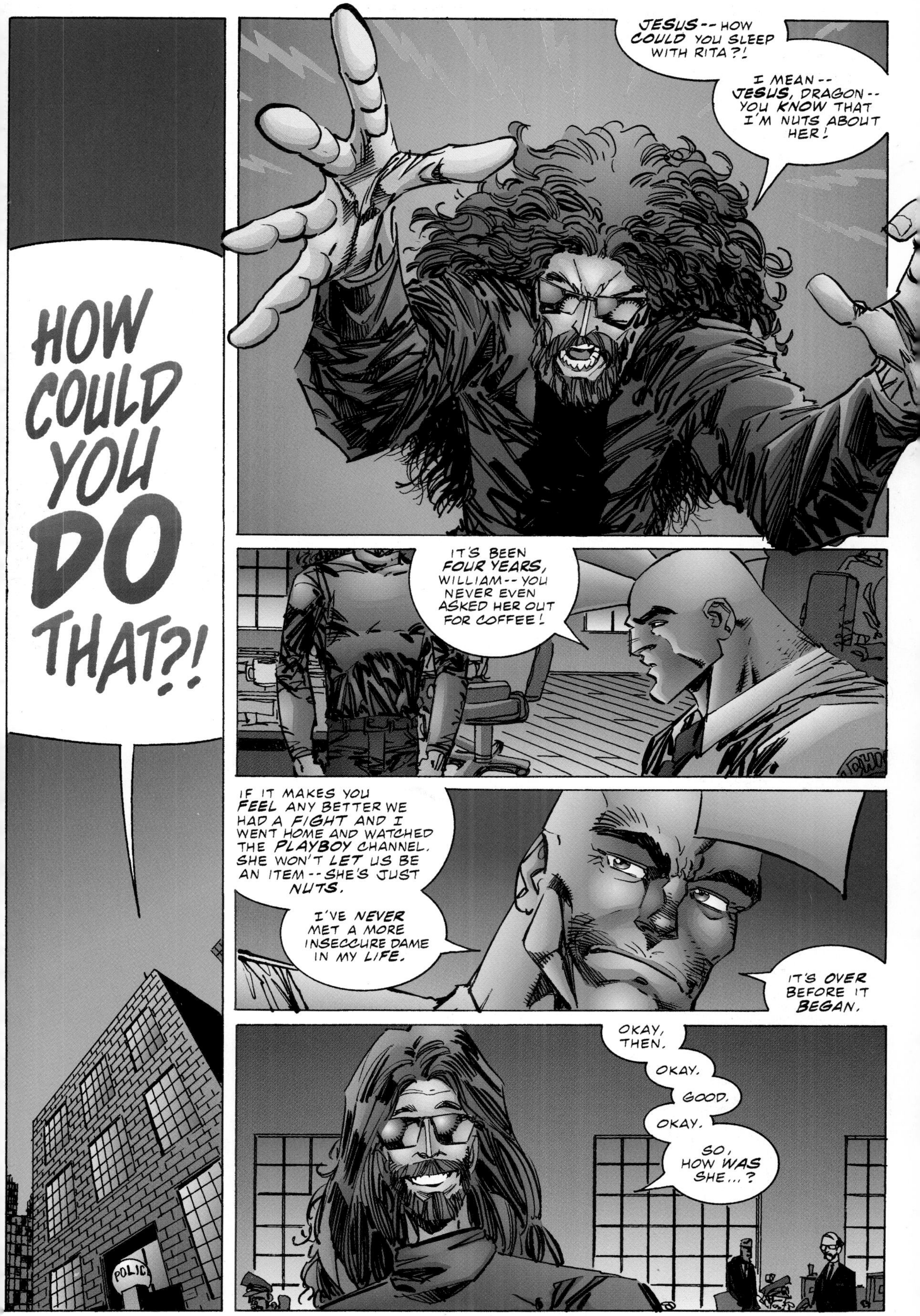
HOW COULD YOU DO THAT?!
JESUS -- HOW COULD YOU SLEEP WITH RITA?!
I MEAN -- JESUS, DRAGON -- YOU KNOW THAT I'M NUTS ABOUT HER!
IT'S BEEN FOUR YEARS, WILLIAM -- YOU NEVER EVEN ASKED HER OUT FOR COFFEE!
IF IT MAKES YOU FEEL ANY BETTER WE HAD A FIGHT AND I WENT HOME AND WATCHED THE PLAYBOY CHANNEL. SHE WON'T LET US BE AN ITEM -- SHE'S JUST NUTS.
I'VE NEVER MET A MORE INSECCURE DAME IN MY LIFE.
IT'S OVER BEFORE IT BEGAN.
OKAY, THEN.
OKAY.
GOOD.
OKAY.
SO, HOW WAS SHE...?
POLIC

SORRY-- SORRY--

AARGH, I DON'T REALLY WANT TO KNOW.

I MEAN-- I DO, BUT, Y'KNOW...,

DRAGON-- HAVE YOU SEEN CHRIS-- HE DIDN'T SHOW UP FOR WORK.

CHRIS...?

CHRIS ROBINSON-- YOU KNOW-- THE GUY I'VE BEEN SEEING...?

YOU KNOW, TALL, DARK, HANDSOME...

YOU JUST DO THIS TO BUG ME--YOU KNOW WHO HE IS, HE WENT WITH US DOWN TO THE UNDERGROUND A WHILE BACK...? REMEMBER?

DON'T GIVE ME THAT LOOK.

ANYWAY, HE'S BEEN SNOOPING INTO PETER KLAPTIN'S DISAPPEARANCE AND I THINK HE MAY HAVE GOTTEN HIMSELF INTO SOME KIND OF TROUBLE.

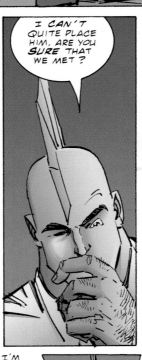

I CAN'T QUITE PLACE HIM, ARE YOU SURE THAT WE MET?

YES, HE USED TO BE PETER KLAPTIN'S BODYGUARD? PETER FIRED HIM AND HE JOINED THE FORCE. YOU'VE GOT TO REMEMBER THAT!

KLAPTIN'S... BODYGUARD...?

ALEX -- I'M NOT SURE HOW TO TELL YOU THIS...

RING! RING!

JUST A SEC!

TELL ME WHAT?!

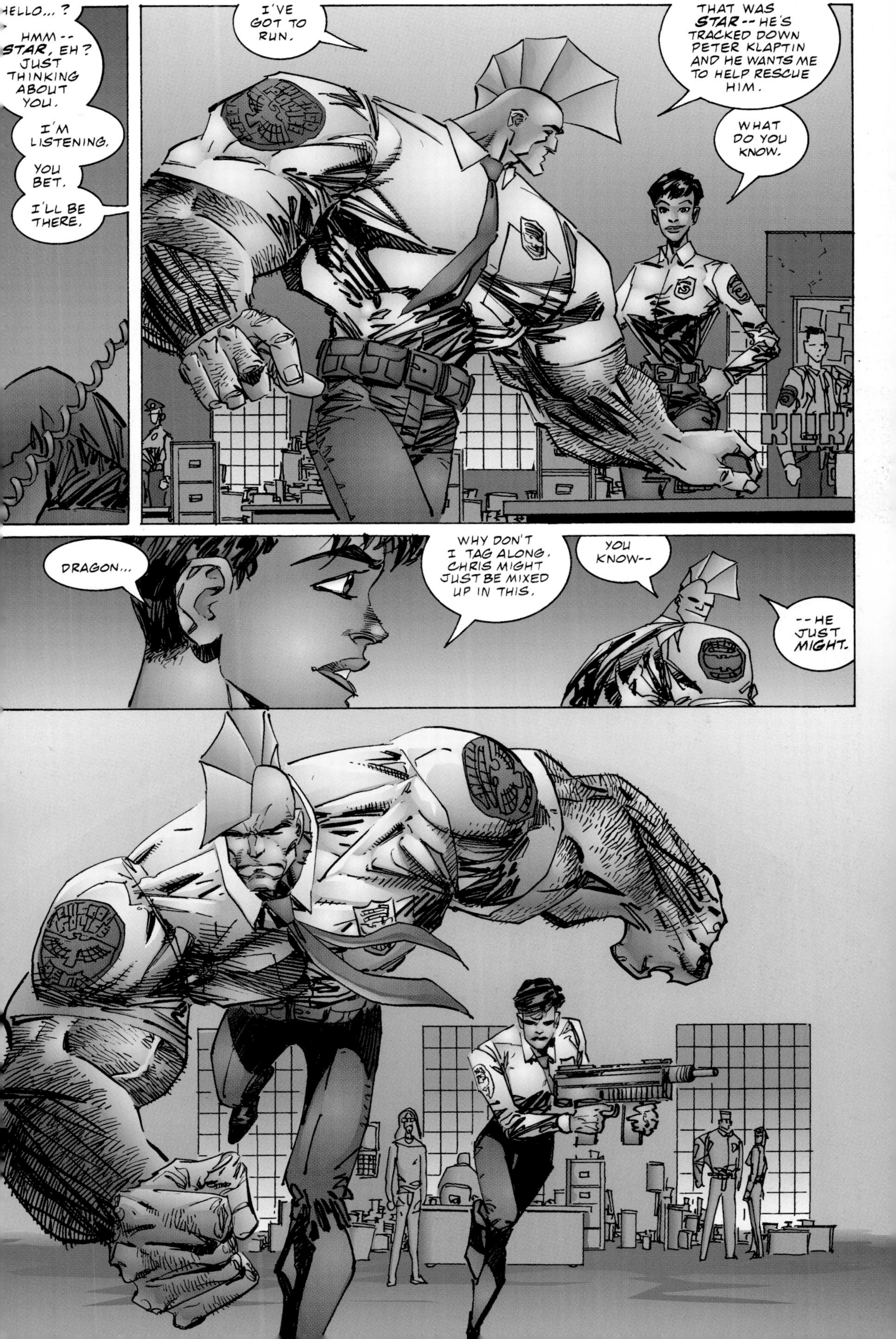
HELLO... ?
HMM -- STAR, EH? JUST THINKING ABOUT YOU.
I'M LISTENING.
YOU BET.
I'LL BE THERE.
I'VE GOT TO RUN.
THAT WAS STAR -- HE'S TRACKED DOWN PETER KLAPTIN AND HE WANTS ME TO HELP RESCUE HIM.
WHAT DO YOU KNOW.
DRAGON...
WHY DON'T I TAG ALONG. CHRIS MIGHT JUST BE MIXED UP IN THIS.
YOU KNOW--
--HE JUST MIGHT.

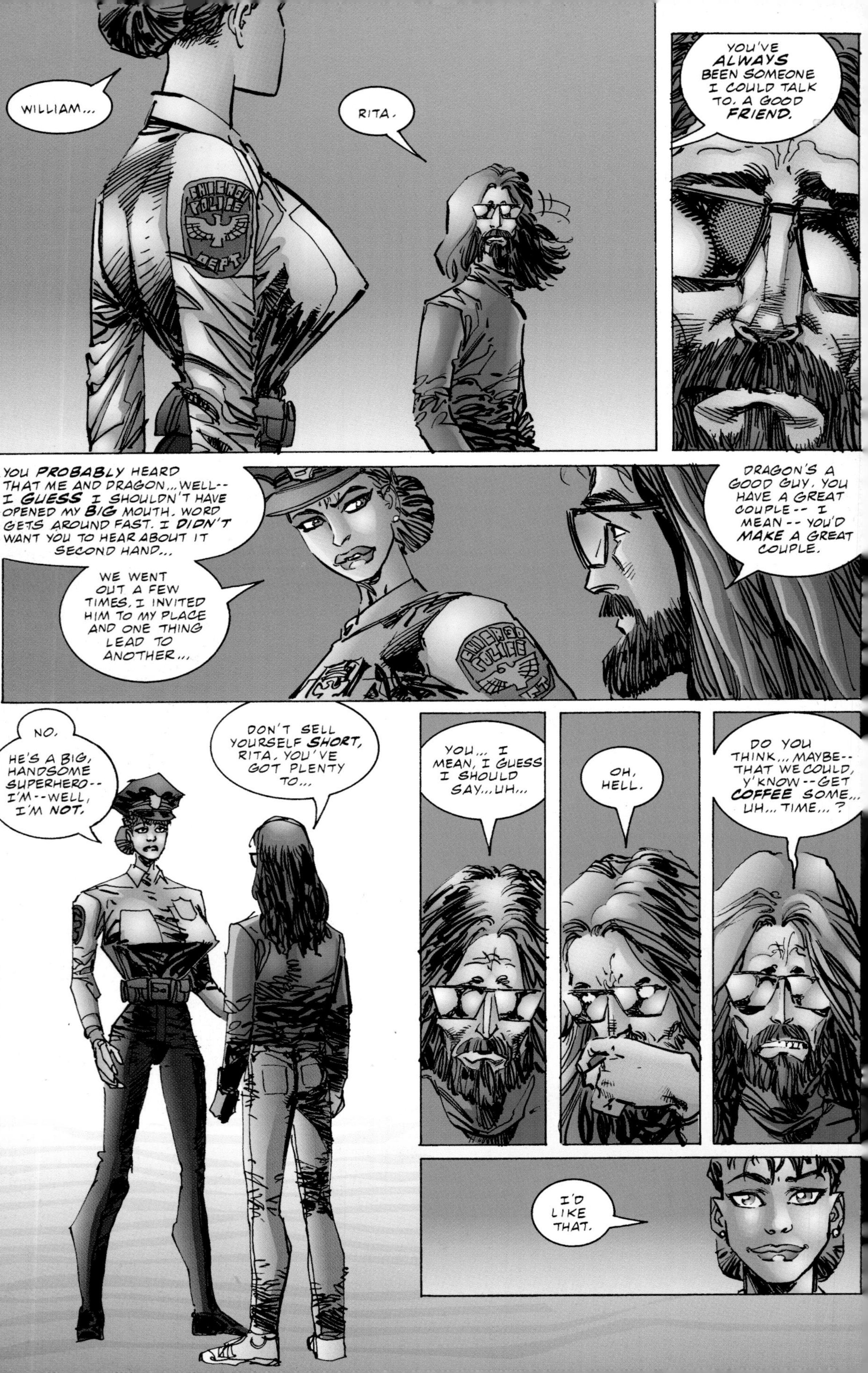
WILLIAM...
RITA.
YOU'VE ALWAYS BEEN SOMEONE I COULD TALK TO. A GOOD FRIEND.
YOU PROBABLY HEARD THAT ME AND DRAGON... WELL-- I GUESS I SHOULDN'T HAVE OPENED MY BIG MOUTH. WORD GETS AROUND FAST. I DIDN'T WANT YOU TO HEAR ABOUT IT SECOND HAND...
WE WENT OUT A FEW TIMES. I INVITED HIM TO MY PLACE AND ONE THING LEAD TO ANOTHER...
DRAGON'S A GOOD GUY. YOU HAVE A GREAT COUPLE -- I MEAN -- YOU'D MAKE A GREAT COUPLE.
NO.
HE'S A BIG, HANDSOME SUPERHERO-- I'M--WELL, I'M NOT.
DON'T SELL YOURSELF SHORT, RITA. YOU'VE GOT PLENTY TO...
YOU... I MEAN, I GUESS I SHOULD SAY... UH...
OH, HELL.
DO YOU THINK... MAYBE-- THAT WE COULD, Y'KNOW--GET COFFEE SOME... UH... TIME...?
I'D LIKE THAT.

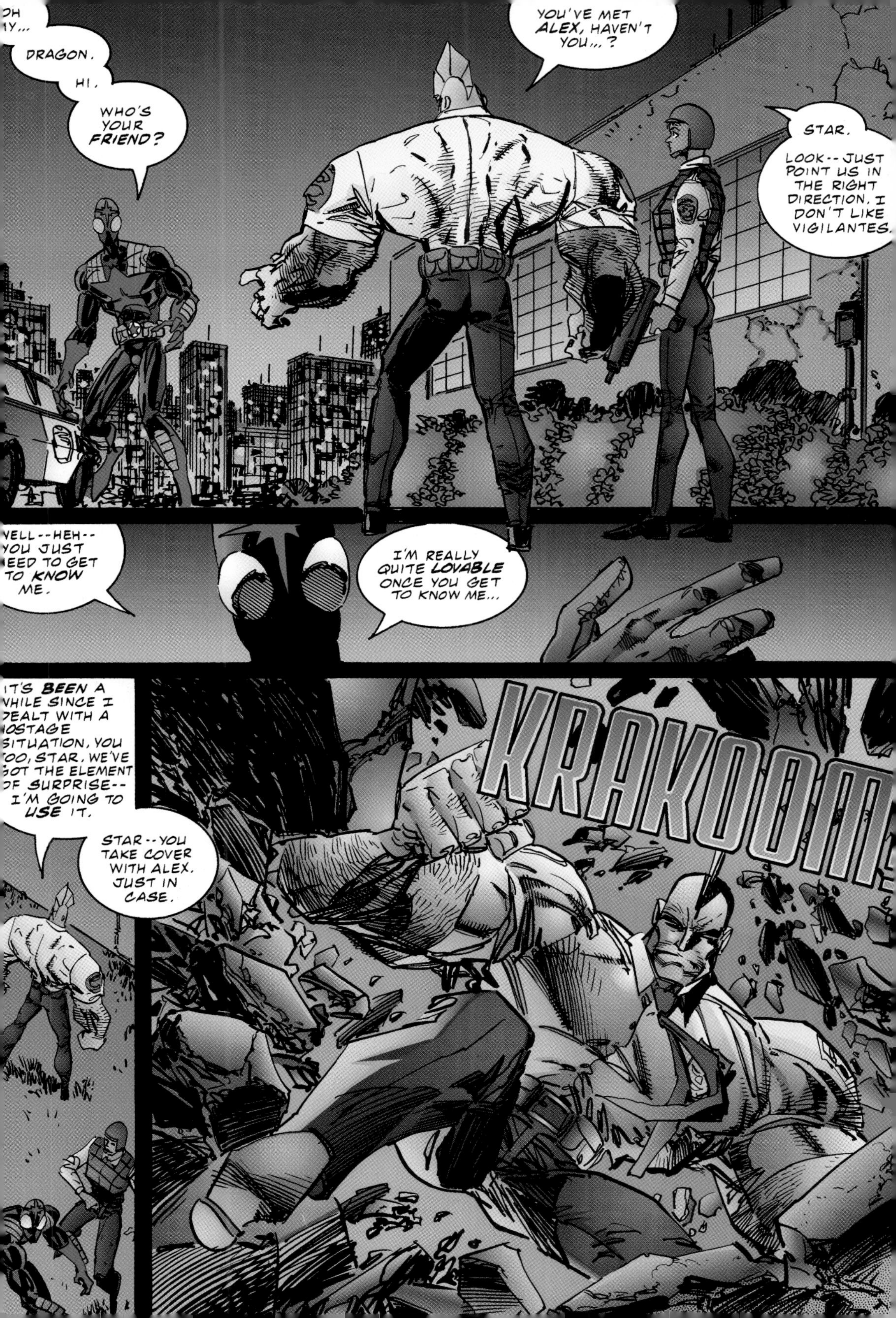
OH
MY...
DRAGON.
HI.
WHO'S YOUR FRIEND?
YOU'VE MET ALEX, HAVEN'T YOU...?
STAR.
LOOK--JUST POINT US IN THE RIGHT DIRECTION. I DON'T LIKE VIGILANTES.
WELL--HEH--YOU JUST NEED TO GET TO KNOW ME.
I'M REALLY QUITE LOVABLE ONCE YOU GET TO KNOW ME...
IT'S BEEN A WHILE SINCE I DEALT WITH A HOSTAGE SITUATION, YOU TOO, STAR. WE'VE GOT THE ELEMENT OF SURPRISE--I'M GOING TO USE IT.
STAR--YOU TAKE COVER WITH ALEX. JUST IN CASE.
KRAKOOM

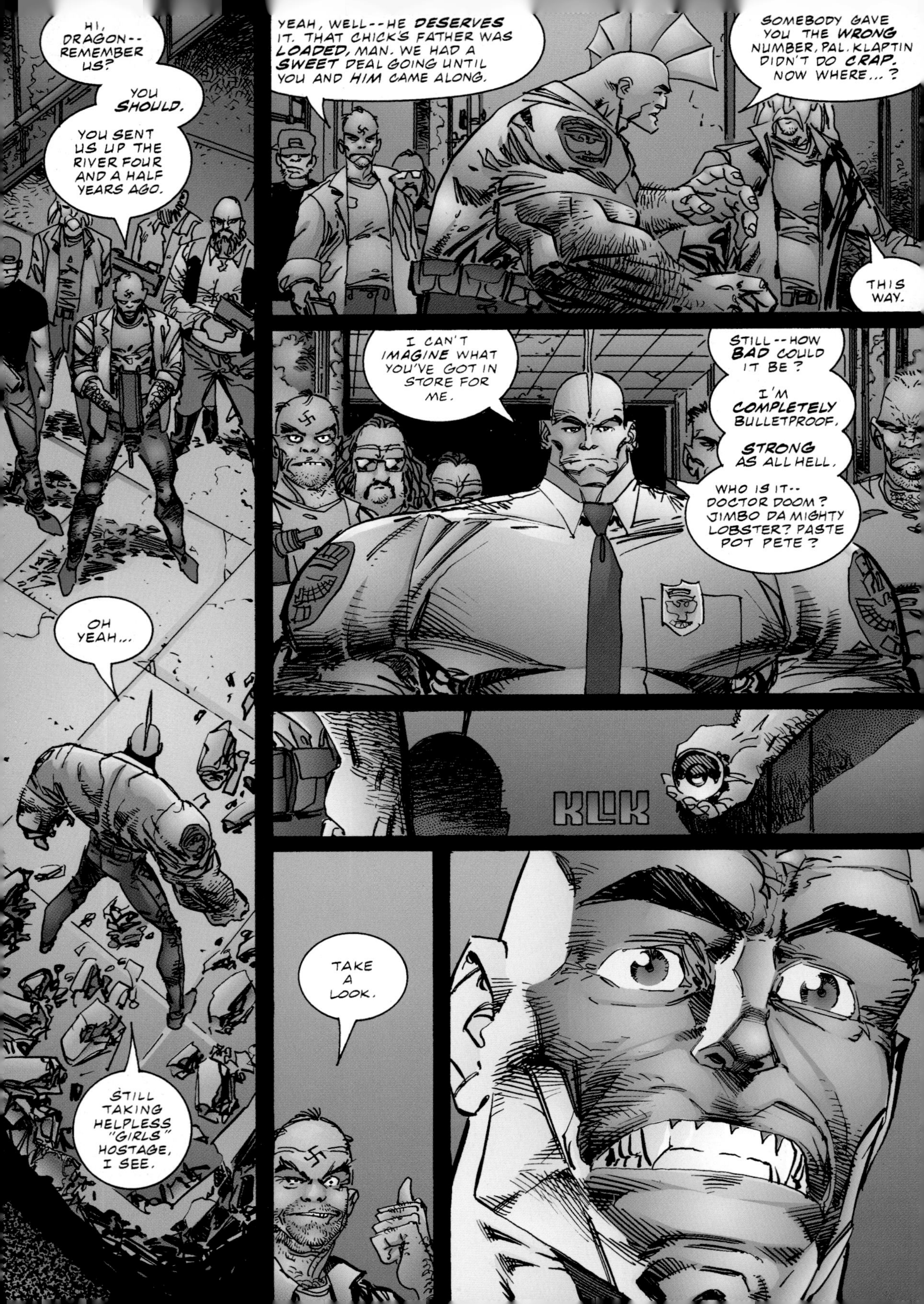

HI, DRAGON-- REMEMBER US?
YOU SHOULD.
YOU SENT US UP THE RIVER FOUR AND A HALF YEARS AGO.
OH YEAH...
STILL TAKING HELPLESS "GIRLS" HOSTAGE, I SEE.
YEAH, WELL--HE DESERVES IT. THAT CHICK'S FATHER WAS LOADED, MAN. WE HAD A SWEET DEAL GOING UNTIL YOU AND HIM CAME ALONG.
SOMEBODY GAVE YOU THE WRONG NUMBER, PAL. KLAPTIN DIDN'T DO CRAP. NOW WHERE...?
THIS WAY.
I CAN'T IMAGINE WHAT YOU'VE GOT IN STORE FOR ME.
STILL--HOW BAD COULD IT BE?
I'M COMPLETELY BULLETPROOF.
STRONG AS ALL HELL.
WHO IS IT-- DOCTOR DOOM? JIMBO DA MIGHTY LOBSTER? PASTE POT PETE?
KLIK
TAKE A LOOK.

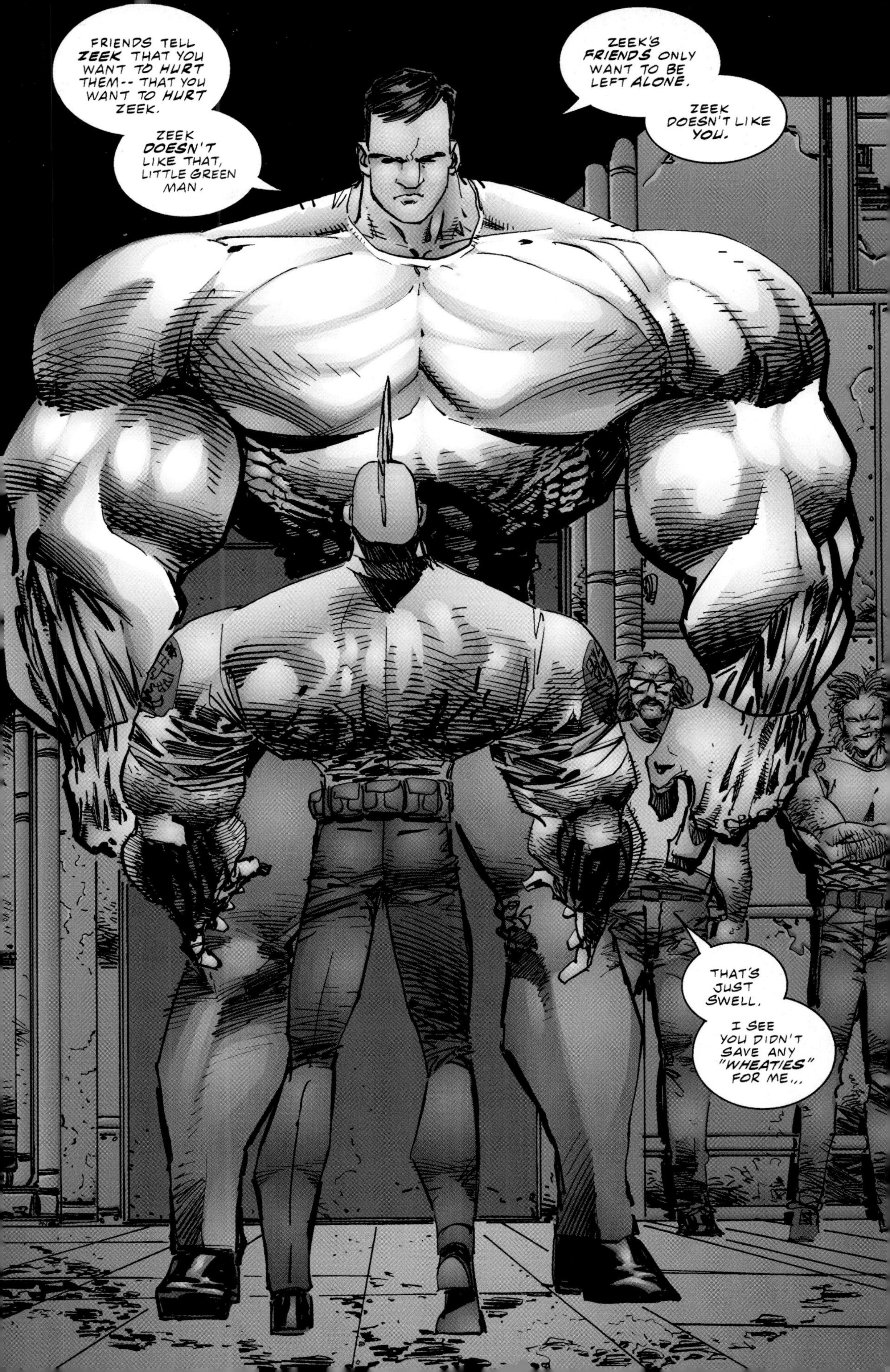
FRIENDS TELL ZEEK THAT YOU WANT TO HURT THEM-- THAT YOU WANT TO HURT ZEEK.
ZEEK DOESN'T LIKE THAT, LITTLE GREEN MAN.
ZEEK'S FRIENDS ONLY WANT TO BE LEFT ALONE.
ZEEK DOESN'T LIKE YOU.
THAT'S JUST SWELL.
I SEE YOU DIDN'T SAVE ANY "WHEATIES" FOR ME...

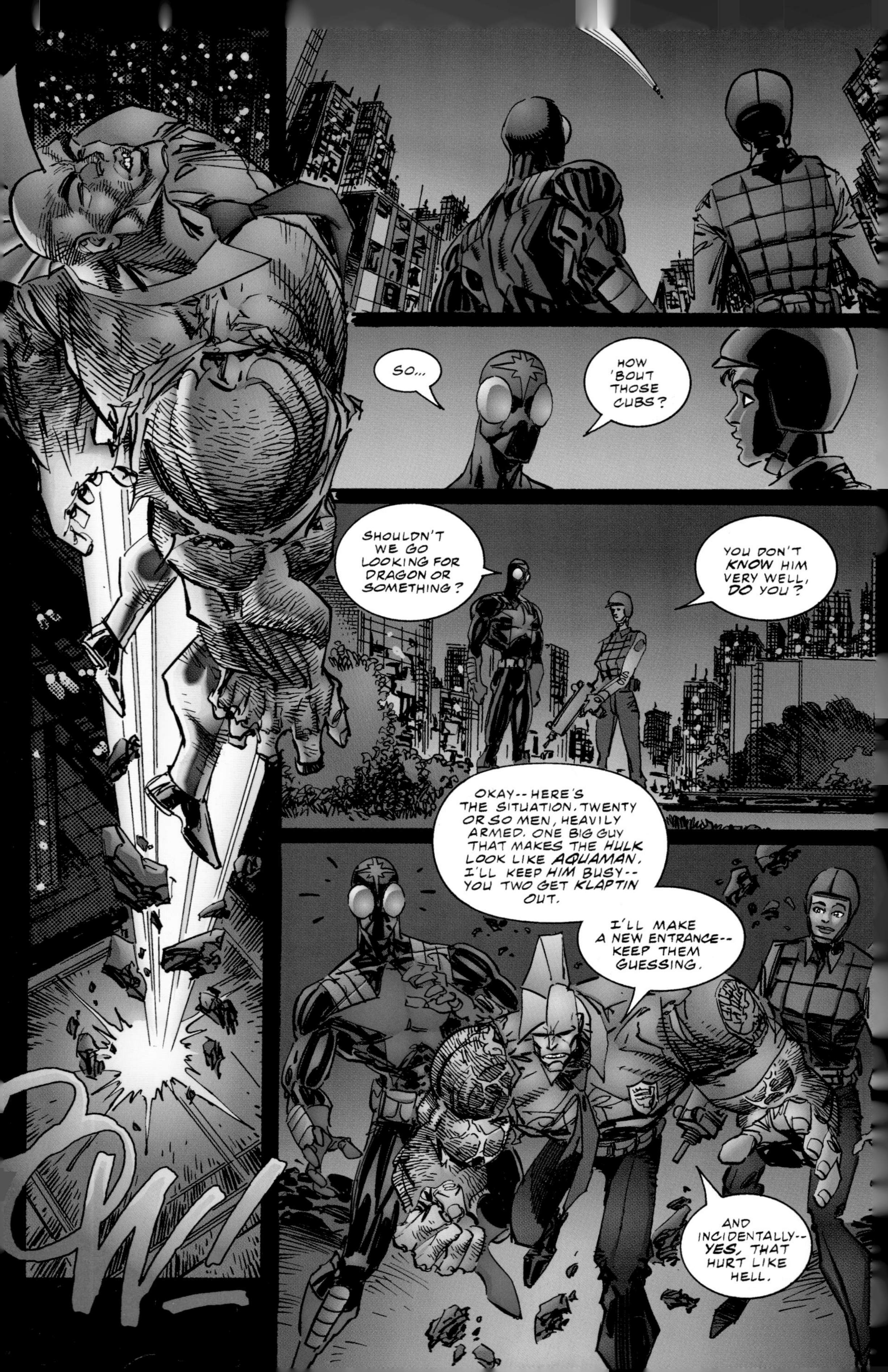

SO...
HOW 'BOUT THOSE CUBS?
SHOULDN'T WE GO LOOKING FOR DRAGON OR SOMETHING?
YOU DON'T KNOW HIM VERY WELL, DO YOU?
OKAY-- HERE'S THE SITUATION. TWENTY OR SO MEN, HEAVILY ARMED. ONE BIG GUY THAT MAKES THE HULK LOOK LIKE AQUAMAN. I'LL KEEP HIM BUSY-- YOU TWO GET KLAPTIN OUT.
I'LL MAKE A NEW ENTRANCE-- KEEP THEM GUESSING.
AND INCIDENTALLY-- YES, THAT HURT LIKE HELL.

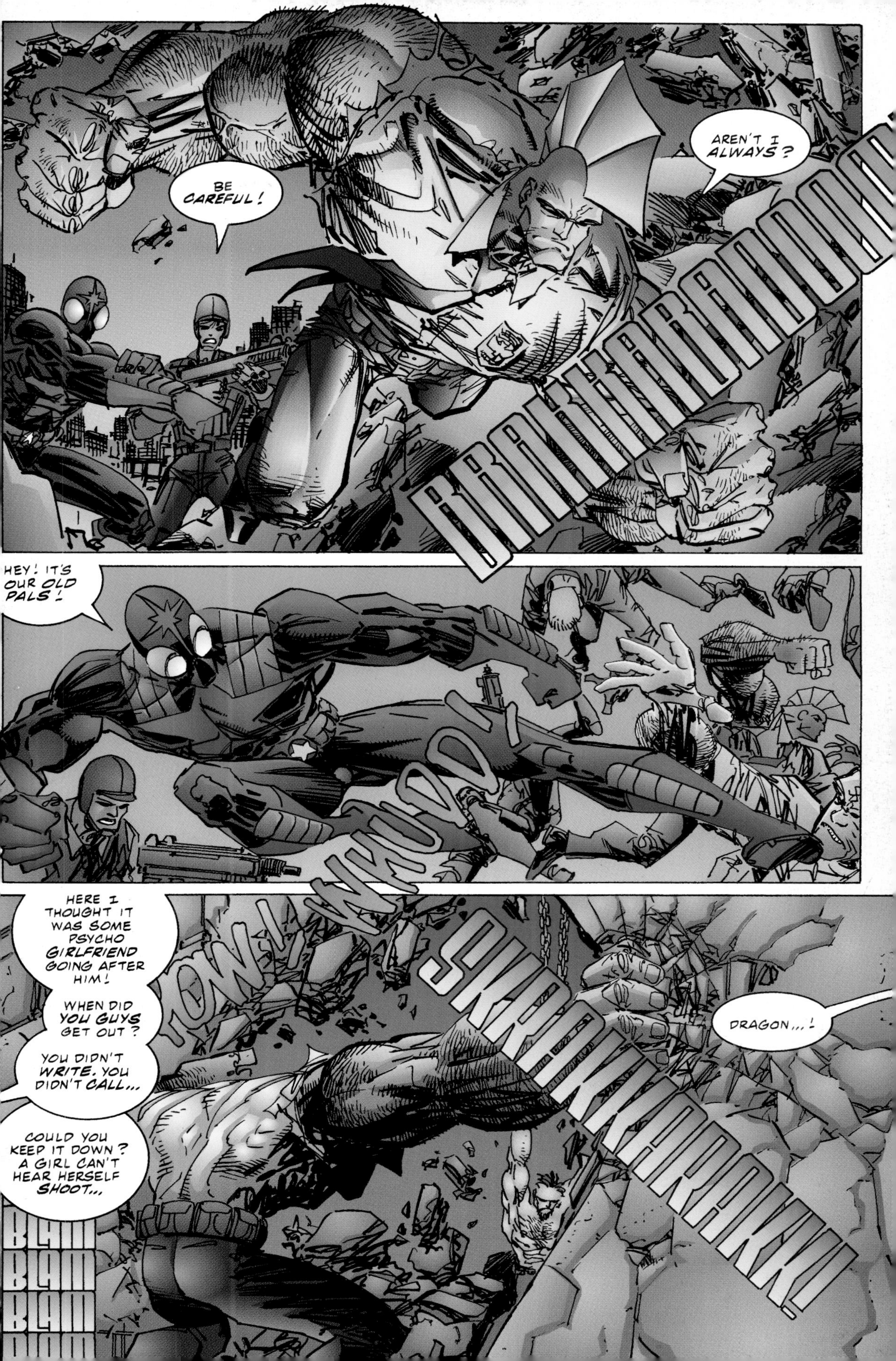
BE CAREFUL!
AREN'T I ALWAYS?
HEY! IT'S OUR OLD PALS!
HERE I THOUGHT IT WAS SOME PSYCHO GIRLFRIEND GOING AFTER HIM!
WHEN DID YOU GUYS GET OUT?
YOU DIDN'T WRITE. YOU DIDN'T CALL...
COULD YOU KEEP IT DOWN? A GIRL CAN'T HEAR HERSELF SHOOT...
DRAGON...!
BLAM
BLAM
BLAM
BLAM

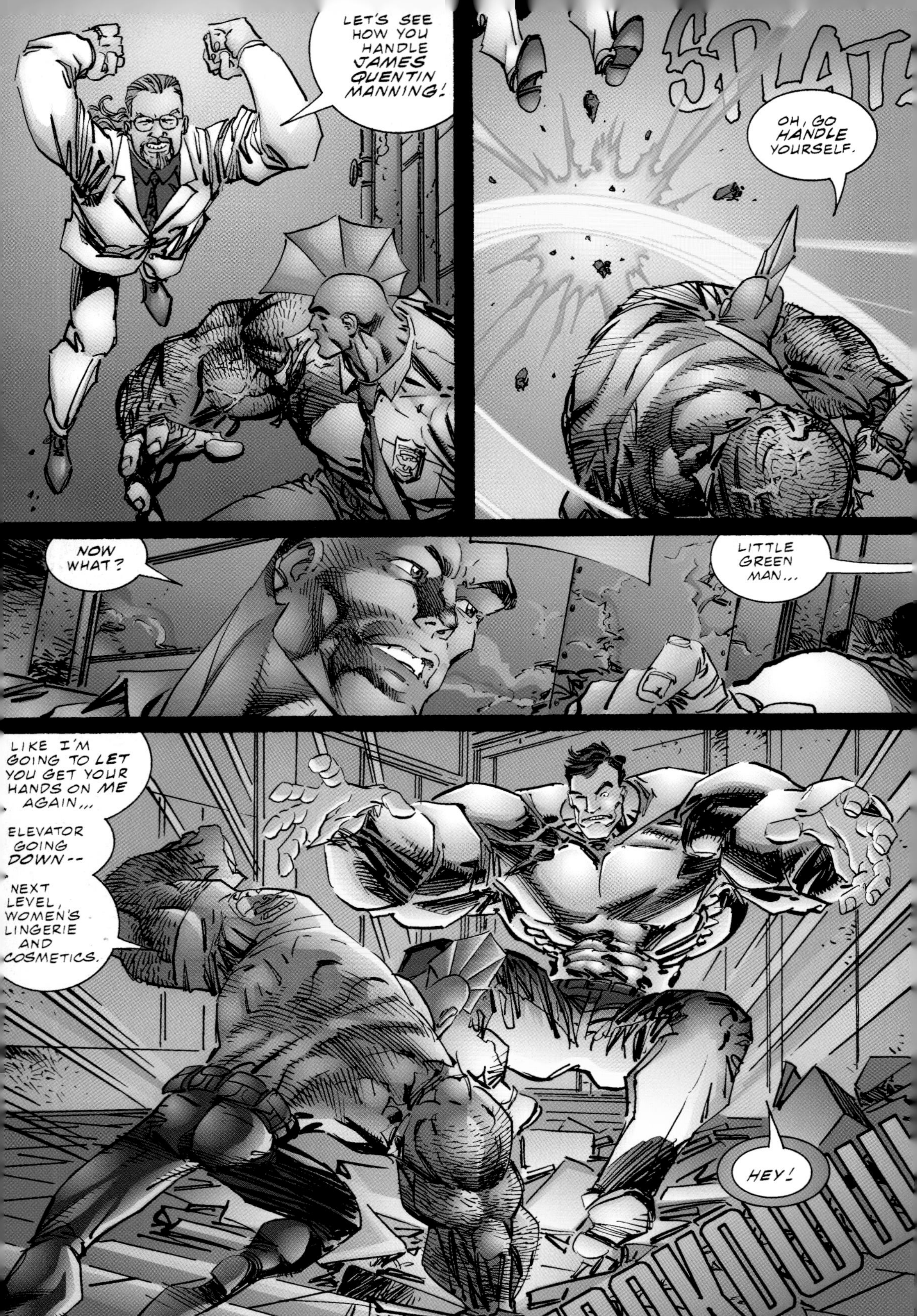
LET'S SEE HOW YOU HANDLE JAMES QUENTIN MANNING!
SPLAT
OH, GO HANDLE YOURSELF.
NOW WHAT?
LITTLE GREEN MAN...
LIKE I'M GOING TO LET YOU GET YOUR HANDS ON ME AGAIN...
ELEVATOR GOING DOWN--
NEXT LEVEL, WOMEN'S LINGERIE AND COSMETICS.
HEY!

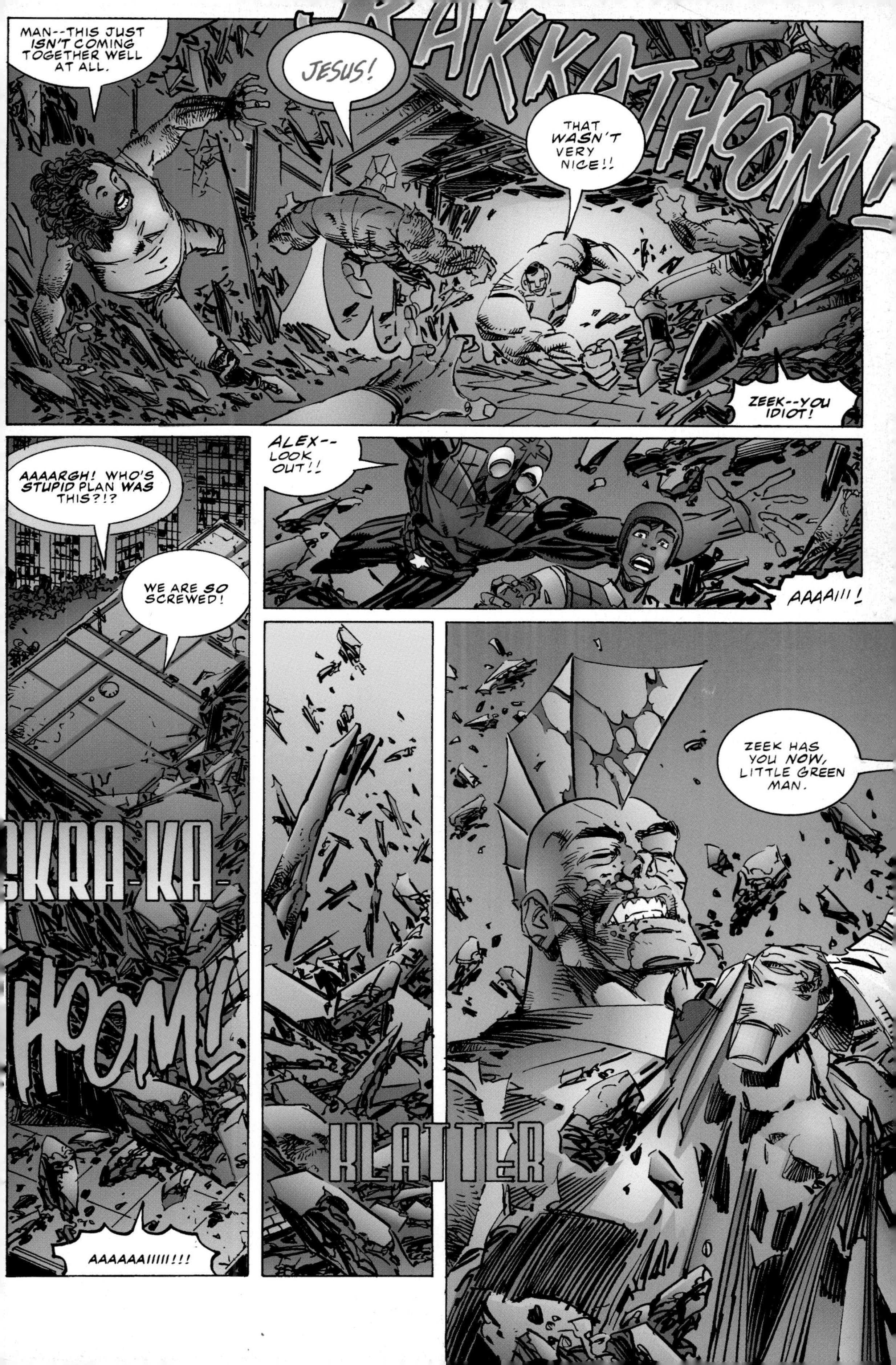

RAKKATHOM!
MAN--THIS JUST ISN'T COMING TOGETHER WELL AT ALL.
JESUS!
THAT WASN'T VERY NICE!!
ZEEK--YOU IDIOT!
AAAARGH! WHO'S STUPID PLAN WAS THIS?!?
WE ARE SO SCREWED!
KRA-KA-
HOOM!
AAAAAAIIIII!!!
ALEX--LOOK OUT!!
AAAAIII!
KLATTER
ZEEK HAS YOU NOW, LITTLE GREEN MAN.

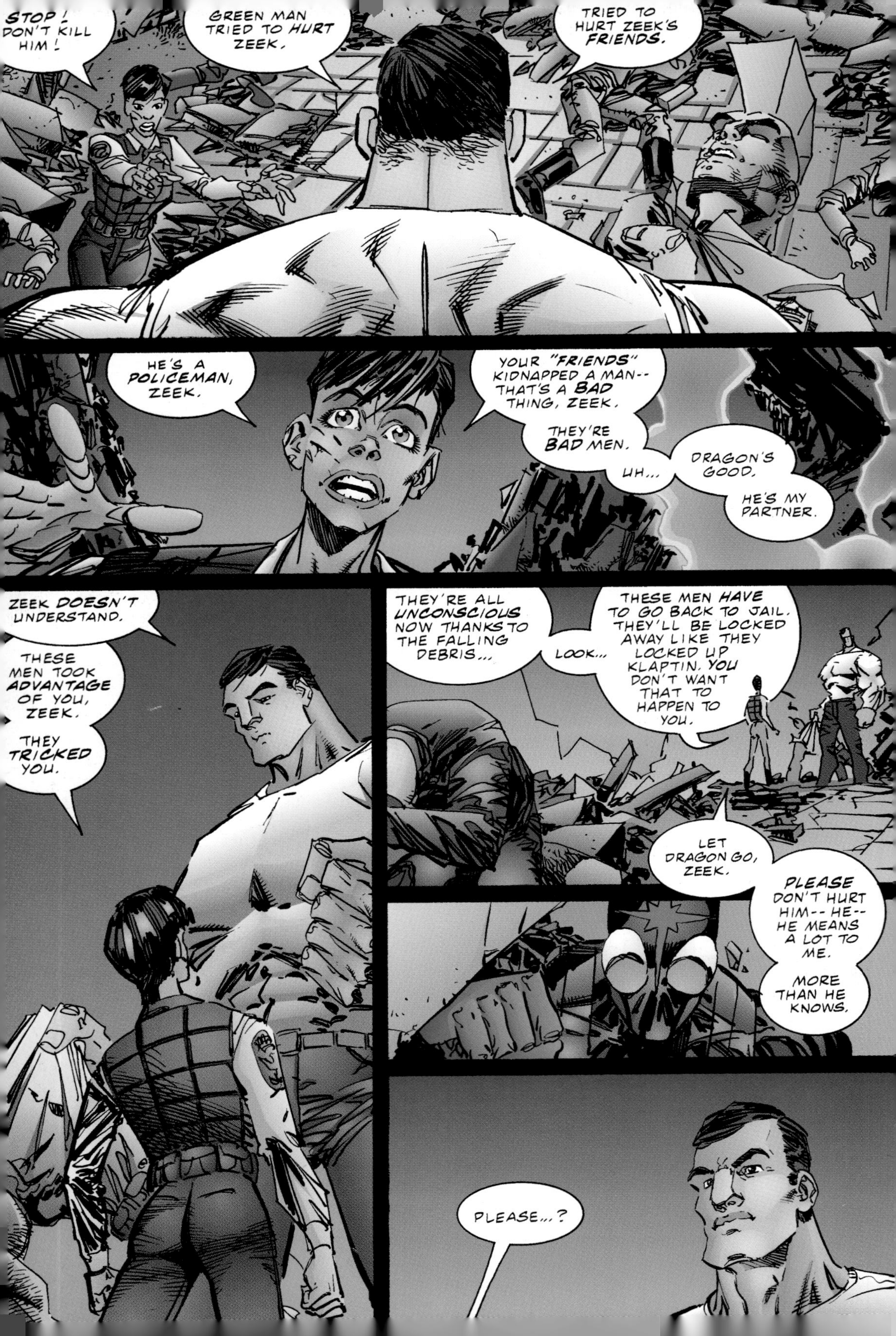
STOP! DON'T KILL HIM!
GREEN MAN TRIED TO HURT ZEEK.
TRIED TO HURT ZEEK'S FRIENDS.
HE'S A POLICEMAN, ZEEK.
YOUR "FRIENDS" KIDNAPPED A MAN-- THAT'S A BAD THING, ZEEK.
THEY'RE BAD MEN.
UH...
DRAGON'S GOOD.
HE'S MY PARTNER.
ZEEK DOESN'T UNDERSTAND.
THESE MEN TOOK ADVANTAGE OF YOU, ZEEK.
THEY TRICKED YOU.
THEY'RE ALL UNCONSCIOUS NOW THANKS TO THE FALLING DEBRIS...
LOOK...
THESE MEN HAVE TO GO BACK TO JAIL. THEY'LL BE LOCKED AWAY LIKE THEY LOCKED UP KLAPTIN. YOU DON'T WANT THAT TO HAPPEN TO YOU.
LET DRAGON GO, ZEEK.
PLEASE DON'T HURT HIM-- HE-- HE MEANS A LOT TO ME.
MORE THAN HE KNOWS.
PLEASE...?

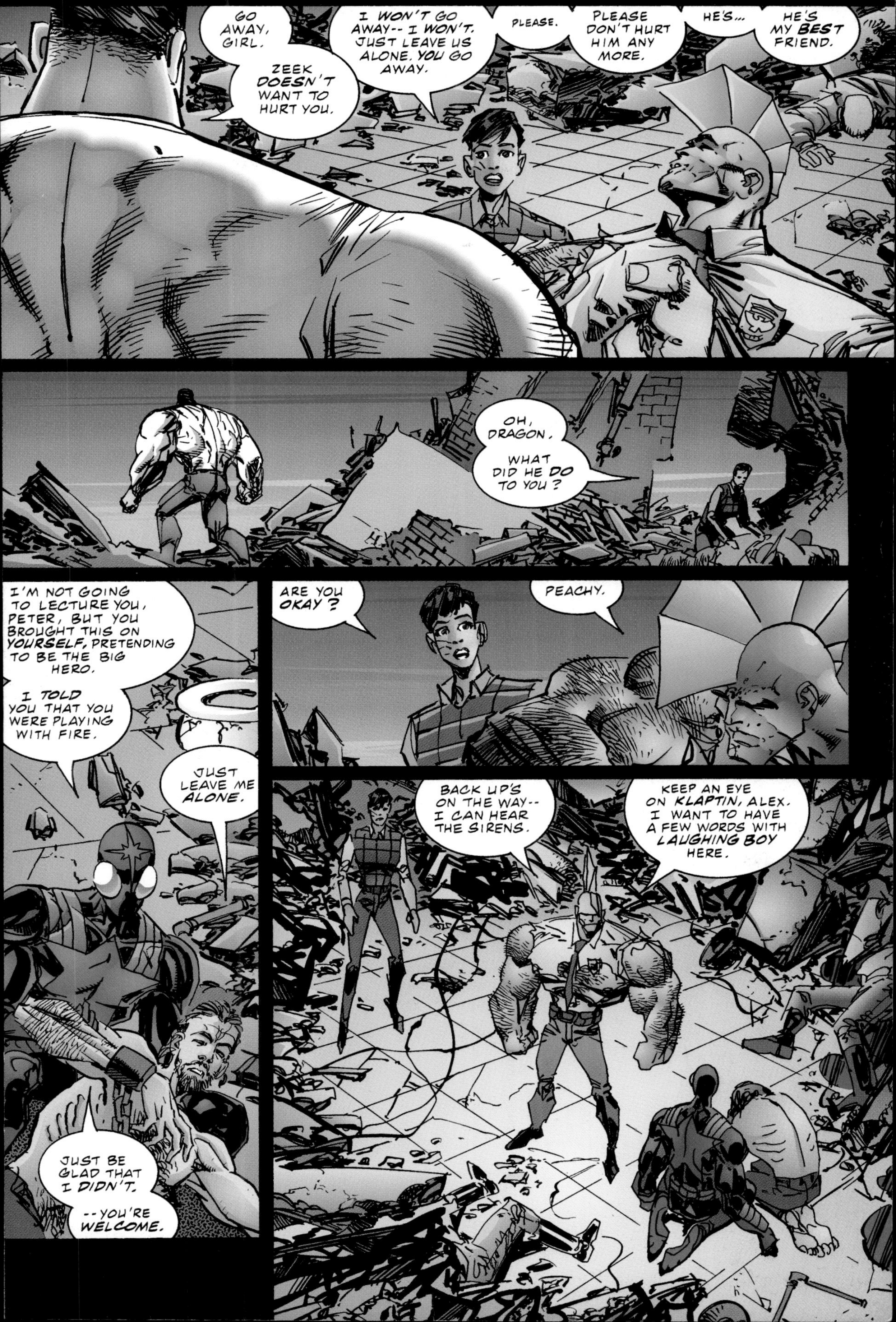
GO AWAY, GIRL.
ZEEK DOESN'T WANT TO HURT YOU.
I WON'T GO AWAY-- I WON'T. JUST LEAVE US ALONE. YOU GO AWAY.
PLEASE.
PLEASE DON'T HURT HIM ANY MORE.
HE'S...
HE'S MY BEST FRIEND.
OH, DRAGON.
WHAT DID HE DO TO YOU?
I'M NOT GOING TO LECTURE YOU, PETER, BUT YOU BROUGHT THIS ON YOURSELF, PRETENDING TO BE THE BIG HERO.
I TOLD YOU THAT YOU WERE PLAYING WITH FIRE.
JUST LEAVE ME ALONE.
JUST BE GLAD THAT I DIDN'T.
--YOU'RE WELCOME.
ARE YOU OKAY?
PEACHY.
BACK UP'S ON THE WAY-- I CAN HEAR THE SIRENS.
KEEP AN EYE ON KLAPTIN, ALEX. I WANT TO HAVE A FEW WORDS WITH LAUGHING BOY HERE.

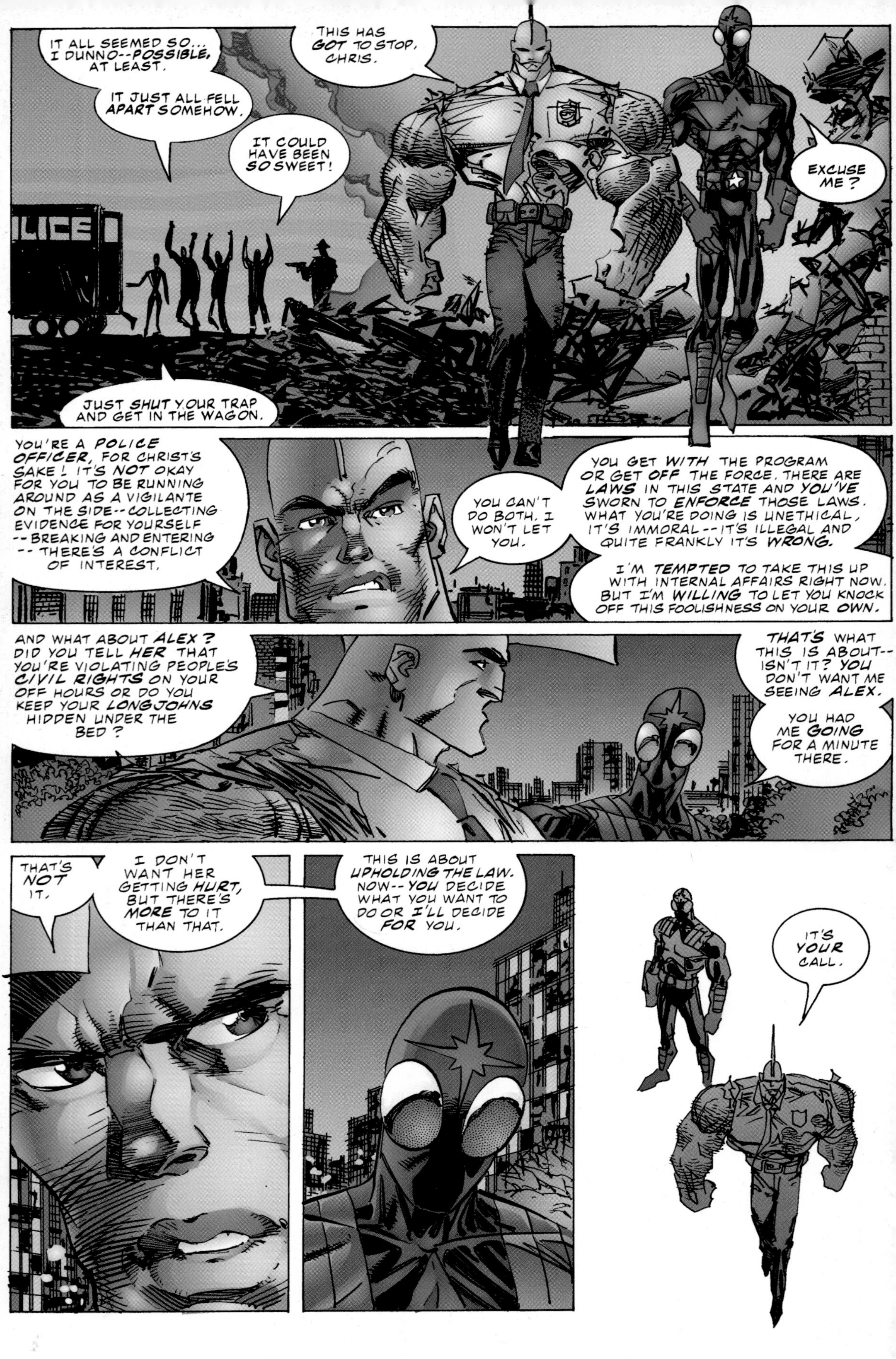
IT ALL SEEMED SO... I DUNNO--POSSIBLE, AT LEAST.
IT JUST ALL FELL APART SOMEHOW.
IT COULD HAVE BEEN SO SWEET!
THIS HAS GOT TO STOP, CHRIS.
EXCUSE ME?
ILICE
JUST SHUT YOUR TRAP AND GET IN THE WAGON.
YOU'RE A POLICE OFFICER, FOR CHRIST'S SAKE! IT'S NOT OKAY FOR YOU TO BE RUNNING AROUND AS A VIGILANTE ON THE SIDE--COLLECTING EVIDENCE FOR YOURSELF --BREAKING AND ENTERING --THERE'S A CONFLICT OF INTEREST.
YOU CAN'T DO BOTH. I WON'T LET YOU.
YOU GET WITH THE PROGRAM OR GET OFF THE FORCE. THERE ARE LAWS IN THIS STATE AND YOU'VE SWORN TO ENFORCE THOSE LAWS. WHAT YOU'RE DOING IS UNETHICAL, IT'S IMMORAL--IT'S ILLEGAL AND QUITE FRANKLY IT'S WRONG.
I'M TEMPTED TO TAKE THIS UP WITH INTERNAL AFFAIRS RIGHT NOW. BUT I'M WILLING TO LET YOU KNOCK OFF THIS FOOLISHNESS ON YOUR OWN.
AND WHAT ABOUT ALEX? DID YOU TELL HER THAT YOU'RE VIOLATING PEOPLE'S CIVIL RIGHTS ON YOUR OFF HOURS OR DO YOU KEEP YOUR LONGJOHNS HIDDEN UNDER THE BED?
THAT'S WHAT THIS IS ABOUT--ISN'T IT? YOU DON'T WANT ME SEEING ALEX.
YOU HAD ME GOING FOR A MINUTE THERE.
THAT'S NOT IT.
I DON'T WANT HER GETTING HURT, BUT THERE'S MORE TO IT THAN THAT.
THIS IS ABOUT UPHOLDING THE LAW. NOW--YOU DECIDE WHAT YOU WANT TO DO OR I'LL DECIDE FOR YOU.
IT'S YOUR CALL.

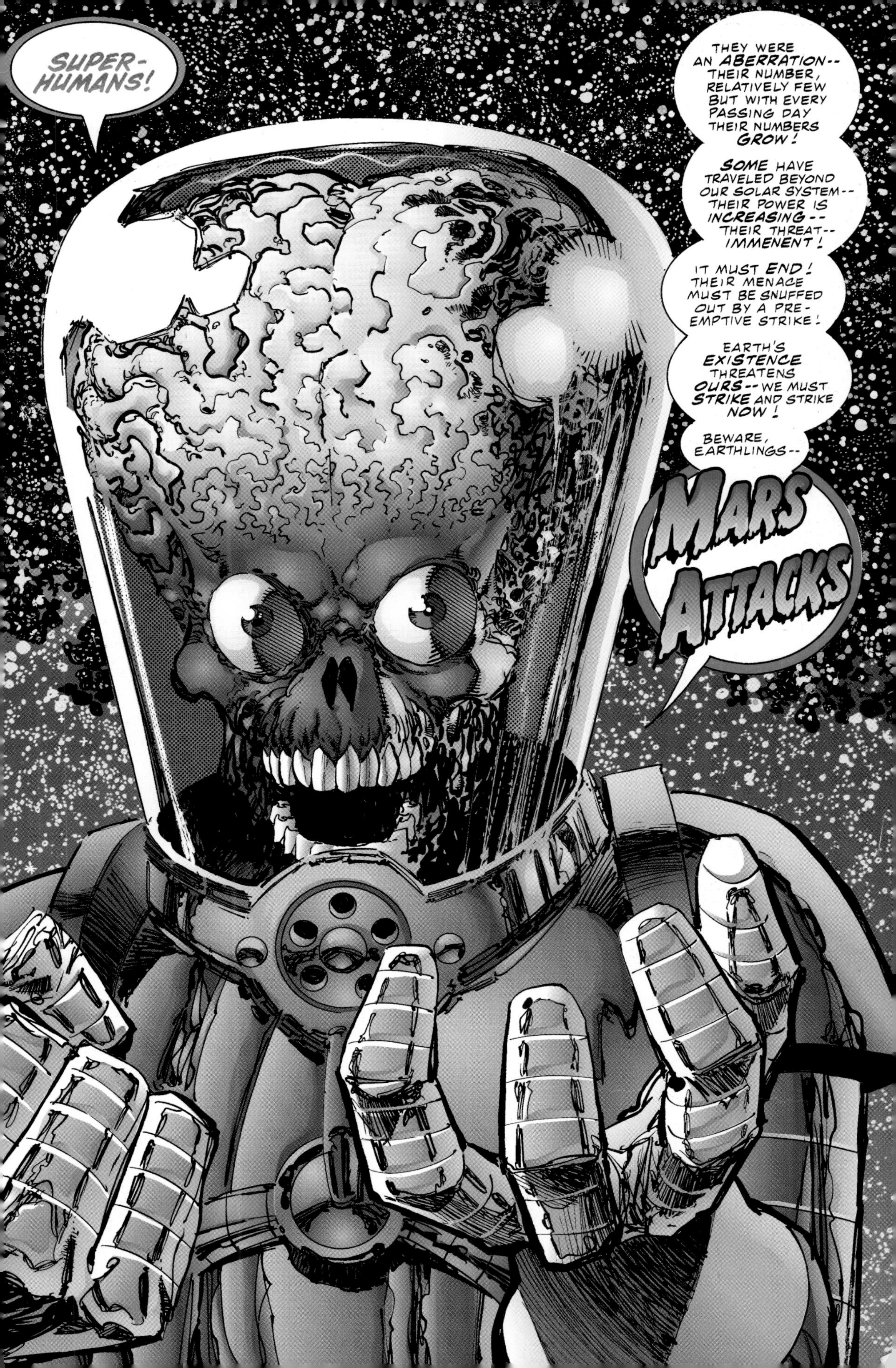
SUPER-HUMANS!
THEY WERE AN ABERRATION-- THEIR NUMBER, RELATIVELY FEW BUT WITH EVERY PASSING DAY THEIR NUMBERS GROW!
SOME HAVE TRAVELED BEYOND OUR SOLAR SYSTEM-- THEIR POWER IS INCREASING-- THEIR THREAT-- IMMENENT!
IT MUST END! THEIR MENACE MUST BE SNUFFED OUT BY A PRE-EMPTIVE STRIKE!
EARTH'S EXISTENCE THREATENS OURS-- WE MUST STRIKE AND STRIKE NOW!
BEWARE, EARTHLINGS--
MARS ATTACKS

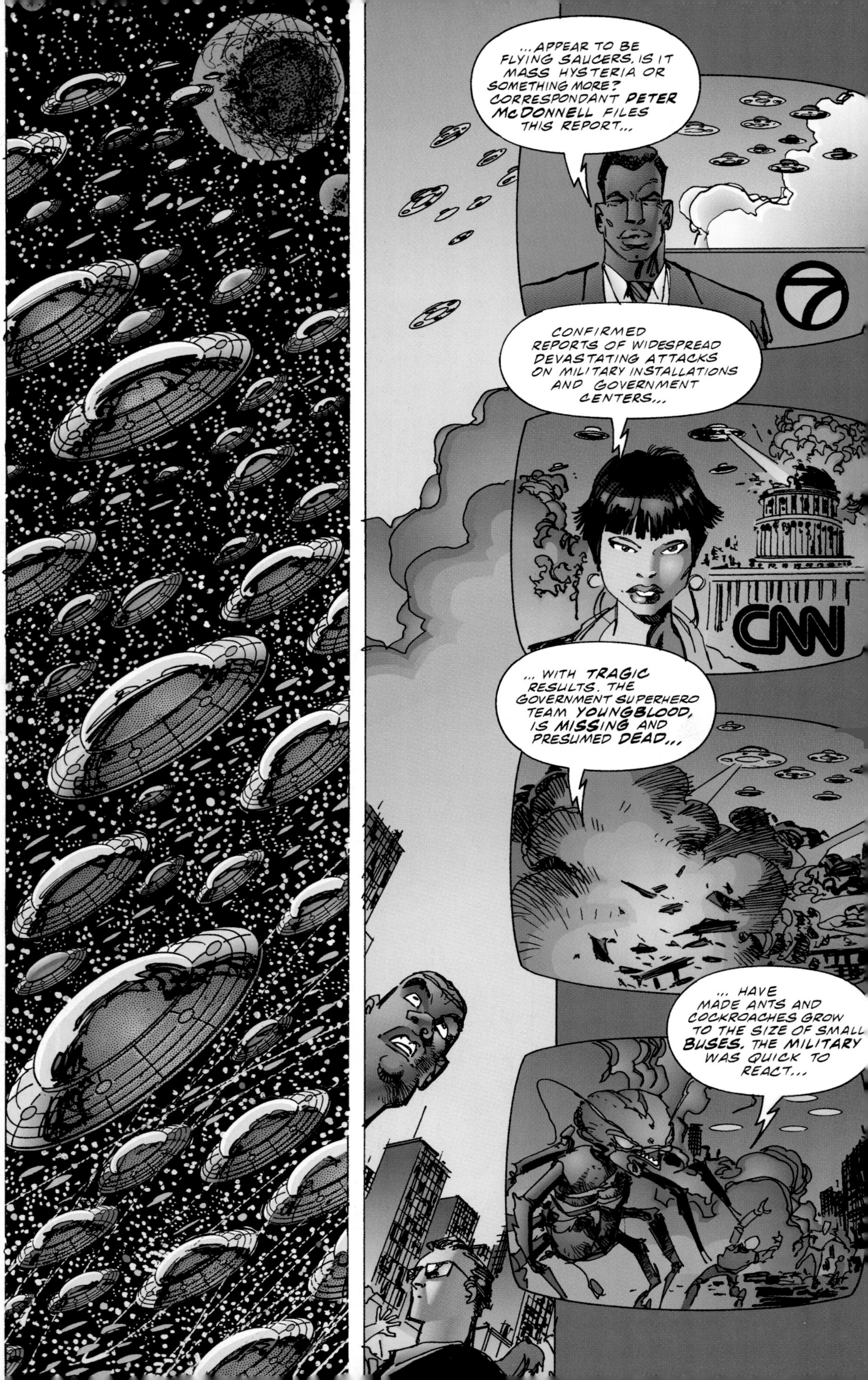
...APPEAR TO BE FLYING SAUCERS. IS IT MASS HYSTERIA OR SOMETHING MORE? CORRESPONDANT PETER McDONNELL FILES THIS REPORT...
CONFIRMED REPORTS OF WIDESPREAD DEVASTATING ATTACKS ON MILITARY INSTALLATIONS AND GOVERNMENT CENTERS...
CNN
... WITH TRAGIC RESULTS. THE GOVERNMENT SUPERHERO TEAM YOUNGBLOOD, IS MISSING AND PRESUMED DEAD...
... HAVE MADE ANTS AND COCKROACHES GROW TO THE SIZE OF SMALL BUSES. THE MILITARY WAS QUICK TO REACT...

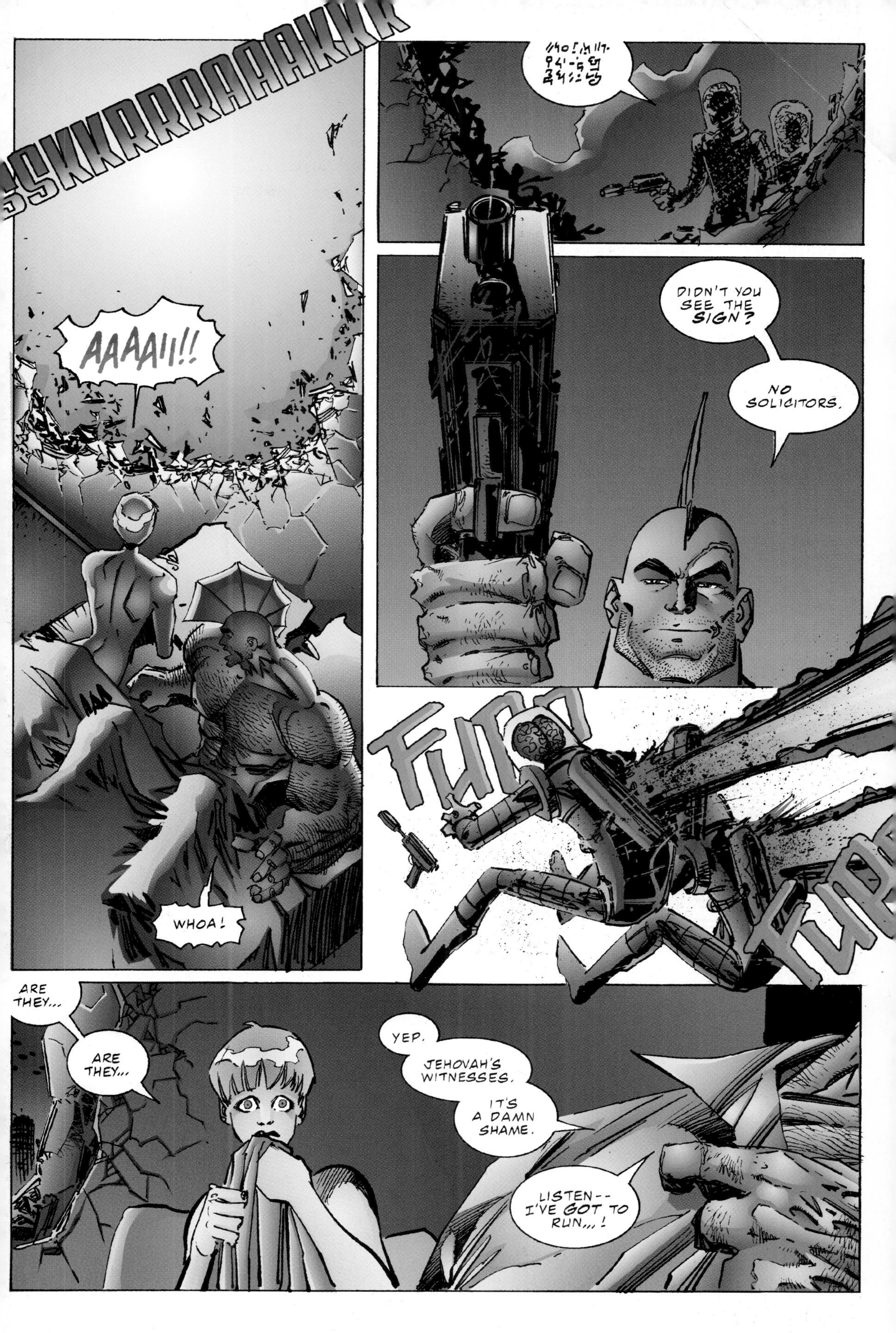
SSKKRRRRAAAKKK
AAAAII!!
WHOA!
DIDN'T YOU SEE THE SIGN?
NO SOLICITORS.
ARE THEY...
ARE THEY...
YEP.
JEHOVAH'S WITNESSES.
IT'S A DAMN SHAME.
LISTEN-- I'VE GOT TO RUN...!

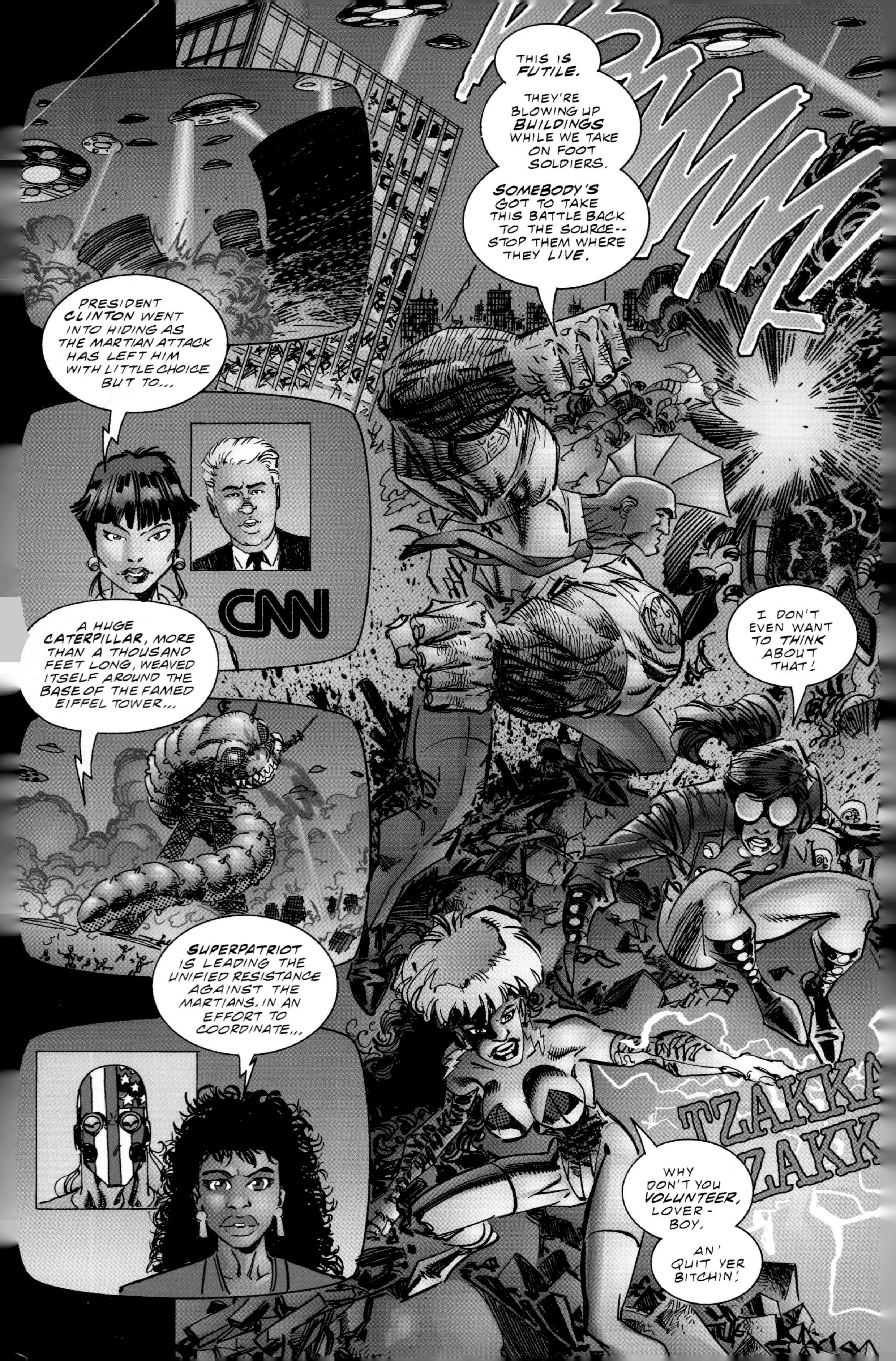
PRESIDENT CLINTON WENT INTO HIDING AS THE MARTIAN ATTACK HAS LEFT HIM WITH LITTLE CHOICE BUT TO...
CNN
A HUGE CATERPILLAR, MORE THAN A THOUSAND FEET LONG, WEAVED ITSELF AROUND THE BASE OF THE FAMED EIFFEL TOWER...
SUPERPATRIOT IS LEADING THE UNIFIED RESISTANCE AGAINST THE MARTIANS. IN AN EFFORT TO COORDINATE...
THIS IS FUTILE.
THEY'RE BLOWING UP BUILDINGS WHILE WE TAKE ON FOOT SOLDIERS.
SOMEBODY'S GOT TO TAKE THIS BATTLE BACK TO THE SOURCE-- STOP THEM WHERE THEY LIVE.
I DON'T EVEN WANT TO THINK ABOUT THAT!
WHY DON'T YOU VOLUNTEER, LOVER-BOY.
AN' QUIT YER BITCHIN'!
TZAKKA
ZAKK

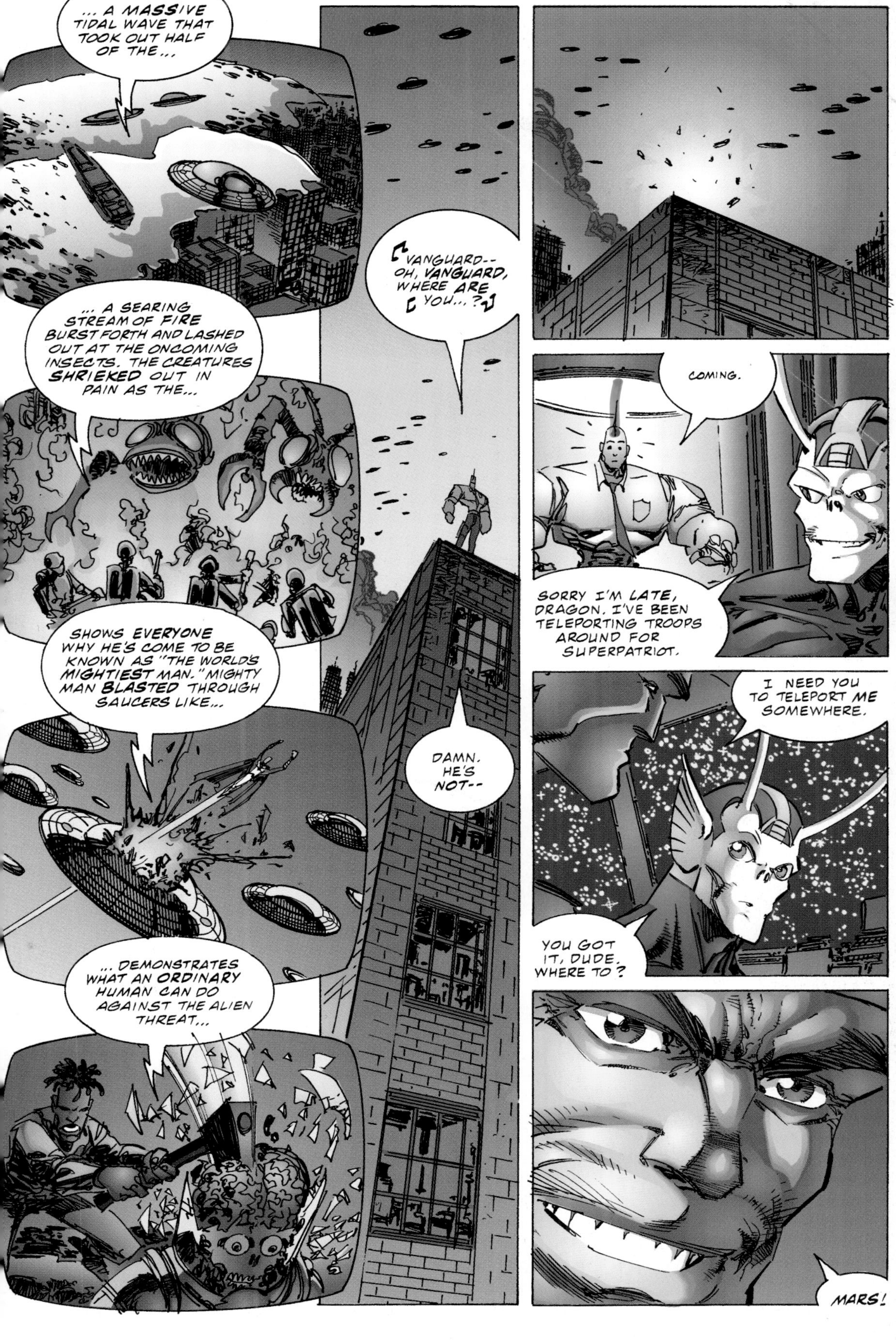
... A MASSIVE TIDAL WAVE THAT TOOK OUT HALF OF THE...
... A SEARING STREAM OF FIRE BURST FORTH AND LASHED OUT AT THE ONCOMING INSECTS. THE CREATURES SHRIEKED OUT IN PAIN AS THE...
SHOWS EVERYONE WHY HE'S COME TO BE KNOWN AS "THE WORLD'S MIGHTIEST MAN." MIGHTY MAN BLASTED THROUGH SAUCERS LIKE...
... DEMONSTRATES WHAT AN ORDINARY HUMAN CAN DO AGAINST THE ALIEN THREAT...
VANGUARD-- OH, VANGUARD, WHERE ARE YOU...?
DAMN. HE'S NOT--
COMING.
SORRY I'M LATE, DRAGON. I'VE BEEN TELEPORTING TROOPS AROUND FOR SUPERPATRIOT.
I NEED YOU TO TELEPORT ME SOMEWHERE.
YOU GOT IT, DUDE. WHERE TO?
MARS!

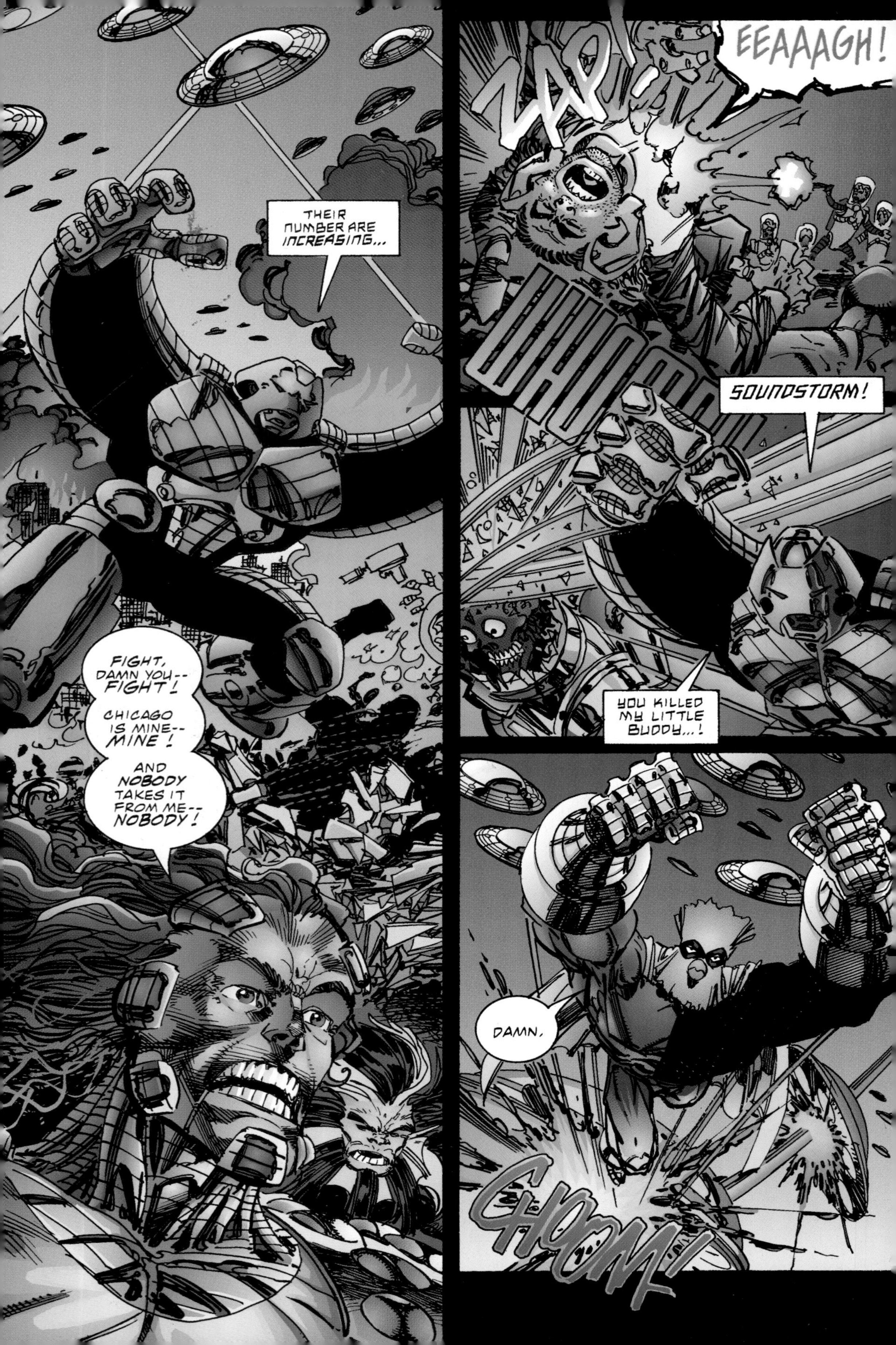
THEIR NUMBER ARE INCREASING...
FIGHT, DAMN YOU--FIGHT!
CHICAGO IS MINE--MINE!
AND NOBODY TAKES IT FROM ME--NOBODY!
ZAP!
EEAAAGH!
SOUNDSTORM!
YOU KILLED MY LITTLE BUDDY...!
DAMN.
CHOOM!

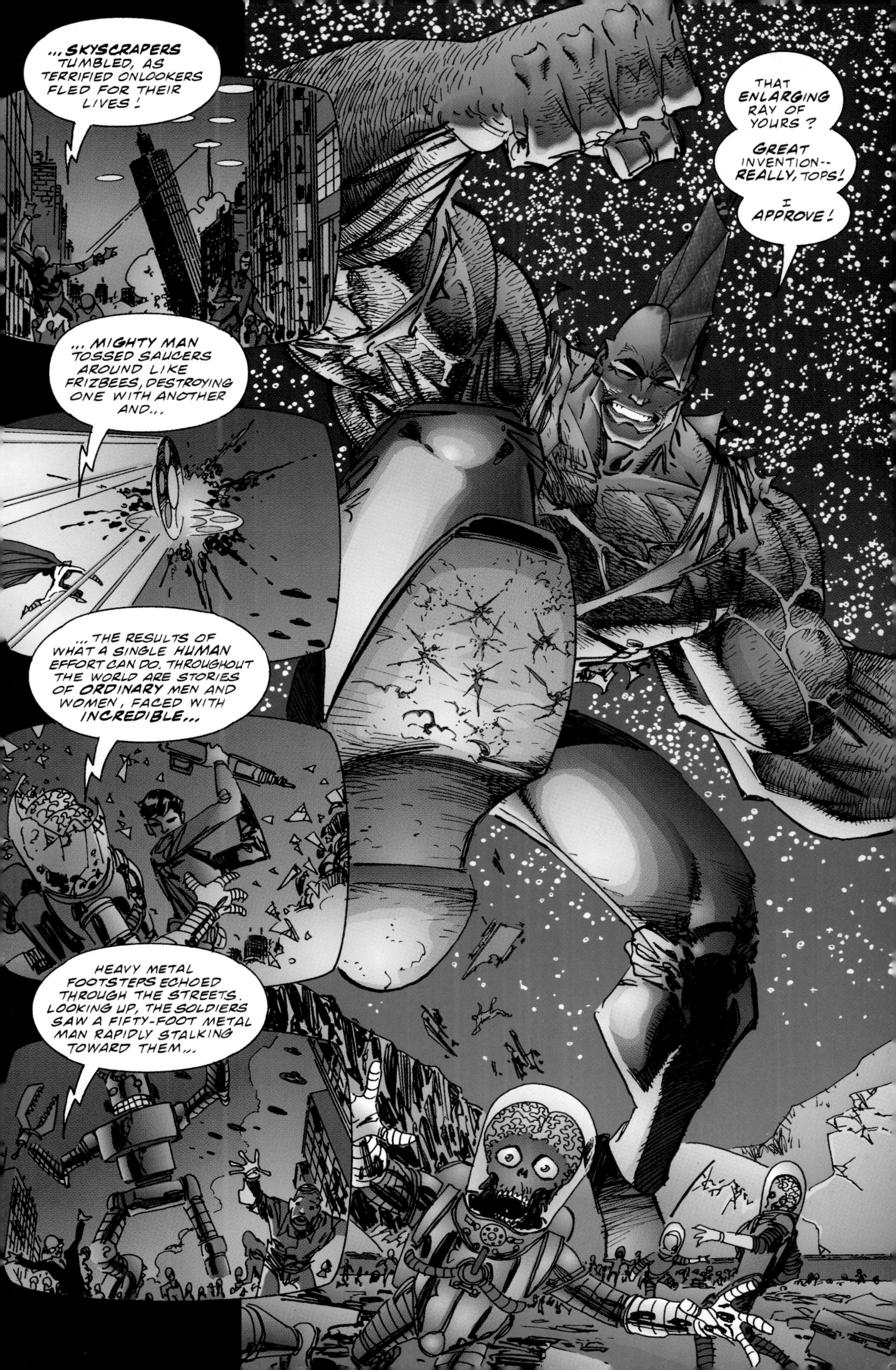
...SKYSCRAPERS TUMBLED, AS TERRIFIED ONLOOKERS FLED FOR THEIR LIVES!
THAT ENLARGING RAY OF YOURS?
GREAT INVENTION-- REALLY, TOPS!
I APPROVE!
...MIGHTY MAN TOSSED SAUCERS AROUND LIKE FRIZBEES, DESTROYING ONE WITH ANOTHER AND...
...THE RESULTS OF WHAT A SINGLE HUMAN EFFORT CAN DO. THROUGHOUT THE WORLD ARE STORIES OF ORDINARY MEN AND WOMEN, FACED WITH INCREDIBLE...
HEAVY METAL FOOTSTEPS ECHOED THROUGH THE STREETS. LOOKING UP, THE SOLDIERS SAW A FIFTY-FOOT METAL MAN RAPIDLY STALKING TOWARD THEM...

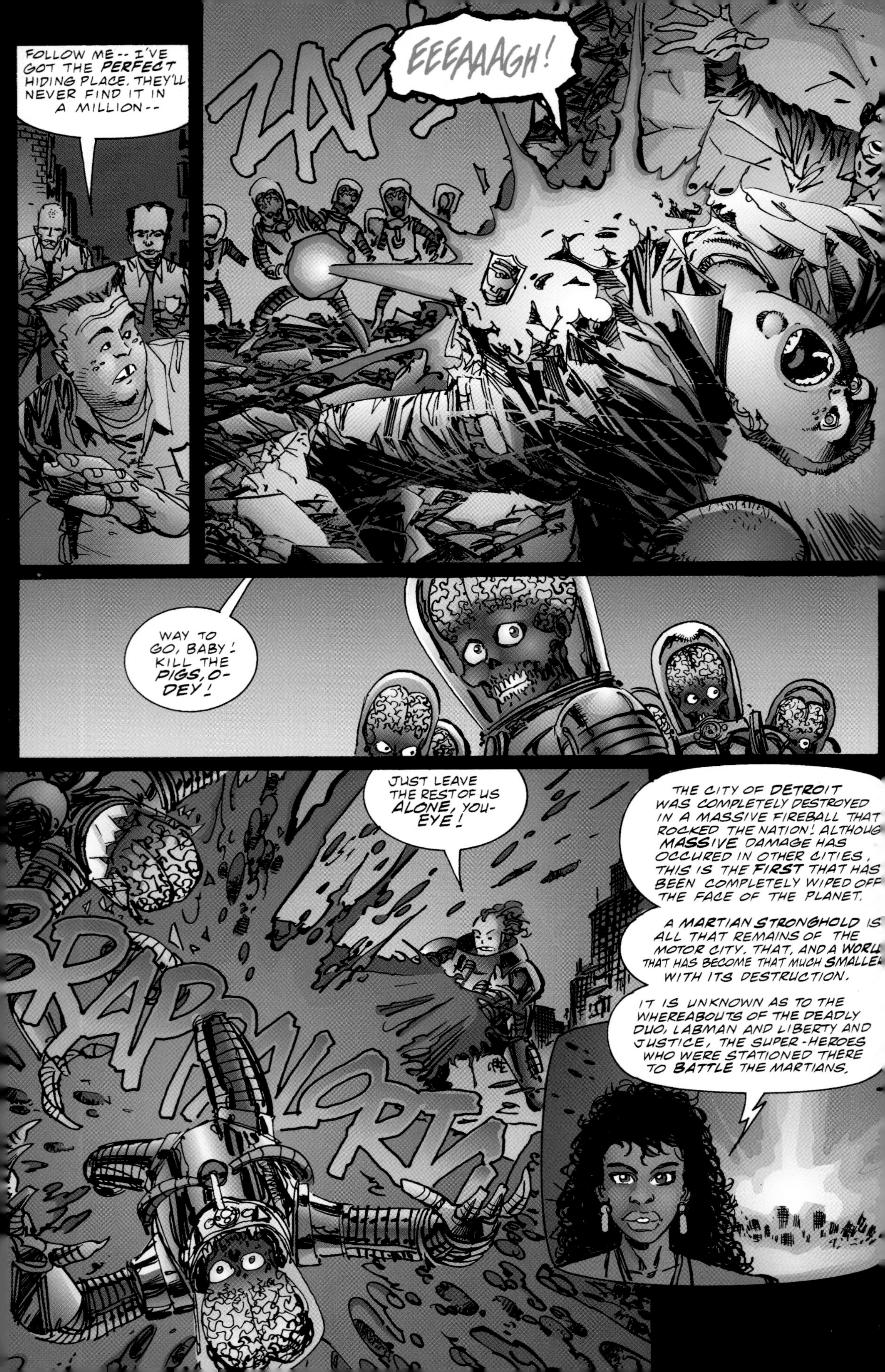
FOLLOW ME -- I'VE GOT THE PERFECT HIDING PLACE. THEY'LL NEVER FIND IT IN A MILLION --
ZAP
EEEAAAGH!
WAY TO GO, BABY! KILL THE PIGS, O-DEY!
JUST LEAVE THE REST OF US ALONE, YOU-EYE!
ZAP
THE CITY OF DETROIT WAS COMPLETELY DESTROYED IN A MASSIVE FIREBALL THAT ROCKED THE NATION! ALTHOUG MASSIVE DAMAGE HAS OCCURED IN OTHER CITIES, THIS IS THE FIRST THAT HAS BEEN COMPLETELY WIPED OFF THE FACE OF THE PLANET.
A MARTIAN STRONGHOLD IS ALL THAT REMAINS OF THE MOTOR CITY. THAT, AND A WORL THAT HAS BECOME THAT MUCH SMALLE WITH ITS DESTRUCTION.
IT IS UNKNOWN AS TO THE WHEREABOUTS OF THE DEADLY DUO, LABMAN AND LIBERTY AND JUSTICE, THE SUPER-HEROES WHO WERE STATIONED THERE TO BATTLE THE MARTIANS.

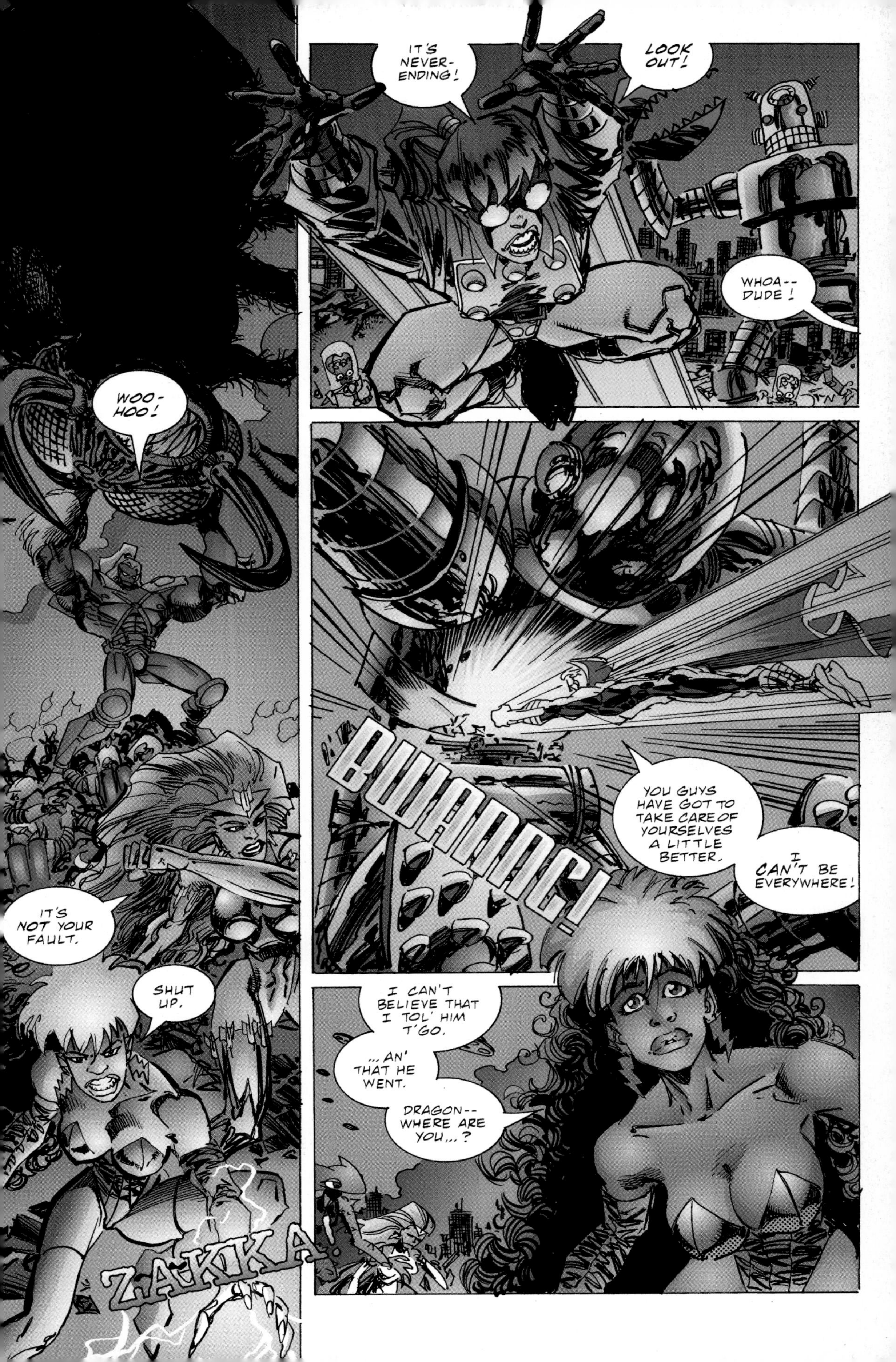
IT'S NEVER-ENDING!
LOOK OUT!
WHOA-- DUDE!
WOO-HOO!
BUDOOOC!
YOU GUYS HAVE GOT TO TAKE CARE OF YOURSELVES A LITTLE BETTER.
I CAN'T BE EVERYWHERE!
IT'S NOT YOUR FAULT.
SHUT UP.
ZAKKA
I CAN'T BELIEVE THAT I TOL' HIM T'GO.
...AN' THAT HE WENT.
DRAGON-- WHERE ARE YOU...?

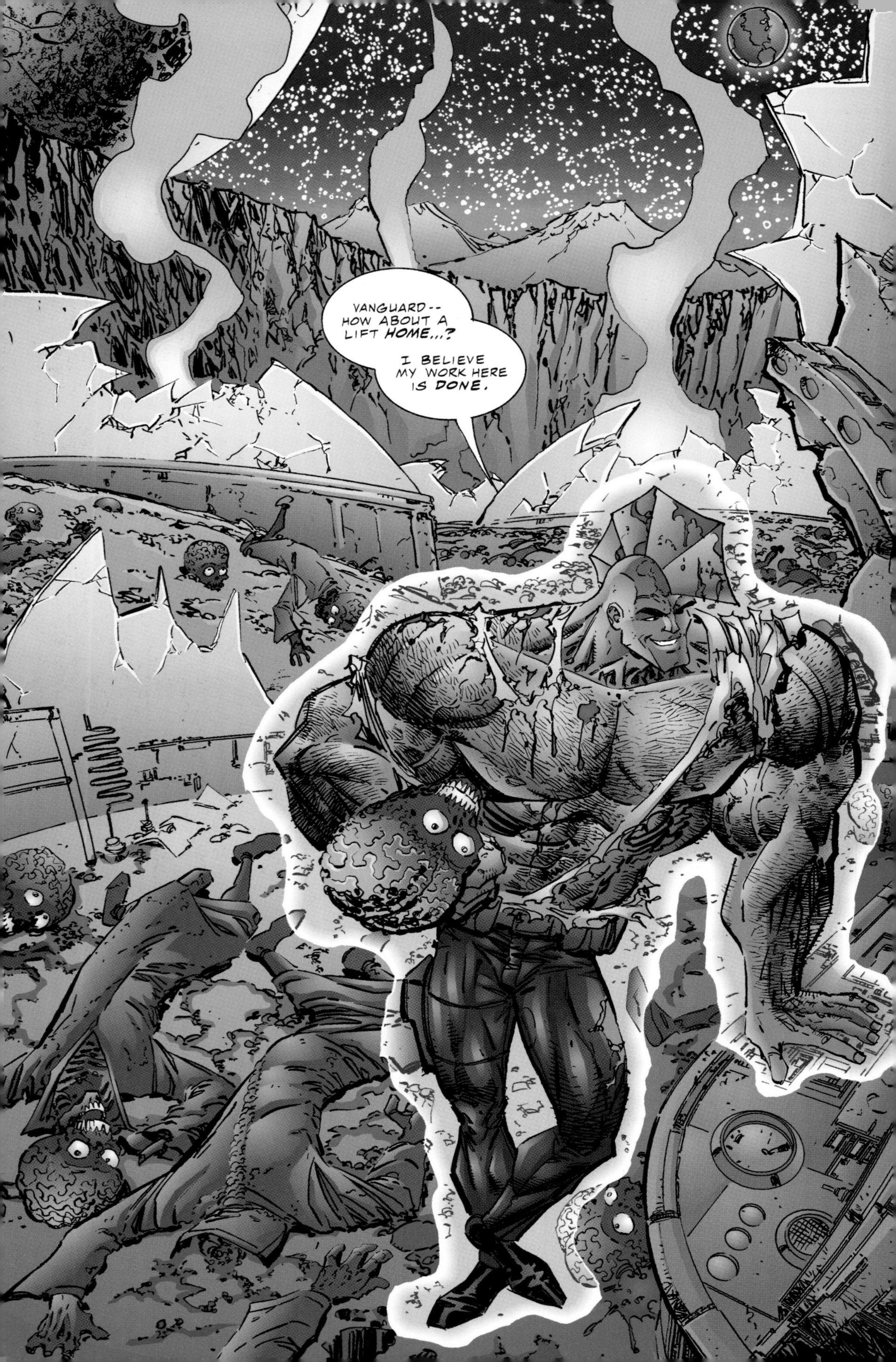
VANGUARD--
HOW ABOUT A
LIFT **HOME**...?
I BELIEVE
MY WORK HERE
IS **DONE**.

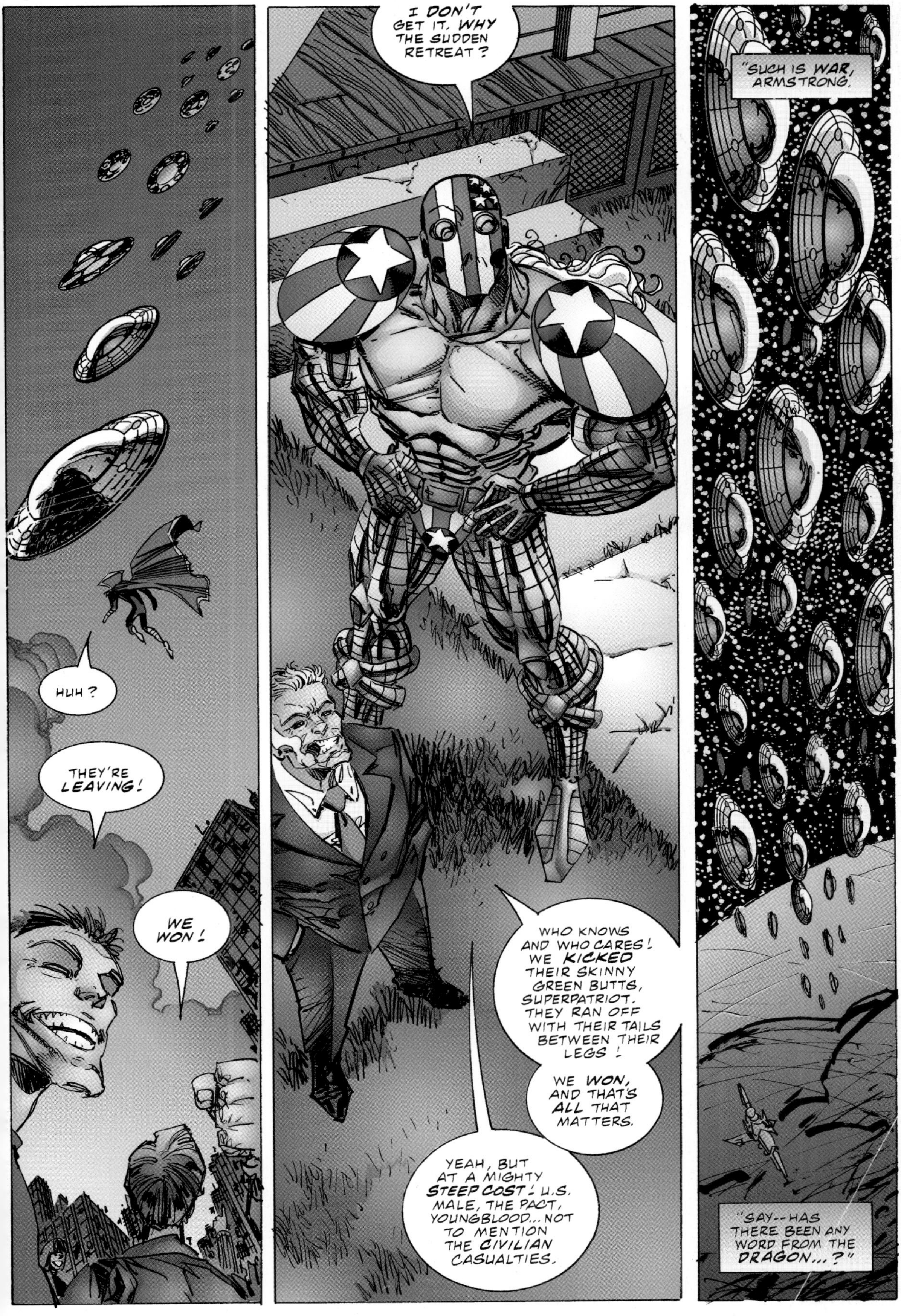
HUH?
THEY'RE LEAVING!
WE WON!
I DON'T GET IT. WHY THE SUDDEN RETREAT?
WHO KNOWS AND WHO CARES! WE KICKED THEIR SKINNY GREEN BUTTS, SUPERPATRIOT. THEY RAN OFF WITH THEIR TAILS BETWEEN THEIR LEGS!
WE WON, AND THAT'S ALL THAT MATTERS.
YEAH, BUT AT A MIGHTY STEEP COST! U.S. MALE, THE PACT, YOUNGBLOOD... NOT TO MENTION THE CIVILIAN CASUALTIES.
"SUCH IS WAR, ARMSTRONG.
"SAY--HAS THERE BEEN ANY WORD FROM THE DRAGON...?"

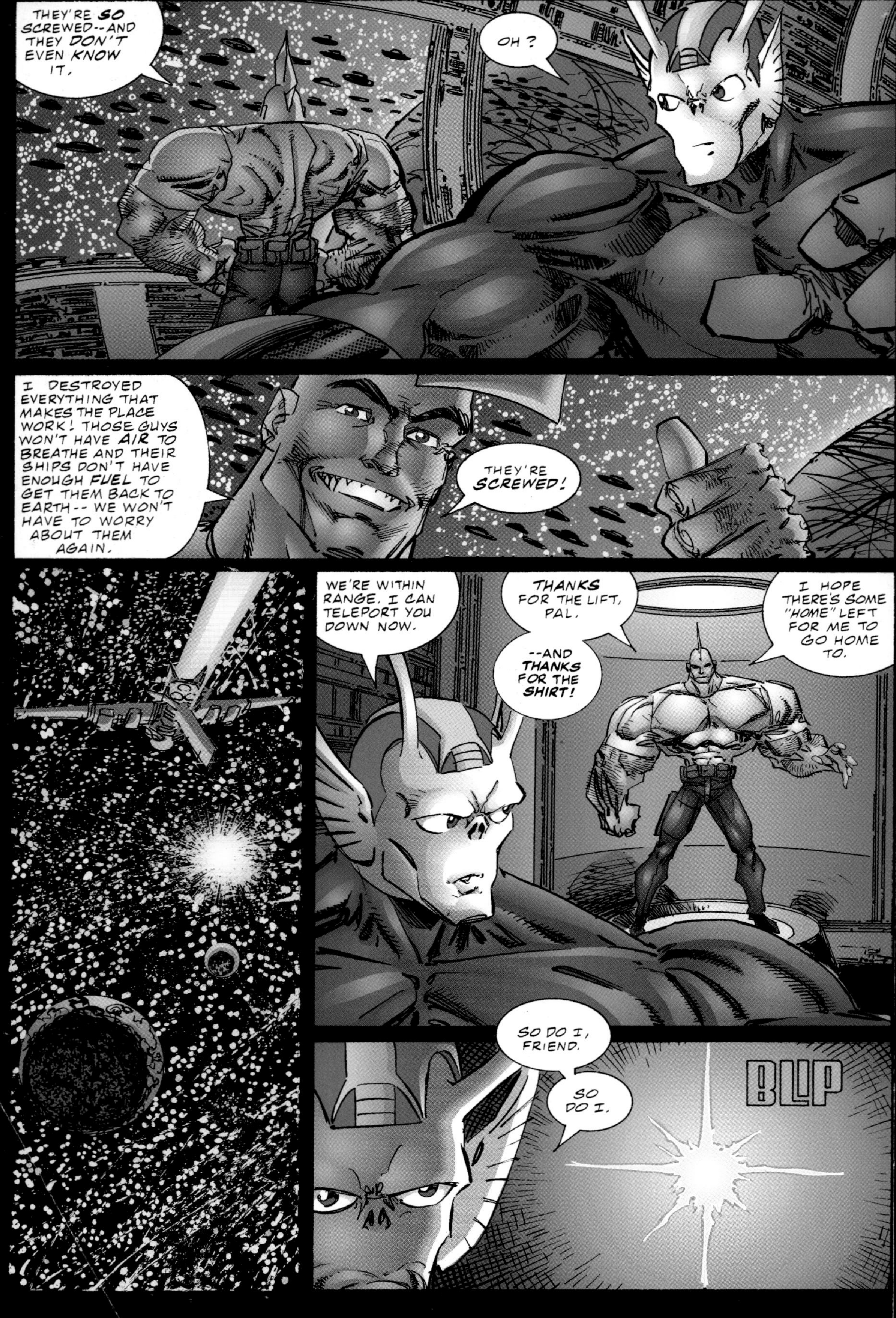

THEY'RE SO SCREWED--AND THEY DON'T EVEN KNOW IT.
OH?
I DESTROYED EVERYTHING THAT MAKES THE PLACE WORK! THOSE GUYS WON'T HAVE AIR TO BREATHE AND THEIR SHIPS DON'T HAVE ENOUGH FUEL TO GET THEM BACK TO EARTH-- WE WON'T HAVE TO WORRY ABOUT THEM AGAIN.
THEY'RE SCREWED!
WE'RE WITHIN RANGE. I CAN TELEPORT YOU DOWN NOW.
THANKS FOR THE LIFT, PAL.
--AND THANKS FOR THE SHIRT!
I HOPE THERE'S SOME "HOME" LEFT FOR ME TO GO HOME TO.
SO DO I, FRIEND.
SO DO I.
BLIP

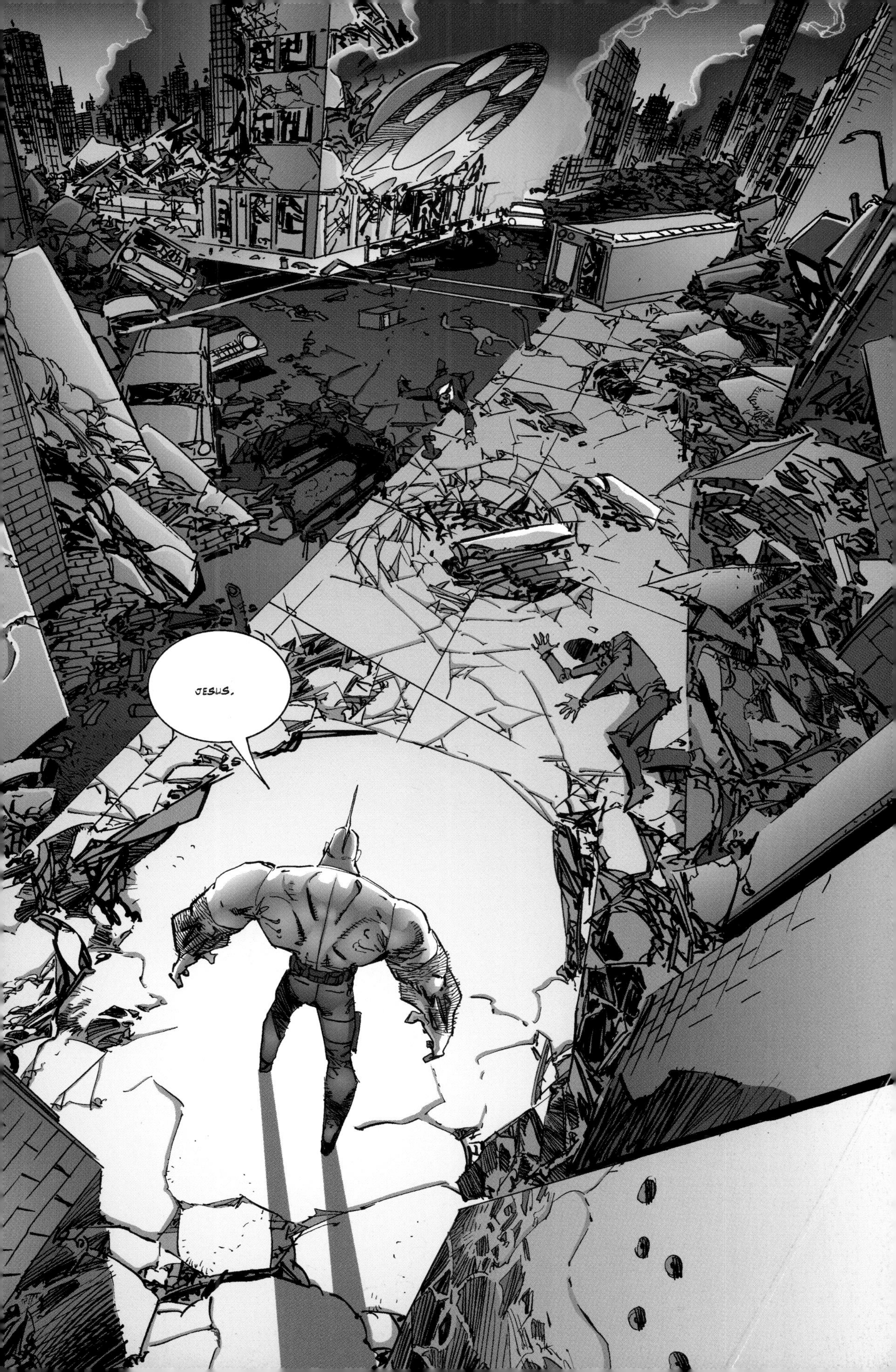
JESUS.

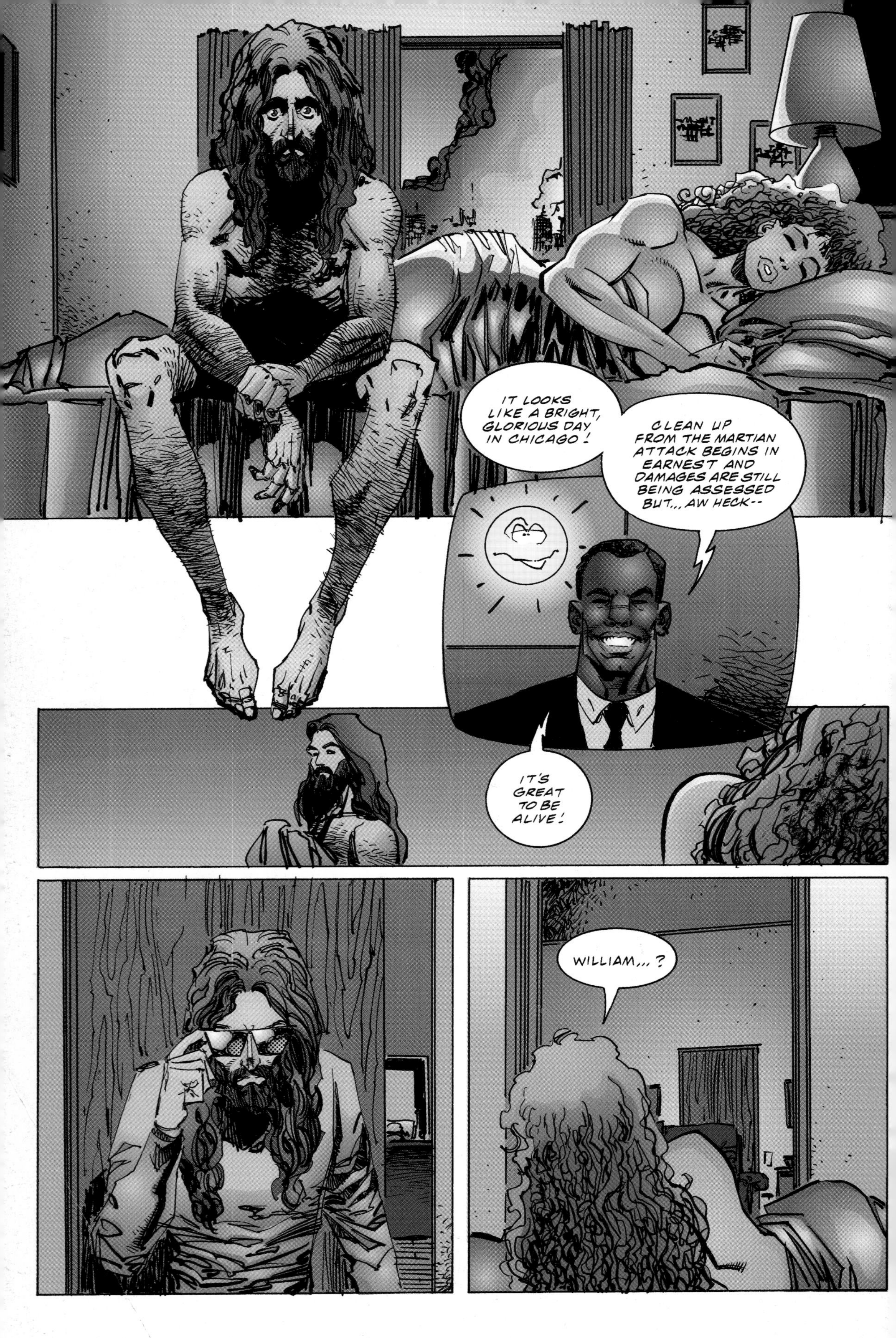
IT LOOKS LIKE A BRIGHT, GLORIOUS DAY IN CHICAGO!
CLEAN UP FROM THE MARTIAN ATTACK BEGINS IN EARNEST AND DAMAGES ARE STILL BEING ASSESSED BUT... AW HECK--
IT'S GREAT TO BE ALIVE!
WILLIAM...?

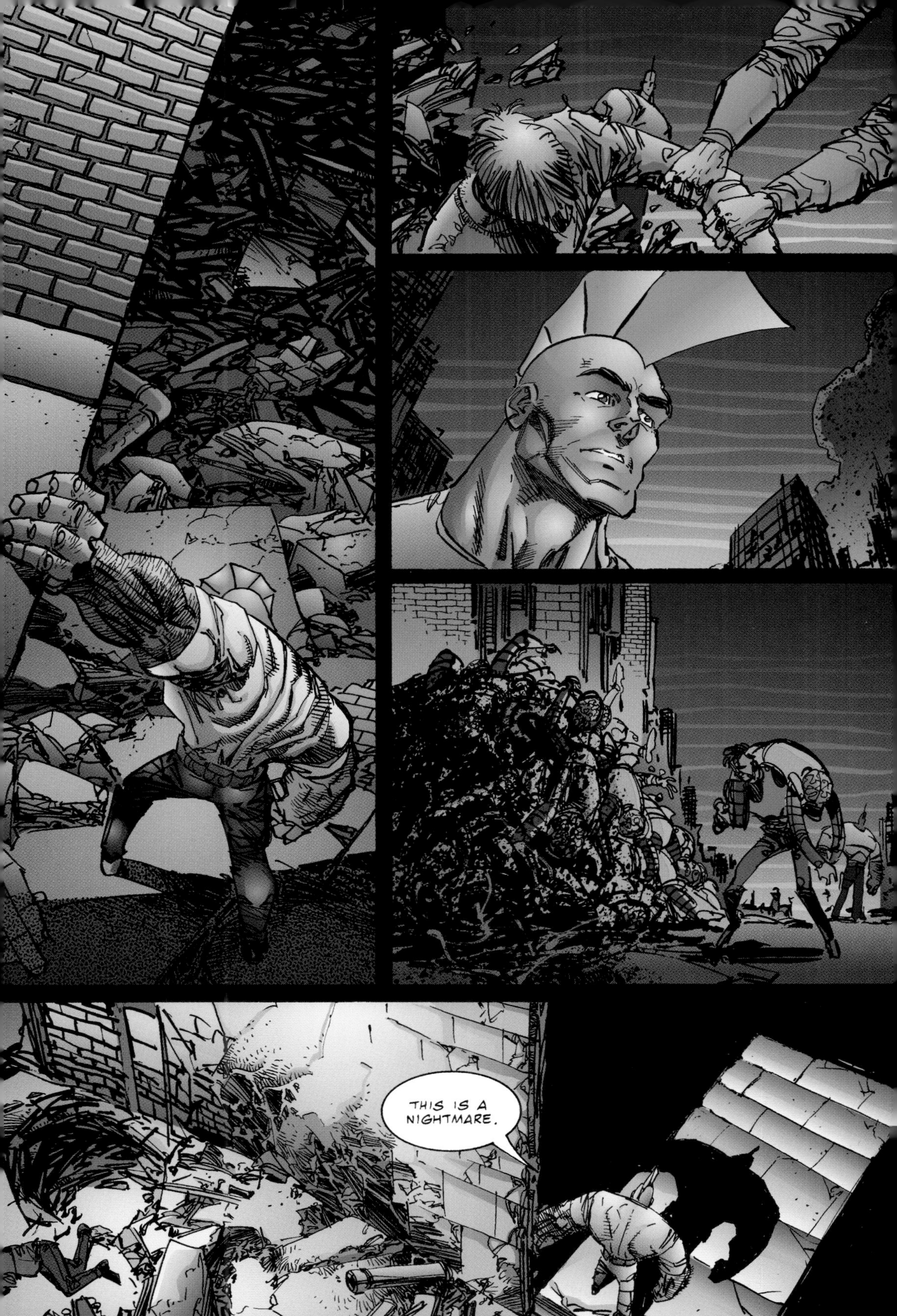
THIS IS A NIGHTMARE.

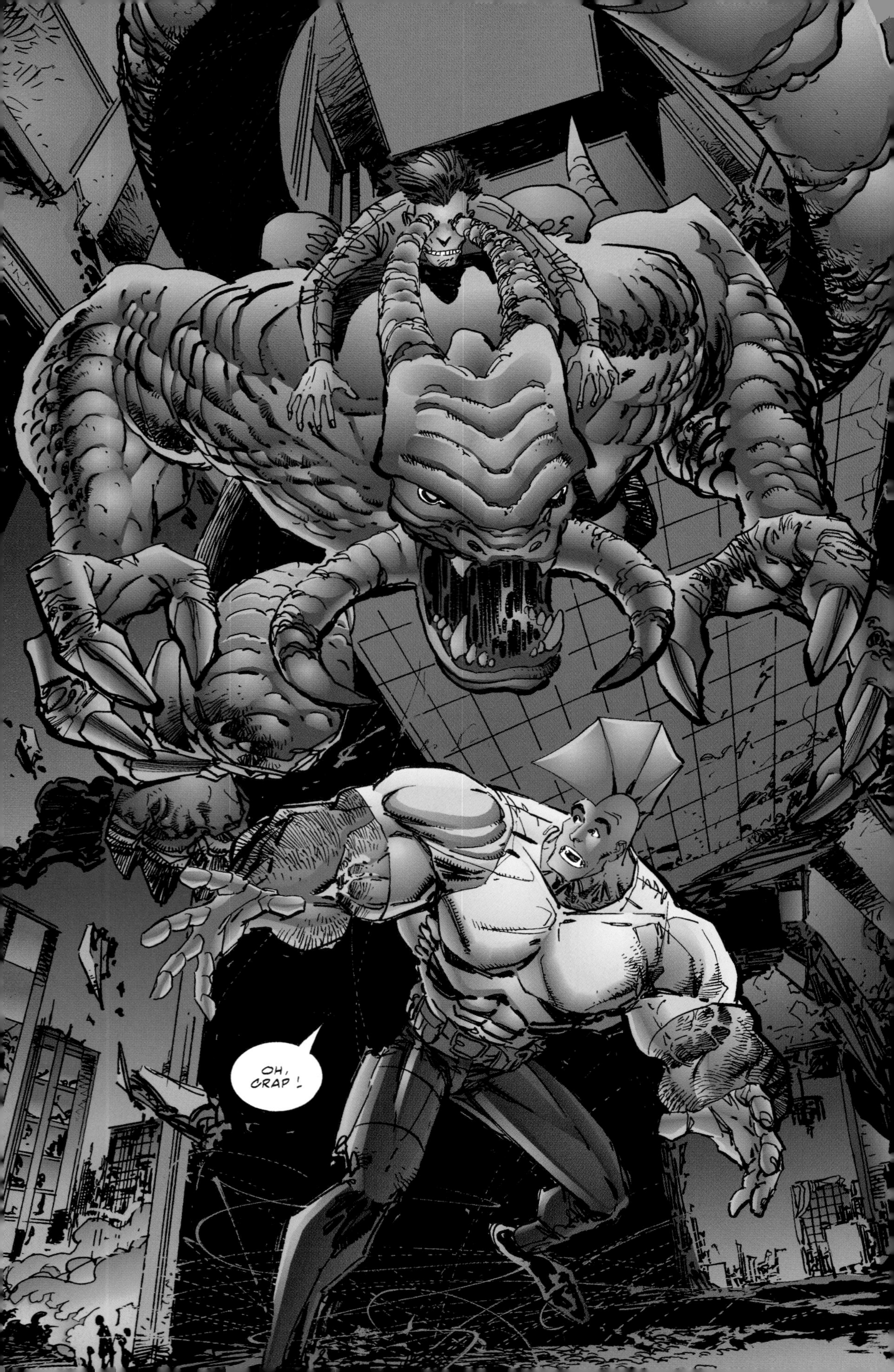
OH, CRAP!

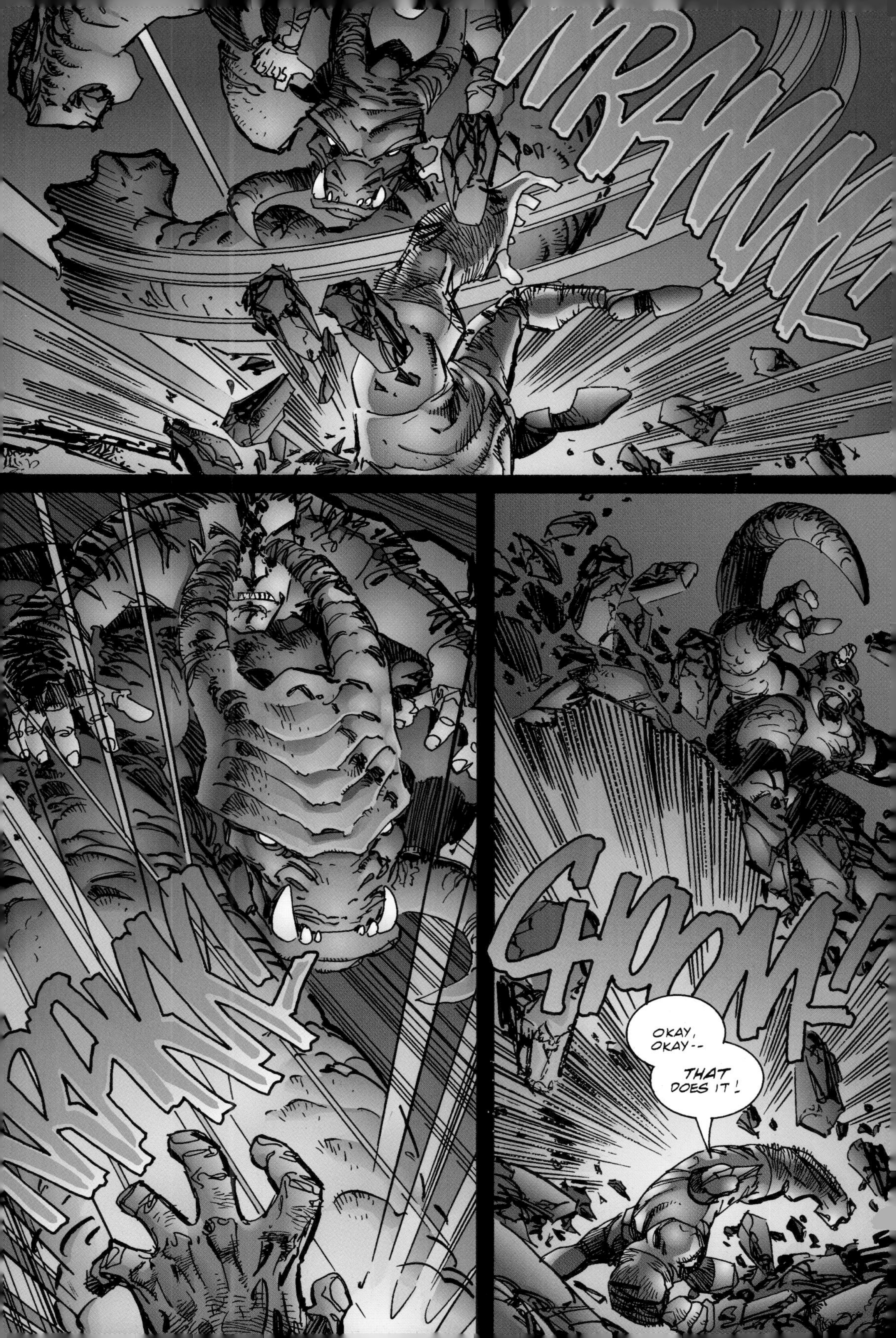
OKAY, OKAY--
THAT DOES IT!

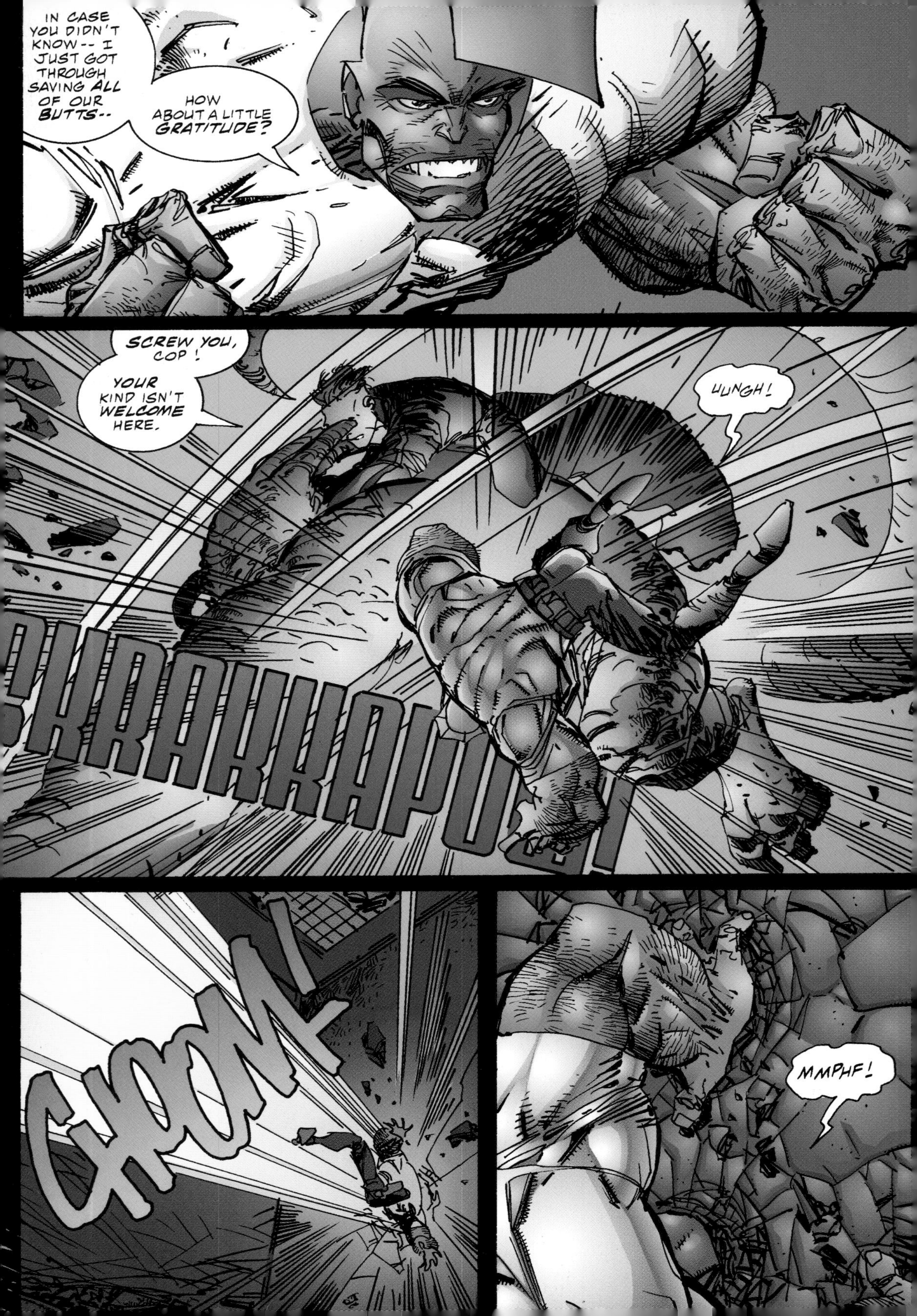

IN CASE YOU DIDN'T KNOW -- I JUST GOT THROUGH SAVING ALL OF OUR BUTTS--
HOW ABOUT A LITTLE GRATITUDE?
SCREW YOU, COP!
YOUR KIND ISN'T WELCOME HERE.
UUNGH!
MMPHF!

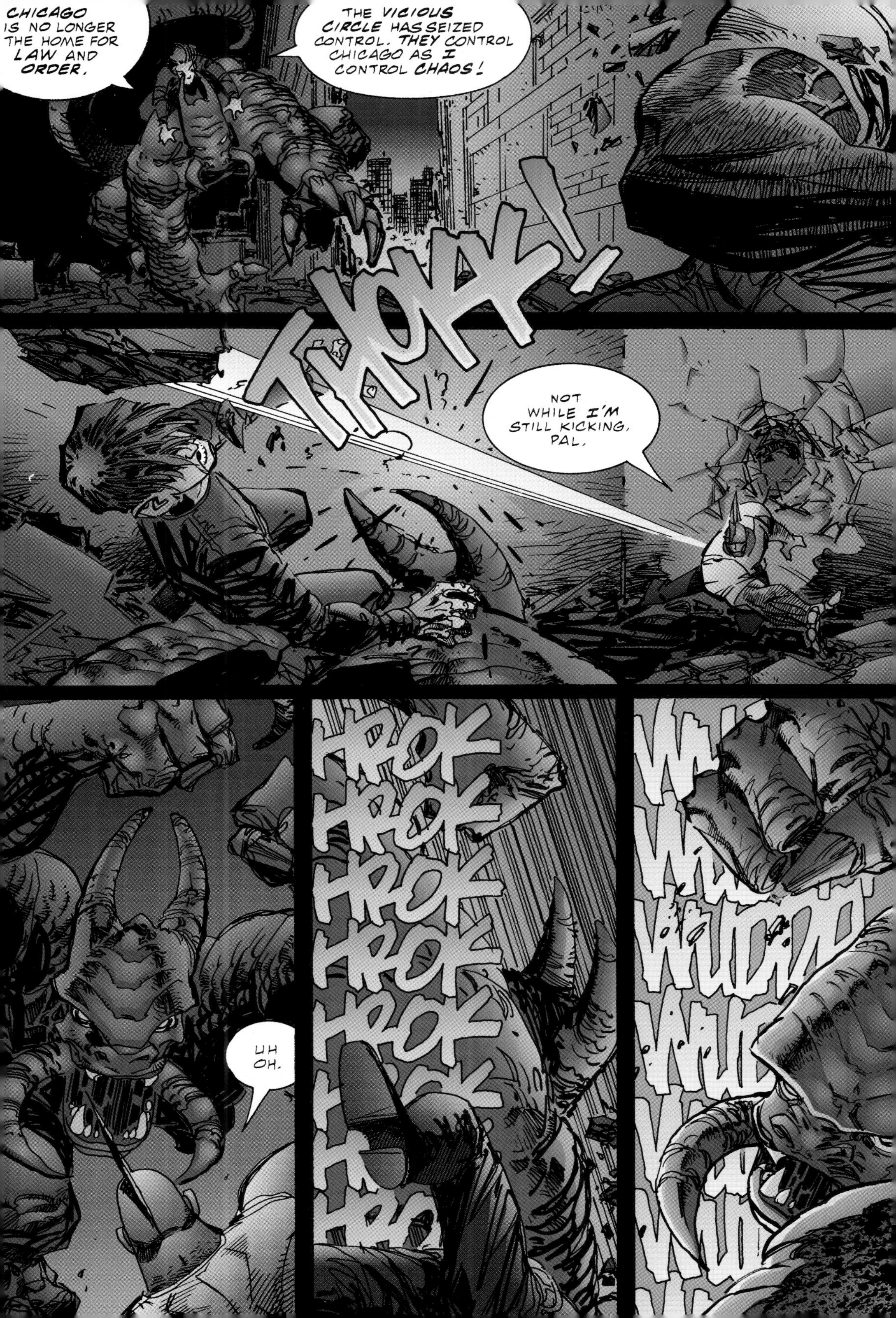

CHICAGO IS NO LONGER THE HOME FOR LAW AND ORDER.
THE VICIOUS CIRCLE HAS SEIZED CONTROL. THEY CONTROL CHICAGO AS I CONTROL CHAOS!
THOKK!
NOT WHILE I'M STILL KICKING, PAL.
UH OH.
HROK HROK HROK HROK HROK

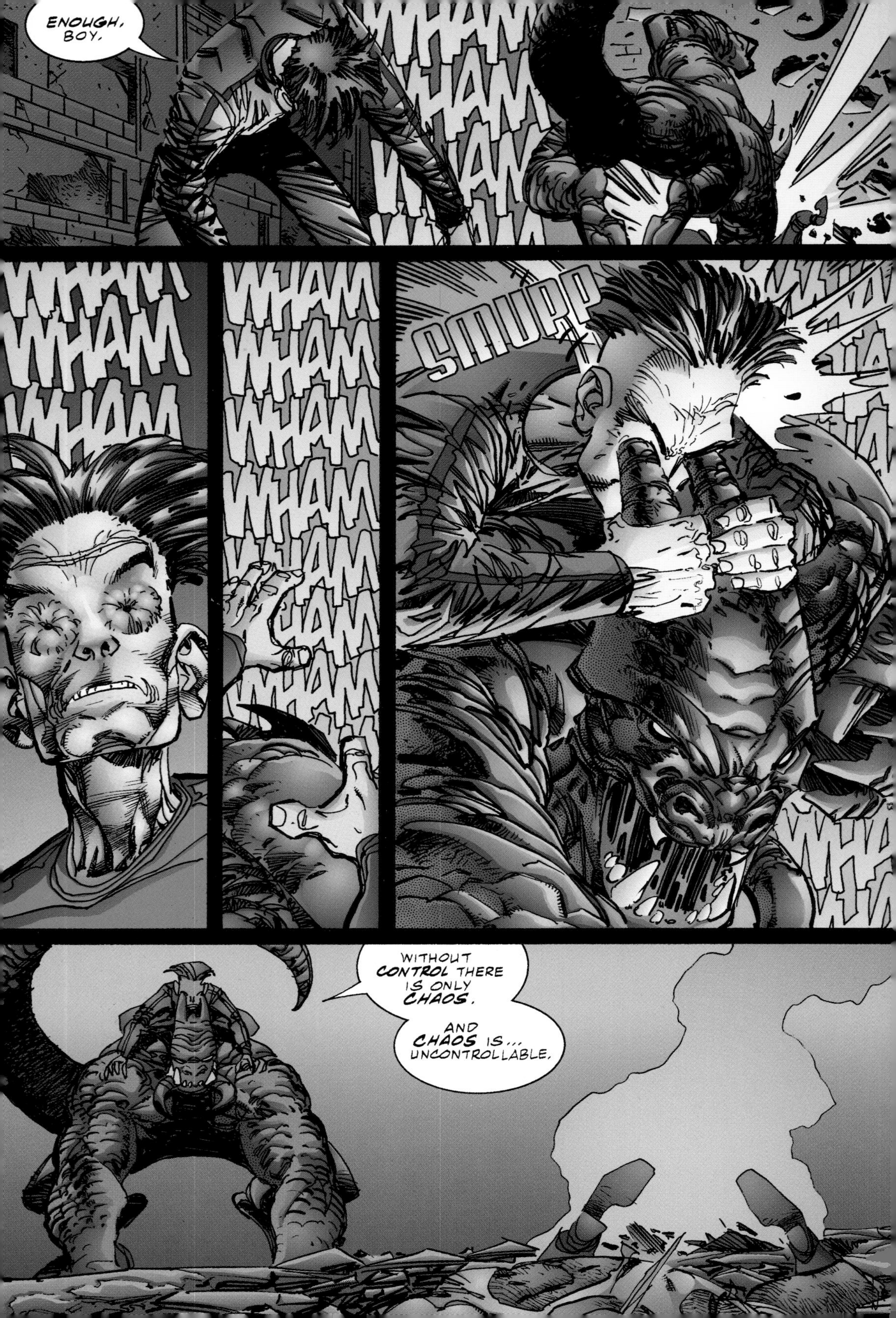
ENOUGH, BOY.
WHAM WHAM WHAM
WHAM WHAM WHAM
WHAM WHAM WHAM WHAM WHAM WHAM WHAM WHAM
SMURP
WITHOUT CONTROL THERE IS ONLY CHAOS.
AND CHAOS IS... UNCONTROLLABLE.

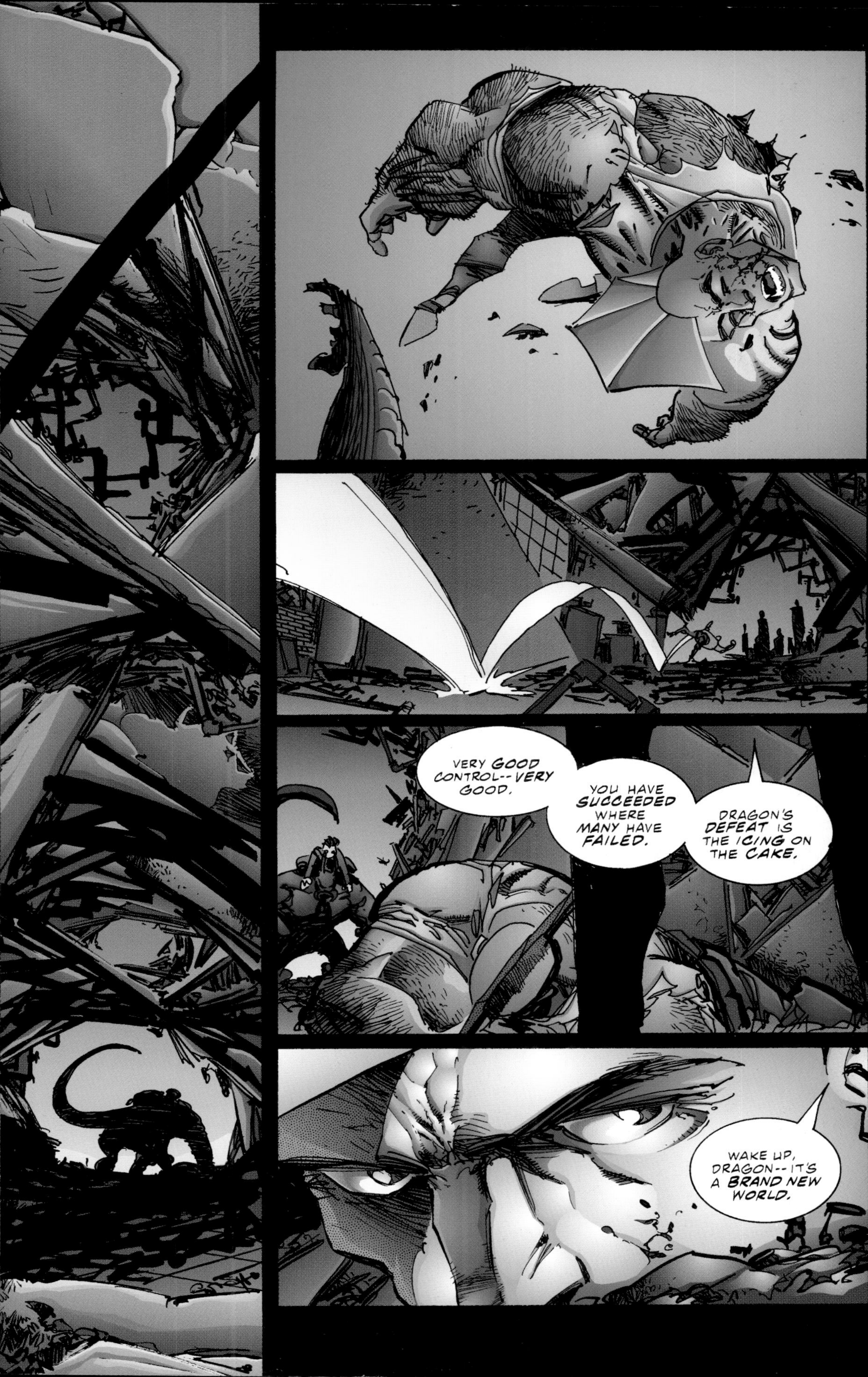
VERY GOOD CONTROL--VERY GOOD.
YOU HAVE SUCCEEDED WHERE MANY HAVE FAILED.
DRAGON'S DEFEAT IS THE ICING ON THE CAKE.
WAKE UP, DRAGON--IT'S A BRAND NEW WORLD.

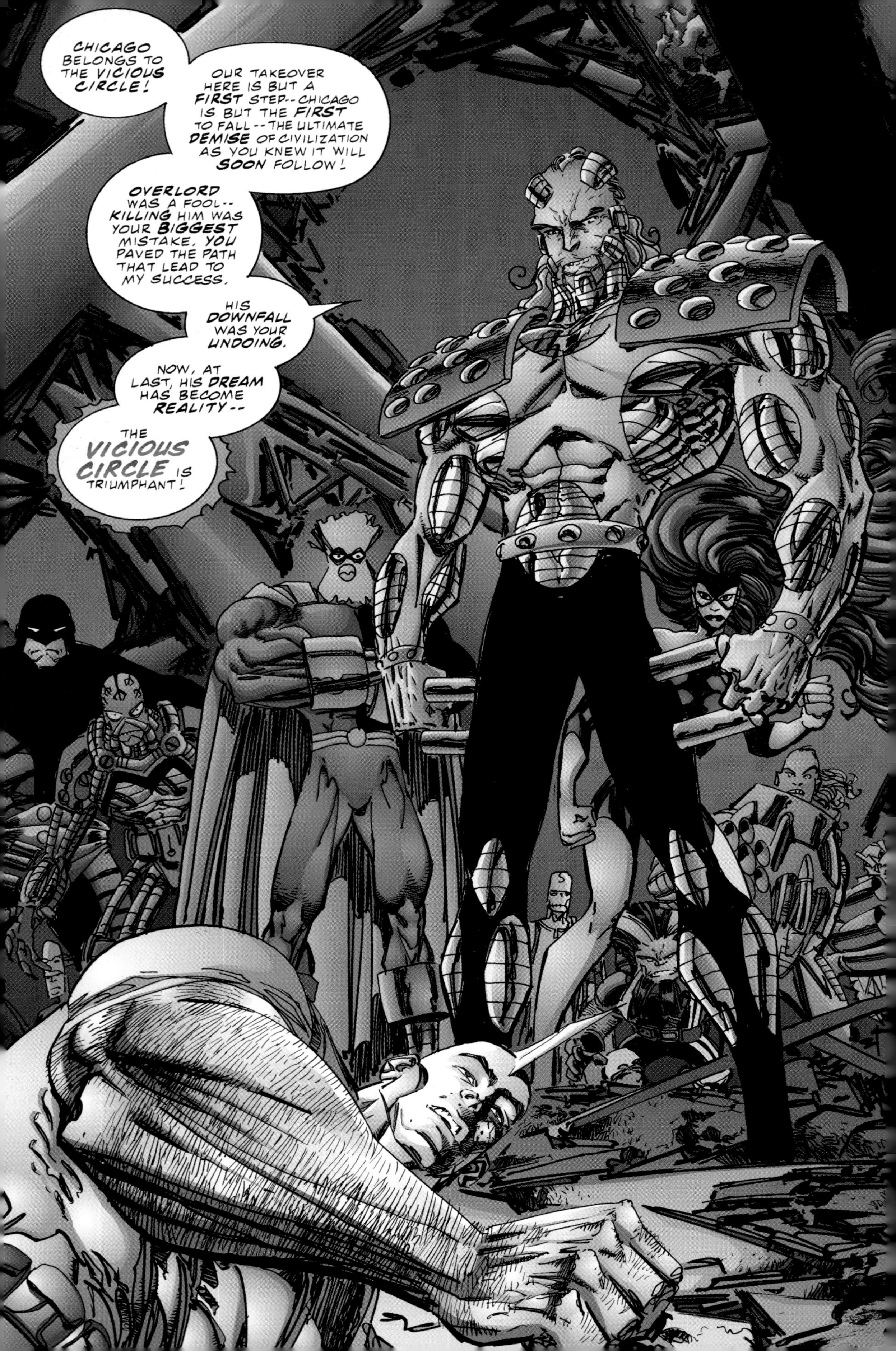
CHICAGO BELONGS TO THE VICIOUS CIRCLE!
OUR TAKEOVER HERE IS BUT A FIRST STEP--CHICAGO IS BUT THE FIRST TO FALL--THE ULTIMATE DEMISE OF CIVILIZATION AS YOU KNEW IT WILL SOON FOLLOW!
OVERLORD WAS A FOOL--KILLING HIM WAS YOUR BIGGEST MISTAKE. YOU PAVED THE PATH THAT LEAD TO MY SUCCESS.
HIS DOWNFALL WAS YOUR UNDOING.
NOW, AT LAST, HIS DREAM HAS BECOME REALITY--
THE VICIOUS CIRCLE IS TRIUMPHANT!

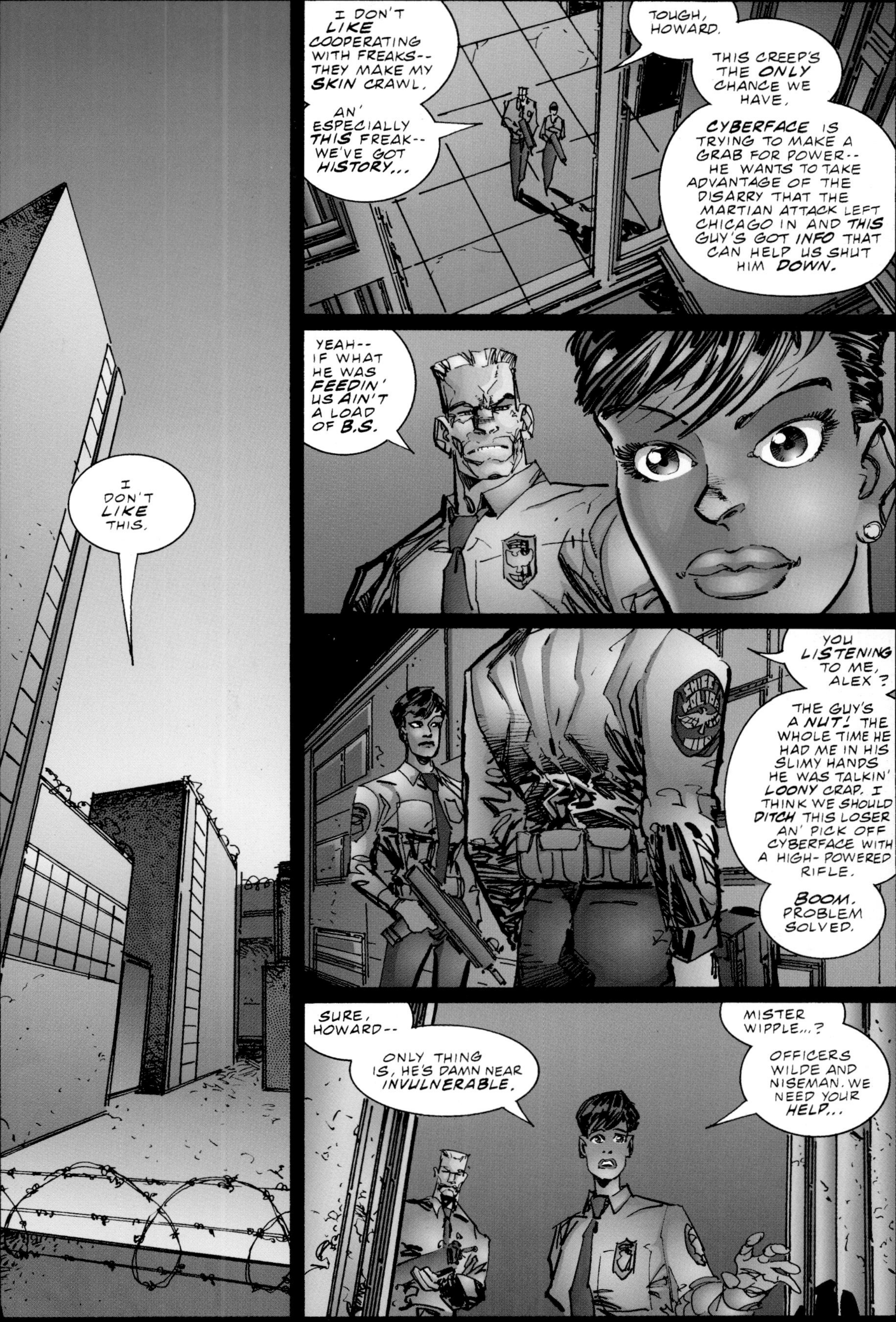
I DON'T LIKE THIS.
I DON'T LIKE COOPERATING WITH FREAKS-- THEY MAKE MY SKIN CRAWL.
AN' ESPECIALLY THIS FREAK-- WE'VE GOT HISTORY...
TOUGH, HOWARD.
THIS CREEP'S THE ONLY CHANCE WE HAVE.
CYBERFACE IS TRYING TO MAKE A GRAB FOR POWER-- HE WANTS TO TAKE ADVANTAGE OF THE DISARRY THAT THE MARTIAN ATTACK LEFT CHICAGO IN AND THIS GUY'S GOT INFO THAT CAN HELP US SHUT HIM DOWN.
YEAH-- IF WHAT HE WAS FEEDIN' US AIN'T A LOAD OF B.S.
YOU LISTENING TO ME, ALEX?
THE GUY'S A NUT! THE WHOLE TIME HE HAD ME IN HIS SLIMY HANDS HE WAS TALKIN' LOONY CRAP. I THINK WE SHOULD DITCH THIS LOSER AN' PICK OFF CYBERFACE WITH A HIGH-POWERED RIFLE.
BOOM. PROBLEM SOLVED.
SURE, HOWARD--
ONLY THING IS, HE'S DAMN NEAR INVULNERABLE.
MISTER WIPPLE...?
OFFICERS WILDE AND NISEMAN. WE NEED YOUR HELP...

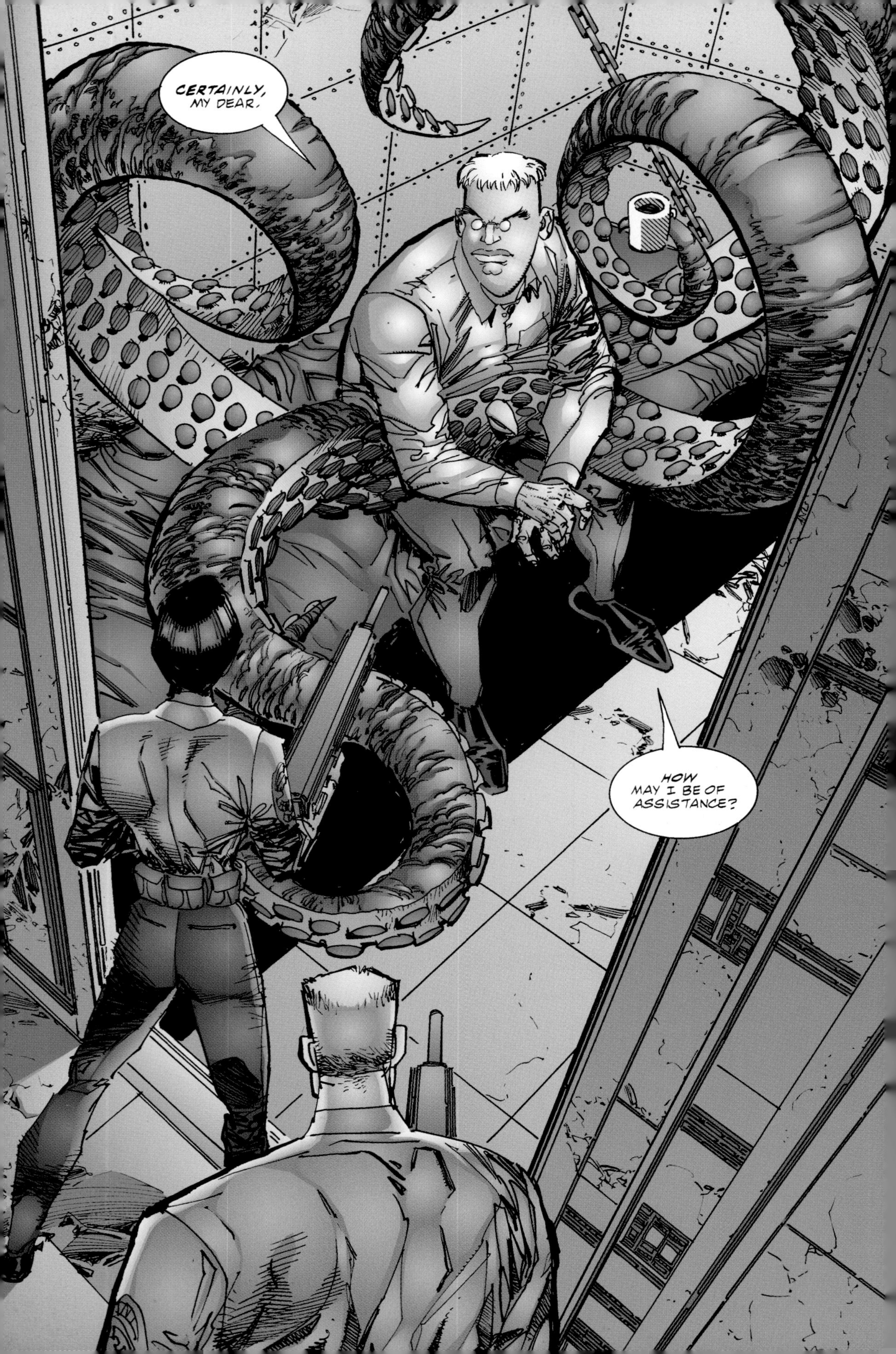
CERTAINLY, MY DEAR.
HOW MAY I BE OF ASSISTANCE?

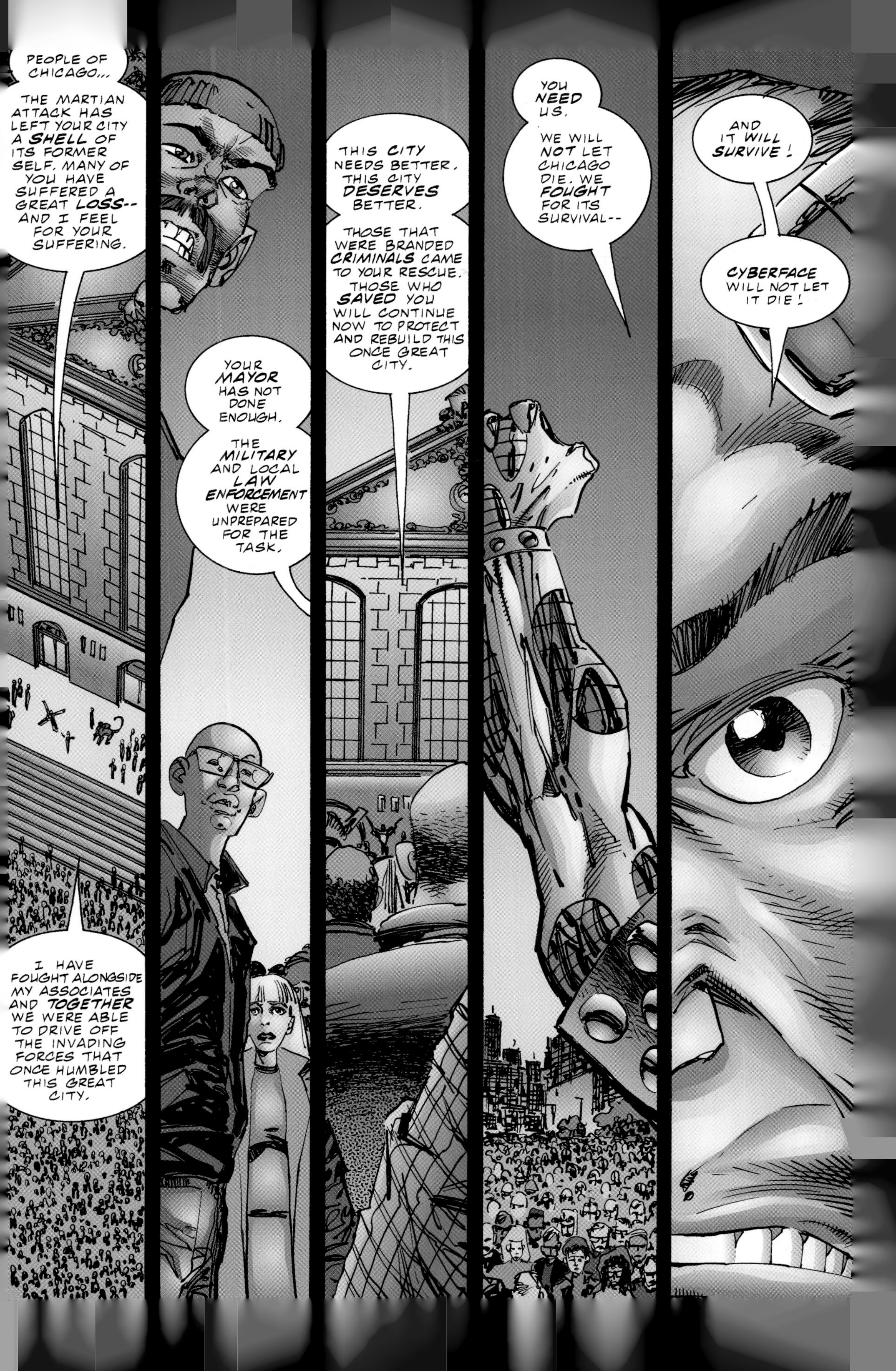
PEOPLE OF CHICAGO...
THE MARTIAN ATTACK HAS LEFT YOUR CITY A SHELL OF ITS FORMER SELF. MANY OF YOU HAVE SUFFERED A GREAT LOSS-- AND I FEEL FOR YOUR SUFFERING.
I HAVE FOUGHT ALONGSIDE MY ASSOCIATES AND TOGETHER WE WERE ABLE TO DRIVE OFF THE INVADING FORCES THAT ONCE HUMBLED THIS GREAT CITY.
YOUR MAYOR HAS NOT DONE ENOUGH.
THE MILITARY AND LOCAL LAW ENFORCEMENT WERE UNPREPARED FOR THE TASK.
THIS CITY NEEDS BETTER. THIS CITY DESERVES BETTER.
THOSE THAT WERE BRANDED CRIMINALS CAME TO YOUR RESCUE. THOSE WHO SAVED YOU WILL CONTINUE NOW TO PROTECT AND REBUILD THIS ONCE GREAT CITY.
YOU NEED US.
WE WILL NOT LET CHICAGO DIE. WE FOUGHT FOR ITS SURVIVAL--
AND IT WILL SURVIVE!
CYBERFACE WILL NOT LET IT DIE!

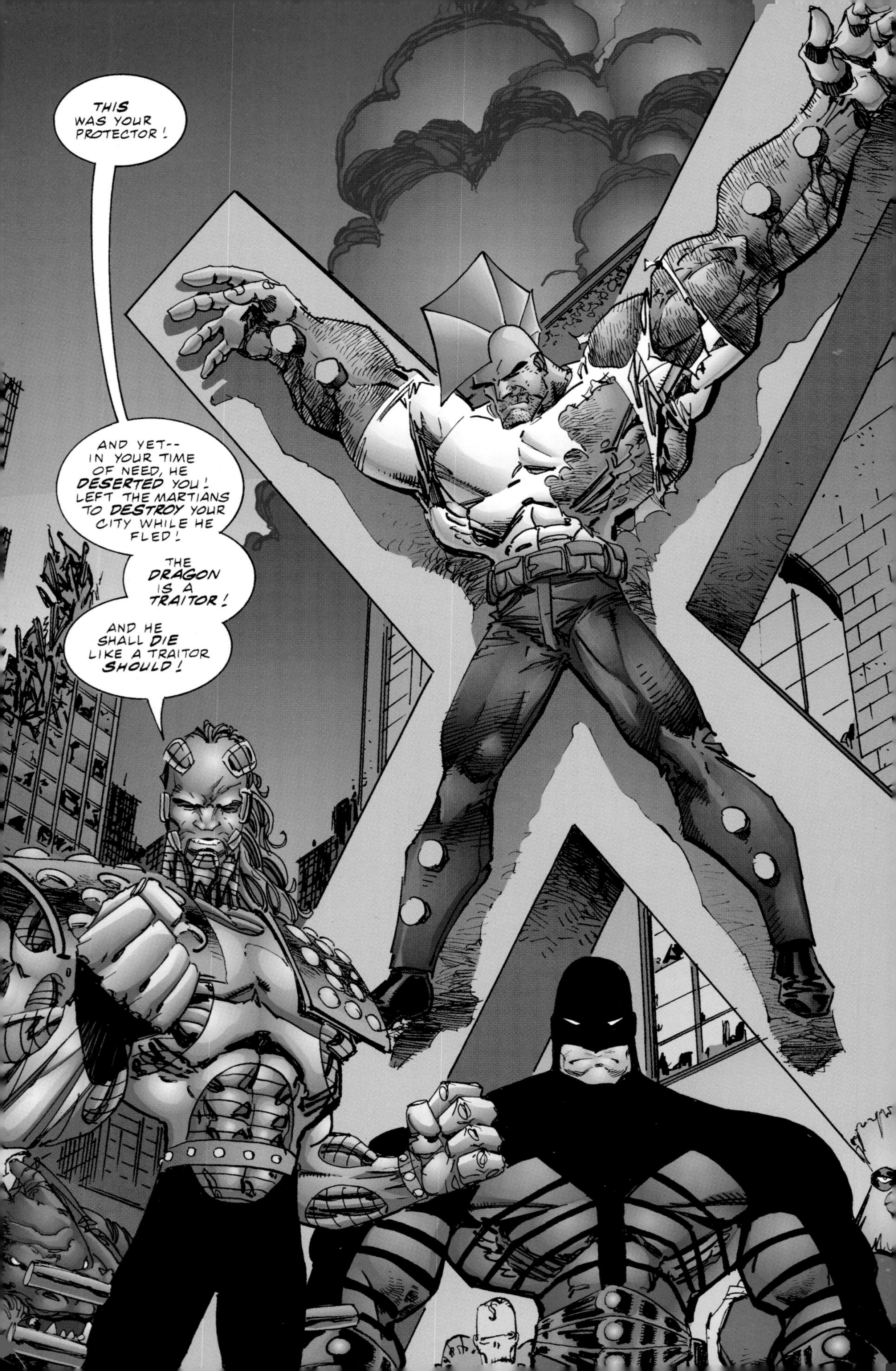

THIS WAS YOUR PROTECTOR!
AND YET-- IN YOUR TIME OF NEED, HE DESERTED YOU! LEFT THE MARTIANS TO DESTROY YOUR CITY WHILE HE FLED!
THE DRAGON IS A TRAITOR!
AND HE SHALL DIE LIKE A TRAITOR SHOULD!

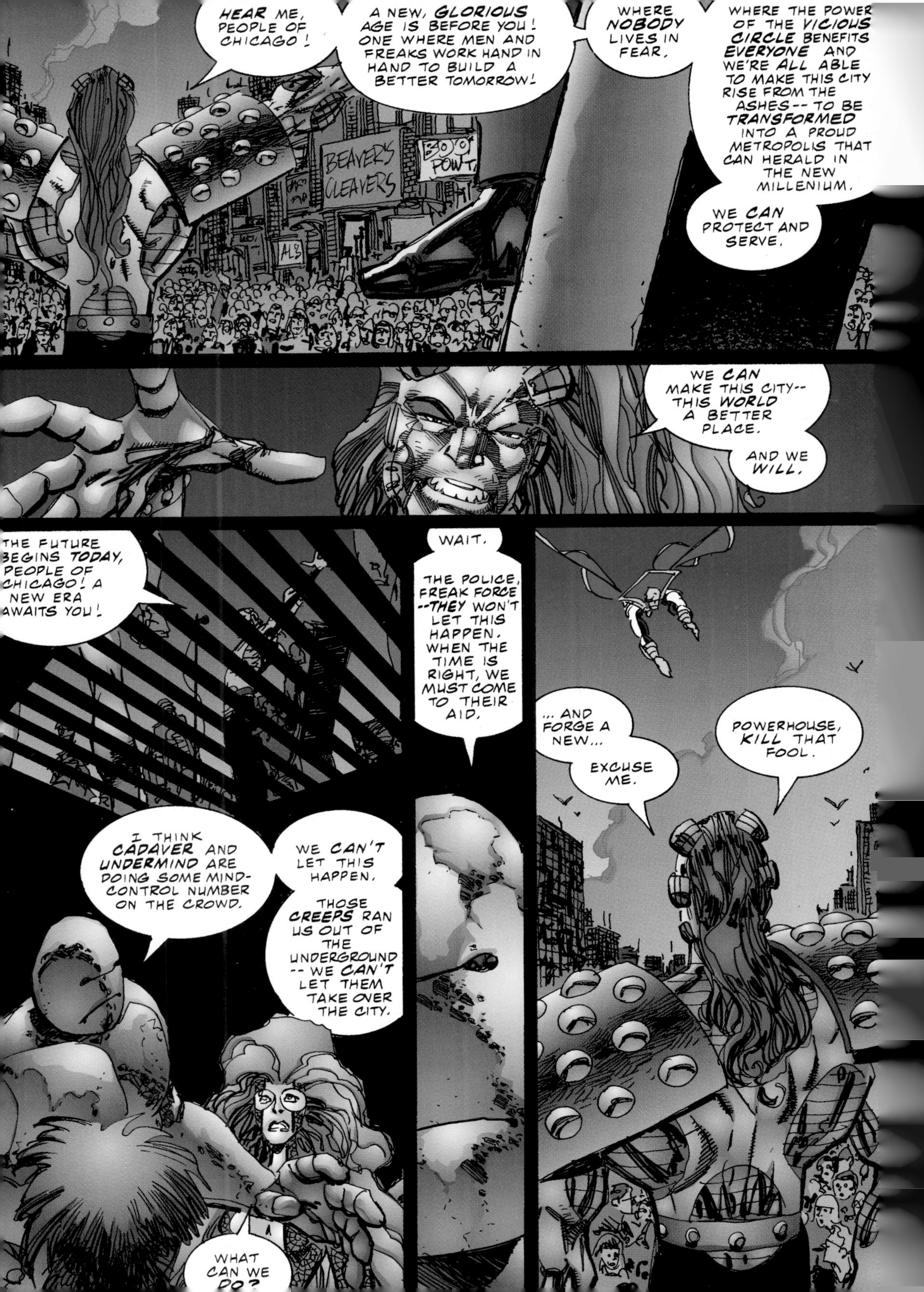
HEAR ME, PEOPLE OF CHICAGO!
A NEW, GLORIOUS AGE IS BEFORE YOU! ONE WHERE MEN AND FREAKS WORK HAND IN HAND TO BUILD A BETTER TOMORROW!
WHERE NOBODY LIVES IN FEAR.
WHERE THE POWER OF THE VICIOUS CIRCLE BENEFITS EVERYONE AND WE'RE ALL ABLE TO MAKE THIS CITY RISE FROM THE ASHES-- TO BE TRANSFORMED INTO A PROUD METROPOLIS THAT CAN HERALD IN THE NEW MILLENIUM.
WE CAN PROTECT AND SERVE.
BEAVER'S CLEAVERS
AL'S
WE CAN MAKE THIS CITY-- THIS WORLD A BETTER PLACE.
AND WE WILL.
THE FUTURE BEGINS TODAY, PEOPLE OF CHICAGO! A NEW ERA AWAITS YOU!
WAIT.
THE POLICE, FREAK FORCE --THEY WON'T LET THIS HAPPEN. WHEN THE TIME IS RIGHT, WE MUST COME TO THEIR AID.
I THINK CADAVER AND UNDERMIND ARE DOING SOME MIND-CONTROL NUMBER ON THE CROWD.
WE CAN'T LET THIS HAPPEN.
THOSE CREEPS RAN US OUT OF THE UNDERGROUND -- WE CAN'T LET THEM TAKE OVER THE CITY.
WHAT CAN WE DO?
... AND FORGE A NEW...
EXCUSE ME.
POWERHOUSE, KILL THAT FOOL.

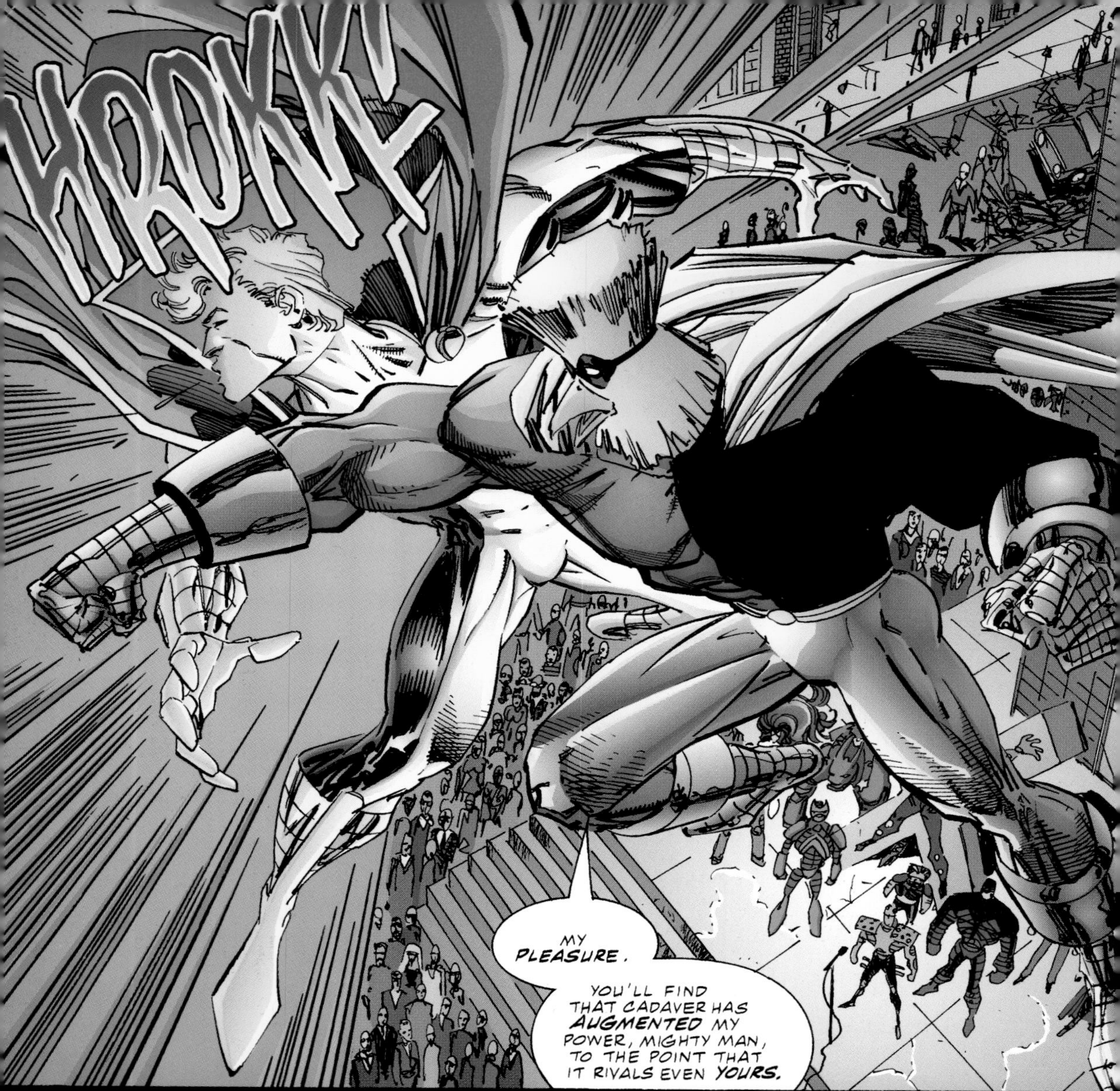
HRKKK!
MY PLEASURE.
YOU'LL FIND THAT CADAVER HAS AUGMENTED MY POWER, MIGHTY MAN, TO THE POINT THAT IT RIVALS EVEN YOURS.

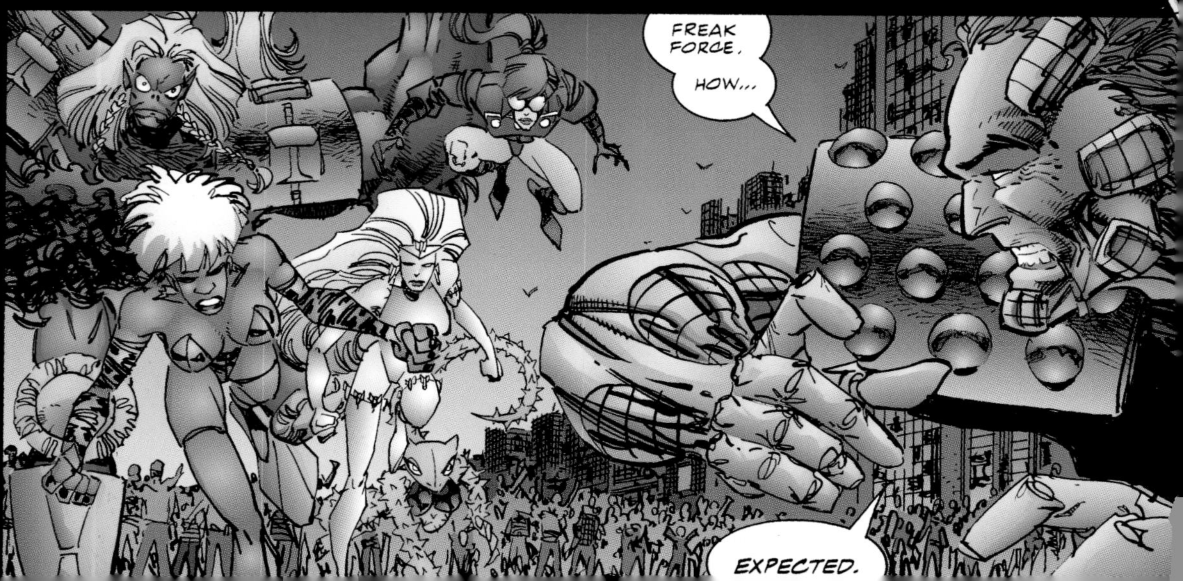
FREAK FORCE.
HOW...
EXPECTED.

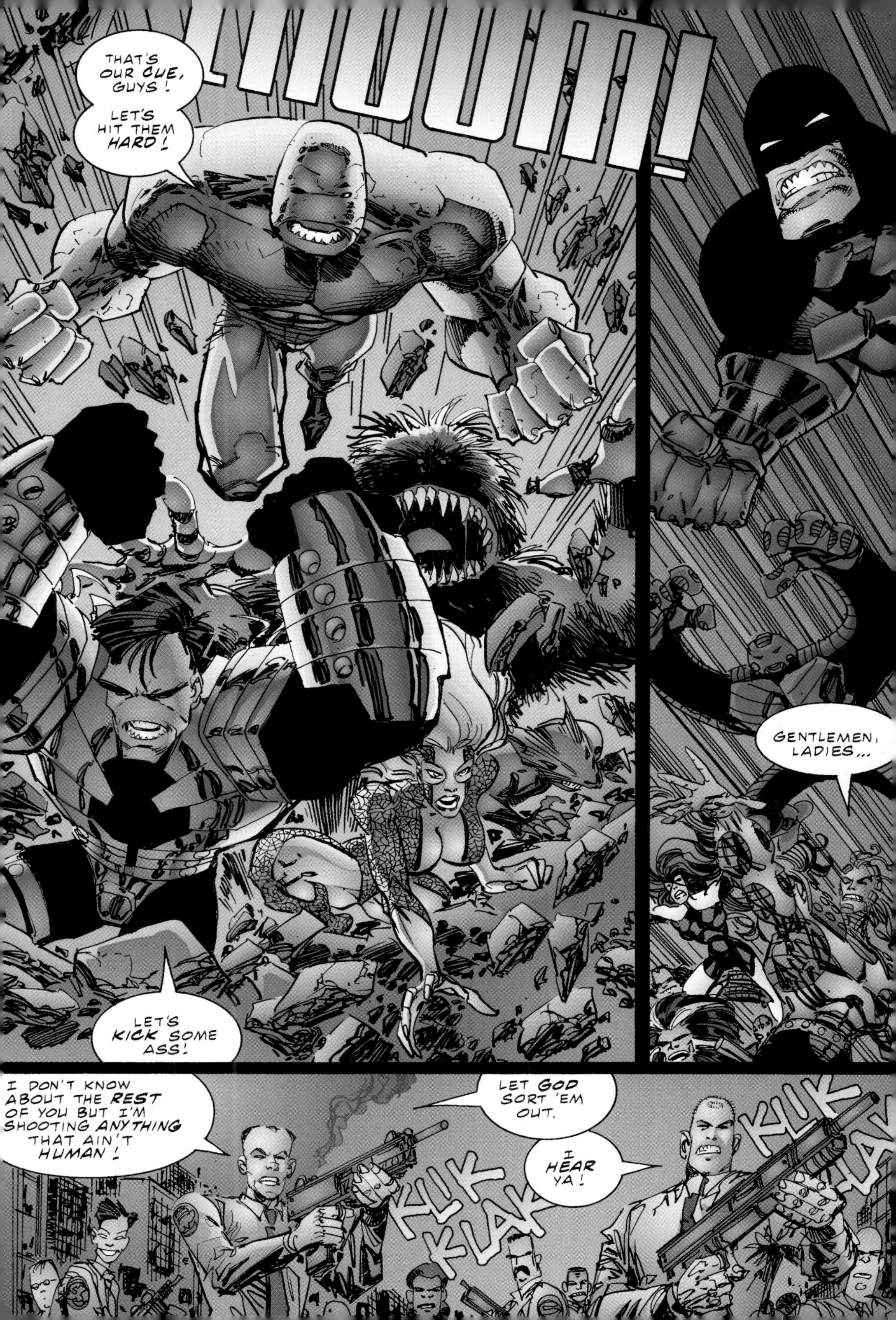
THAT'S OUR CUE, GUYS!
LET'S HIT THEM HARD!
LET'S KICK SOME ASS!
GENTLEMEN, LADIES...
I DON'T KNOW ABOUT THE REST OF YOU BUT I'M SHOOTING ANYTHING THAT AIN'T HUMAN!
LET GOD SORT 'EM OUT.
I HEAR YA!
KLIK KLAK
KLIK KLAK
KLIK

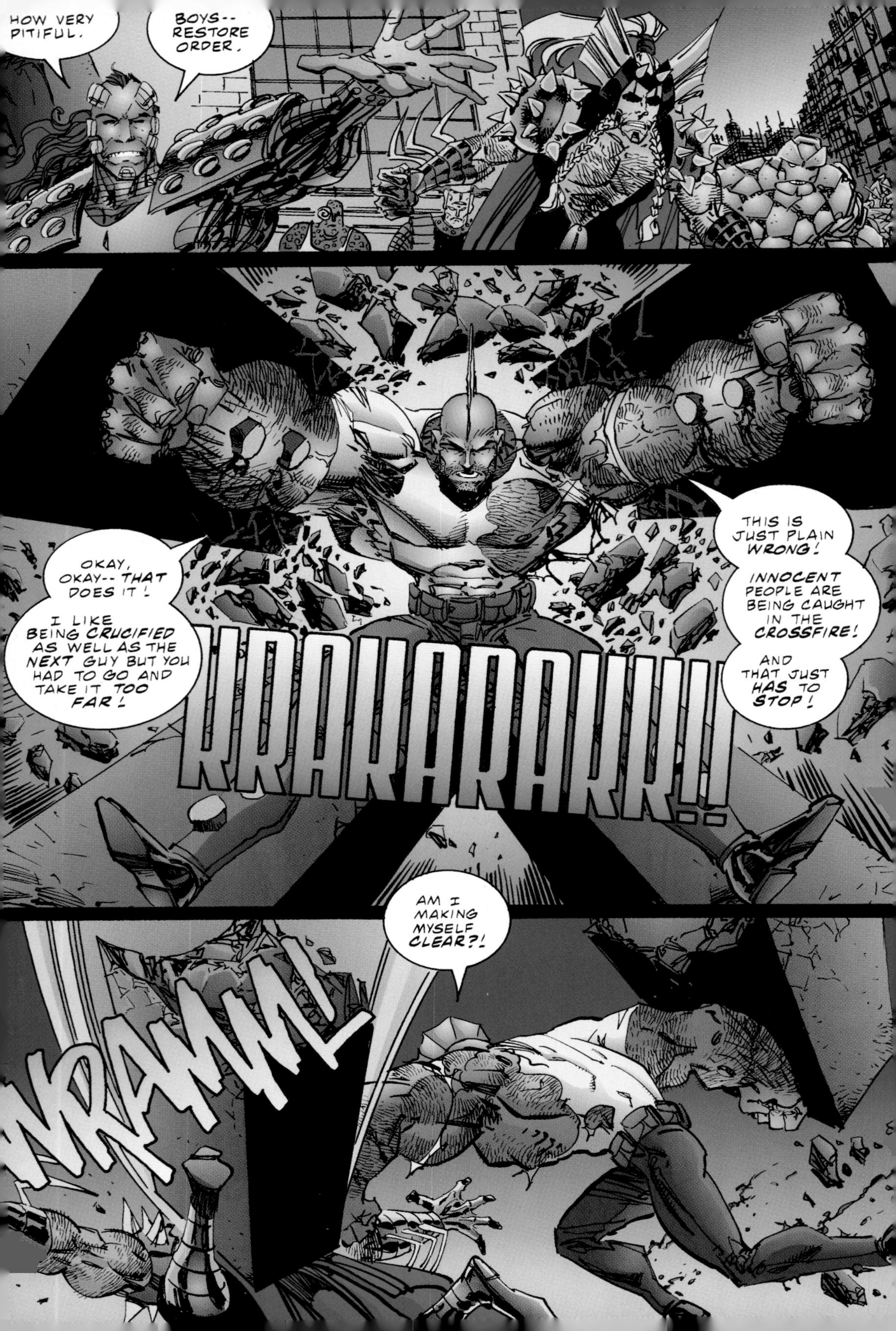
HOW VERY PITIFUL.
BOYS-- RESTORE ORDER.
OKAY, OKAY-- THAT DOES IT!
I LIKE BEING CRUCIFIED AS WELL AS THE NEXT GUY BUT YOU HAD TO GO AND TAKE IT TOO FAR!
KRAKARAKK!!!
THIS IS JUST PLAIN WRONG!
INNOCENT PEOPLE ARE BEING CAUGHT IN THE CROSSFIRE!
AND THAT JUST HAS TO STOP!
AM I MAKING MYSELF CLEAR?!
WRAMM!

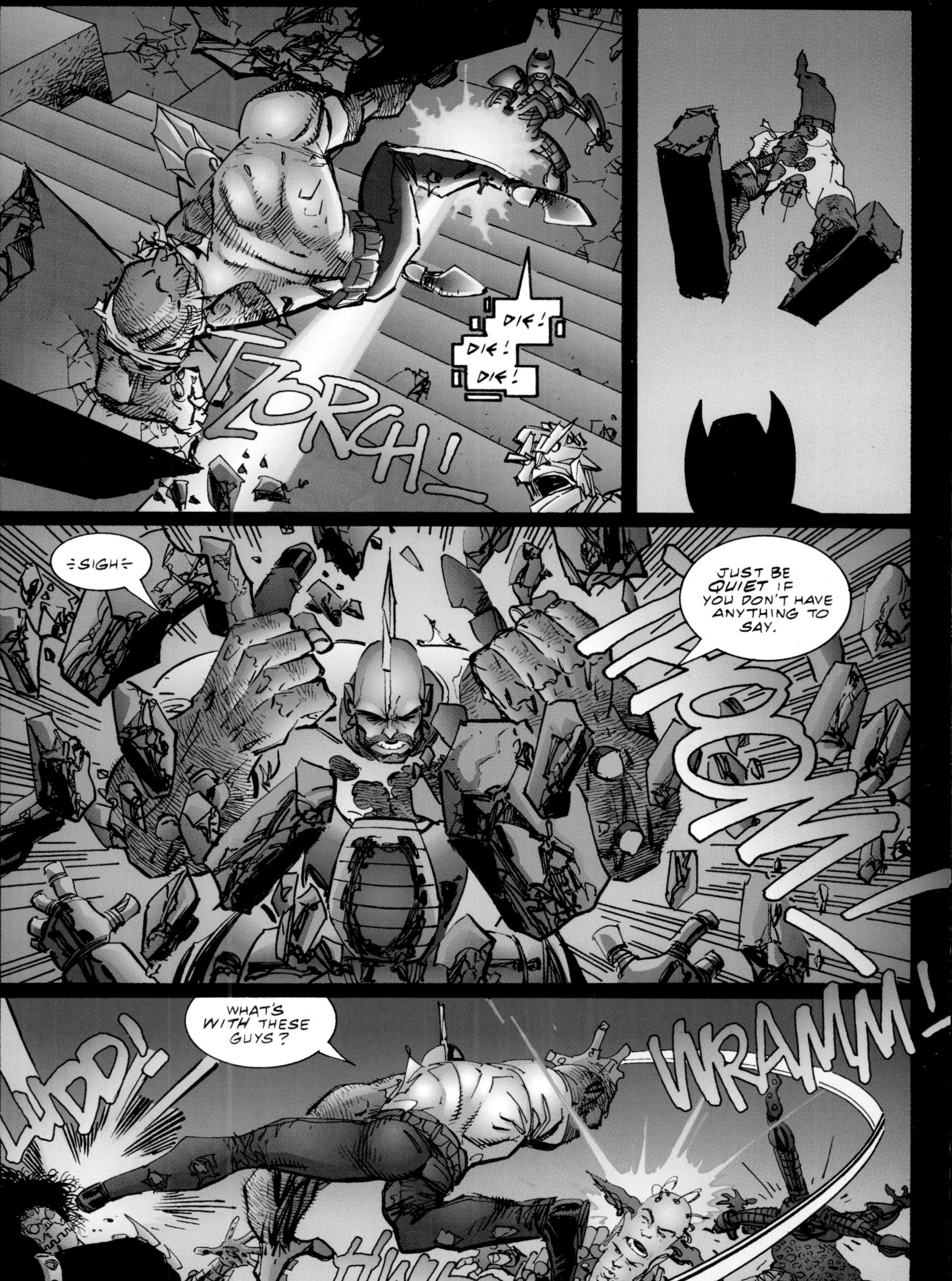
DIE! DIE! DIE!
TZORCH!
=SIGH=
JUST BE QUIET IF YOU DON'T HAVE ANYTHING TO SAY.
WHAT'S WITH THESE GUYS?
VRAMM!

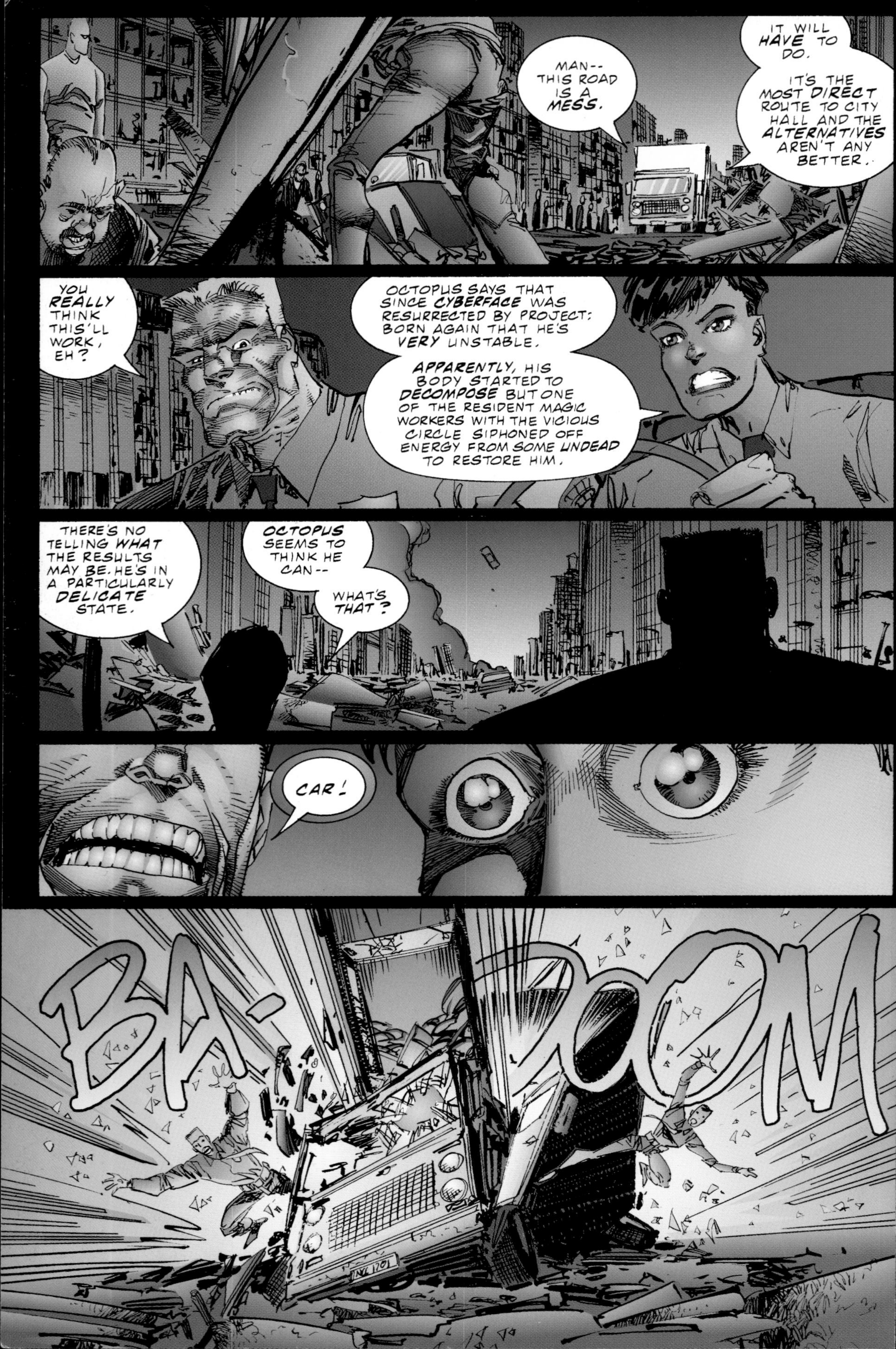

MAN-- THIS ROAD IS A MESS.
IT WILL HAVE TO DO.
IT'S THE MOST DIRECT ROUTE TO CITY HALL AND THE ALTERNATIVES AREN'T ANY BETTER.
YOU REALLY THINK THIS'LL WORK, EH?
OCTOPUS SAYS THAT SINCE CYBERFACE WAS RESURRECTED BY PROJECT: BORN AGAIN THAT HE'S VERY UNSTABLE.
APPARENTLY, HIS BODY STARTED TO DECOMPOSE BUT ONE OF THE RESIDENT MAGIC WORKERS WITH THE VICIOUS CIRCLE SIPHONED OFF ENERGY FROM SOME UNDEAD TO RESTORE HIM.
THERE'S NO TELLING WHAT THE RESULTS MAY BE. HE'S IN A PARTICULARLY DELICATE STATE.
OCTOPUS SEEMS TO THINK HE CAN--
WHAT'S THAT?
CAR!
BA-BOOM

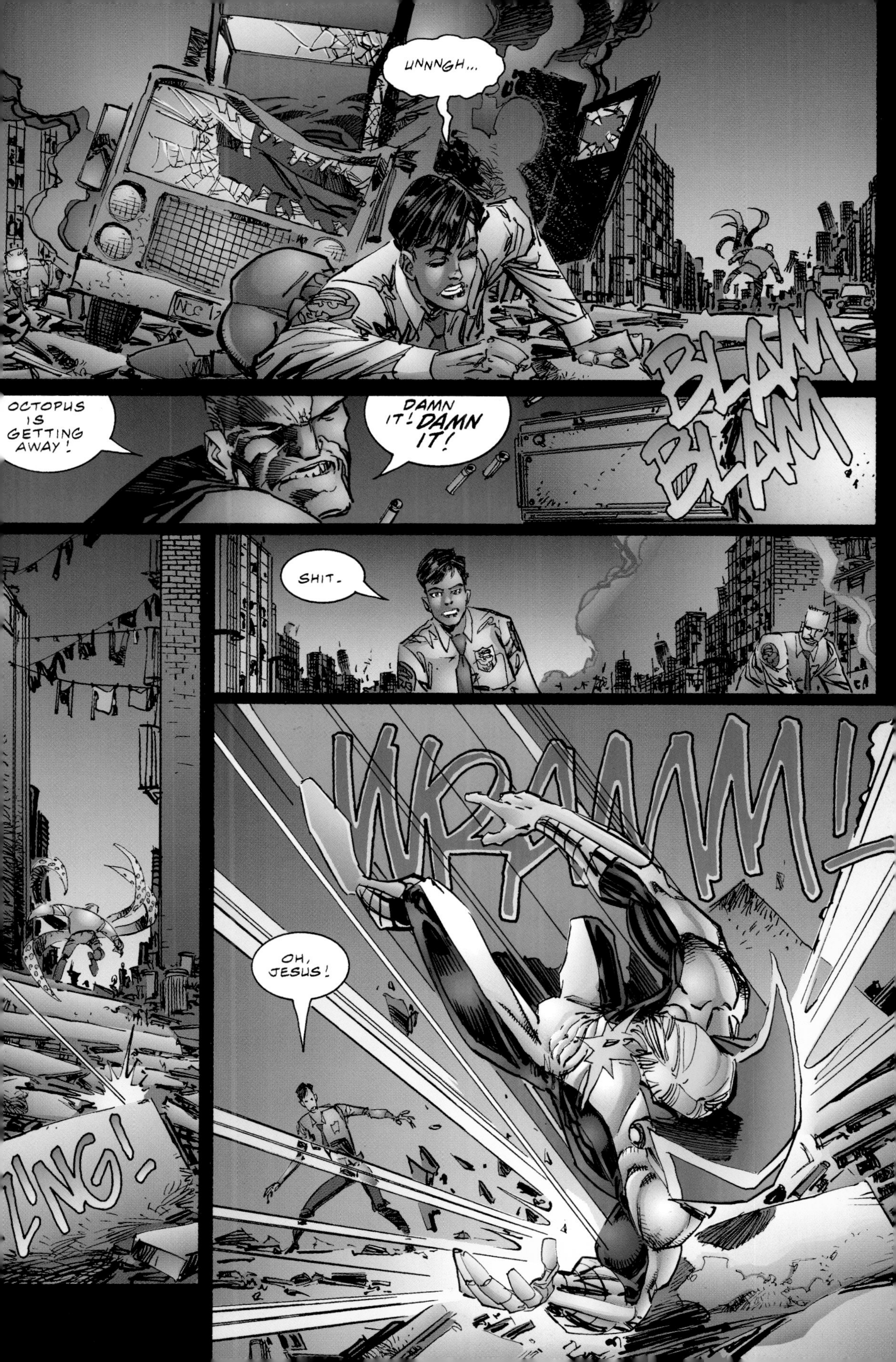
UNNNGH...
BLAM BLAM
OCTOPUS IS GETTING AWAY!
DAMN IT! DAMN IT!
SHIT.
WRAAAM!
OH, JESUS!
ZING!

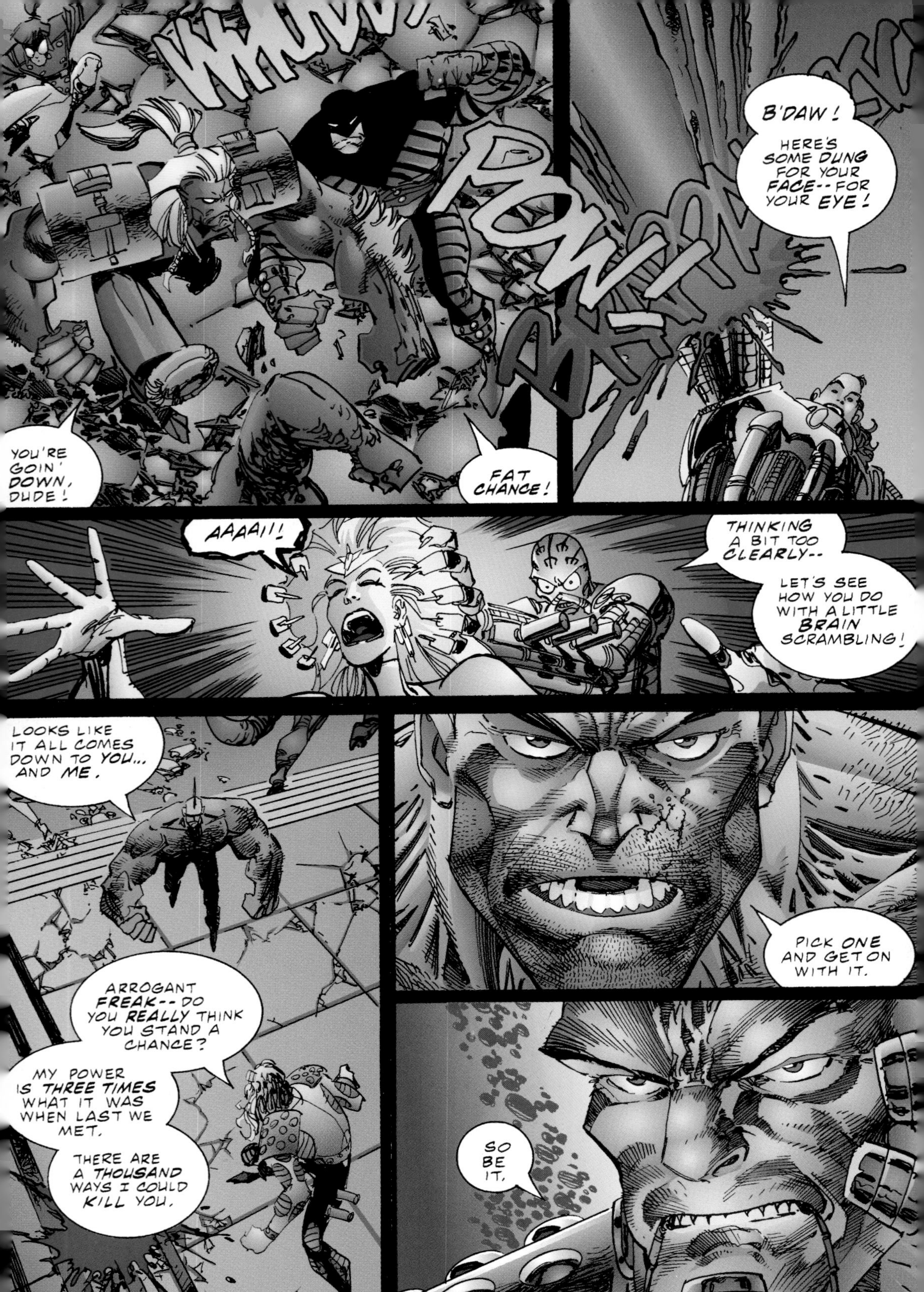
YOU'RE GOIN' DOWN, DUDE!
FAT CHANCE!
B'DAW!
HERE'S SOME DUNG FOR YOUR FACE-- FOR YOUR EYE!
AAAAII!
THINKING A BIT TOO CLEARLY--
LET'S SEE HOW YOU DO WITH A LITTLE BRAIN SCRAMBLING!
LOOKS LIKE IT ALL COMES DOWN TO YOU... AND ME.
PICK ONE AND GET ON WITH IT.
ARROGANT FREAK-- DO YOU REALLY THINK YOU STAND A CHANCE?
MY POWER IS THREE TIMES WHAT IT WAS WHEN LAST WE MET.
THERE ARE A THOUSAND WAYS I COULD KILL YOU.
SO BE IT.

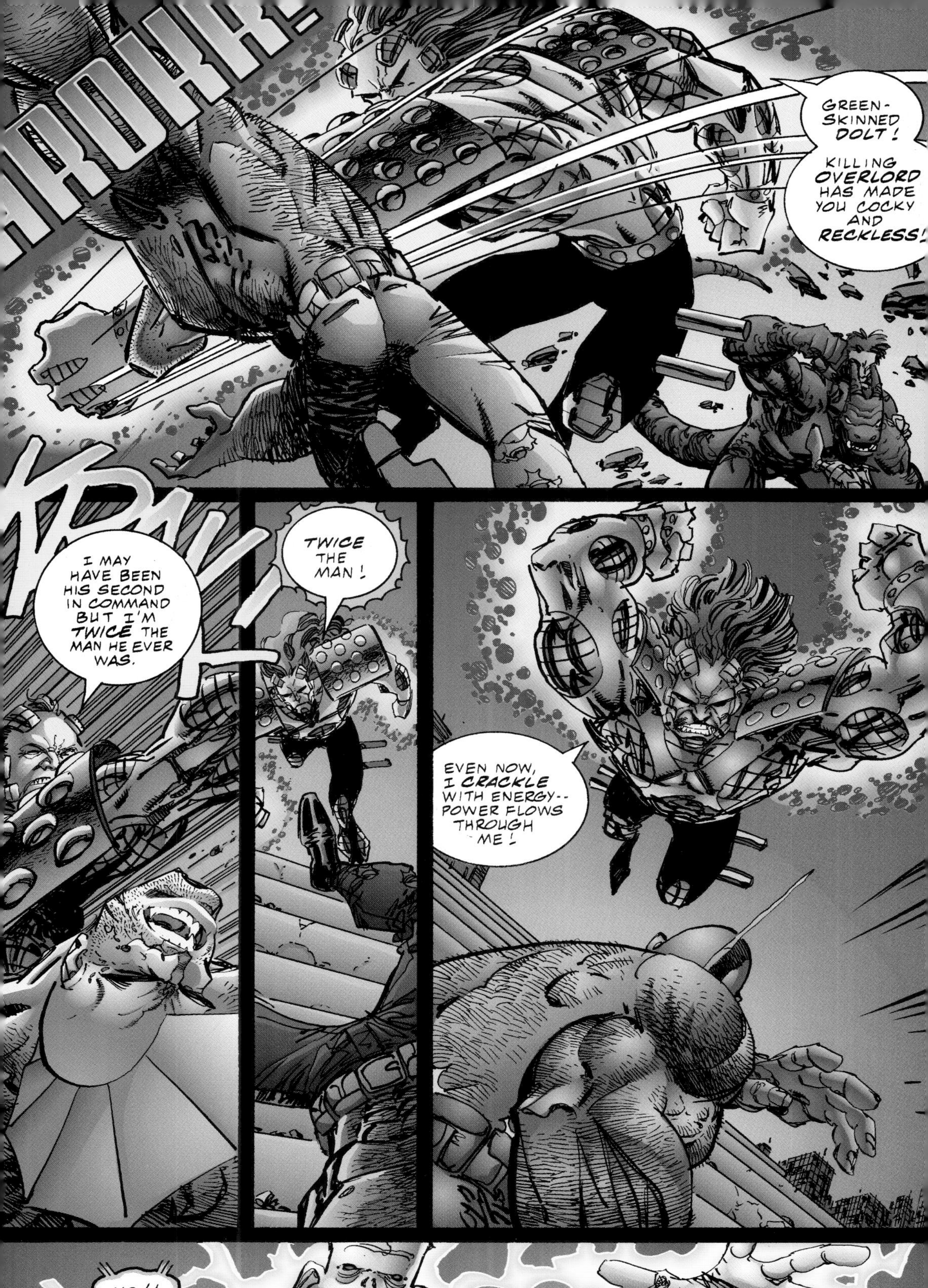
AROKK!
GREEN-SKINNED DOLT!
KILLING OVERLORD HAS MADE YOU COCKY AND RECKLESS!
I MAY HAVE BEEN HIS SECOND IN COMMAND BUT I'M TWICE THE MAN HE EVER WAS.
TWICE THE MAN!
EVEN NOW, I CRACKLE WITH ENERGY-- POWER FLOWS THROUGH ME!
NO!!
DON'T!

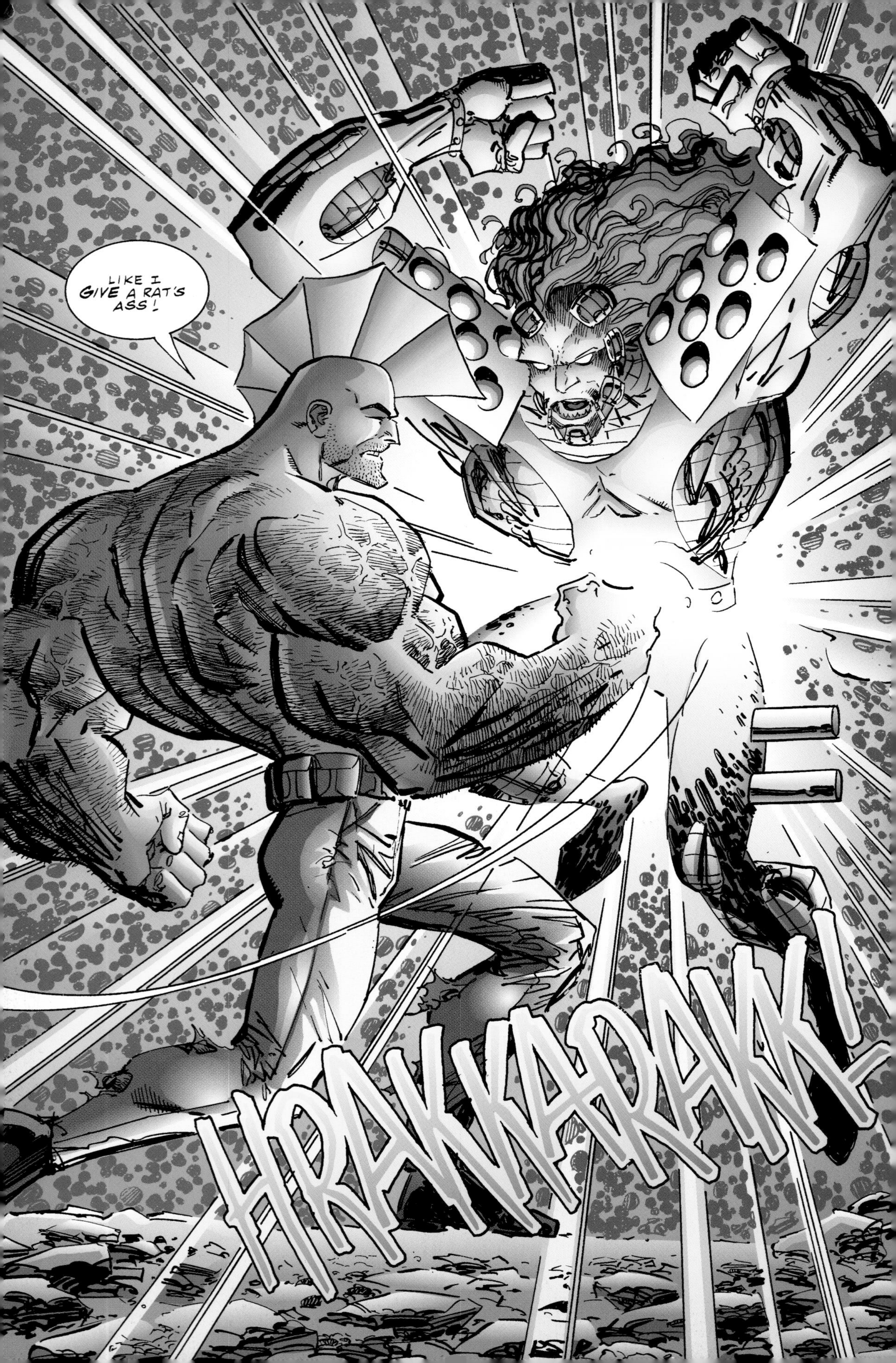
LIKE I GIVE A RAT'S ASS!
HRAKKARAKK!

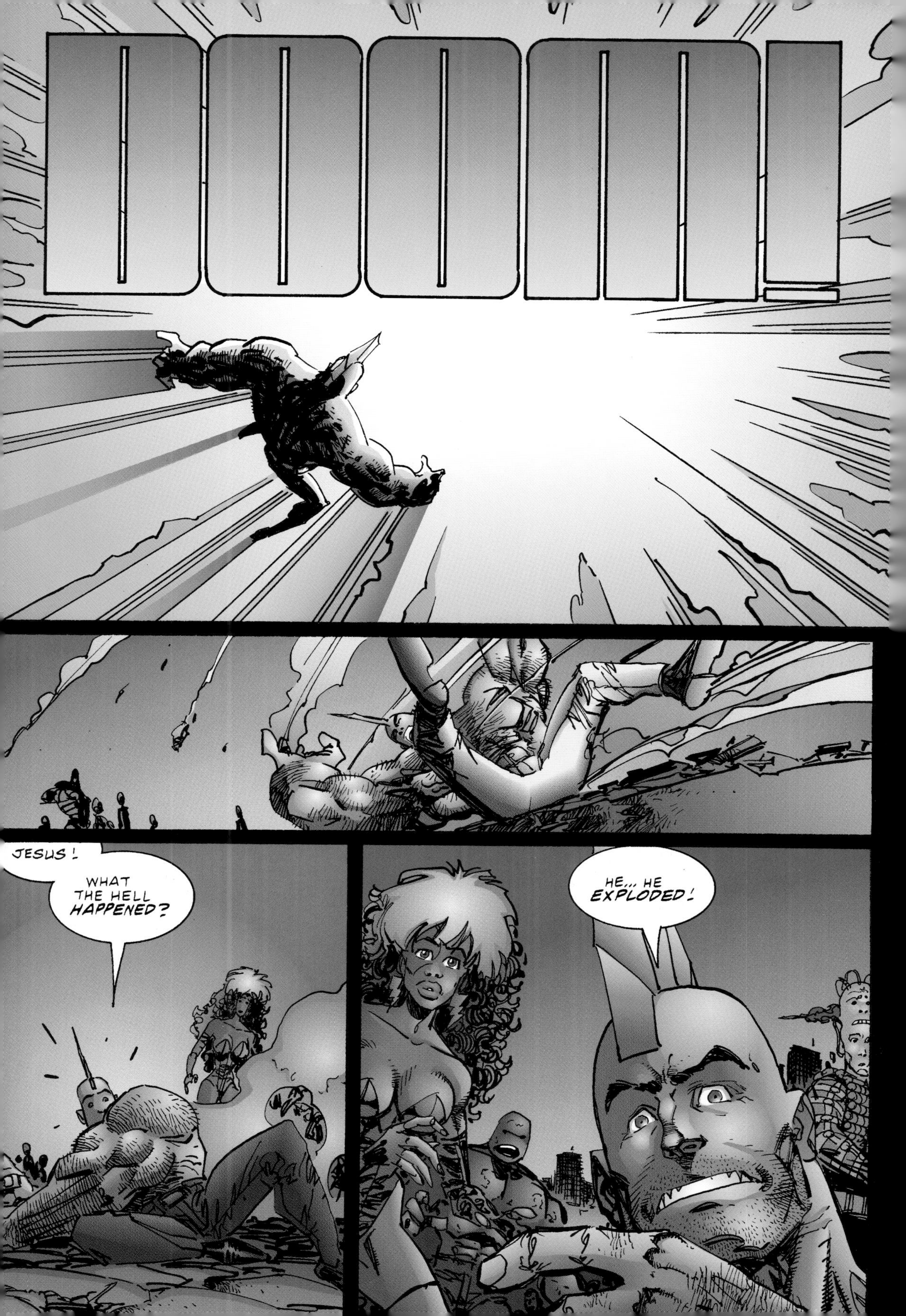
DOOOM!
JESUS!
WHAT THE HELL HAPPENED?
HE... HE EXPLODED!

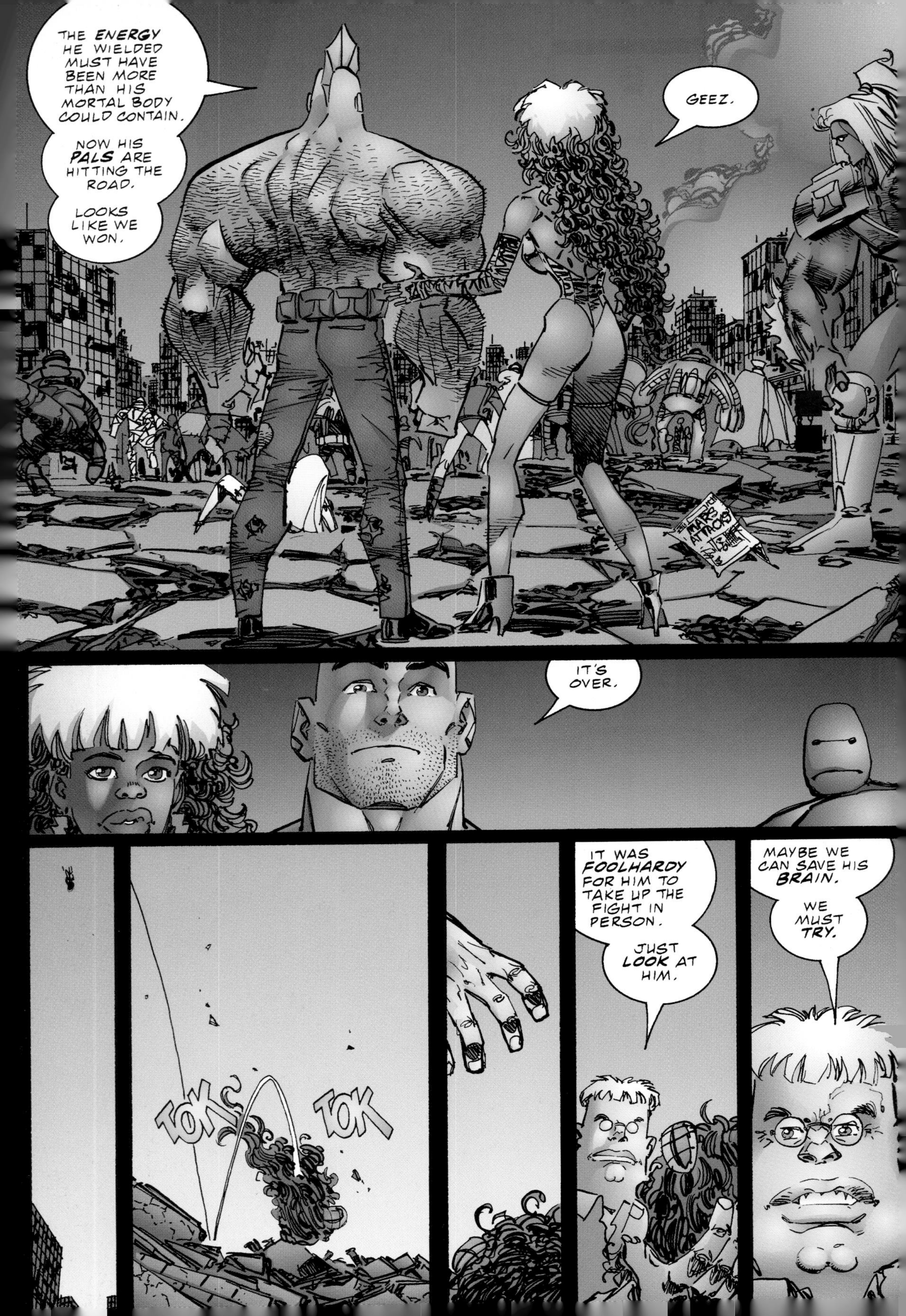
THE ENERGY HE WIELDED MUST HAVE BEEN MORE THAN HIS MORTAL BODY COULD CONTAIN.
NOW HIS PALS ARE HITTING THE ROAD.
LOOKS LIKE WE WON.
GEEZ.
MARS ATTACKS
IT'S OVER.
TOK
TOK
IT WAS FOOLHARDY FOR HIM TO TAKE UP THE FIGHT IN PERSON.
JUST LOOK AT HIM.
MAYBE WE CAN SAVE HIS BRAIN.
WE MUST TRY.

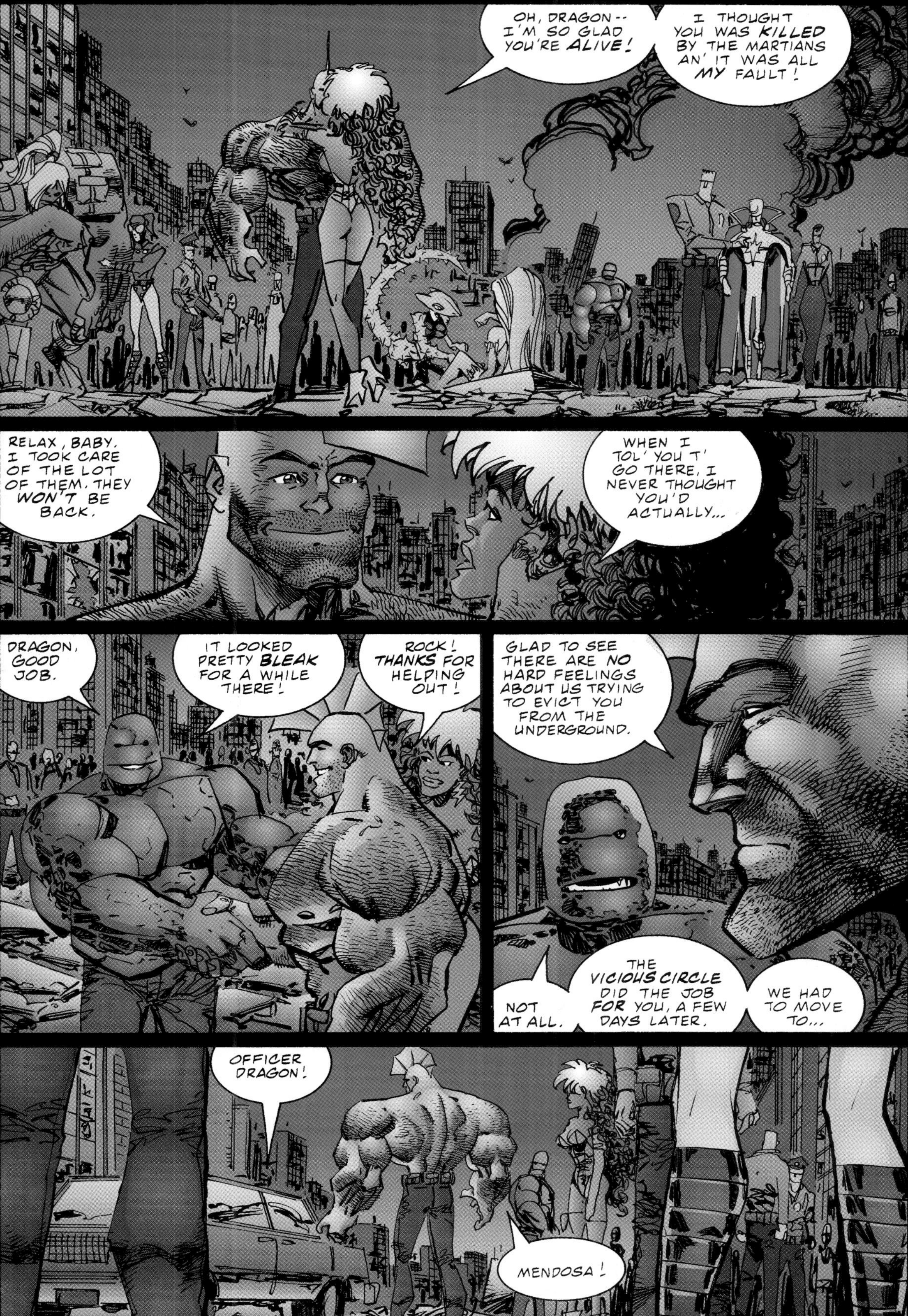
OH, DRAGON-- I'M SO GLAD YOU'RE ALIVE!
I THOUGHT YOU WAS KILLED BY THE MARTIANS AN' IT WAS ALL MY FAULT!
RELAX, BABY. I TOOK CARE OF THE LOT OF THEM. THEY WON'T BE BACK.
WHEN I TOL' YOU T' GO THERE, I NEVER THOUGHT YOU'D ACTUALLY...
DRAGON, GOOD JOB.
IT LOOKED PRETTY BLEAK FOR A WHILE THERE!
ROCK! THANKS FOR HELPING OUT!
GLAD TO SEE THERE ARE NO HARD FEELINGS ABOUT US TRYING TO EVICT YOU FROM THE UNDERGROUND.
NOT AT ALL.
THE VICIOUS CIRCLE DID THE JOB FOR YOU, A FEW DAYS LATER.
WE HAD TO MOVE TO...
OFFICER DRAGON!
MENDOSA!

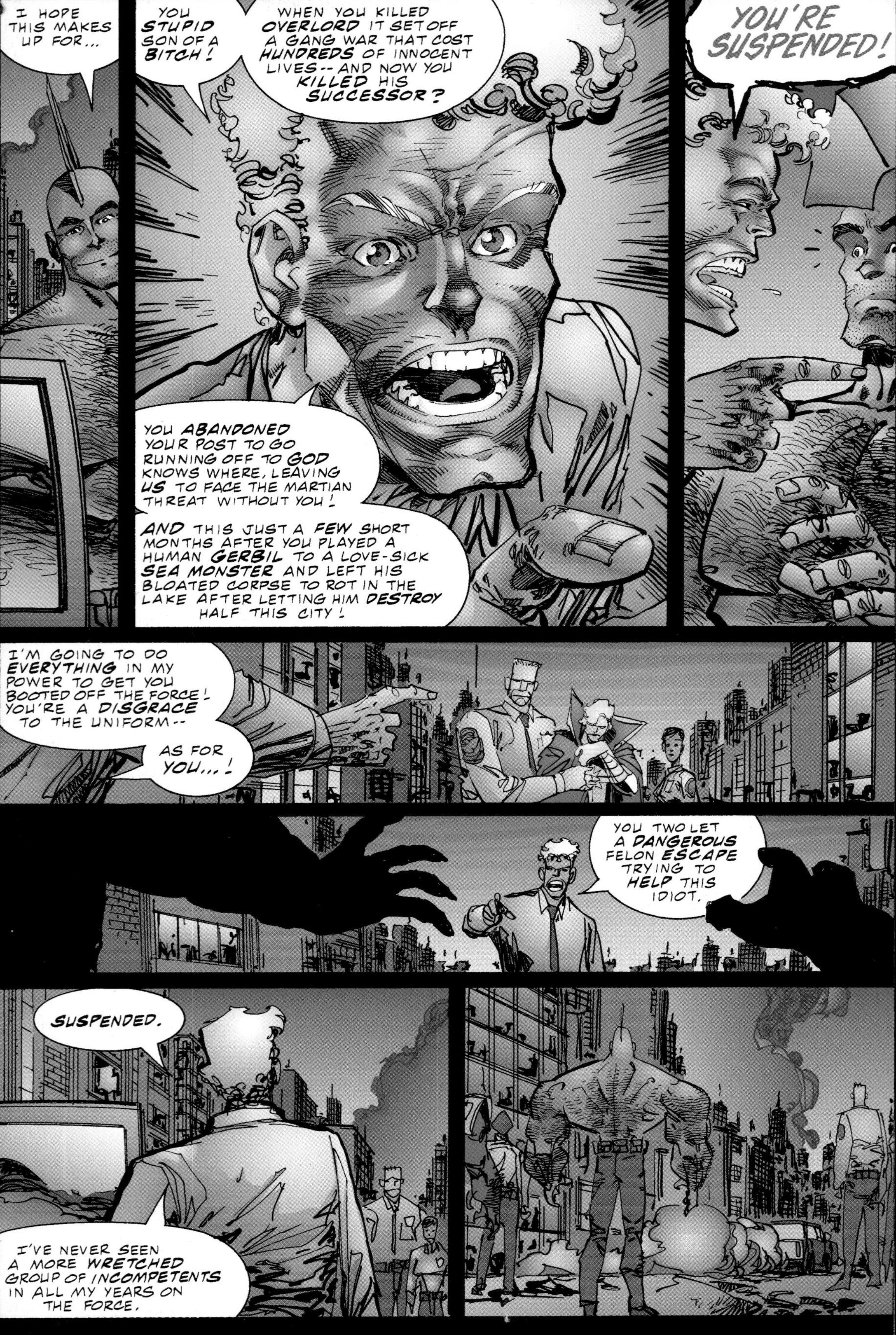
I HOPE THIS MAKES UP FOR...
YOU STUPID SON OF A BITCH!
WHEN YOU KILLED OVERLORD IT SET OFF A GANG WAR THAT COST HUNDREDS OF INNOCENT LIVES -- AND NOW YOU KILLED HIS SUCCESSOR?
YOU ABANDONED YOUR POST TO GO RUNNING OFF TO GOD KNOWS WHERE, LEAVING US TO FACE THE MARTIAN THREAT WITHOUT YOU!
AND THIS JUST A FEW SHORT MONTHS AFTER YOU PLAYED A HUMAN GERBIL TO A LOVE-SICK SEA MONSTER AND LEFT HIS BLOATED CORPSE TO ROT IN THE LAKE AFTER LETTING HIM DESTROY HALF THIS CITY!
YOU'RE SUSPENDED!
I'M GOING TO DO EVERYTHING IN MY POWER TO GET YOU BOOTED OFF THE FORCE! YOU'RE A DISGRACE TO THE UNIFORM --
AS FOR YOU...!
YOU TWO LET A DANGEROUS FELON ESCAPE TRYING TO HELP THIS IDIOT.
SUSPENDED.
I'VE NEVER SEEN A MORE WRETCHED GROUP OF INCOMPETENTS IN ALL MY YEARS ON THE FORCE.

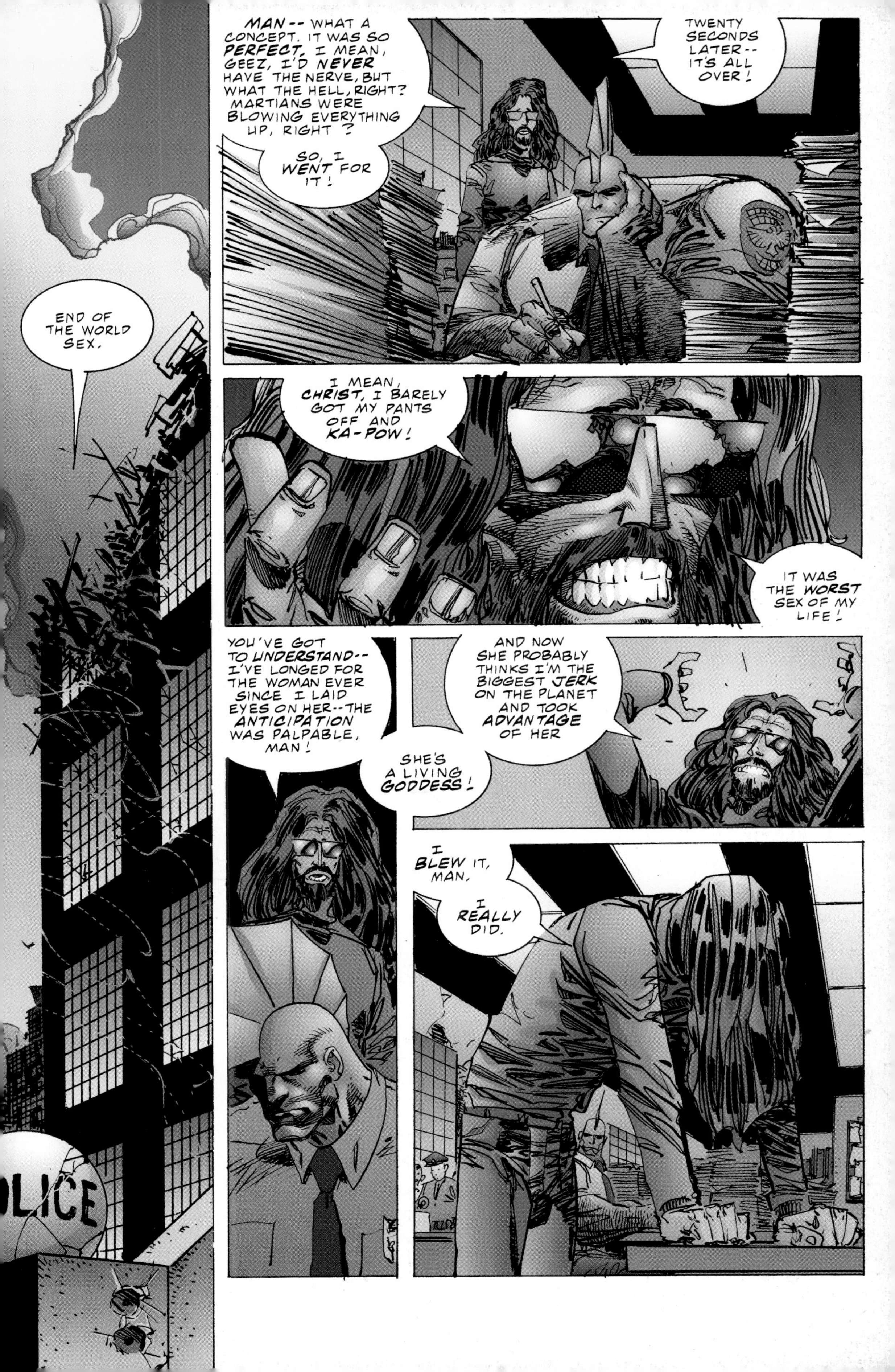

END OF THE WORLD SEX.
MAN-- WHAT A CONCEPT. IT WAS SO PERFECT. I MEAN, GEEZ, I'D NEVER HAVE THE NERVE, BUT WHAT THE HELL, RIGHT? MARTIANS WERE BLOWING EVERYTHING UP, RIGHT?
SO, I WENT FOR IT!
TWENTY SECONDS LATER-- IT'S ALL OVER!
I MEAN, CHRIST, I BARELY GOT MY PANTS OFF AND KA-POW!
IT WAS THE WORST SEX OF MY LIFE!
YOU'VE GOT TO UNDERSTAND-- I'VE LONGED FOR THE WOMAN EVER SINCE I LAID EYES ON HER--THE ANTICIPATION WAS PALPABLE, MAN!
SHE'S A LIVING GODDESS!
AND NOW SHE PROBABLY THINKS I'M THE BIGGEST JERK ON THE PLANET AND TOOK ADVANTAGE OF HER
I BLEW IT, MAN.
I REALLY DID.
OLICE

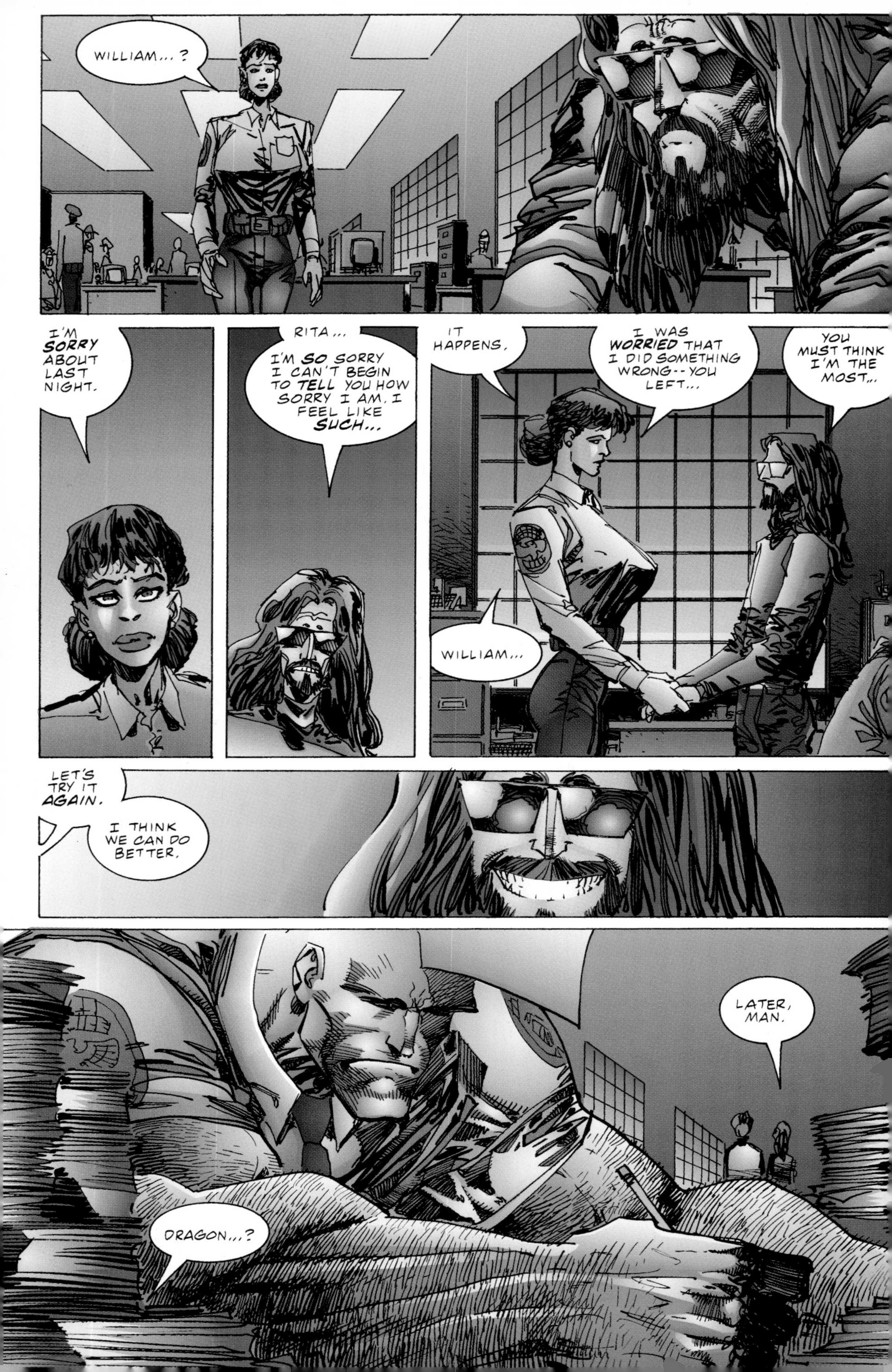
WILLIAM...?
I'M SORRY ABOUT LAST NIGHT.
RITA...
I'M SO SORRY I CAN'T BEGIN TO TELL YOU HOW SORRY I AM. I FEEL LIKE SUCH...
IT HAPPENS.
I WAS WORRIED THAT I DID SOMETHING WRONG--YOU LEFT...
YOU MUST THINK I'M THE MOST...
WILLIAM...
LET'S TRY IT AGAIN.
I THINK WE CAN DO BETTER.
LATER, MAN.
DRAGON...?

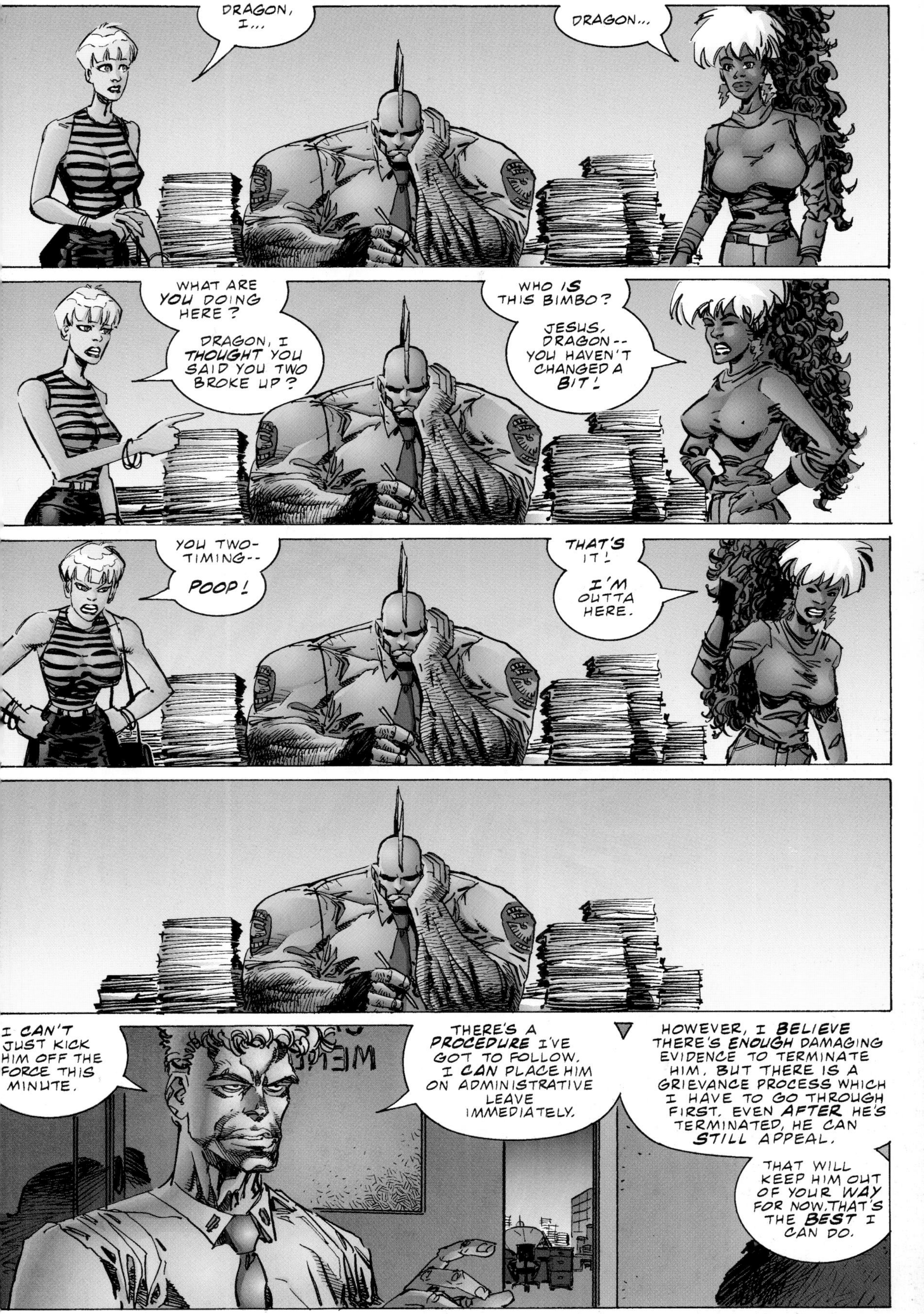

DRAGON, I...
DRAGON...
WHAT ARE YOU DOING HERE?
DRAGON, I THOUGHT YOU SAID YOU TWO BROKE UP?
WHO IS THIS BIMBO?
JESUS, DRAGON-- YOU HAVEN'T CHANGED A BIT!
YOU TWO-TIMING-- POOP!
THAT'S IT! I'M OUTTA HERE.
I CAN'T JUST KICK HIM OFF THE FORCE THIS MINUTE.
THERE'S A PROCEDURE I'VE GOT TO FOLLOW. I CAN PLACE HIM ON ADMINISTRATIVE LEAVE IMMEDIATELY.
HOWEVER, I BELIEVE THERE'S ENOUGH DAMAGING EVIDENCE TO TERMINATE HIM. BUT THERE IS A GRIEVANCE PROCESS WHICH I HAVE TO GO THROUGH FIRST. EVEN AFTER HE'S TERMINATED, HE CAN STILL APPEAL.
THAT WILL KEEP HIM OUT OF YOUR WAY FOR NOW. THAT'S THE BEST I CAN DO.

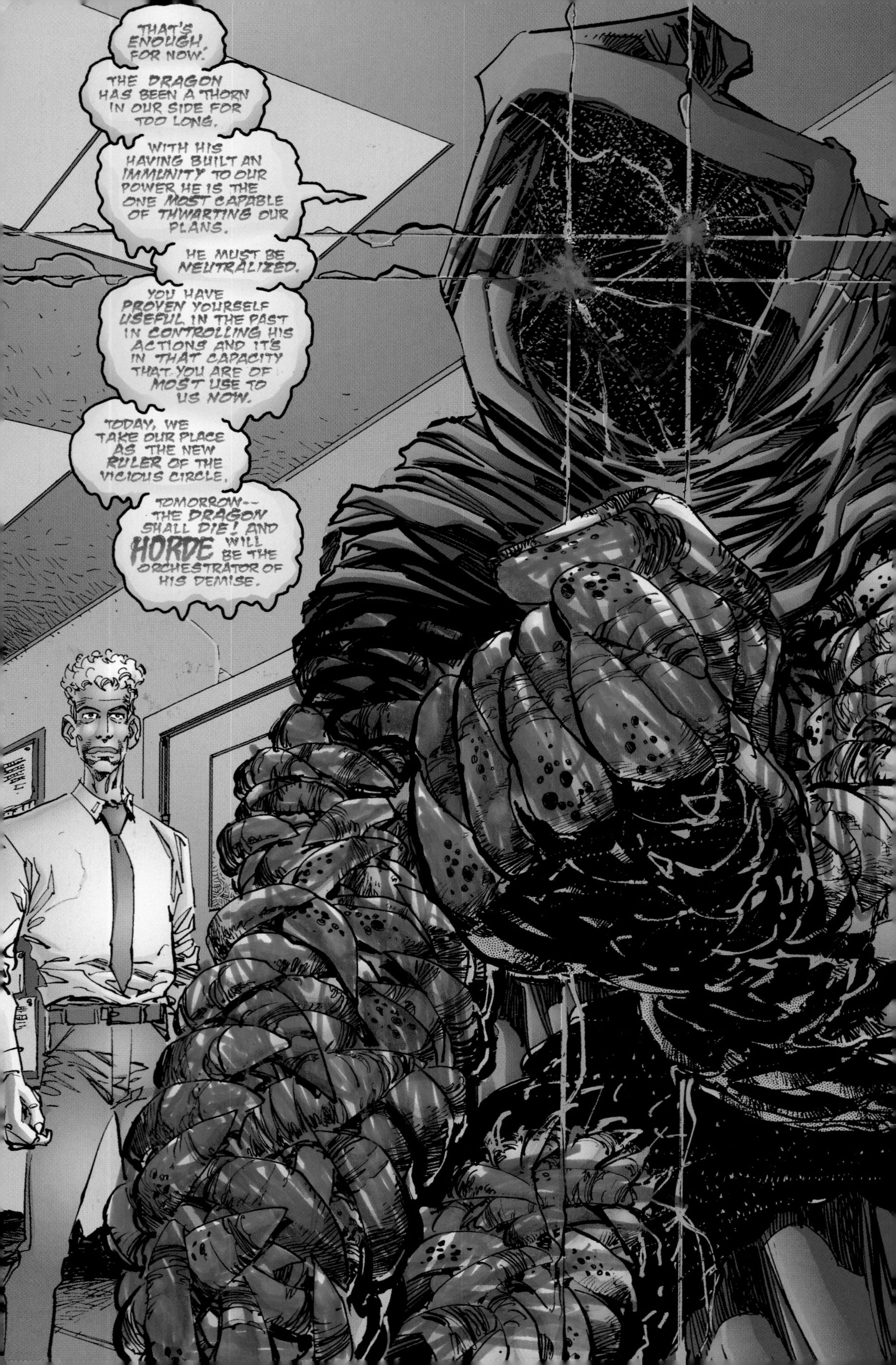

THAT'S ENOUGH FOR NOW.
THE DRAGON HAS BEEN A THORN IN OUR SIDE FOR TOO LONG.
WITH HIS HAVING BUILT AN IMMUNITY TO OUR POWER HE IS THE ONE MOST CAPABLE OF THWARTING OUR PLANS.
HE MUST BE NEUTRALIZED.
YOU HAVE PROVEN YOURSELF USEFUL IN THE PAST IN CONTROLLING HIS ACTIONS AND IT'S IN THAT CAPACITY THAT YOU ARE OF MOST USE TO US NOW.
TODAY, WE TAKE OUR PLACE AS THE NEW RULER OF THE VICIOUS CIRCLE.
TOMORROW-- THE DRAGON SHALL DIE! AND HORDE WILL BE THE ORCHESTRATOR OF HIS DEMISE.

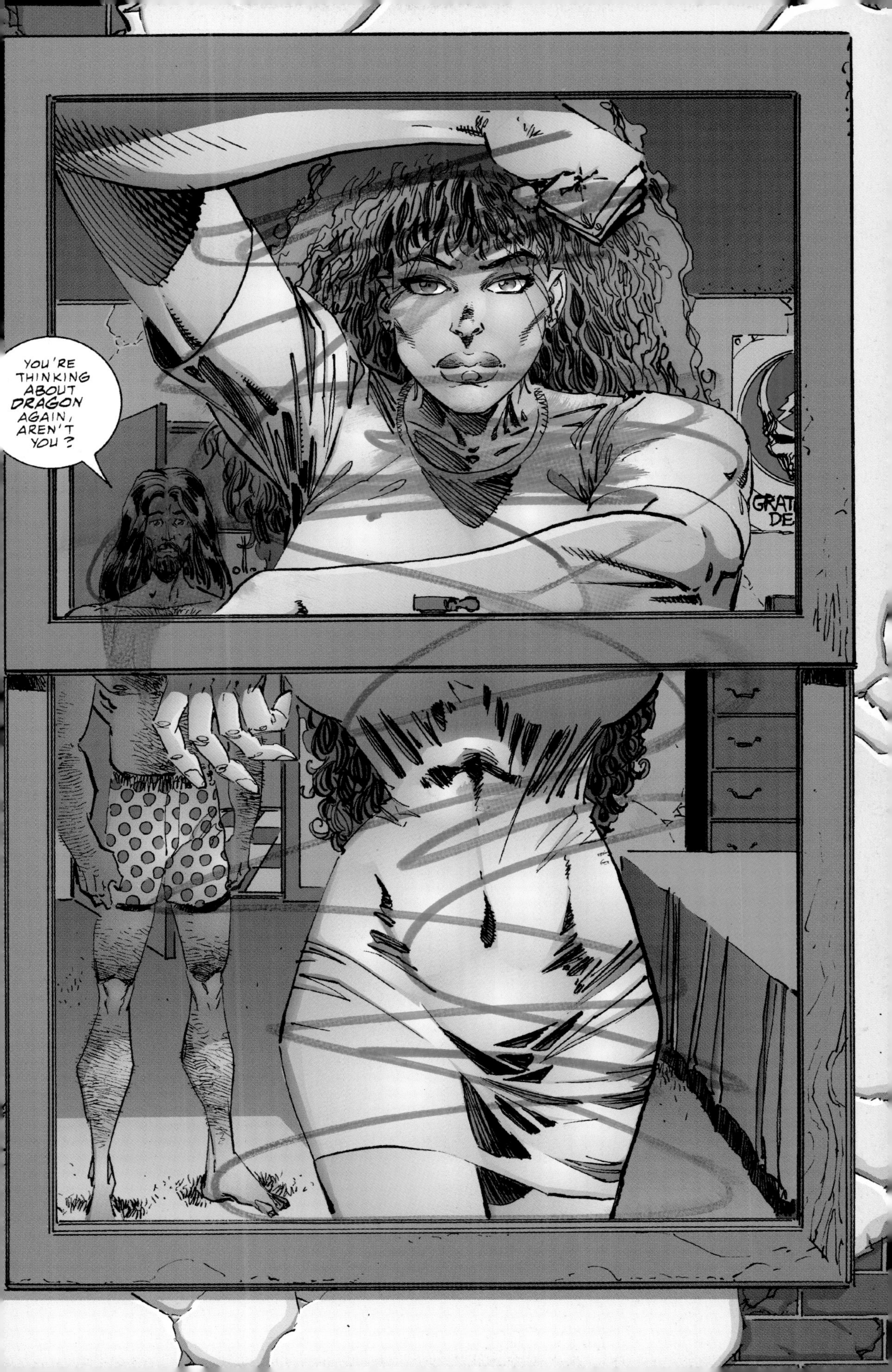
YOU'RE THINKING ABOUT DRAGON AGAIN, AREN'T YOU?

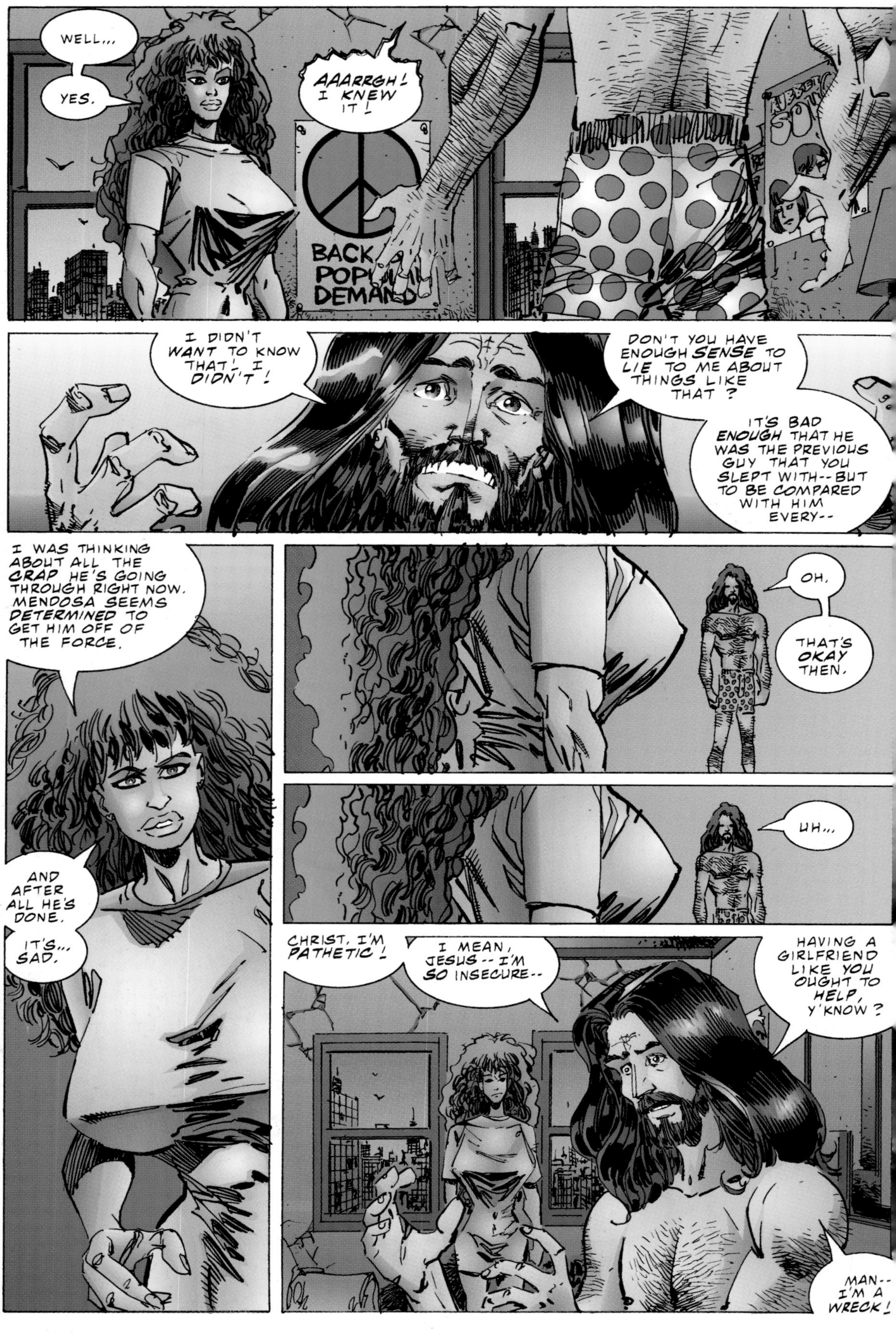
WELL...
YES.
AAARRGH! I KNEW IT!
BACK BY POPULAR DEMAND
I DIDN'T WANT TO KNOW THAT! I DIDN'T!
DON'T YOU HAVE ENOUGH SENSE TO LIE TO ME ABOUT THINGS LIKE THAT?
IT'S BAD ENOUGH THAT HE WAS THE PREVIOUS GUY THAT YOU SLEPT WITH--BUT TO BE COMPARED WITH HIM EVERY--
I WAS THINKING ABOUT ALL THE CRAP HE'S GOING THROUGH RIGHT NOW. MENDOSA SEEMS DETERMINED TO GET HIM OFF OF THE FORCE.
AND AFTER ALL HE'S DONE.
IT'S... SAD.
OH.
THAT'S OKAY THEN.
UH...
CHRIST, I'M PATHETIC!
I MEAN, JESUS -- I'M SO INSECURE--
HAVING A GIRLFRIEND LIKE YOU OUGHT TO HELP, Y'KNOW?
MAN-- I'M A WRECK!

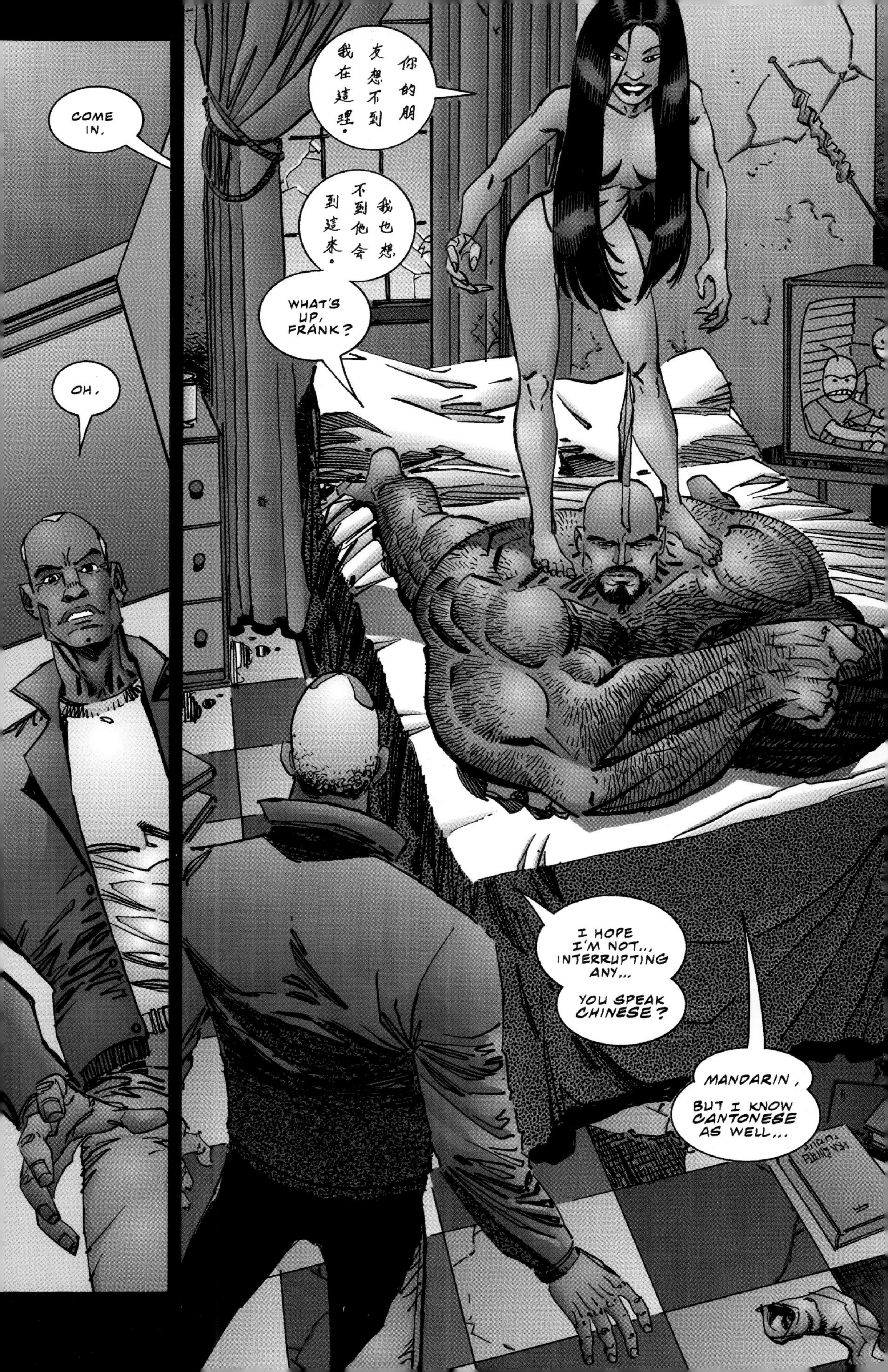
COME IN.
OH.
你的朋友想不到我在這理。
我也想不到他会到這來。
WHAT'S UP, FRANK?
I HOPE I'M NOT... INTERRUPTING ANY...
YOU SPEAK CHINESE?
MANDARIN,
BUT I KNOW CANTONESE AS WELL...

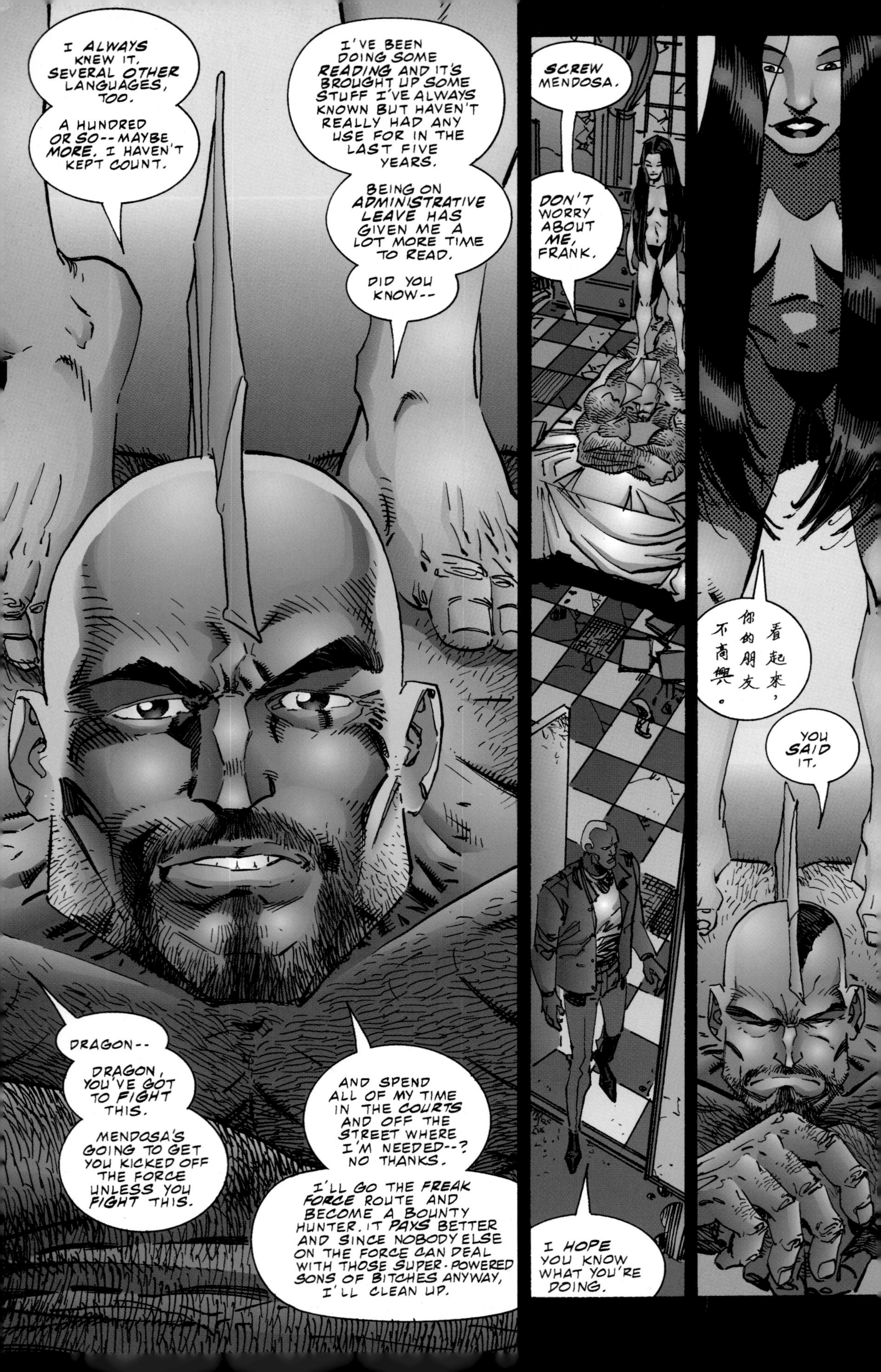

I ALWAYS KNEW IT, SEVERAL OTHER LANGUAGES, TOO.
A HUNDRED OR SO--MAYBE MORE. I HAVEN'T KEPT COUNT.
I'VE BEEN DOING SOME READING AND IT'S BROUGHT UP SOME STUFF I'VE ALWAYS KNOWN BUT HAVEN'T REALLY HAD ANY USE FOR IN THE LAST FIVE YEARS.
BEING ON ADMINISTRATIVE LEAVE HAS GIVEN ME A LOT MORE TIME TO READ.
DID YOU KNOW--
DRAGON--
DRAGON, YOU'VE GOT TO FIGHT THIS.
MENDOSA'S GOING TO GET YOU KICKED OFF THE FORCE UNLESS YOU FIGHT THIS.
AND SPEND ALL OF MY TIME IN THE COURTS AND OFF THE STREET WHERE I'M NEEDED--? NO THANKS.
I'LL GO THE FREAK FORCE ROUTE AND BECOME A BOUNTY HUNTER. IT PAYS BETTER AND SINCE NOBODY ELSE ON THE FORCE CAN DEAL WITH THOSE SUPER-POWERED SONS OF BITCHES ANYWAY, I'LL CLEAN UP.
SCREW MENDOSA.
DON'T WORRY ABOUT ME, FRANK.
I HOPE YOU KNOW WHAT YOU'RE DOING.
看起來，你的朋友不高興。
YOU SAID IT.

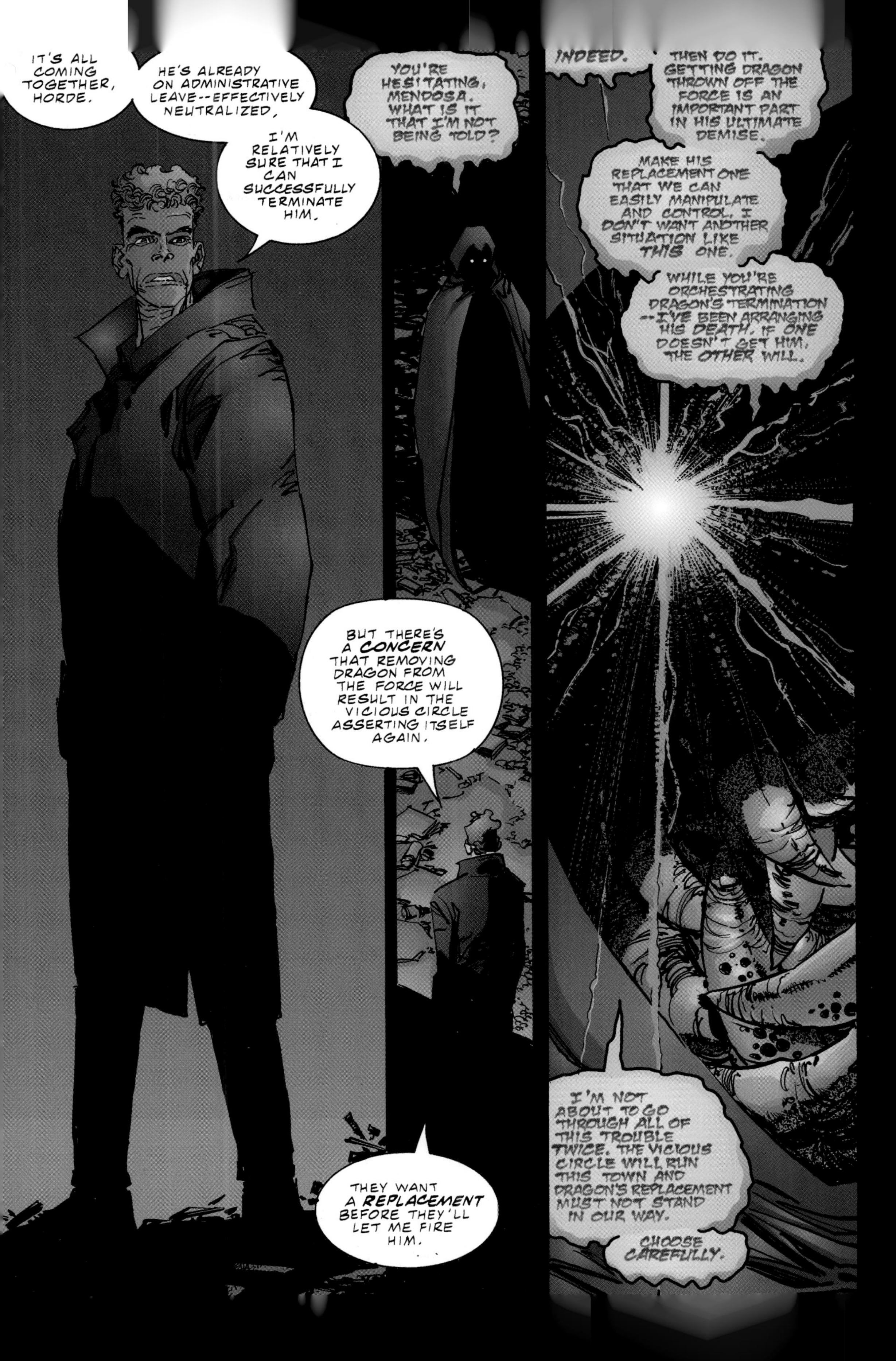
IT'S ALL COMING TOGETHER, HORDE.
HE'S ALREADY ON ADMINISTRATIVE LEAVE--EFFECTIVELY NEUTRALIZED,
I'M RELATIVELY SURE THAT I CAN SUCCESSFULLY TERMINATE HIM.
YOU'RE HESITATING, MENDOSA. WHAT IS IT THAT I'M NOT BEING TOLD?
BUT THERE'S A CONCERN THAT REMOVING DRAGON FROM THE FORCE WILL RESULT IN THE VICIOUS CIRCLE ASSERTING ITSELF AGAIN.
THEY WANT A REPLACEMENT BEFORE THEY'LL LET ME FIRE HIM.
INDEED.
THEN DO IT. GETTING DRAGON THROWN OFF THE FORCE IS AN IMPORTANT PART IN HIS ULTIMATE DEMISE.
MAKE HIS REPLACEMENT ONE THAT WE CAN EASILY MANIPULATE AND CONTROL. I DON'T WANT ANOTHER SITUATION LIKE THIS ONE.
WHILE YOU'RE ORCHESTRATING DRAGON'S TERMINATION --I'VE BEEN ARRANGING HIS DEATH. IF ONE DOESN'T GET HIM, THE OTHER WILL.
I'M NOT ABOUT TO GO THROUGH ALL OF THIS TROUBLE TWICE. THE VICIOUS CIRCLE WILL RUN THIS TOWN AND DRAGON'S REPLACEMENT MUST NOT STAND IN OUR WAY.
CHOOSE CAREFULLY.

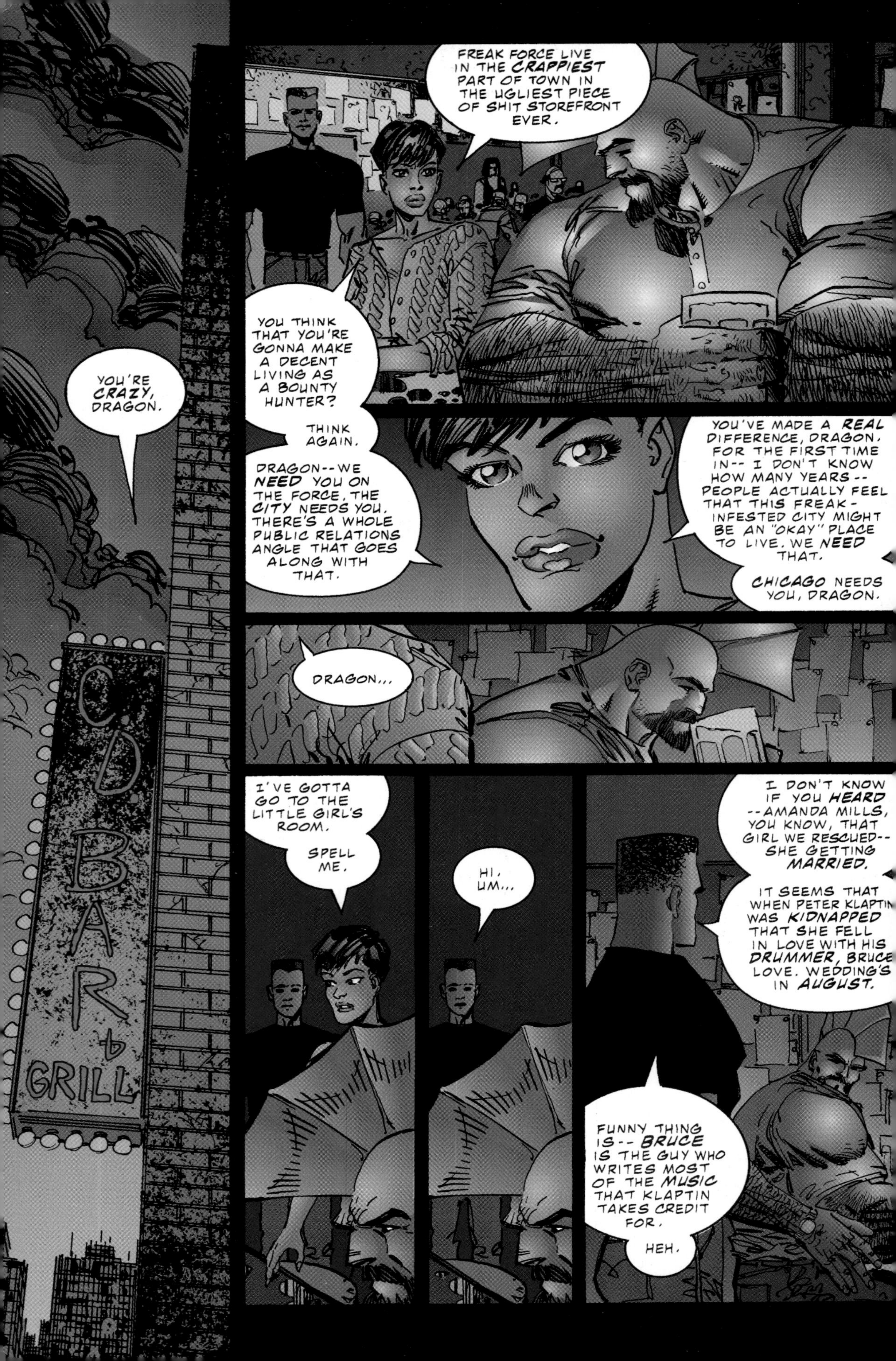
FREAK FORCE LIVE IN THE CRAPPIEST PART OF TOWN IN THE UGLIEST PIECE OF SHIT STOREFRONT EVER.
YOU'RE CRAZY, DRAGON.
YOU THINK THAT YOU'RE GONNA MAKE A DECENT LIVING AS A BOUNTY HUNTER?
THINK AGAIN.
DRAGON--WE NEED YOU ON THE FORCE, THE CITY NEEDS YOU. THERE'S A WHOLE PUBLIC RELATIONS ANGLE THAT GOES ALONG WITH THAT.
YOU'VE MADE A REAL DIFFERENCE, DRAGON. FOR THE FIRST TIME IN-- I DON'T KNOW HOW MANY YEARS -- PEOPLE ACTUALLY FEEL THAT THIS FREAK-INFESTED CITY MIGHT BE AN "OKAY" PLACE TO LIVE. WE NEED THAT.
CHICAGO NEEDS YOU, DRAGON.
CD BAR & GRILL
DRAGON...
I'VE GOTTA GO TO THE LITTLE GIRL'S ROOM.
SPELL ME.
HI, UM...
I DON'T KNOW IF YOU HEARD --AMANDA MILLS, YOU KNOW, THAT GIRL WE RESCUED-- SHE GETTING MARRIED.
IT SEEMS THAT WHEN PETER KLAPTIN WAS KIDNAPPED THAT SHE FELL IN LOVE WITH HIS DRUMMER, BRUCE LOVE. WEDDING'S IN AUGUST.
FUNNY THING IS -- BRUCE IS THE GUY WHO WRITES MOST OF THE MUSIC THAT KLAPTIN TAKES CREDIT FOR.
HEH.

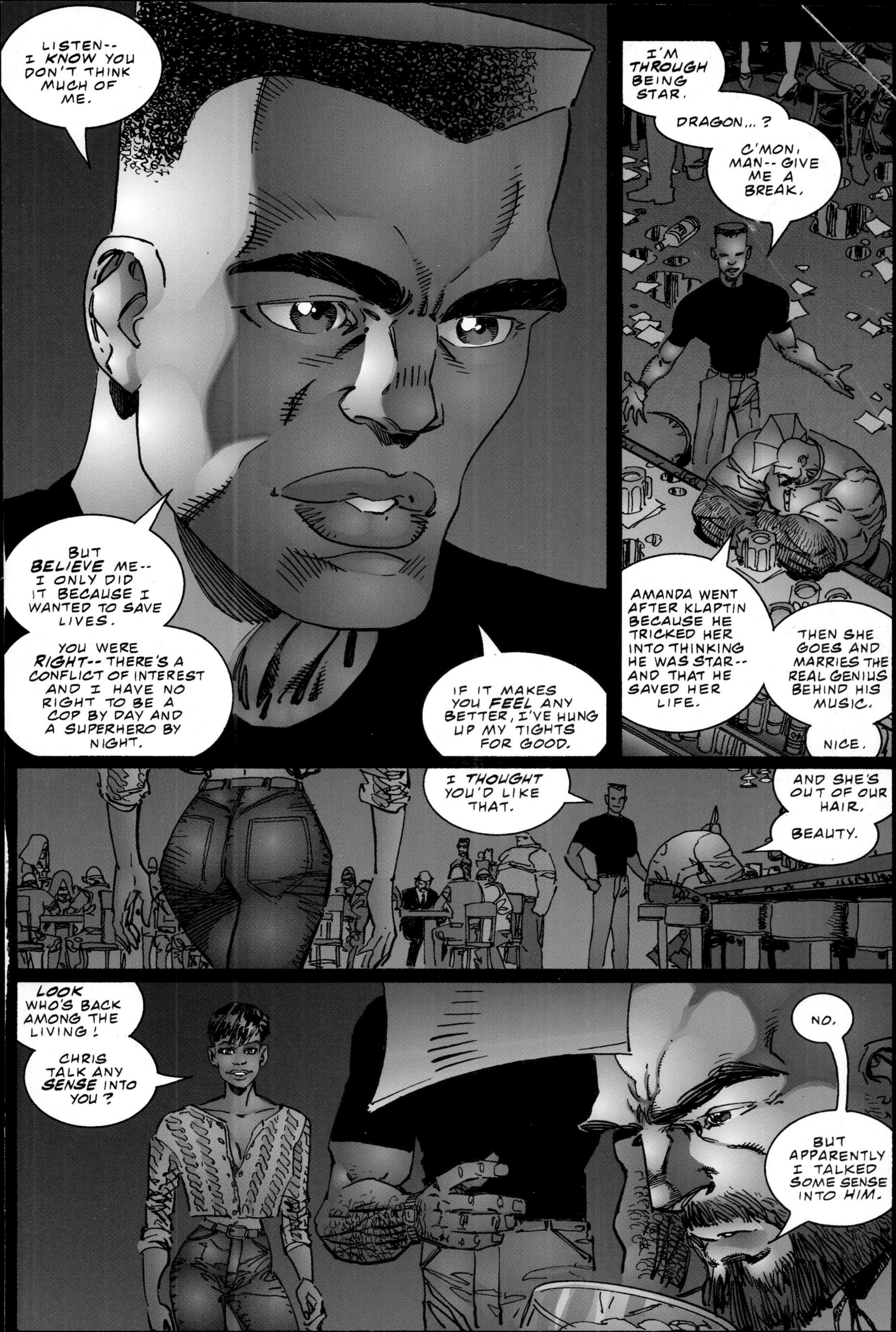
LISTEN-- I KNOW YOU DON'T THINK MUCH OF ME.
BUT BELIEVE ME-- I ONLY DID IT BECAUSE I WANTED TO SAVE LIVES.
YOU WERE RIGHT-- THERE'S A CONFLICT OF INTEREST AND I HAVE NO RIGHT TO BE A COP BY DAY AND A SUPERHERO BY NIGHT.
IF IT MAKES YOU FEEL ANY BETTER, I'VE HUNG UP MY TIGHTS FOR GOOD.
I'M THROUGH BEING STAR.
DRAGON... ?
C'MON, MAN-- GIVE ME A BREAK.
AMANDA WENT AFTER KLAPTIN BECAUSE HE TRICKED HER INTO THINKING HE WAS STAR-- AND THAT HE SAVED HER LIFE.
THEN SHE GOES AND MARRIES THE REAL GENIUS BEHIND HIS MUSIC.
NICE.
I THOUGHT YOU'D LIKE THAT.
AND SHE'S OUT OF OUR HAIR.
BEAUTY.
LOOK WHO'S BACK AMONG THE LIVING!
CHRIS TALK ANY SENSE INTO YOU?
NO.
BUT APPARENTLY I TALKED SOME SENSE INTO HIM.

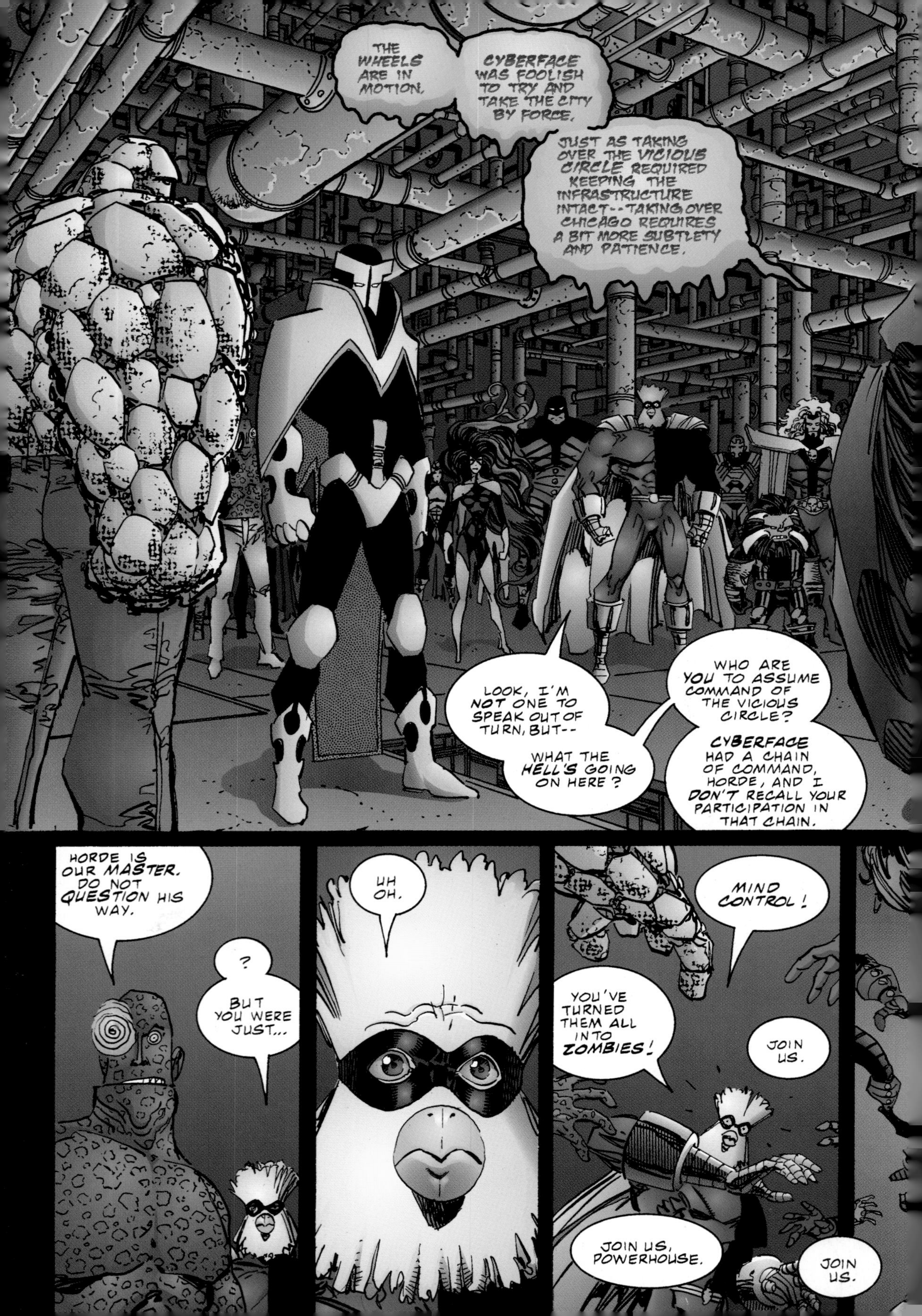
THE WHEELS ARE IN MOTION.
CYBERFACE WAS FOOLISH TO TRY AND TAKE THE CITY BY FORCE.
JUST AS TAKING OVER THE VICIOUS CIRCLE REQUIRED KEEPING THE INFRASTRUCTURE INTACT--TAKING OVER CHICAGO REQUIRES A BIT MORE SUBTLETY AND PATIENCE.
LOOK, I'M NOT ONE TO SPEAK OUT OF TURN, BUT--
WHAT THE HELL'S GOING ON HERE?
WHO ARE YOU TO ASSUME COMMAND OF THE VICIOUS CIRCLE?
CYBERFACE HAD A CHAIN OF COMMAND, HORDE, AND I DON'T RECALL YOUR PARTICIPATION IN THAT CHAIN.
HORDE IS OUR MASTER. DO NOT QUESTION HIS WAY.
?
BUT YOU WERE JUST...
UH OH.
MIND CONTROL!
YOU'VE TURNED THEM ALL INTO ZOMBIES!
JOIN US.
JOIN US, POWERHOUSE.
JOIN US.

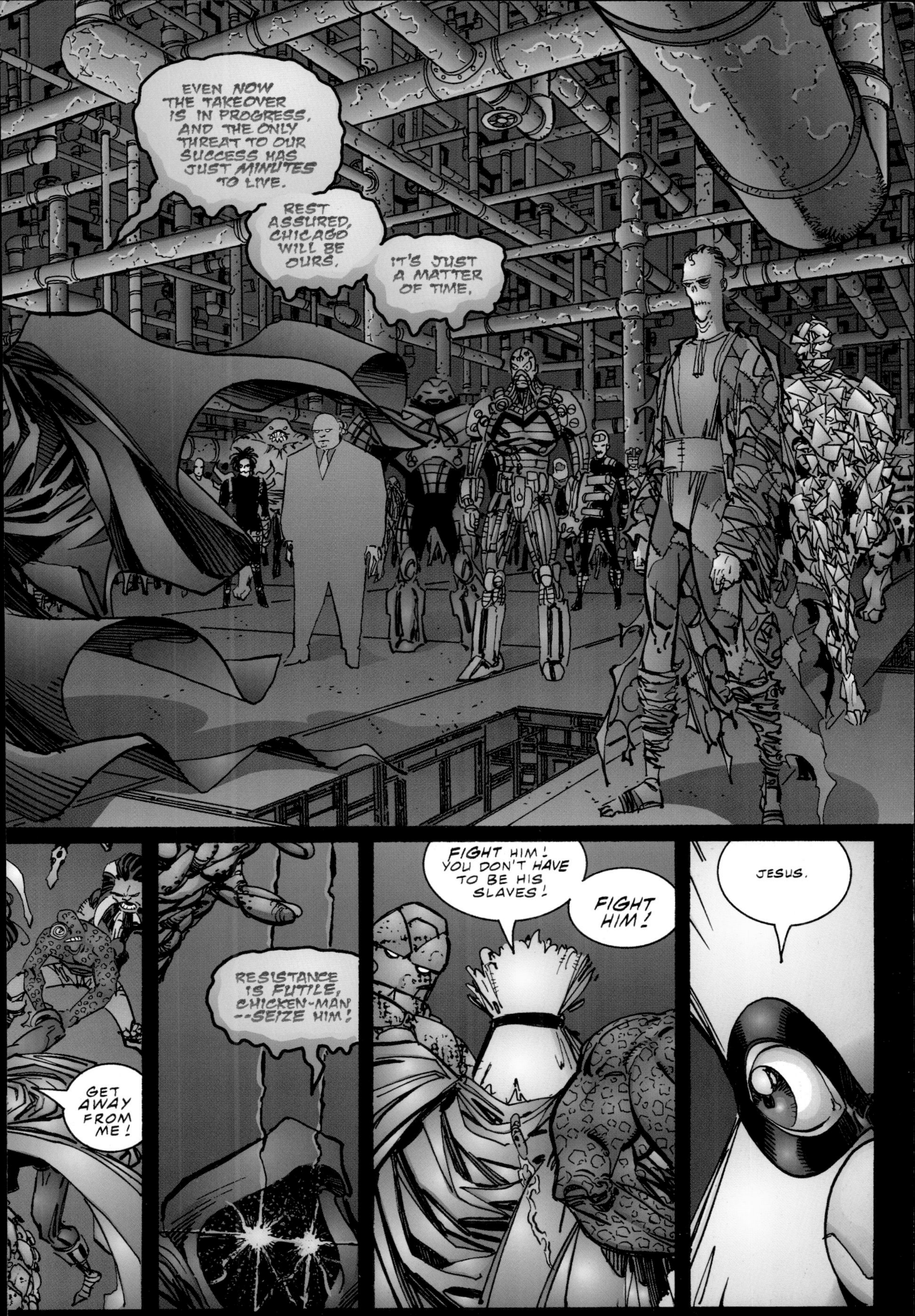
EVEN NOW THE TAKEOVER IS IN PROGRESS, AND THE ONLY THREAT TO OUR SUCCESS HAS JUST MINUTES TO LIVE.
REST ASSURED, CHICAGO WILL BE OURS.
IT'S JUST A MATTER OF TIME.
GET AWAY FROM ME!
RESISTANCE IS FUTILE, CHICKEN-MAN --SEIZE HIM!
FIGHT HIM! YOU DON'T HAVE TO BE HIS SLAVES!
FIGHT HIM!
JESUS.

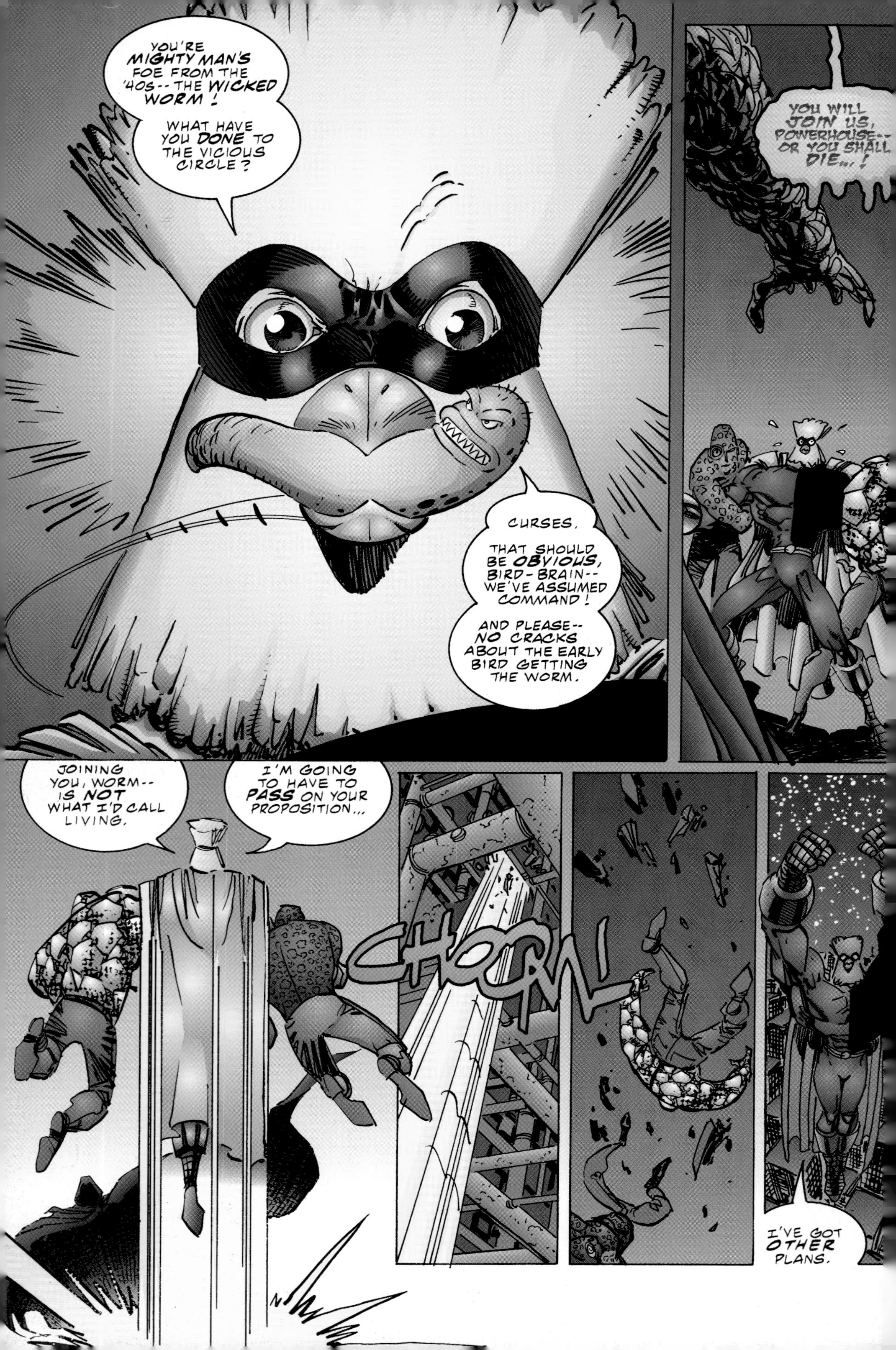
YOU'RE MIGHTY MAN'S FOE FROM THE '40S-- THE WICKED WORM!
WHAT HAVE YOU DONE TO THE VICIOUS CIRCLE?
CURSES.
THAT SHOULD BE OBVIOUS, BIRD-BRAIN-- WE'VE ASSUMED COMMAND!
AND PLEASE-- NO CRACKS ABOUT THE EARLY BIRD GETTING THE WORM.
YOU WILL JOIN US, POWERHOUSE-- OR YOU SHALL DIE...!
JOINING YOU, WORM-- IS NOT WHAT I'D CALL LIVING.
I'M GOING TO HAVE TO PASS ON YOUR PROPOSITION...
I'VE GOT OTHER PLANS.

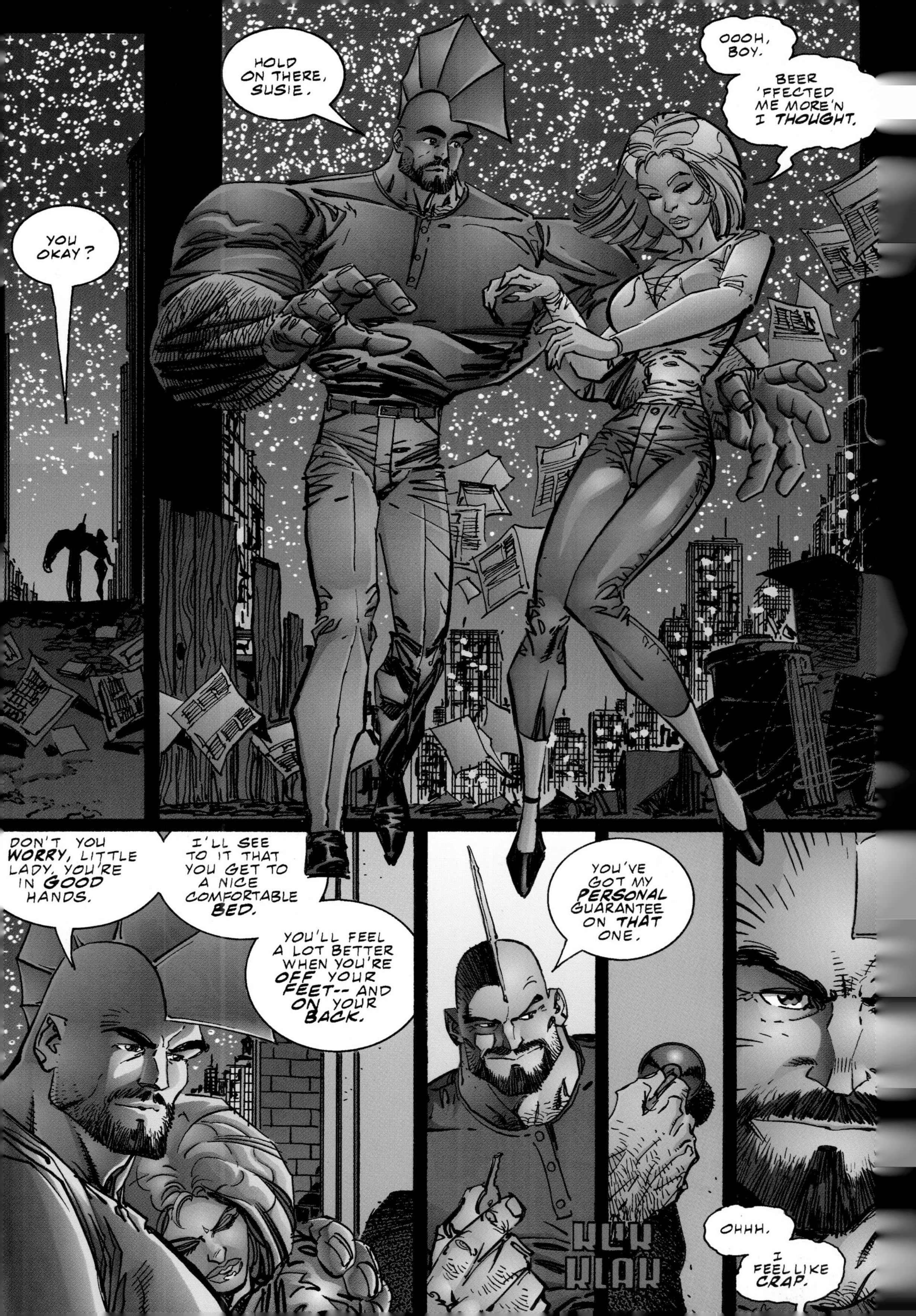
YOU OKAY?
HOLD ON THERE, SUSIE.
OOOH, BOY.
BEER 'FFECTED ME MORE'N I THOUGHT.
DON'T YOU WORRY, LITTLE LADY. YOU'RE IN GOOD HANDS.
I'LL SEE TO IT THAT YOU GET TO A NICE COMFORTABLE BED.
YOU'LL FEEL A LOT BETTER WHEN YOU'RE OFF YOUR FEET-- AND ON YOUR BACK.
YOU'VE GOT MY PERSONAL GUARANTEE ON THAT ONE.
KLIK KLAK
OHHH.
I FEEL LIKE CRAP.

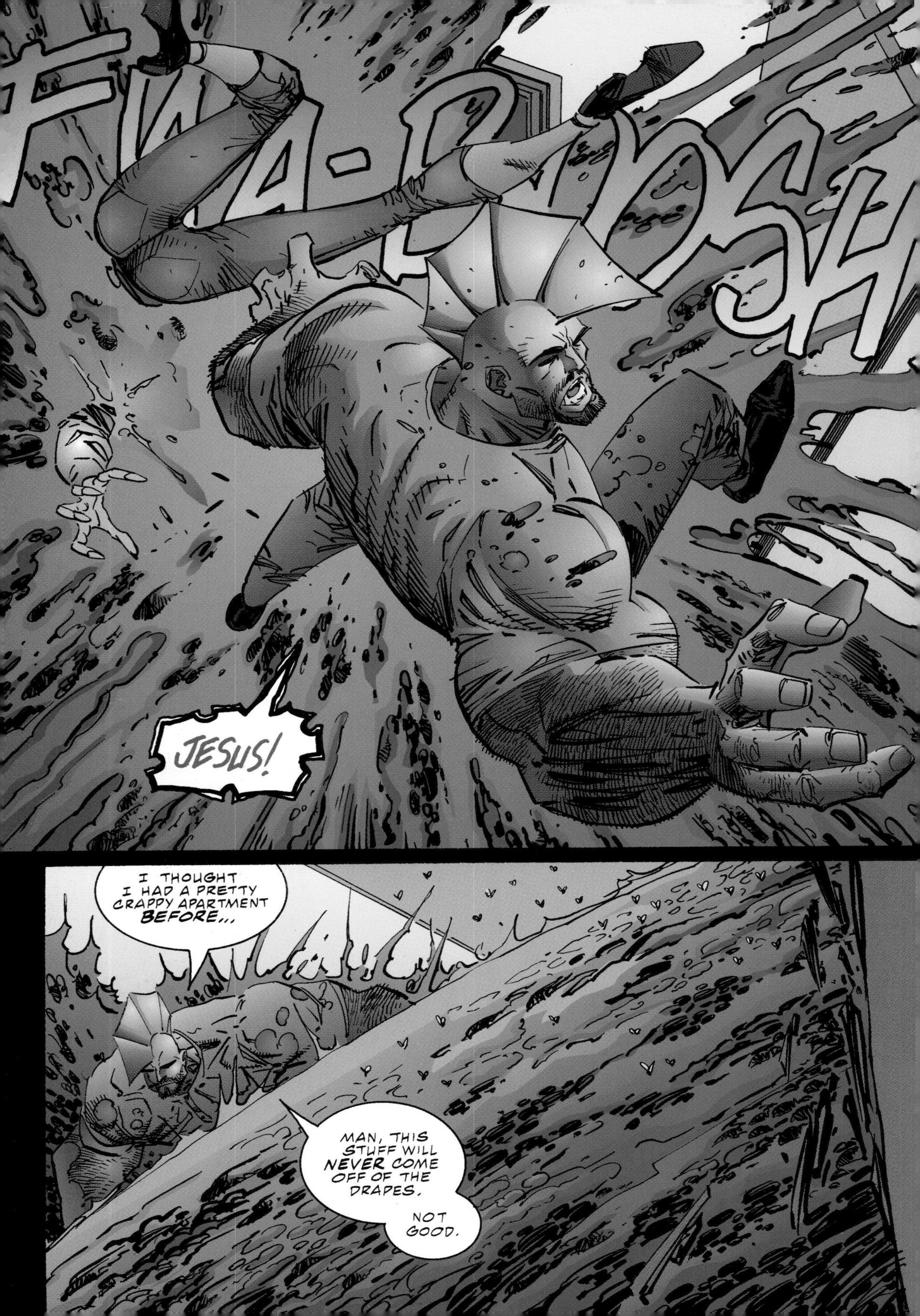
FWA-DOOSH
JESUS!
I THOUGHT I HAD A PRETTY CRAPPY APARTMENT BEFORE...
MAN, THIS STUFF WILL NEVER COME OFF OF THE DRAPES.
NOT GOOD.

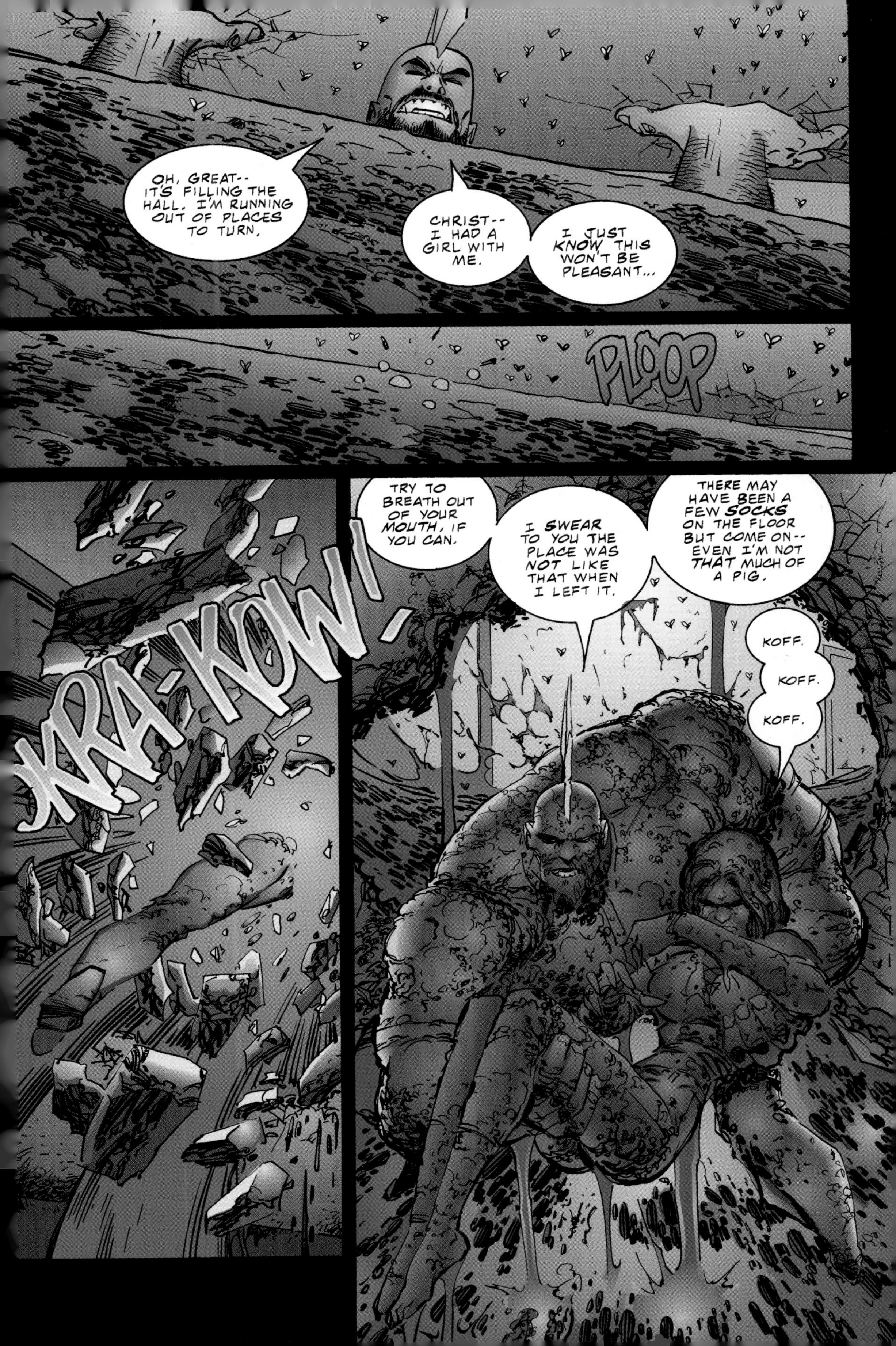

OH, GREAT--
IT'S FILLING THE HALL. I'M RUNNING OUT OF PLACES TO TURN.
CHRIST--
I HAD A GIRL WITH ME.
I JUST KNOW THIS WON'T BE PLEASANT...
PLOOP
KRA-KOW!
TRY TO BREATH OUT OF YOUR MOUTH, IF YOU CAN.
I SWEAR TO YOU THE PLACE WAS NOT LIKE THAT WHEN I LEFT IT.
THERE MAY HAVE BEEN A FEW SOCKS ON THE FLOOR BUT COME ON--
EVEN I'M NOT THAT MUCH OF A PIG.
KOFF.
KOFF.
KOFF.

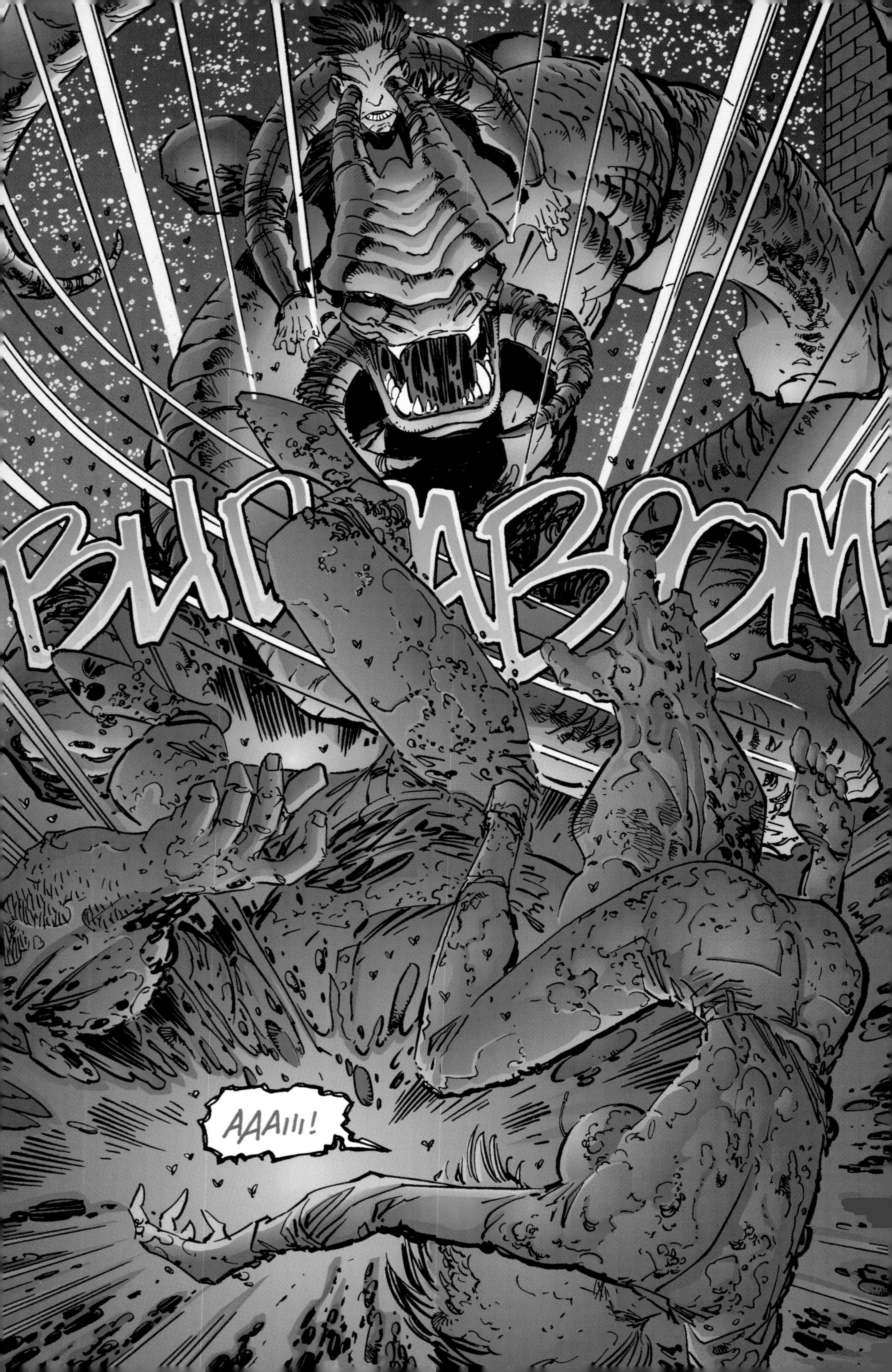
BU ABOOM
AAAIII!

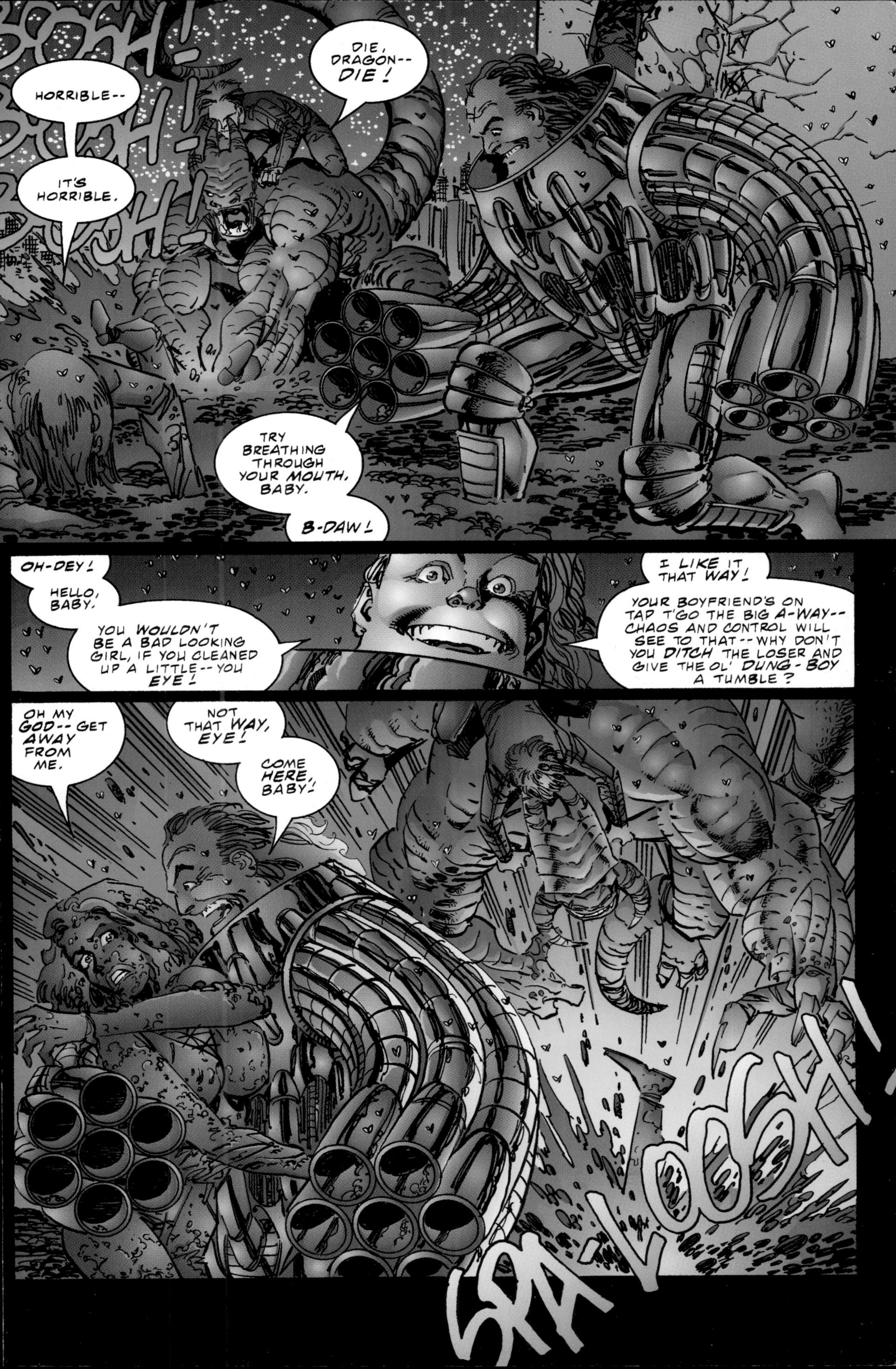

HORRIBLE--
IT'S HORRIBLE.
DIE, DRAGON-- DIE!
TRY BREATHING THROUGH YOUR MOUTH, BABY.
B-DAW!
OH-DEY!
HELLO, BABY.
YOU WOULDN'T BE A BAD LOOKING GIRL, IF YOU CLEANED UP A LITTLE-- YOU EYE!
I LIKE IT THAT WAY!
YOUR BOYFRIEND'S ON TAP T'GO THE BIG A-WAY-- CHAOS AND CONTROL WILL SEE TO THAT-- WHY DON'T YOU DITCH THE LOSER AND GIVE THE OL' DUNG-BOY A TUMBLE?
OH MY GOD-- GET AWAY FROM ME.
NOT THAT WAY, EYE!
COME HERE, BABY!

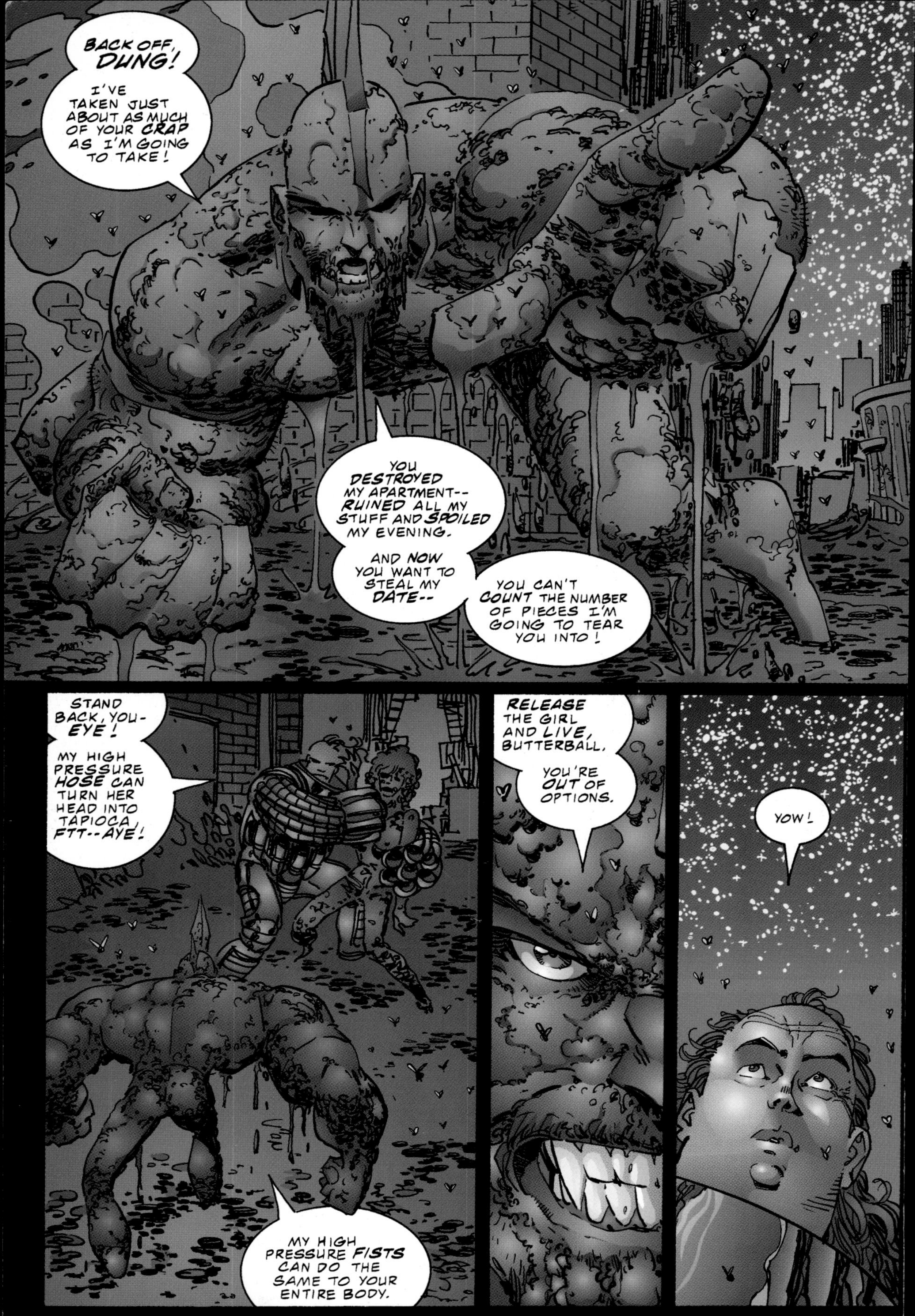
BACK OFF, DUNG!
I'VE TAKEN JUST ABOUT AS MUCH OF YOUR CRAP AS I'M GOING TO TAKE!
YOU DESTROYED MY APARTMENT-- RUINED ALL MY STUFF AND SPOILED MY EVENING.
AND NOW YOU WANT TO STEAL MY DATE--
YOU CAN'T COUNT THE NUMBER OF PIECES I'M GOING TO TEAR YOU INTO!
STAND BACK, YOU-EYE!
MY HIGH PRESSURE HOSE CAN TURN HER HEAD INTO TAPIOCA, FTT--AYE!
MY HIGH PRESSURE FISTS CAN DO THE SAME TO YOUR ENTIRE BODY.
RELEASE THE GIRL AND LIVE, BUTTERBALL.
YOU'RE OUT OF OPTIONS.
YOW!

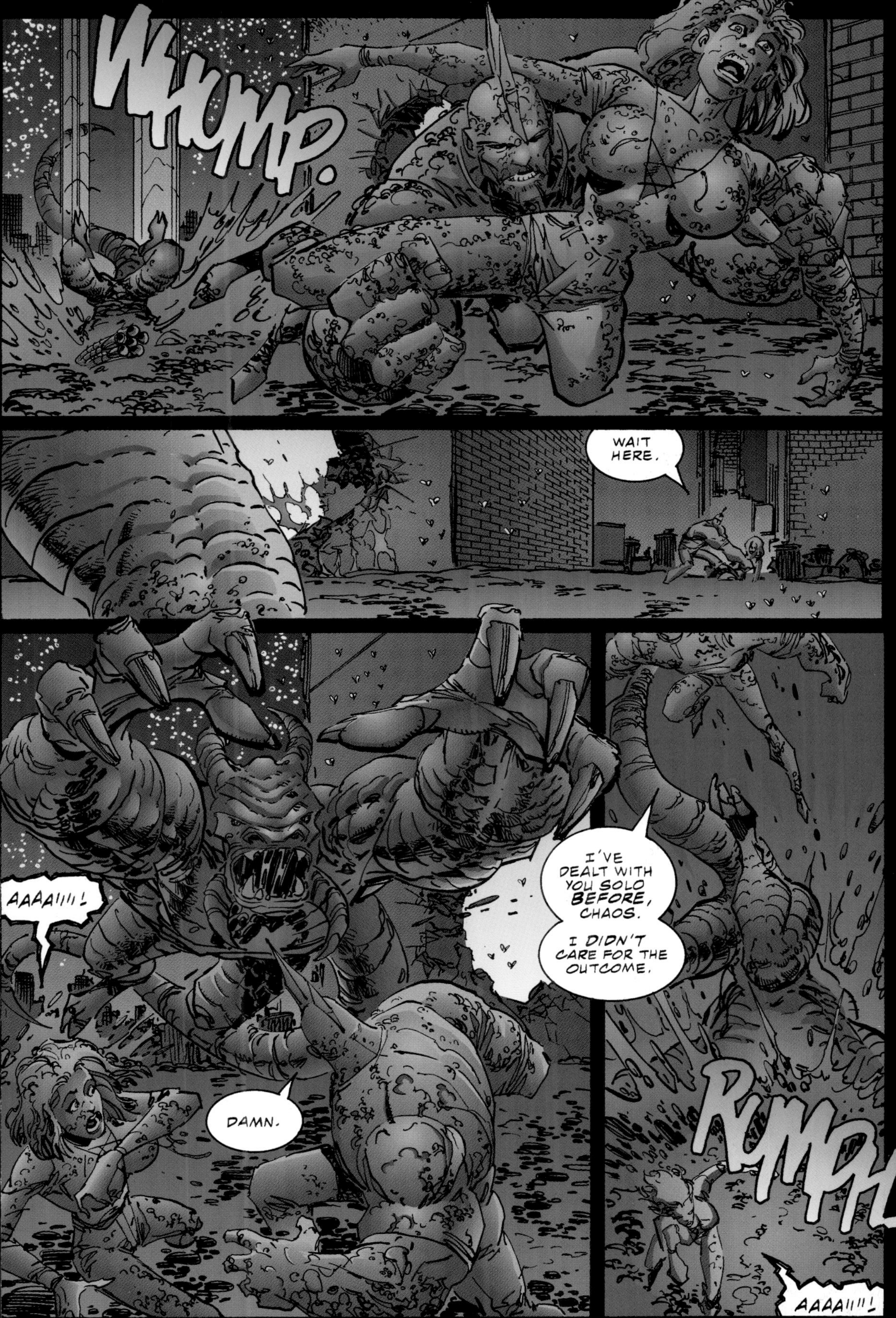
WHUMP!
WAIT HERE.
AAAAIIII!
I'VE DEALT WITH YOU SOLO BEFORE, CHAOS.
I DIDN'T CARE FOR THE OUTCOME.
DAMN.
RUMPH!
AAAAIIII!

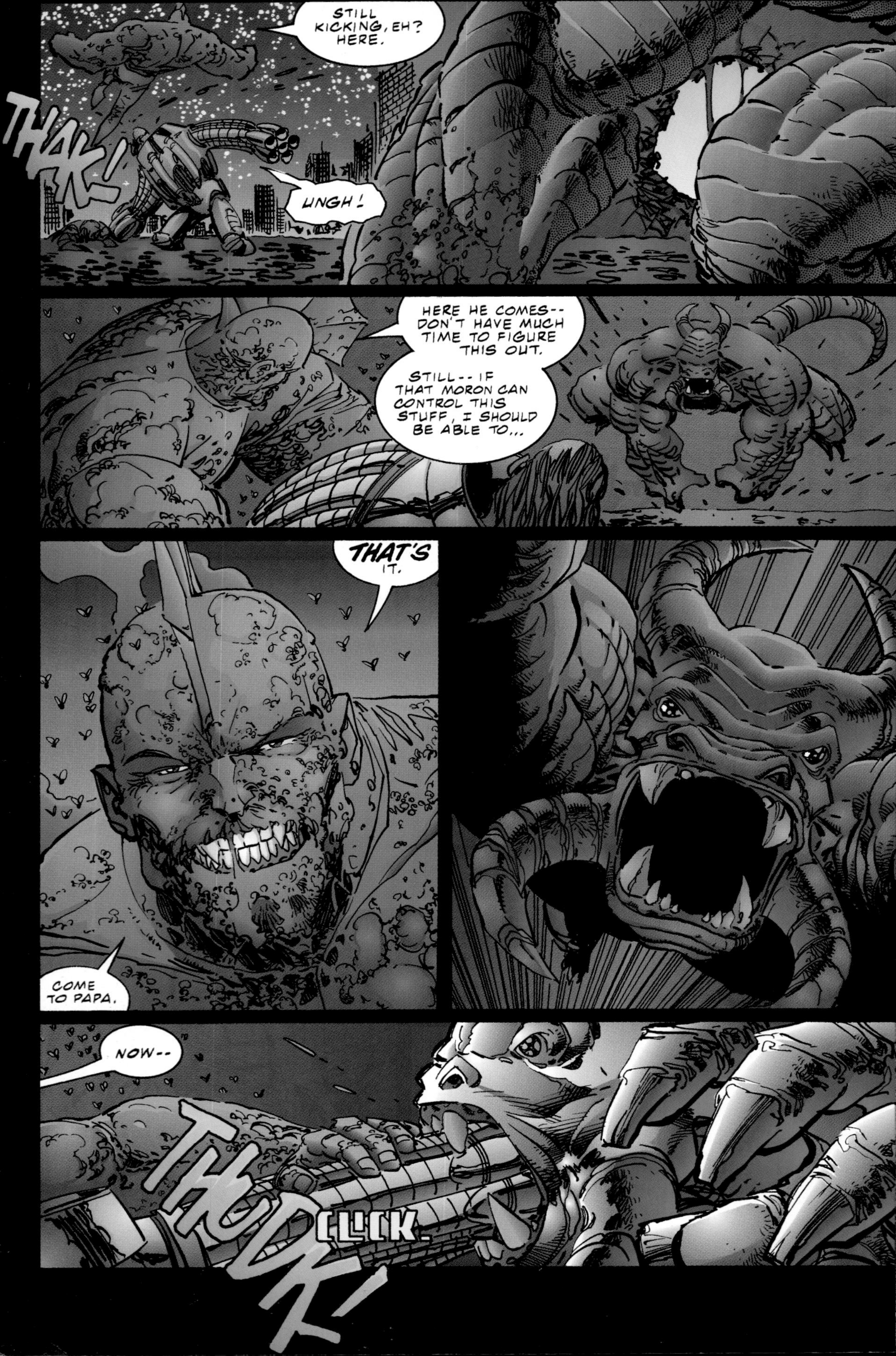
STILL KICKING, EH? HERE.
THAK!
UNGH!
HERE HE COMES-- DON'T HAVE MUCH TIME TO FIGURE THIS OUT.
STILL-- IF THAT MORON CAN CONTROL THIS STUFF, I SHOULD BE ABLE TO...
THAT'S IT.
COME TO PAPA.
NOW--
THUNK!
CLICK.

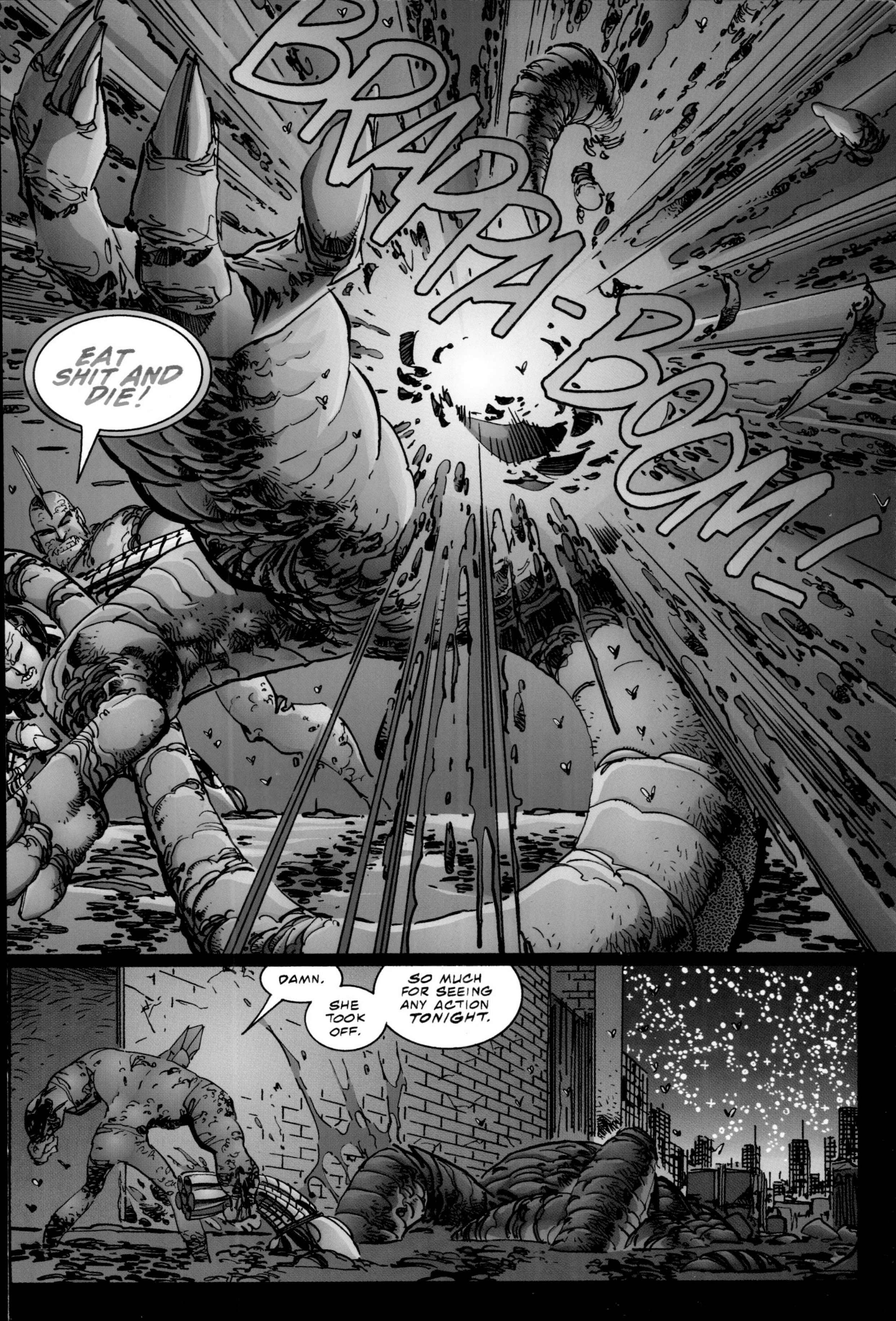
BRAPA-BOOM!!
EAT SHIT AND DIE!
DAMN.
SHE TOOK OFF.
SO MUCH FOR SEEING ANY ACTION TONIGHT.

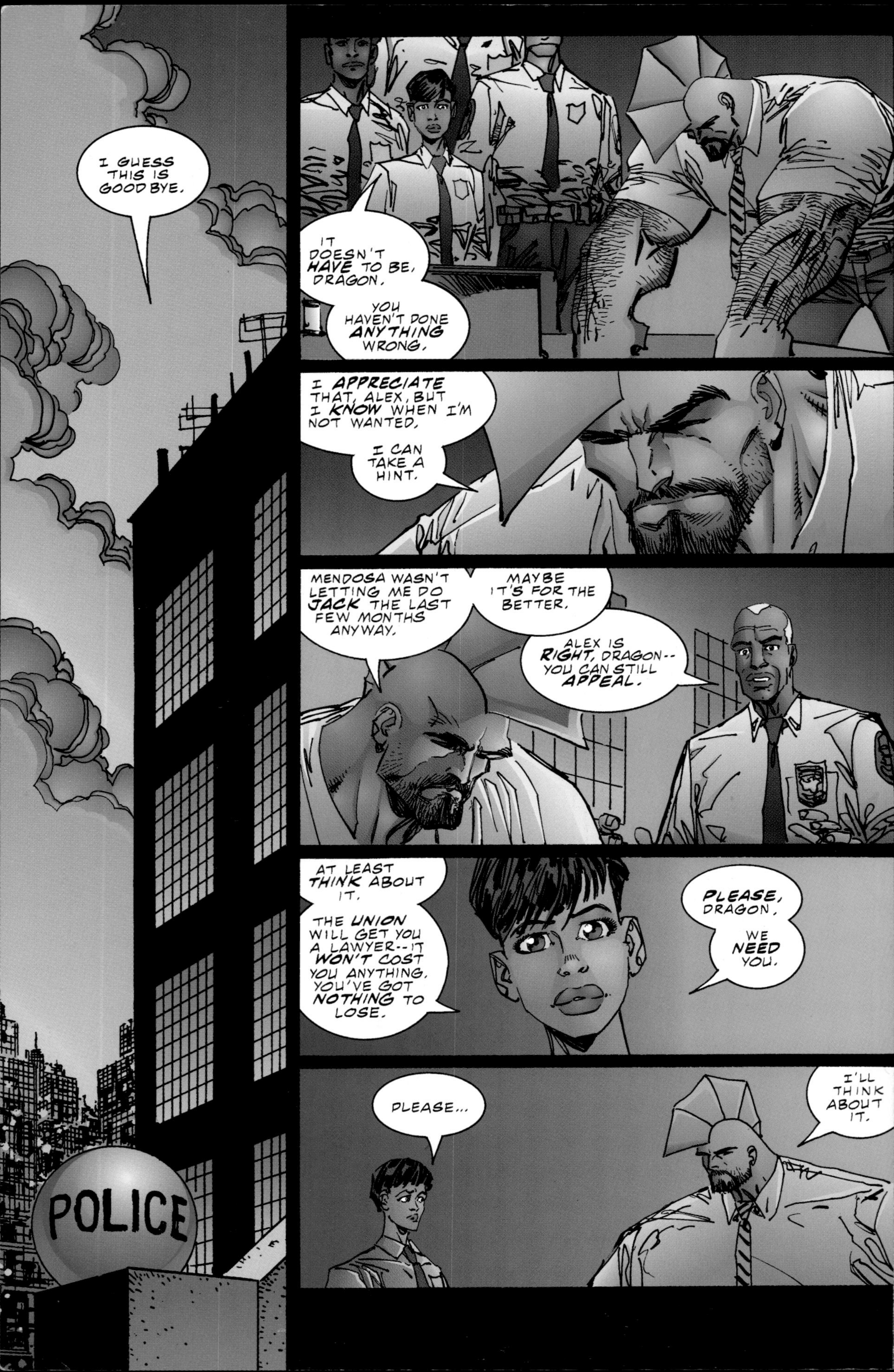
I GUESS THIS IS GOODBYE.
IT DOESN'T HAVE TO BE, DRAGON.
YOU HAVEN'T DONE ANYTHING WRONG.
I APPRECIATE THAT, ALEX, BUT I KNOW WHEN I'M NOT WANTED.
I CAN TAKE A HINT.
MENDOSA WASN'T LETTING ME DO JACK THE LAST FEW MONTHS ANYWAY.
MAYBE IT'S FOR THE BETTER.
ALEX IS RIGHT, DRAGON-- YOU CAN STILL APPEAL.
AT LEAST THINK ABOUT IT.
THE UNION WILL GET YOU A LAWYER--IT WON'T COST YOU ANYTHING. YOU'VE GOT NOTHING TO LOSE.
PLEASE, DRAGON.
WE NEED YOU.
PLEASE...
I'LL THINK ABOUT IT.
POLICE

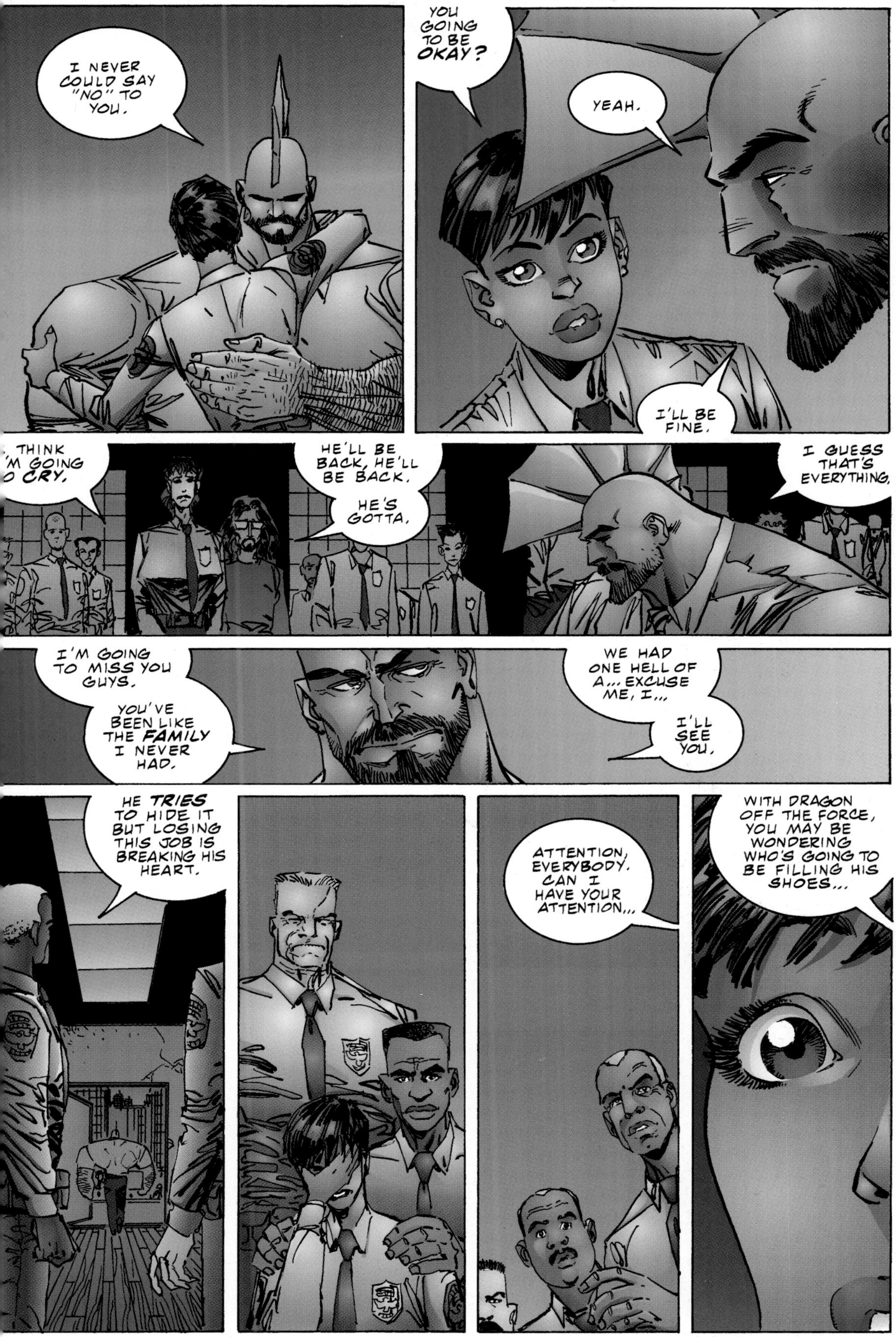
I NEVER COULD SAY "NO" TO YOU.
YOU GOING TO BE OKAY?
YEAH.
I'LL BE FINE.
THINK 'M GOING O CRY.
HE'LL BE BACK, HE'LL BE BACK.
HE'S GOTTA.
I GUESS THAT'S EVERYTHING.
I'M GOING TO MISS YOU GUYS.
YOU'VE BEEN LIKE THE FAMILY I NEVER HAD.
WE HAD ONE HELL OF A... EXCUSE ME, I...
I'LL SEE YOU.
HE TRIES TO HIDE IT BUT LOSING THIS JOB IS BREAKING HIS HEART.
ATTENTION, EVERYBODY. CAN I HAVE YOUR ATTENTION...
WITH DRAGON OFF THE FORCE, YOU MAY BE WONDERING WHO'S GOING TO BE FILLING HIS SHOES...

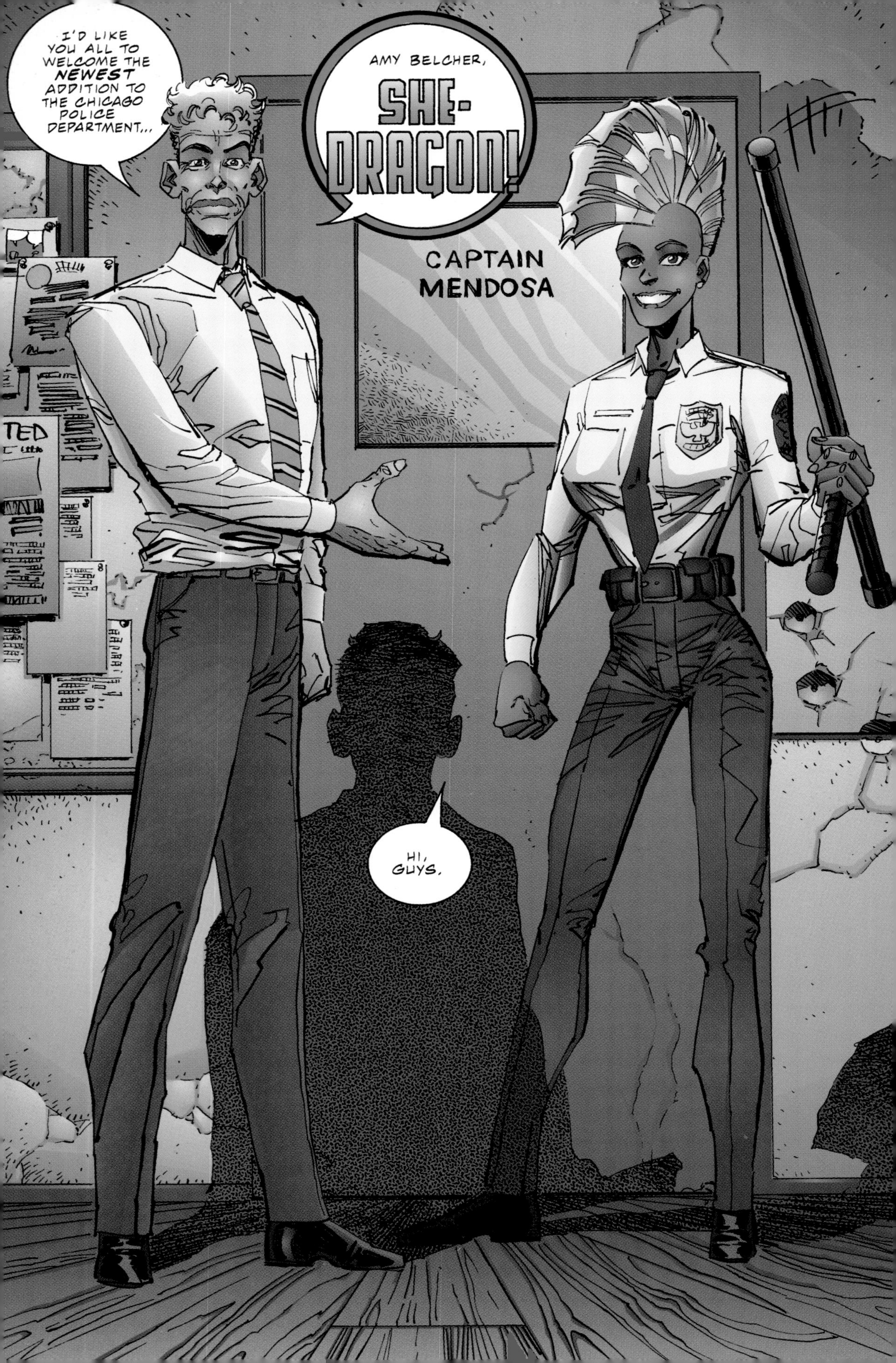
I'D LIKE YOU ALL TO WELCOME THE NEWEST ADDITION TO THE CHICAGO POLICE DEPARTMENT...
AMY BELCHER, SHE-DRAGON!
CAPTAIN MENDOSA
HI, GUYS.

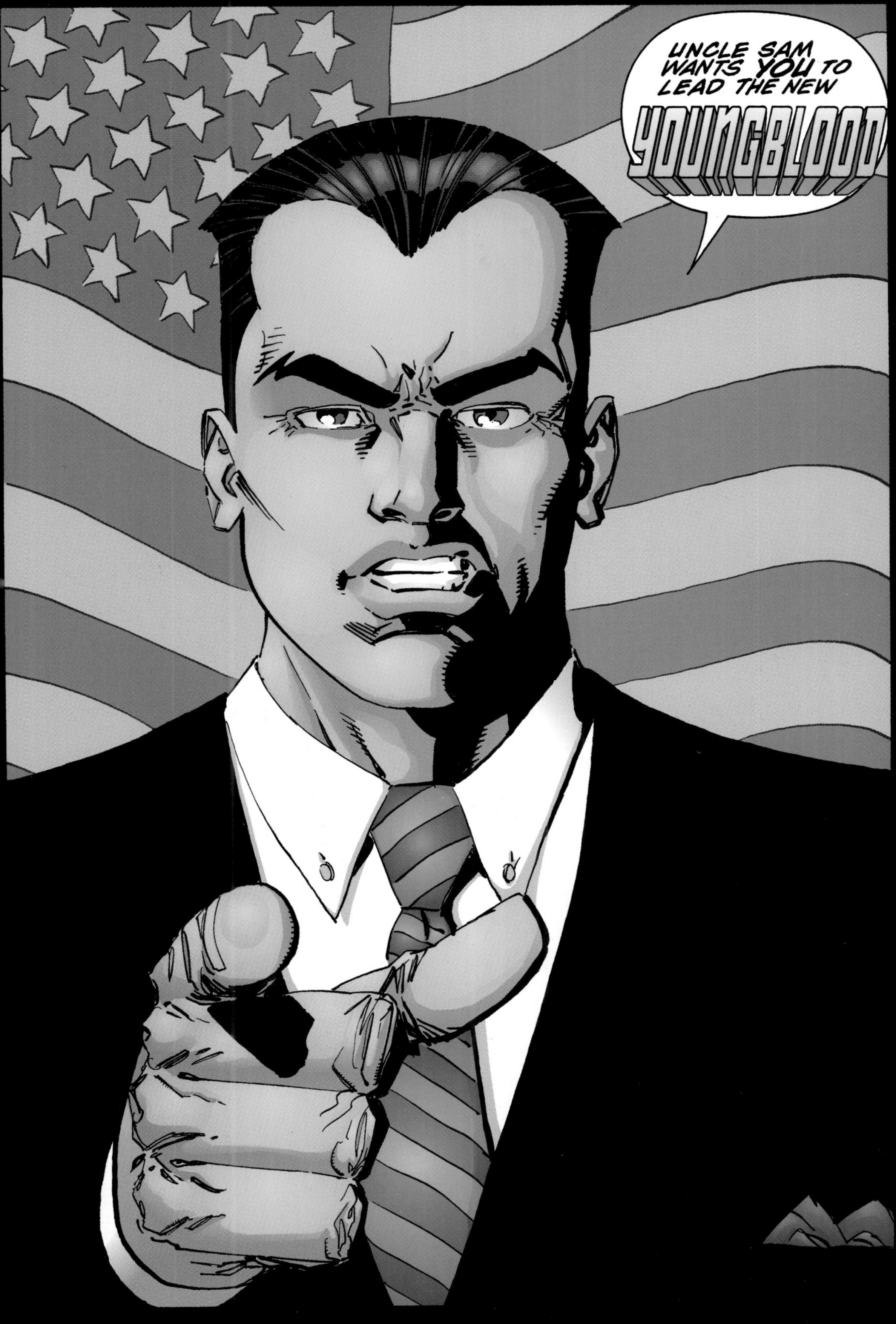
UNCLE SAM WANTS YOU TO LEAD THE NEW
YOUNGBLOOD

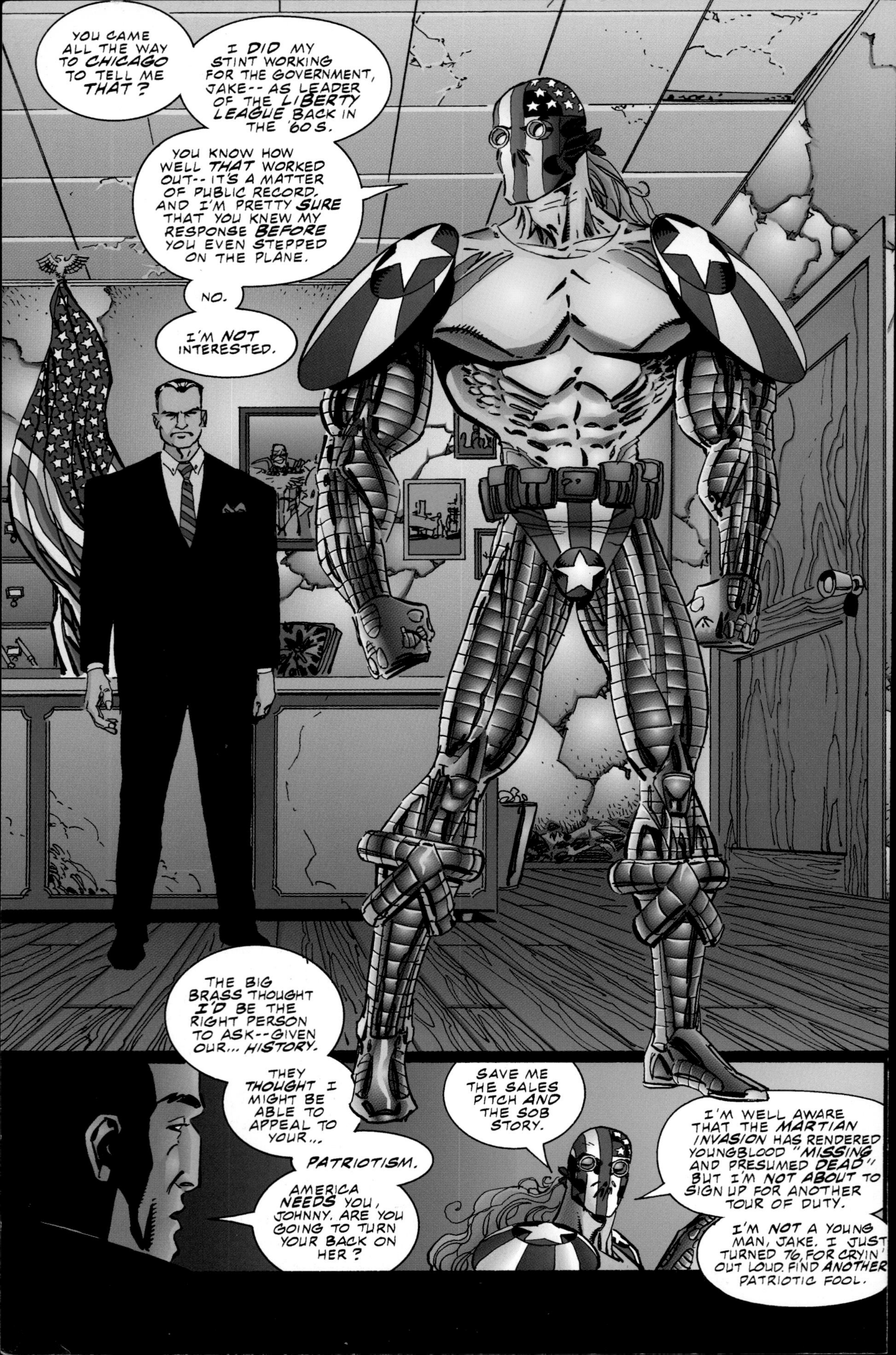
YOU CAME ALL THE WAY TO CHICAGO TO TELL ME THAT?
I DID MY STINT WORKING FOR THE GOVERNMENT, JAKE-- AS LEADER OF THE LIBERTY LEAGUE BACK IN THE '60S.
YOU KNOW HOW WELL THAT WORKED OUT-- IT'S A MATTER OF PUBLIC RECORD. AND I'M PRETTY SURE THAT YOU KNEW MY RESPONSE BEFORE YOU EVEN STEPPED ON THE PLANE.
NO.
I'M NOT INTERESTED.
THE BIG BRASS THOUGHT I'D BE THE RIGHT PERSON TO ASK--GIVEN OUR... HISTORY.
THEY THOUGHT I MIGHT BE ABLE TO APPEAL TO YOUR...
PATRIOTISM.
AMERICA NEEDS YOU, JOHNNY. ARE YOU GOING TO TURN YOUR BACK ON HER?
SAVE ME THE SALES PITCH AND THE SOB STORY.
I'M WELL AWARE THAT THE MARTIAN INVASION HAS RENDERED YOUNGBLOOD "MISSING AND PRESUMED DEAD," BUT I'M NOT ABOUT TO SIGN UP FOR ANOTHER TOUR OF DUTY.
I'M NOT A YOUNG MAN, JAKE. I JUST TURNED 76, FOR CRYIN' OUT LOUD. FIND ANOTHER PATRIOTIC FOOL.

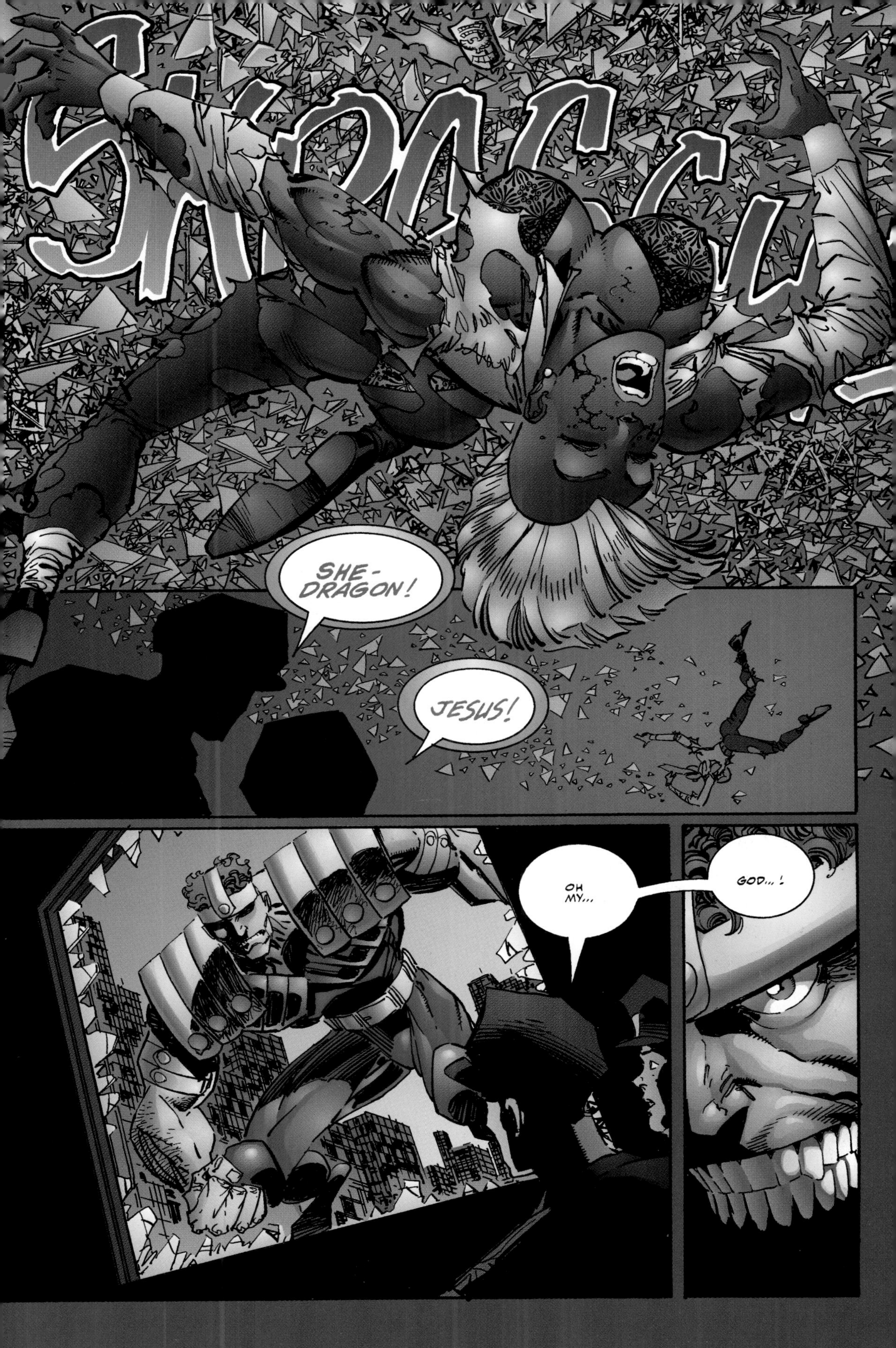
SHE-
DRAGON!
JESUS!
OH
MY...
GOD...!

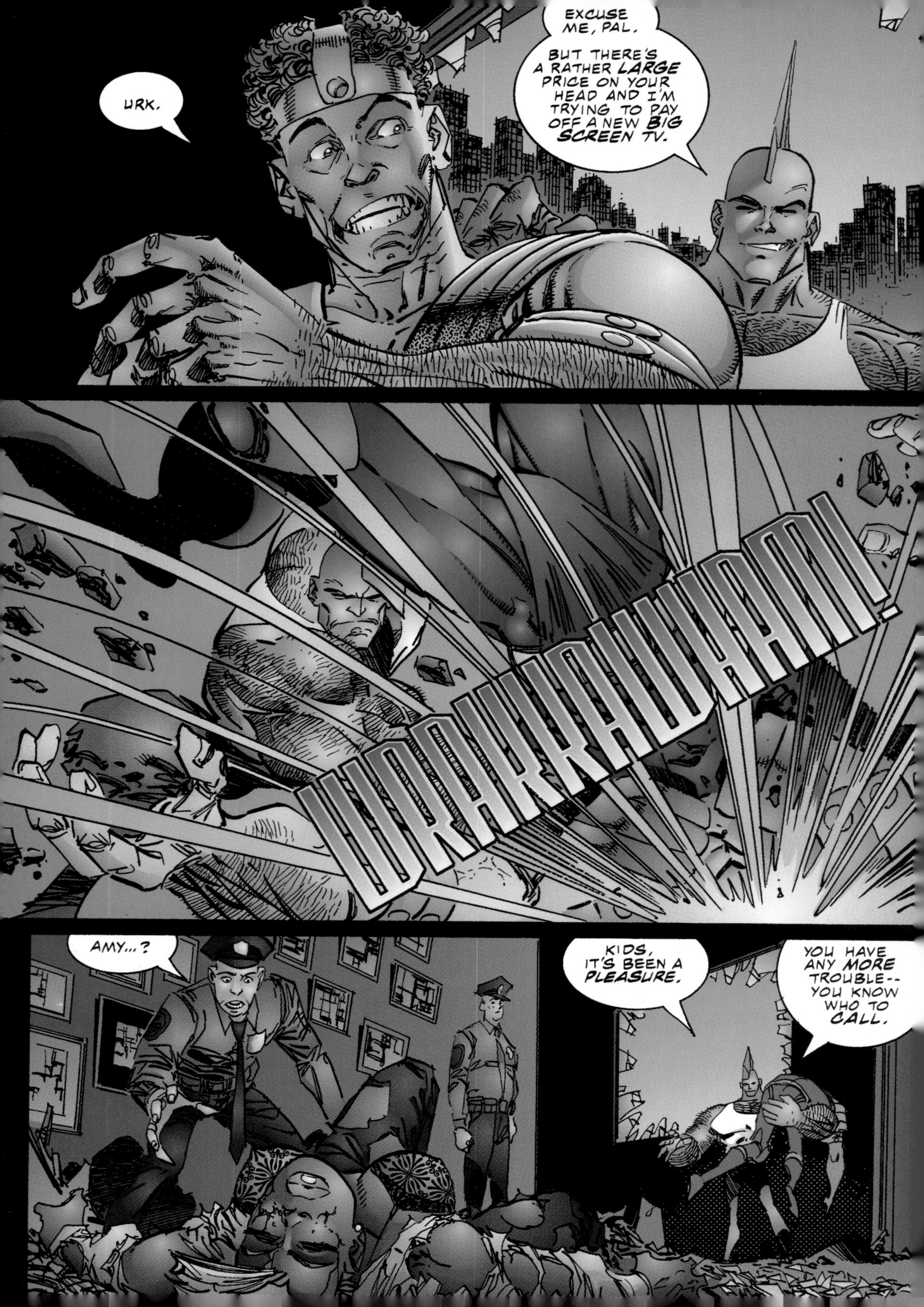
URK.
EXCUSE ME, PAL. BUT THERE'S A RATHER LARGE PRICE ON YOUR HEAD AND I'M TRYING TO PAY OFF A NEW BIG SCREEN TV.
DRAKKAWAM!
AMY...?
KIDS, IT'S BEEN A PLEASURE.
YOU HAVE ANY MORE TROUBLE-- YOU KNOW WHO TO CALL.

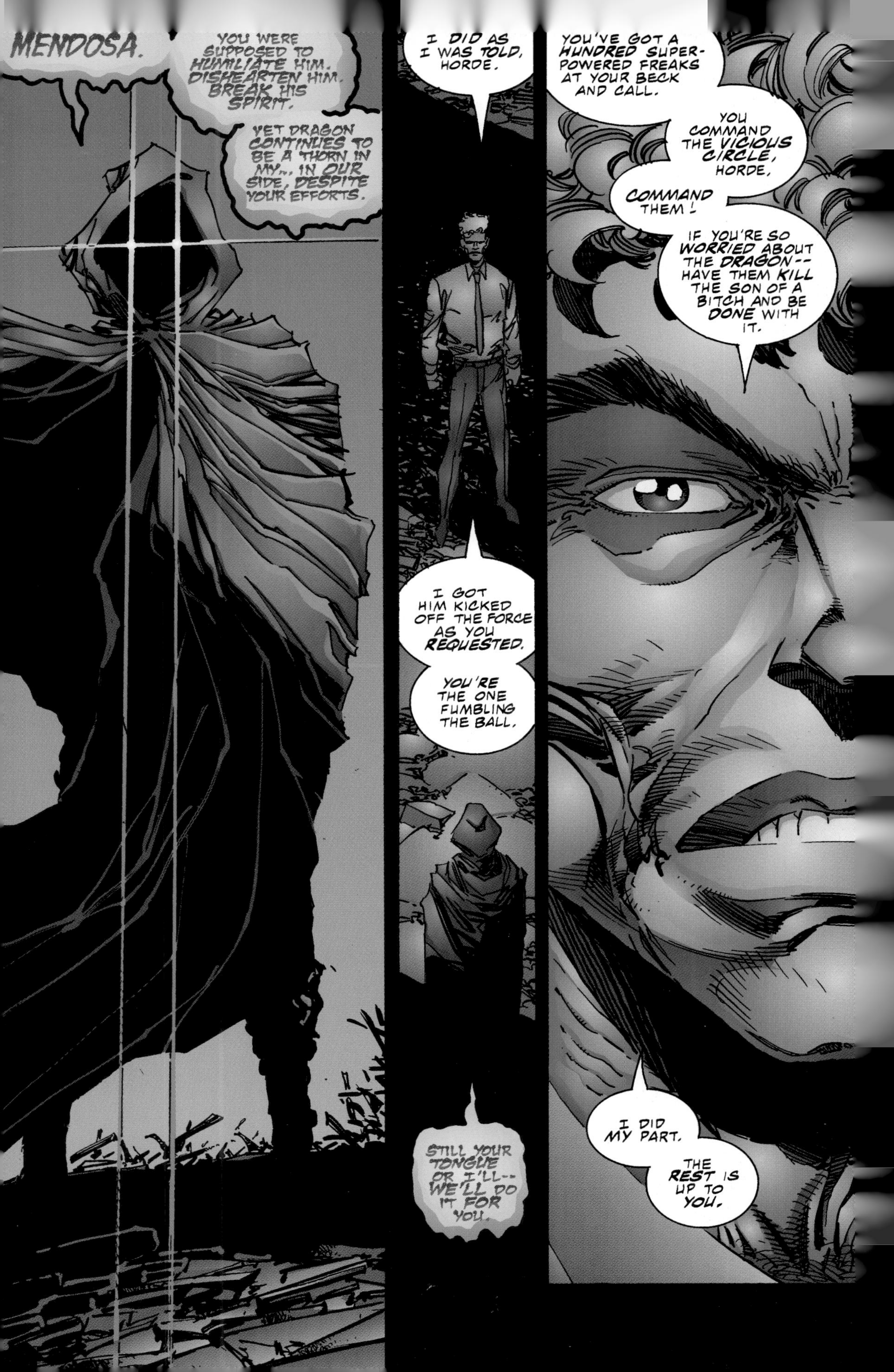
MENDOSA.
YOU WERE SUPPOSED TO HUMILIATE HIM. DISHEARTEN HIM. BREAK HIS SPIRIT.
YET DRAGON CONTINUES TO BE A THORN IN MY... IN OUR SIDE, DESPITE YOUR EFFORTS.
I DID AS I WAS TOLD, HORDE.
I GOT HIM KICKED OFF THE FORCE AS YOU REQUESTED.
YOU'RE THE ONE FUMBLING THE BALL.
STILL YOUR TONGUE OR I'LL-- WE'LL DO IT FOR YOU.
YOU'VE GOT A HUNDRED SUPER-POWERED FREAKS AT YOUR BECK AND CALL.
YOU COMMAND THE VICIOUS CIRCLE, HORDE.
COMMAND THEM!
IF YOU'RE SO WORRIED ABOUT THE DRAGON--HAVE THEM KILL THE SON OF A BITCH AND BE DONE WITH IT.
I DID MY PART.
THE REST IS UP TO YOU.

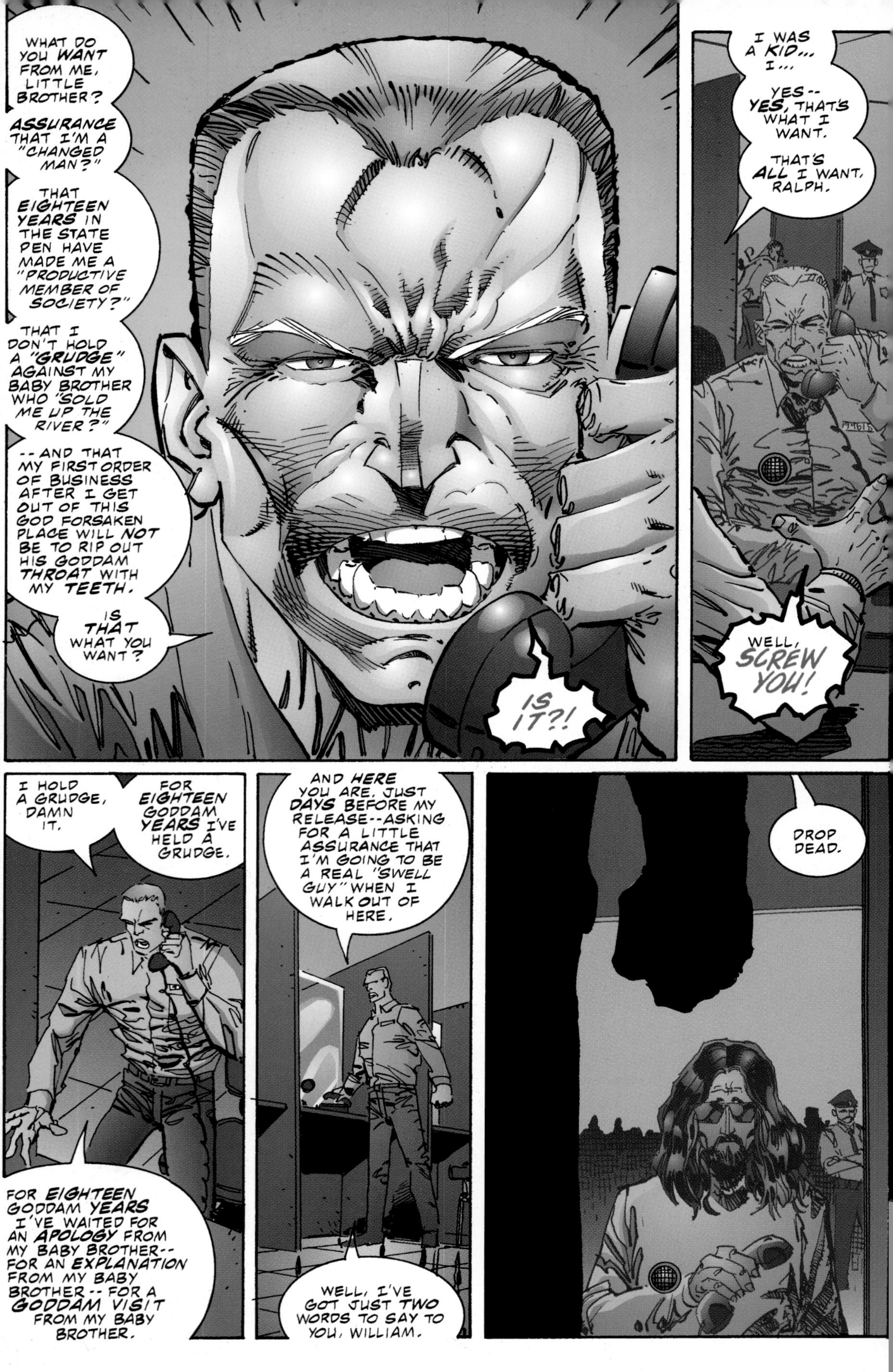
WHAT DO YOU WANT FROM ME, LITTLE BROTHER?
ASSURANCE THAT I'M A "CHANGED MAN?"
THAT EIGHTEEN YEARS IN THE STATE PEN HAVE MADE ME A "PRODUCTIVE MEMBER OF SOCIETY?"
THAT I DON'T HOLD A "GRUDGE" AGAINST MY BABY BROTHER WHO "SOLD ME UP THE RIVER?"
--AND THAT MY FIRST ORDER OF BUSINESS AFTER I GET OUT OF THIS GOD FORSAKEN PLACE WILL NOT BE TO RIP OUT HIS GODDAM THROAT WITH MY TEETH.
IS THAT WHAT YOU WANT?
IS IT?!
I WAS A KID... I...
YES-- YES, THAT'S WHAT I WANT.
THAT'S ALL I WANT, RALPH.
WELL, SCREW YOU!
I HOLD A GRUDGE, DAMN IT.
FOR EIGHTEEN GODDAM YEARS I'VE HELD A GRUDGE.
FOR EIGHTEEN GODDAM YEARS I'VE WAITED FOR AN APOLOGY FROM MY BABY BROTHER-- FOR AN EXPLANATION FROM MY BABY BROTHER-- FOR A GODDAM VISIT FROM MY BABY BROTHER.
AND HERE YOU ARE, JUST DAYS BEFORE MY RELEASE--ASKING FOR A LITTLE ASSURANCE THAT I'M GOING TO BE A REAL "SWELL GUY" WHEN I WALK OUT OF HERE.
WELL, I'VE GOT JUST TWO WORDS TO SAY TO YOU, WILLIAM.
DROP DEAD.

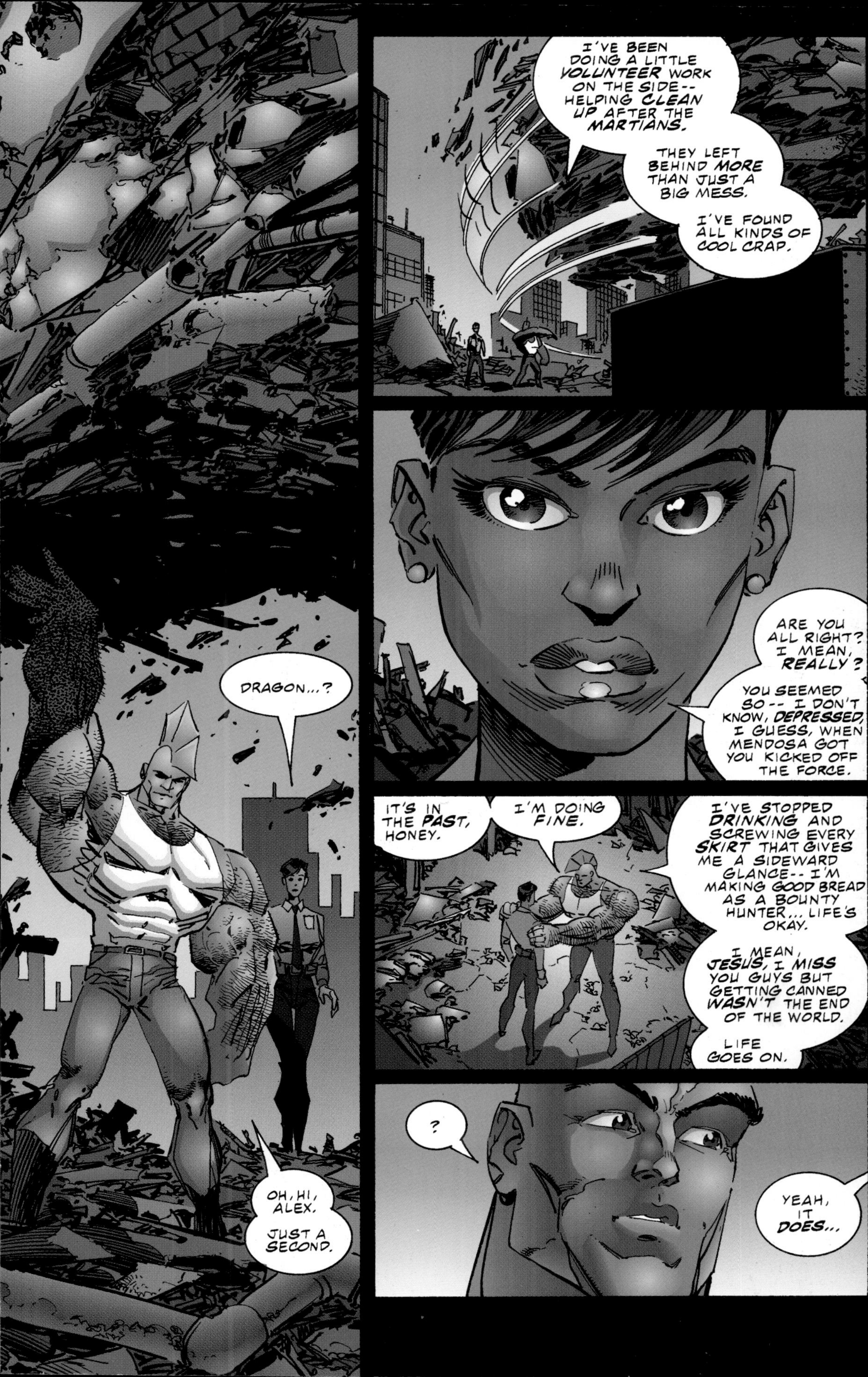
I'VE BEEN DOING A LITTLE VOLUNTEER WORK ON THE SIDE-- HELPING CLEAN UP AFTER THE MARTIANS.
THEY LEFT BEHIND MORE THAN JUST A BIG MESS.
I'VE FOUND ALL KINDS OF COOL CRAP.
DRAGON...?
OH, HI, ALEX.
JUST A SECOND.
ARE YOU ALL RIGHT? I MEAN, REALLY?
YOU SEEMED SO-- I DON'T KNOW, DEPRESSED, I GUESS, WHEN MENDOSA GOT YOU KICKED OFF THE FORCE.
IT'S IN THE PAST, HONEY.
I'M DOING FINE.
I'VE STOPPED DRINKING AND SCREWING EVERY SKIRT THAT GIVES ME A SIDEWARD GLANCE-- I'M MAKING GOOD BREAD AS A BOUNTY HUNTER... LIFE'S OKAY.
I MEAN, JESUS, I MISS YOU GUYS BUT GETTING CANNED WASN'T THE END OF THE WORLD.
LIFE GOES ON.
?
YEAH, IT DOES...

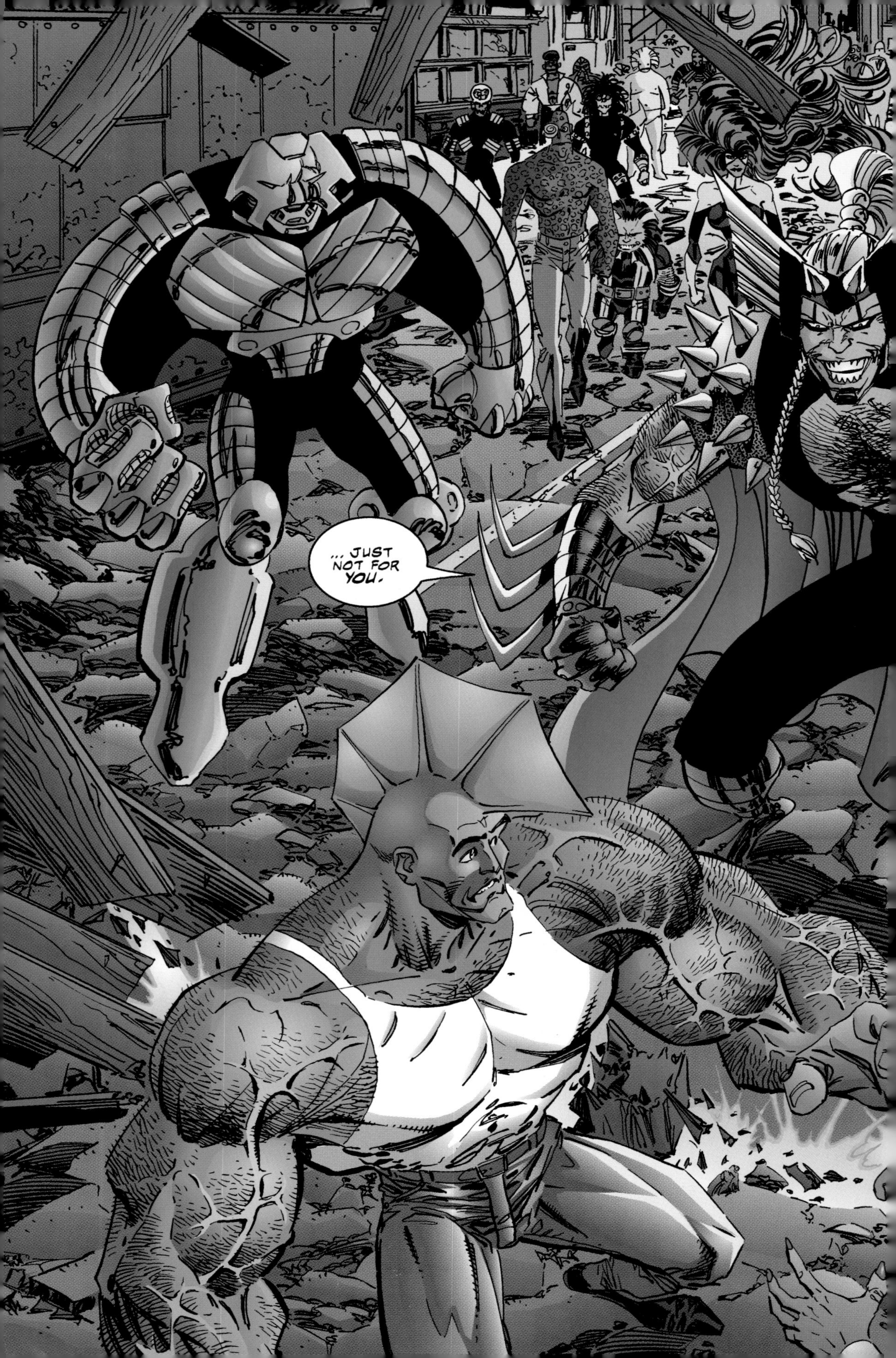
... JUST NOT FOR YOU.

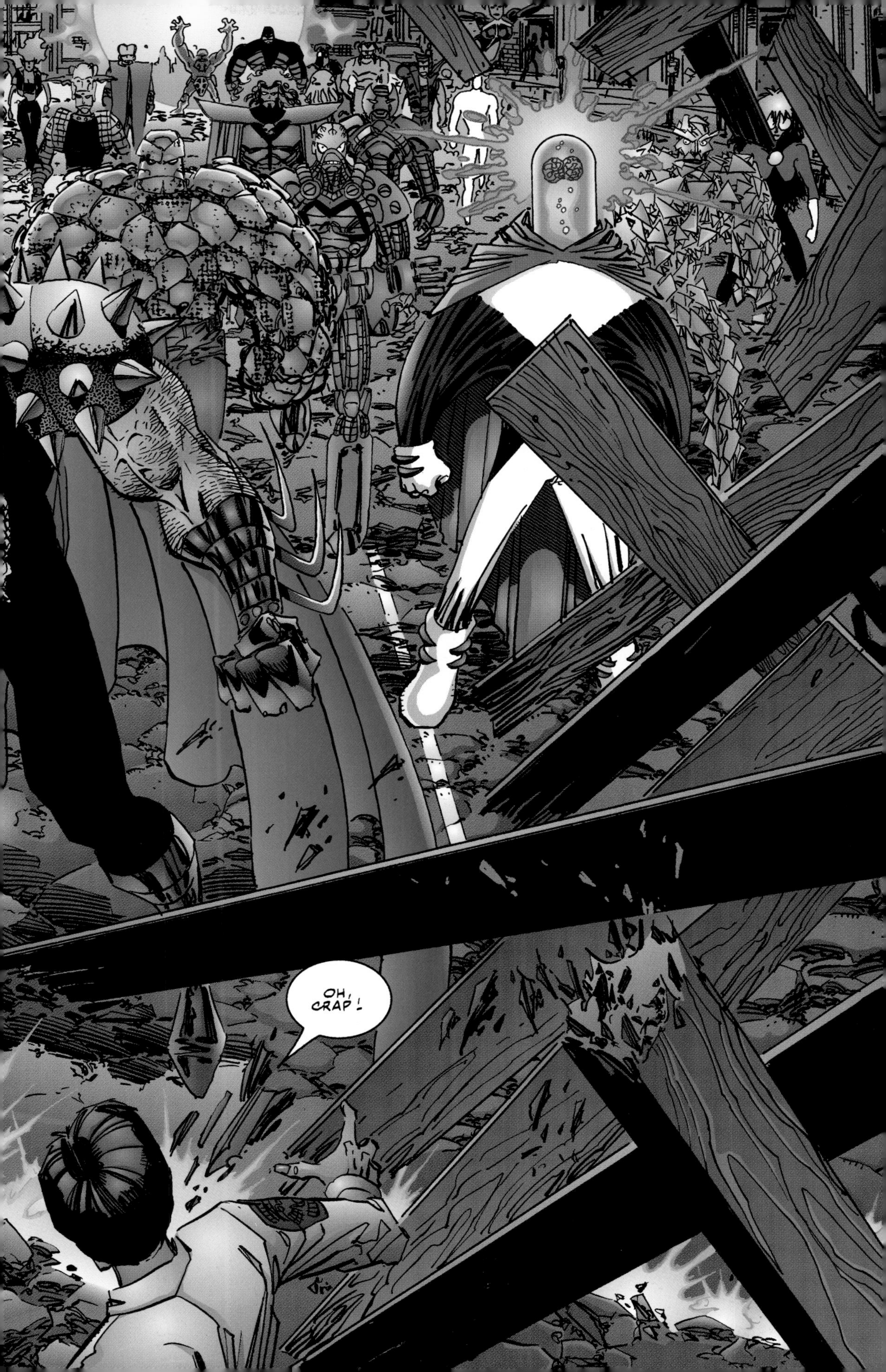
OH, CRAP!

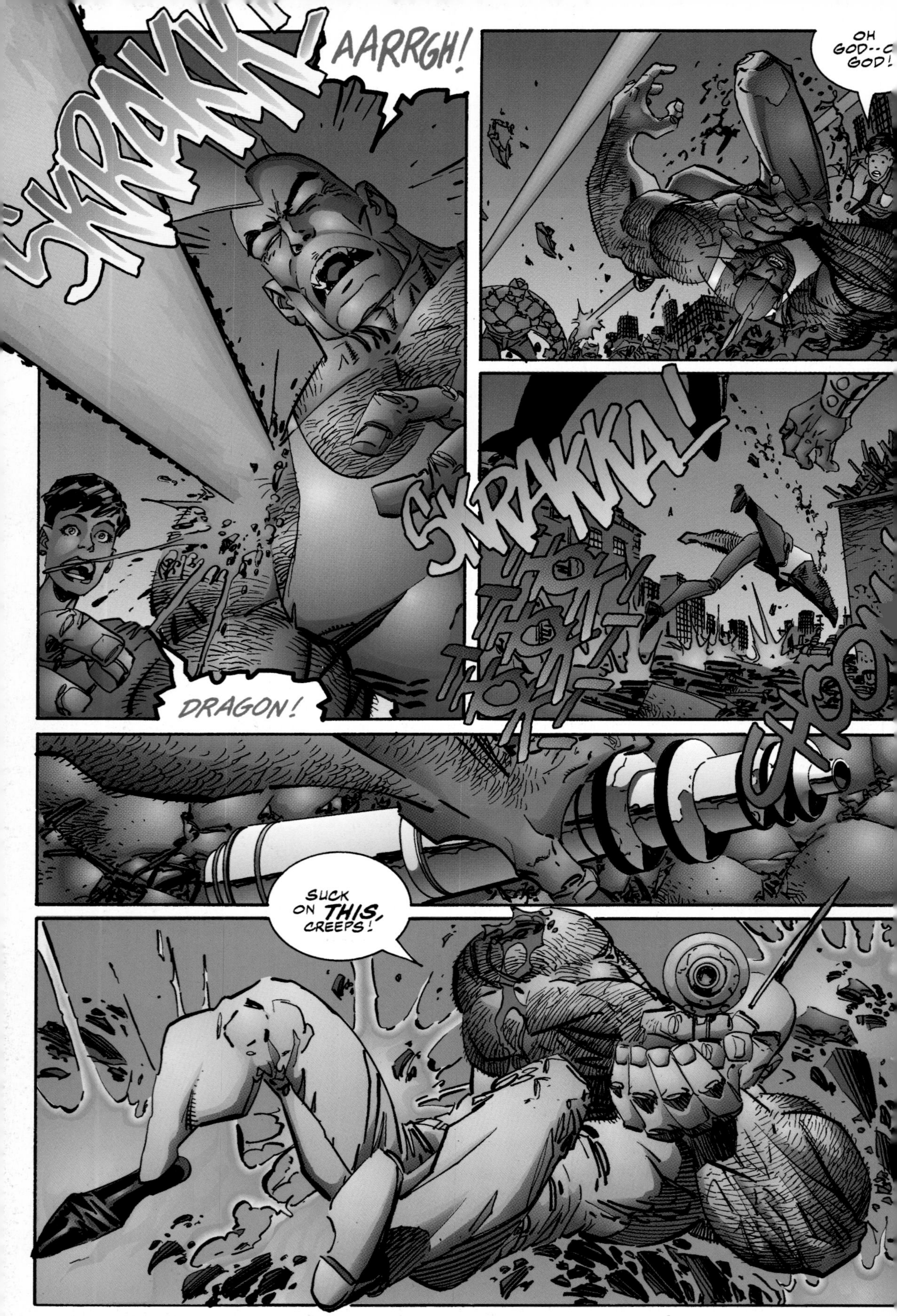
SKRAKK!
AARRGH!
DRAGON!
OH GOD--O GOD!
SKRAKKA!
THOK! THOK! THOK!
SUCK ON THIS, CREEPS!

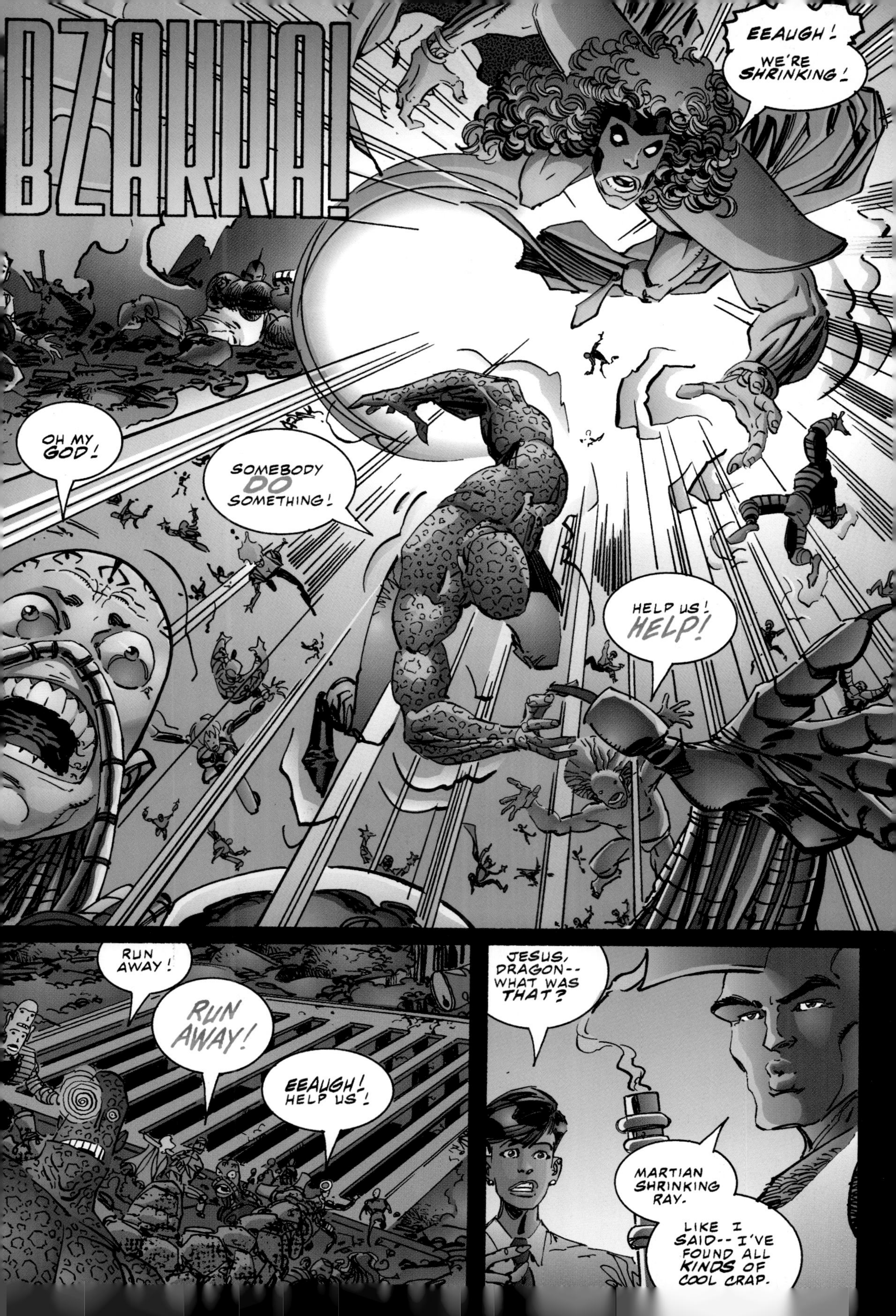
BZAKKA!
EEAUGH! WE'RE SHRINKING!
OH MY GOD!
SOMEBODY DO SOMETHING!
HELP US! HELP!
RUN AWAY!
RUN AWAY!
EEAUGH! HELP US!
JESUS, DRAGON-- WHAT WAS THAT?
MARTIAN SHRINKING RAY.
LIKE I SAID-- I'VE FOUND ALL KINDS OF COOL CRAP.

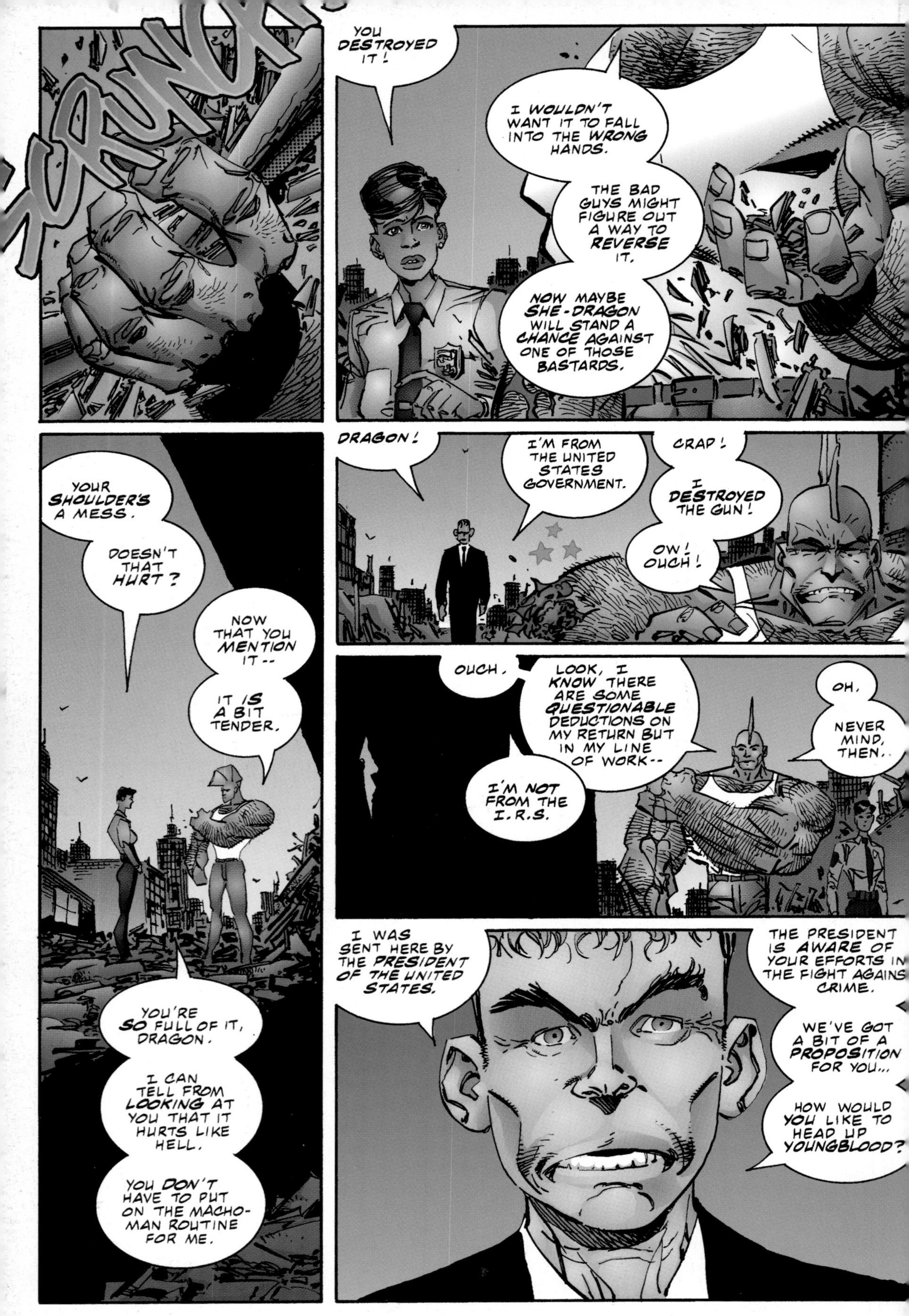

KRUNCH
YOU DESTROYED IT!
I WOULDN'T WANT IT TO FALL INTO THE WRONG HANDS.
THE BAD GUYS MIGHT FIGURE OUT A WAY TO REVERSE IT.
NOW MAYBE SHE-DRAGON WILL STAND A CHANCE AGAINST ONE OF THOSE BASTARDS.
YOUR SHOULDER'S A MESS.
DOESN'T THAT HURT?
NOW THAT YOU MENTION IT --
IT IS A BIT TENDER.
YOU'RE SO FULL OF IT, DRAGON.
I CAN TELL FROM LOOKING AT YOU THAT IT HURTS LIKE HELL.
YOU DON'T HAVE TO PUT ON THE MACHO-MAN ROUTINE FOR ME.
DRAGON!
I'M FROM THE UNITED STATES GOVERNMENT.
CRAP!
I DESTROYED THE GUN!
OW! OUCH!
OUCH.
LOOK, I KNOW THERE ARE SOME QUESTIONABLE DEDUCTIONS ON MY RETURN BUT IN MY LINE OF WORK--
I'M NOT FROM THE I.R.S.
OH.
NEVER MIND, THEN.
I WAS SENT HERE BY THE PRESIDENT OF THE UNITED STATES.
THE PRESIDENT IS AWARE OF YOUR EFFORTS IN THE FIGHT AGAINS CRIME.
WE'VE GOT A BIT OF A PROPOSITION FOR YOU...
HOW WOULD YOU LIKE TO HEAD UP YOUNGBLOOD?

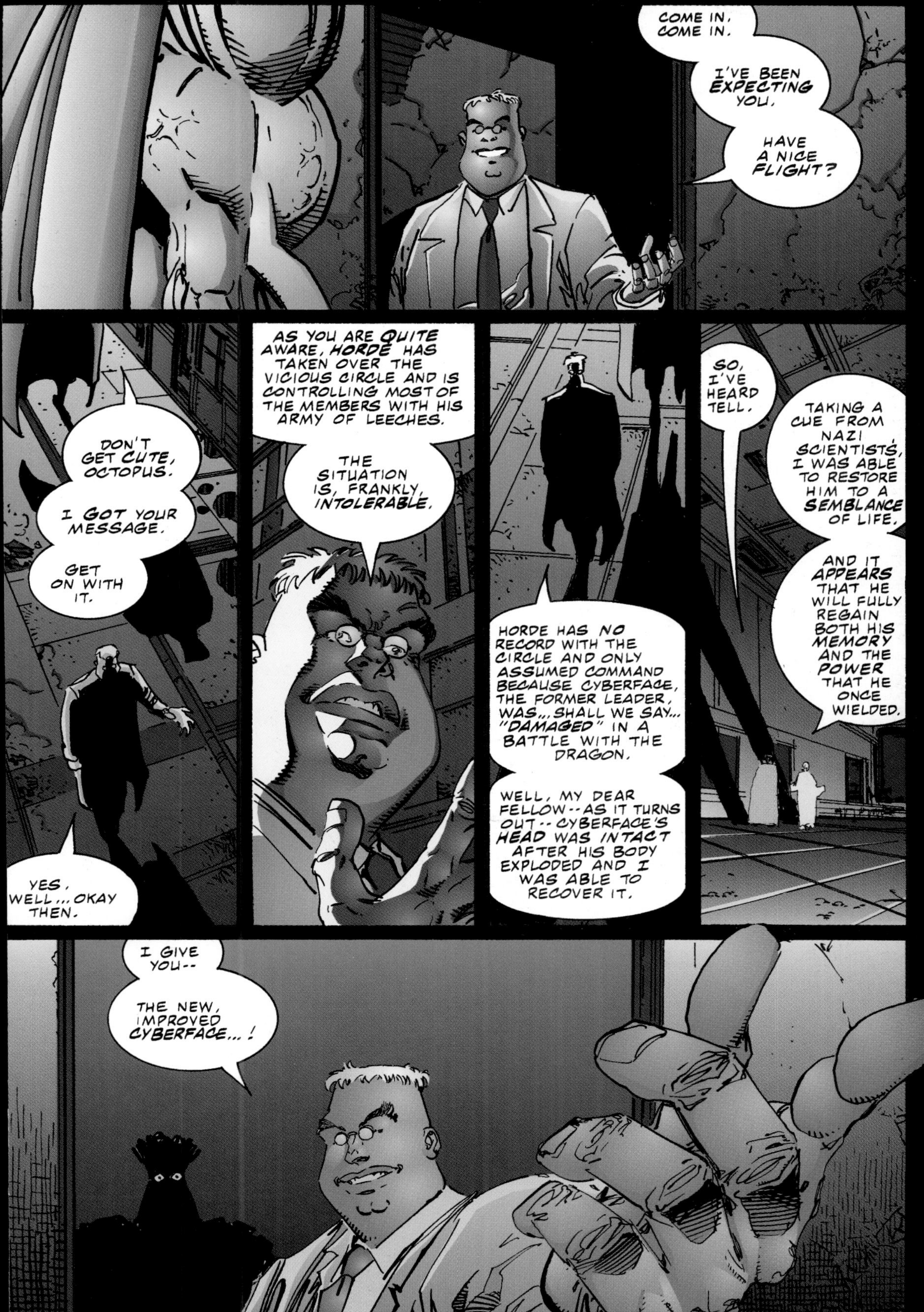

COME IN, COME IN.
I'VE BEEN EXPECTING YOU.
HAVE A NICE FLIGHT?
DON'T GET CUTE, OCTOPUS.
I GOT YOUR MESSAGE.
GET ON WITH IT.
YES. WELL... OKAY THEN.
AS YOU ARE QUITE AWARE, HORDE HAS TAKEN OVER THE VICIOUS CIRCLE AND IS CONTROLLING MOST OF THE MEMBERS WITH HIS ARMY OF LEECHES.
THE SITUATION IS, FRANKLY, INTOLERABLE.
SO, I'VE HEARD TELL.
HORDE HAS NO RECORD WITH THE CIRCLE AND ONLY ASSUMED COMMAND BECAUSE CYBERFACE, THE FORMER LEADER, WAS... SHALL WE SAY... "DAMAGED" IN A BATTLE WITH THE DRAGON.
WELL, MY DEAR FELLOW--AS IT TURNS OUT--CYBERFACE'S HEAD WAS INTACT AFTER HIS BODY EXPLODED AND I WAS ABLE TO RECOVER IT.
TAKING A CUE FROM NAZI SCIENTISTS, I WAS ABLE TO RESTORE HIM TO A SEMBLANCE OF LIFE.
AND IT APPEARS THAT HE WILL FULLY REGAIN BOTH HIS MEMORY AND THE POWER THAT HE ONCE WIELDED.
I GIVE YOU--
THE NEW, IMPROVED CYBERFACE...!

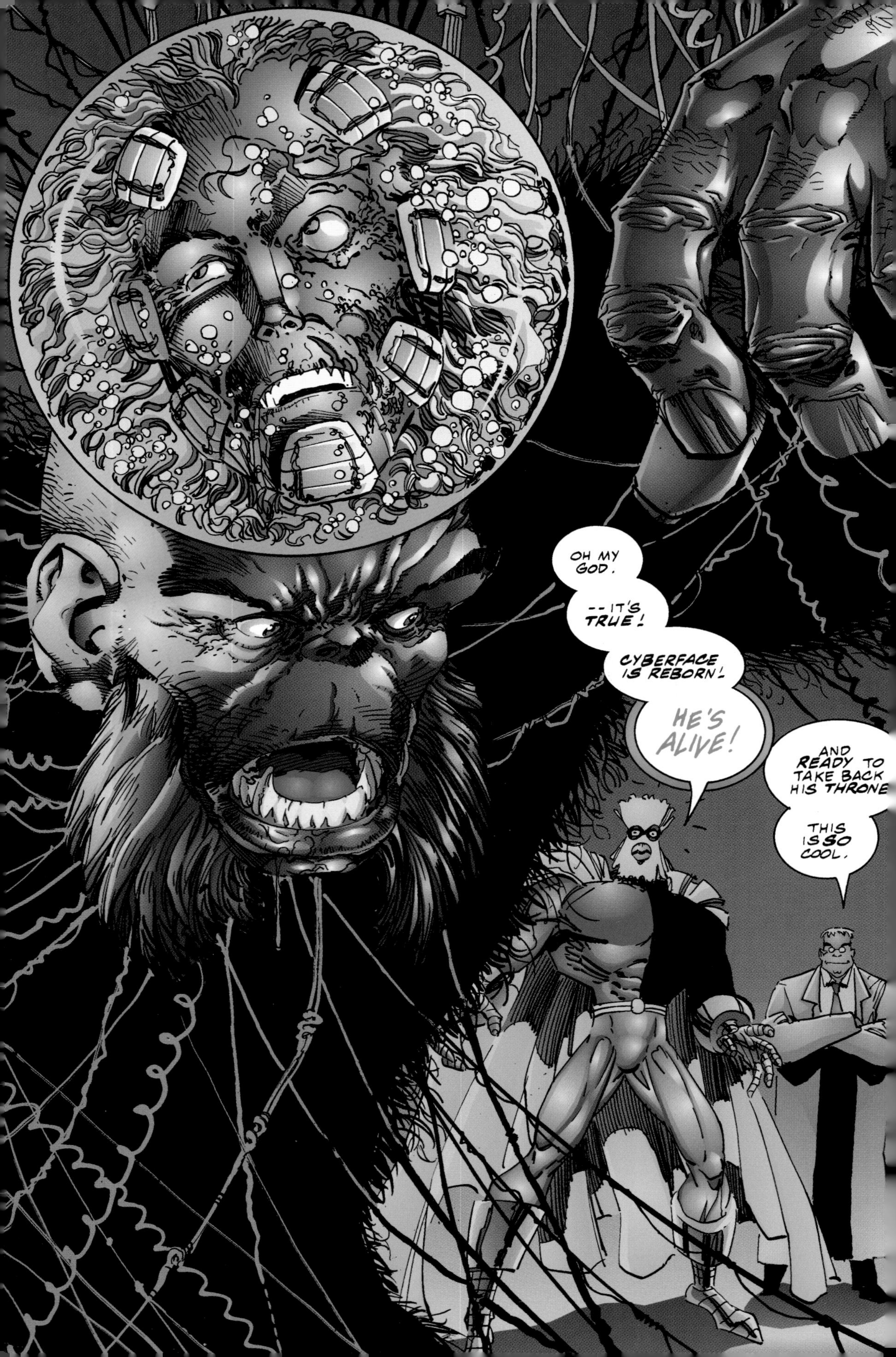
OH MY GOD.
-- IT'S TRUE!
CYBERFACE IS REBORN!
HE'S ALIVE!
AND READY TO TAKE BACK HIS THRONE
THIS IS SO COOL.

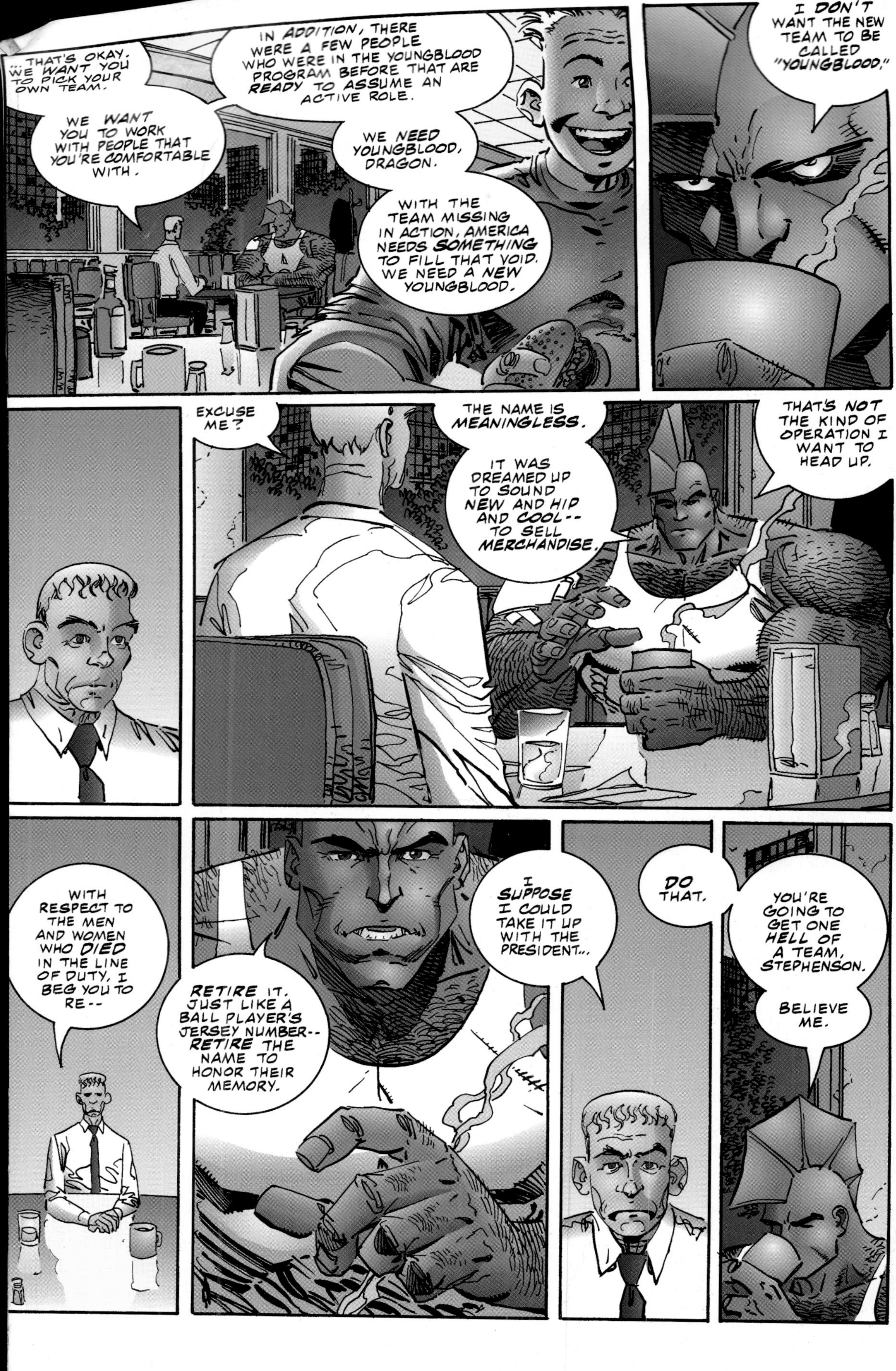
...THAT'S OKAY. WE WANT YOU TO PICK YOUR OWN TEAM.
WE WANT YOU TO WORK WITH PEOPLE THAT YOU'RE COMFORTABLE WITH.
IN ADDITION, THERE WERE A FEW PEOPLE WHO WERE IN THE YOUNGBLOOD PROGRAM BEFORE THAT ARE READY TO ASSUME AN ACTIVE ROLE.
WE NEED YOUNGBLOOD, DRAGON.
WITH THE TEAM MISSING IN ACTION, AMERICA NEEDS SOMETHING TO FILL THAT VOID. WE NEED A NEW YOUNGBLOOD.
I DON'T WANT THE NEW TEAM TO BE CALLED "YOUNGBLOOD."
EXCUSE ME?
THE NAME IS MEANINGLESS.
IT WAS DREAMED UP TO SOUND NEW AND HIP AND COOL-- TO SELL MERCHANDISE.
THAT'S NOT THE KIND OF OPERATION I WANT TO HEAD UP.
WITH RESPECT TO THE MEN AND WOMEN WHO DIED IN THE LINE OF DUTY, I BEG YOU TO RE--
RETIRE IT. JUST LIKE A BALL PLAYER'S JERSEY NUMBER-- RETIRE THE NAME TO HONOR THEIR MEMORY.
I SUPPOSE I COULD TAKE IT UP WITH THE PRESIDENT...
DO THAT.
YOU'RE GOING TO GET ONE HELL OF A TEAM, STEPHENSON.
BELIEVE ME.

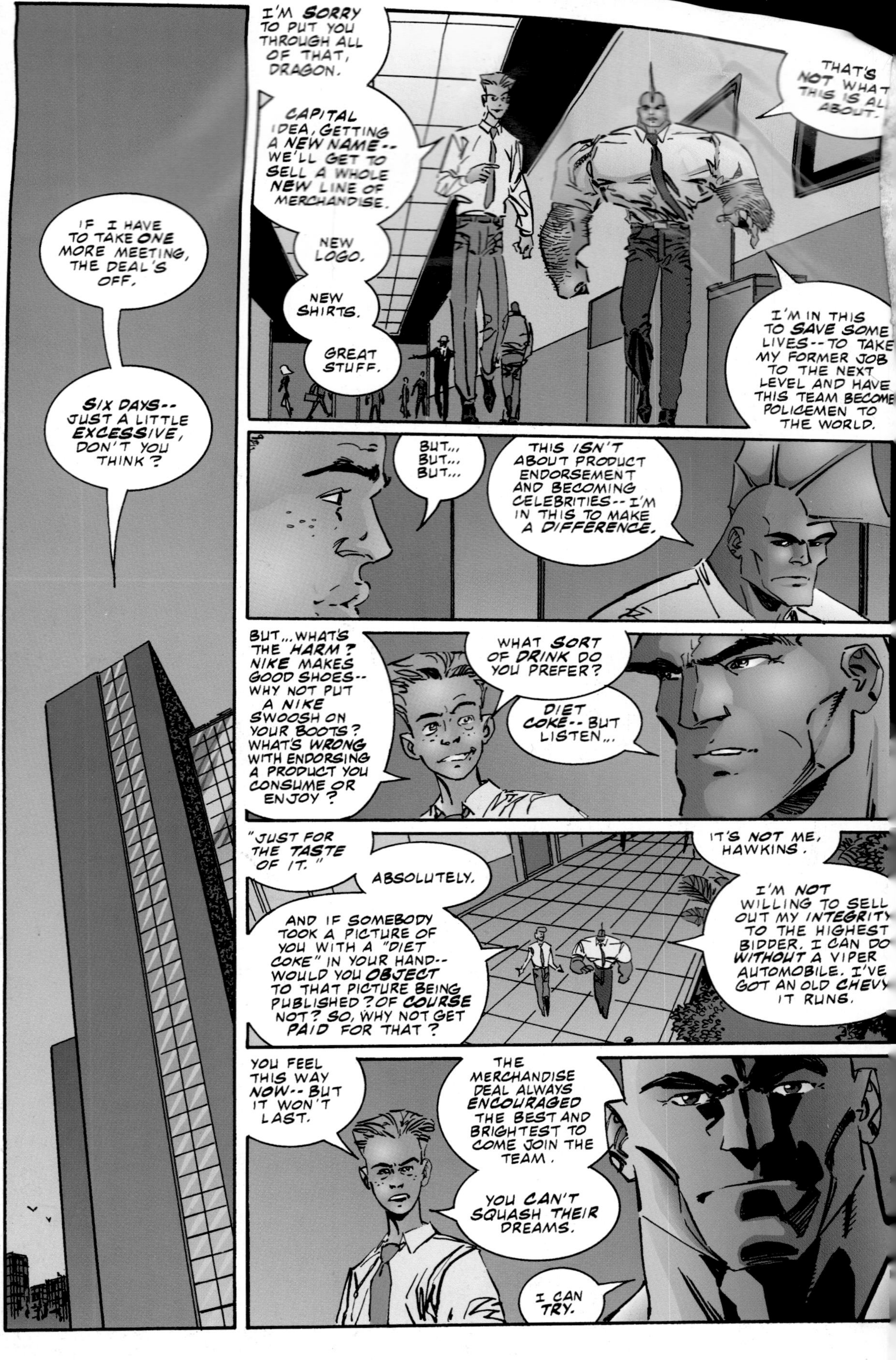
IF I HAVE TO TAKE ONE MORE MEETING, THE DEAL'S OFF.
SIX DAYS-- JUST A LITTLE EXCESSIVE, DON'T YOU THINK?
I'M SORRY TO PUT YOU THROUGH ALL OF THAT, DRAGON.
CAPITAL IDEA, GETTING A NEW NAME-- WE'LL GET TO SELL A WHOLE NEW LINE OF MERCHANDISE.
NEW LOGO.
NEW SHIRTS.
GREAT STUFF.
THAT'S NOT WHAT THIS IS ALL ABOUT.
I'M IN THIS TO SAVE SOME LIVES--TO TAKE MY FORMER JOB TO THE NEXT LEVEL AND HAVE THIS TEAM BECOME POLICEMEN TO THE WORLD.
BUT... BUT... BUT...
THIS ISN'T ABOUT PRODUCT ENDORSEMENT AND BECOMING CELEBRITIES-- I'M IN THIS TO MAKE A DIFFERENCE.
BUT... WHAT'S THE HARM? NIKE MAKES GOOD SHOES-- WHY NOT PUT A NIKE SWOOSH ON YOUR BOOTS? WHAT'S WRONG WITH ENDORSING A PRODUCT YOU CONSUME OR ENJOY?
WHAT SORT OF DRINK DO YOU PREFER?
DIET COKE-- BUT LISTEN...
"JUST FOR THE TASTE OF IT."
ABSOLUTELY.
AND IF SOMEBODY TOOK A PICTURE OF YOU WITH A "DIET COKE" IN YOUR HAND-- WOULD YOU OBJECT TO THAT PICTURE BEING PUBLISHED? OF COURSE NOT? SO, WHY NOT GET PAID FOR THAT?
IT'S NOT ME, HAWKINS.
I'M NOT WILLING TO SELL OUT MY INTEGRITY TO THE HIGHEST BIDDER. I CAN DO WITHOUT A VIPER AUTOMOBILE. I'VE GOT AN OLD CHEVY. IT RUNS.
YOU FEEL THIS WAY NOW-- BUT IT WON'T LAST.
THE MERCHANDISE DEAL ALWAYS ENCOURAGED THE BEST AND BRIGHTEST TO COME JOIN THE TEAM.
YOU CAN'T SQUASH THEIR DREAMS.
I CAN TRY.

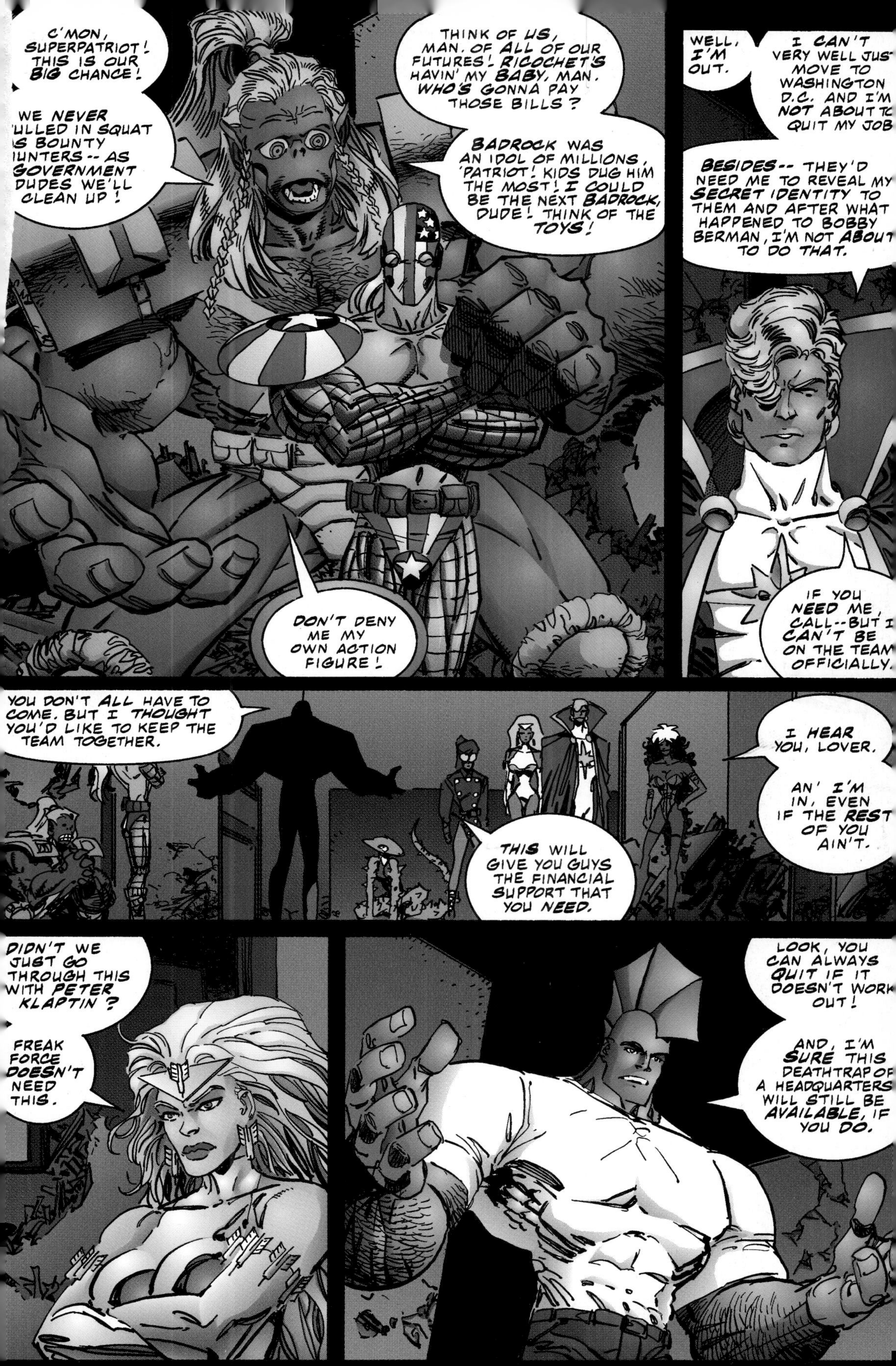
C'MON, SUPERPATRIOT! THIS IS OUR BIG CHANCE!
WE NEVER ULLED IN SQUAT AS BOUNTY UNTERS -- AS GOVERNMENT DUDES WE'LL CLEAN UP!
THINK OF US, MAN. OF ALL OF OUR FUTURES! RICOCHET'S HAVIN' MY BABY, MAN. WHO'S GONNA PAY THOSE BILLS?
BADROCK WAS AN IDOL OF MILLIONS, 'PATRIOT! KIDS DUG HIM THE MOST! I COULD BE THE NEXT BADROCK, DUDE! THINK OF THE TOYS!
DON'T DENY ME MY OWN ACTION FIGURE!
WELL, I'M OUT.
I CAN'T VERY WELL JUST MOVE TO WASHINGTON D.C. AND I'M NOT ABOUT TO QUIT MY JOB
BESIDES -- THEY'D NEED ME TO REVEAL MY SECRET IDENTITY TO THEM AND AFTER WHAT HAPPENED TO BOBBY BERMAN, I'M NOT ABOUT TO DO THAT.
IF YOU NEED ME, CALL -- BUT I CAN'T BE ON THE TEAM OFFICIALLY.
YOU DON'T ALL HAVE TO COME. BUT I THOUGHT YOU'D LIKE TO KEEP THE TEAM TOGETHER.
THIS WILL GIVE YOU GUYS THE FINANCIAL SUPPORT THAT YOU NEED.
I HEAR YOU, LOVER.
AN' I'M IN, EVEN IF THE REST OF YOU AIN'T.
DIDN'T WE JUST GO THROUGH THIS WITH PETER KLAPTIN?
FREAK FORCE DOESN'T NEED THIS.
LOOK, YOU CAN ALWAYS QUIT IF IT DOESN'T WORK OUT!
AND, I'M SURE THIS DEATHTRAP OF A HEADQUARTERS WILL STILL BE AVAILABLE, IF YOU DO.

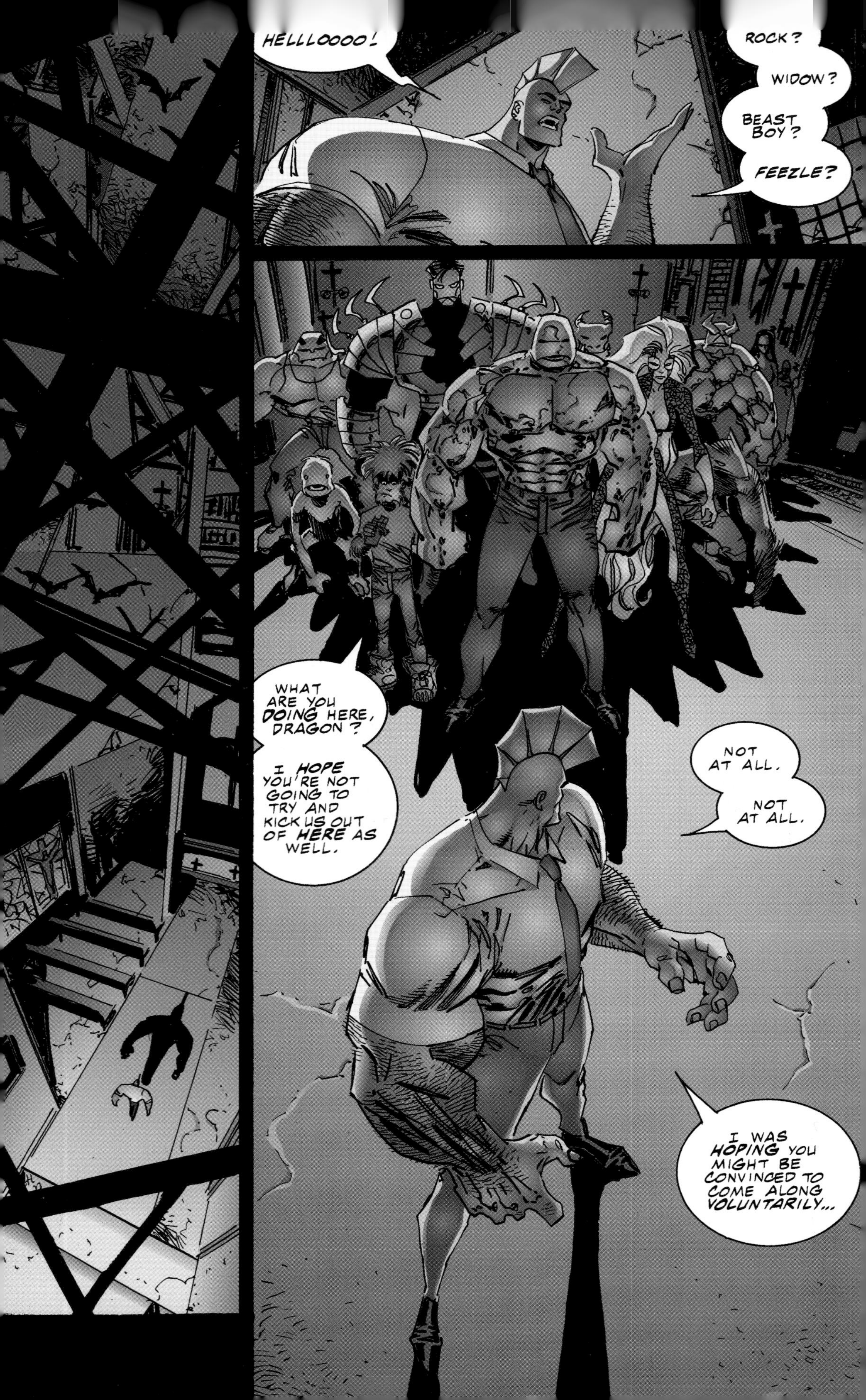

HELLLOOOO!
ROCK?
WIDOW?
BEAST BOY?
FEEZLE?
WHAT ARE YOU DOING HERE, DRAGON?
I HOPE YOU'RE NOT GOING TO TRY AND KICK US OUT OF HERE AS WELL.
NOT AT ALL.
NOT AT ALL.
I WAS HOPING YOU MIGHT BE CONVINCED TO COME ALONG VOLUNTARILY...

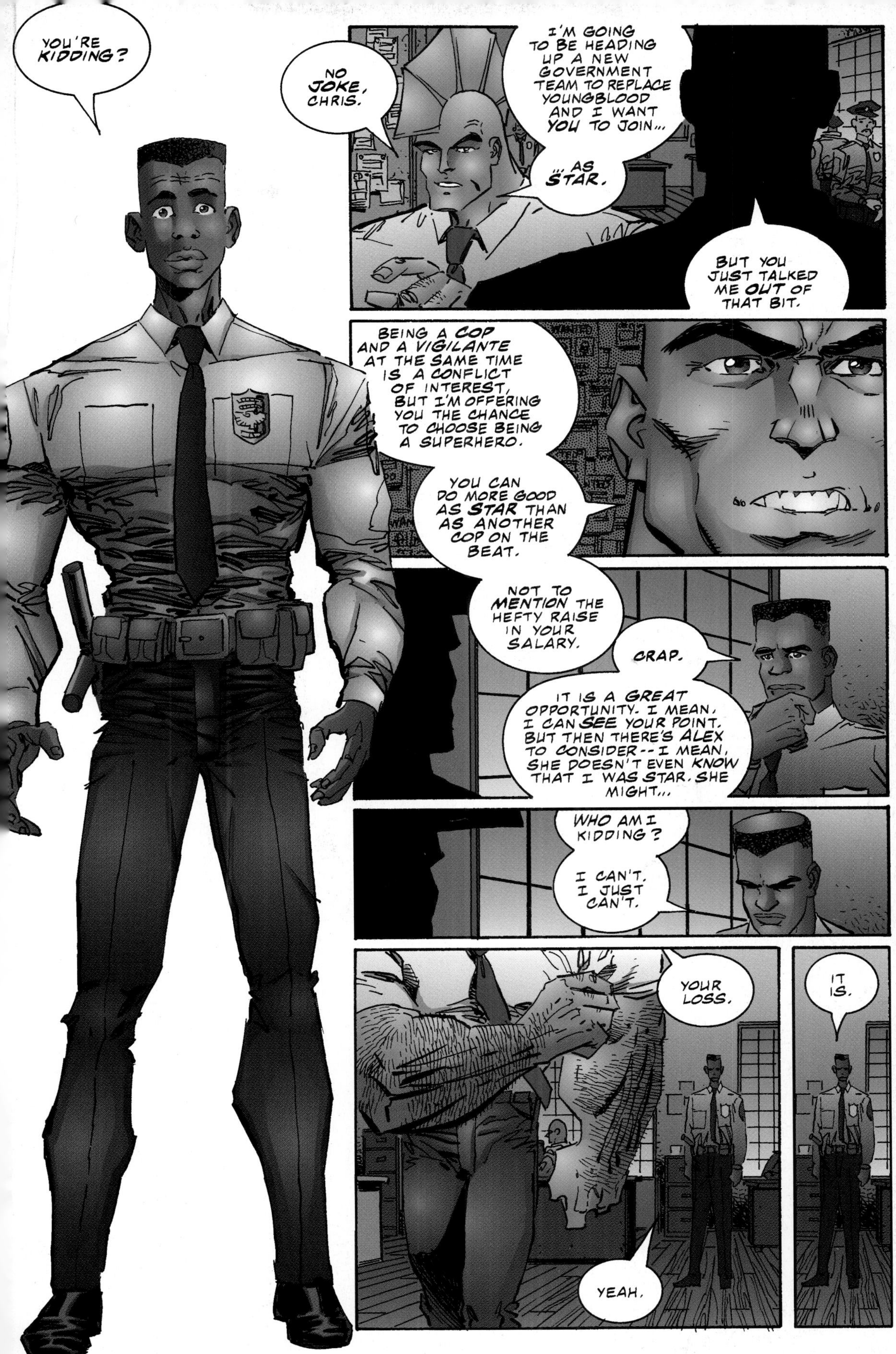
YOU'RE KIDDING?
NO JOKE, CHRIS.
I'M GOING TO BE HEADING UP A NEW GOVERNMENT TEAM TO REPLACE YOUNGBLOOD AND I WANT YOU TO JOIN...
...AS STAR.
BUT YOU JUST TALKED ME OUT OF THAT BIT.
BEING A COP AND A VIGILANTE AT THE SAME TIME IS A CONFLICT OF INTEREST, BUT I'M OFFERING YOU THE CHANCE TO CHOOSE BEING A SUPERHERO.
YOU CAN DO MORE GOOD AS STAR THAN AS ANOTHER COP ON THE BEAT.
NOT TO MENTION THE HEFTY RAISE IN YOUR SALARY.
CRAP.
IT IS A GREAT OPPORTUNITY. I MEAN, I CAN SEE YOUR POINT. BUT THEN THERE'S ALEX TO CONSIDER--I MEAN, SHE DOESN'T EVEN KNOW THAT I WAS STAR. SHE MIGHT...
WHO AM I KIDDING?
I CAN'T. I JUST CAN'T.
YOUR LOSS.
YEAH.
IT IS.

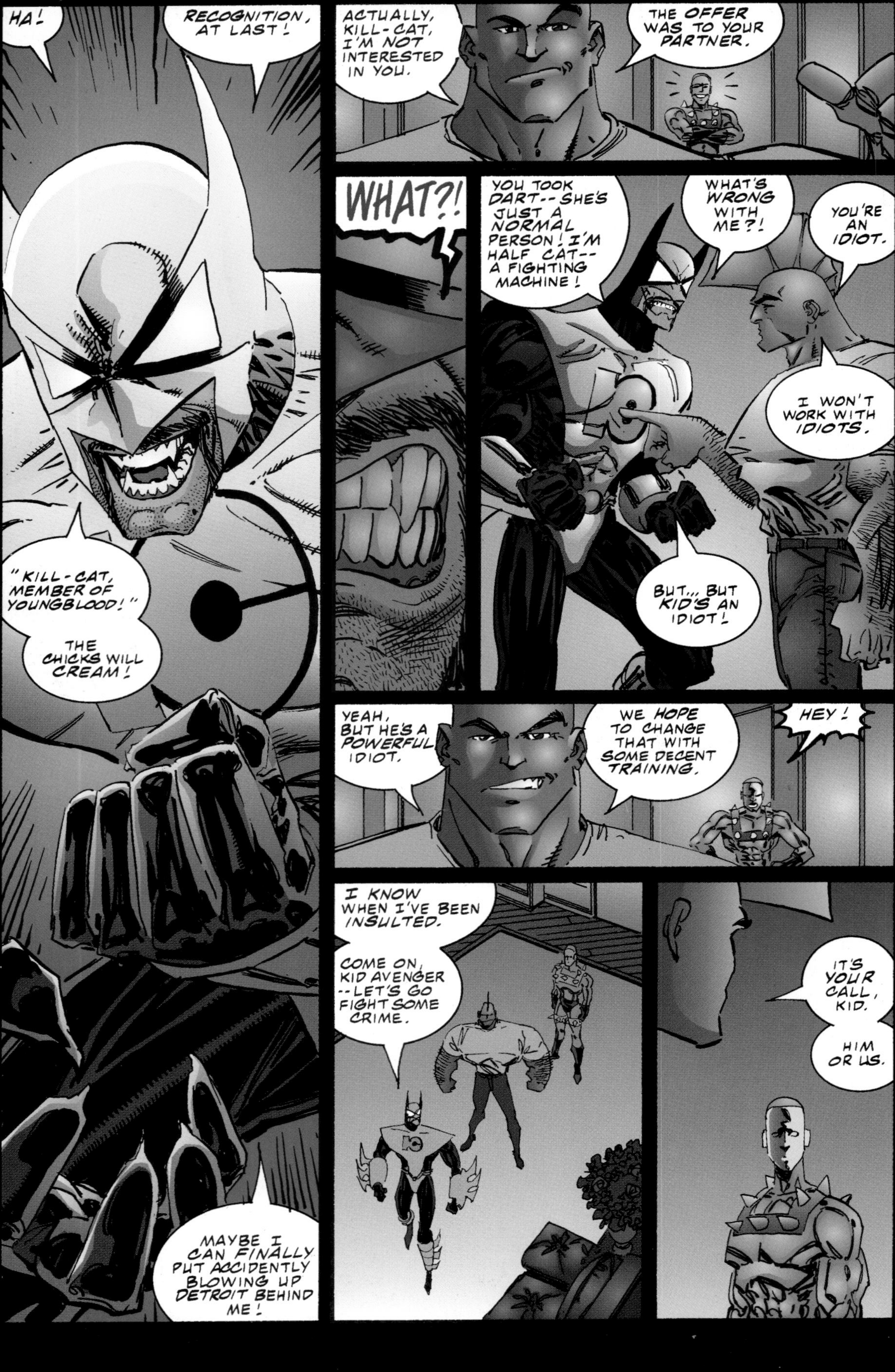
HA!
RECOGNITION, AT LAST!
"KILL-CAT, MEMBER OF YOUNGBLOOD!"
THE CHICKS WILL CREAM!
MAYBE I CAN FINALLY PUT ACCIDENTLY BLOWING UP DETROIT BEHIND ME!
ACTUALLY, KILL-CAT, I'M NOT INTERESTED IN YOU.
THE OFFER WAS TO YOUR PARTNER.
WHAT?!
YOU TOOK DART-- SHE'S JUST A NORMAL PERSON! I'M HALF CAT-- A FIGHTING MACHINE!
WHAT'S WRONG WITH ME?!
YOU'RE AN IDIOT.
I WON'T WORK WITH IDIOTS.
BUT... BUT KID'S AN IDIOT!
YEAH, BUT HE'S A POWERFUL IDIOT.
WE HOPE TO CHANGE THAT WITH SOME DECENT TRAINING.
HEY!
I KNOW WHEN I'VE BEEN INSULTED.
COME ON, KID AVENGER --LET'S GO FIGHT SOME CRIME.
IT'S YOUR CALL, KID.
HIM OR US.

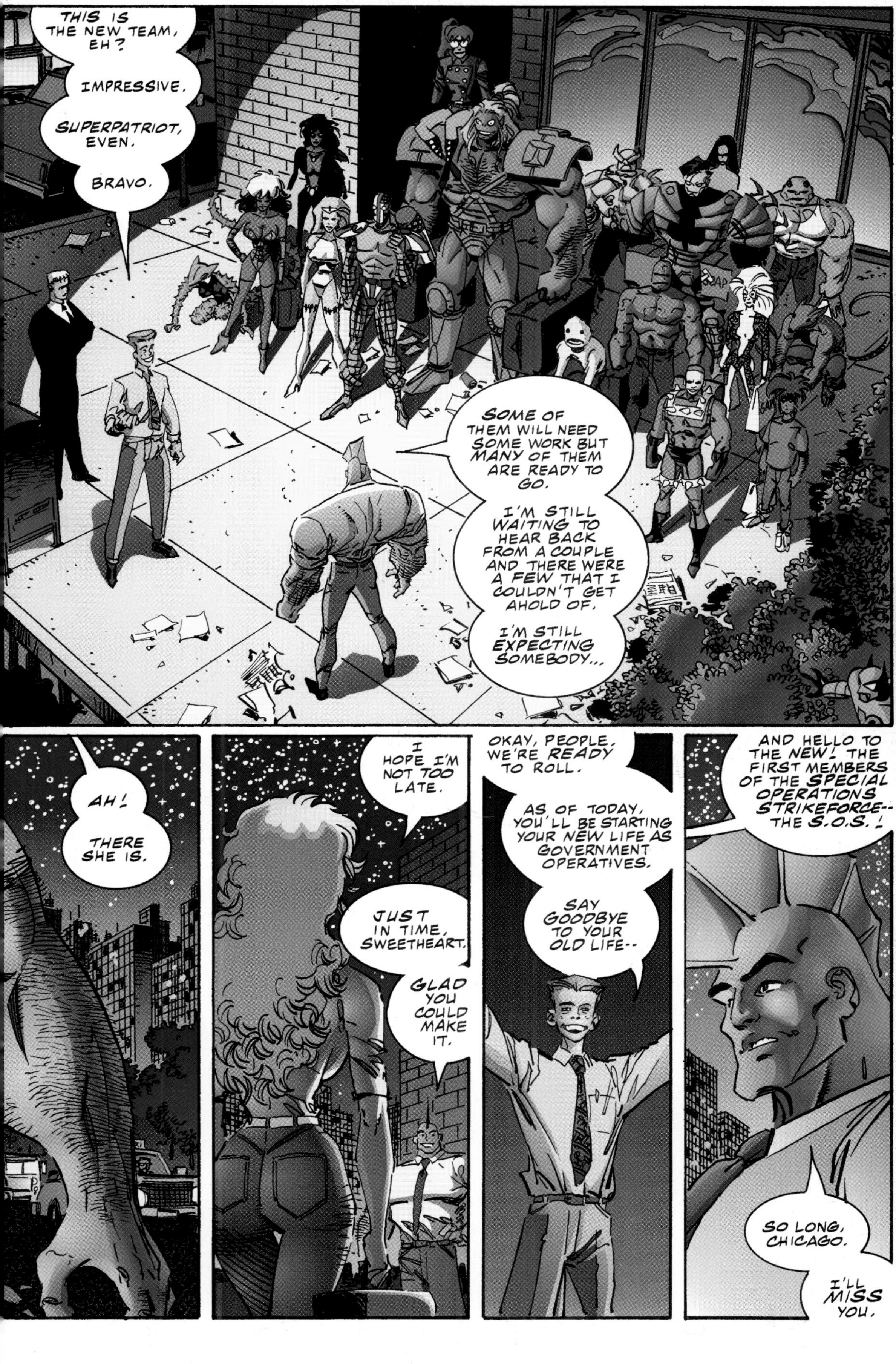
THIS IS THE NEW TEAM, EH?
IMPRESSIVE.
SUPERPATRIOT, EVEN.
BRAVO.
SOME OF THEM WILL NEED SOME WORK BUT MANY OF THEM ARE READY TO GO.
I'M STILL WAITING TO HEAR BACK FROM A COUPLE AND THERE WERE A FEW THAT I COULDN'T GET AHOLD OF.
I'M STILL EXPECTING SOMEBODY...
AH!
THERE SHE IS.
I HOPE I'M NOT TOO LATE.
JUST IN TIME, SWEETHEART.
GLAD YOU COULD MAKE IT.
OKAY, PEOPLE, WE'RE READY TO ROLL.
AS OF TODAY, YOU'LL BE STARTING YOUR NEW LIFE AS GOVERNMENT OPERATIVES.
SAY GOODBYE TO YOUR OLD LIFE--
AND HELLO TO THE NEW! THE FIRST MEMBERS OF THE SPECIAL OPERATIONS STRIKEFORCE-- THE S.O.S.!
SO LONG, CHICAGO.
I'LL MISS YOU.

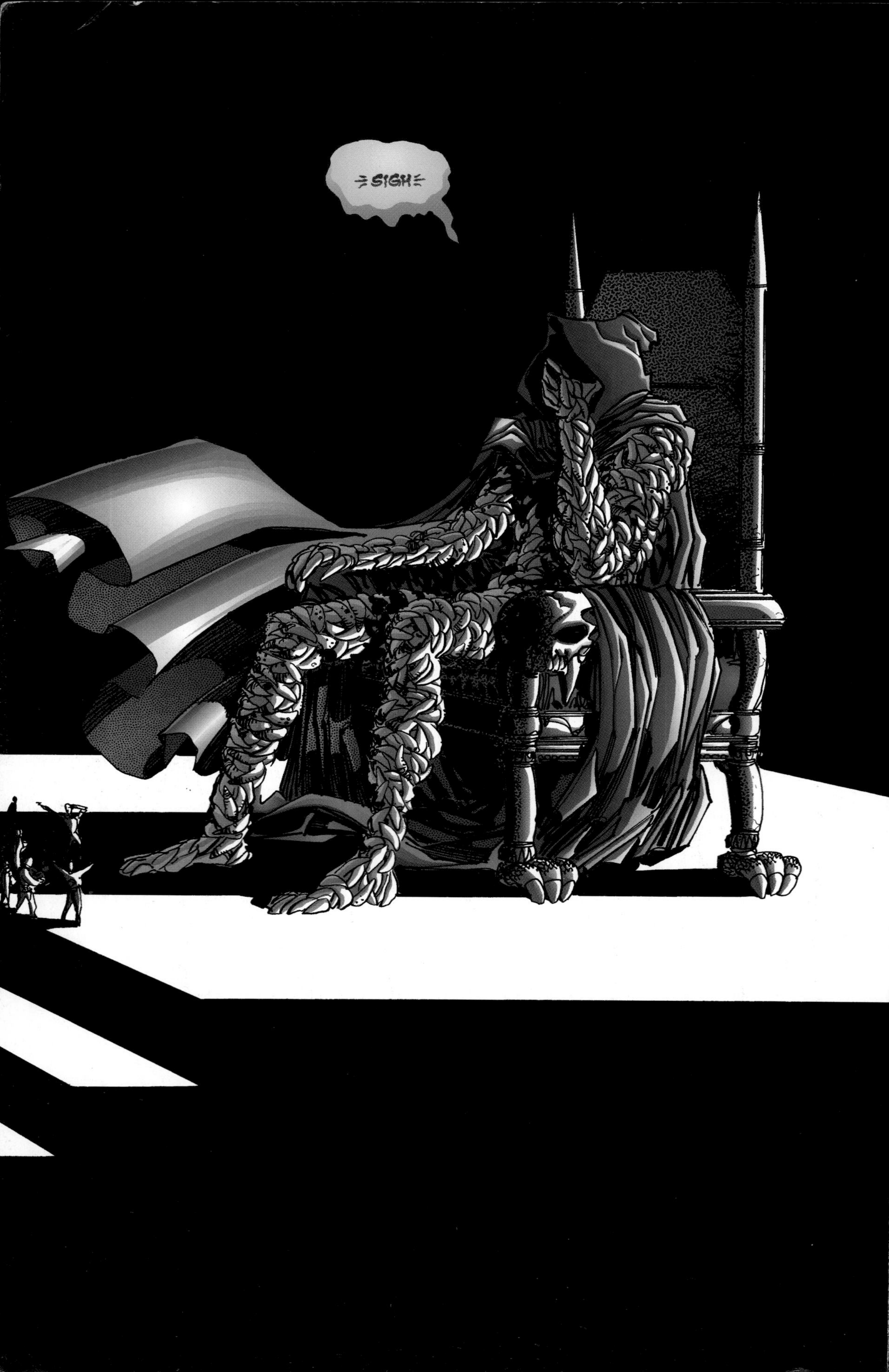
SIGH

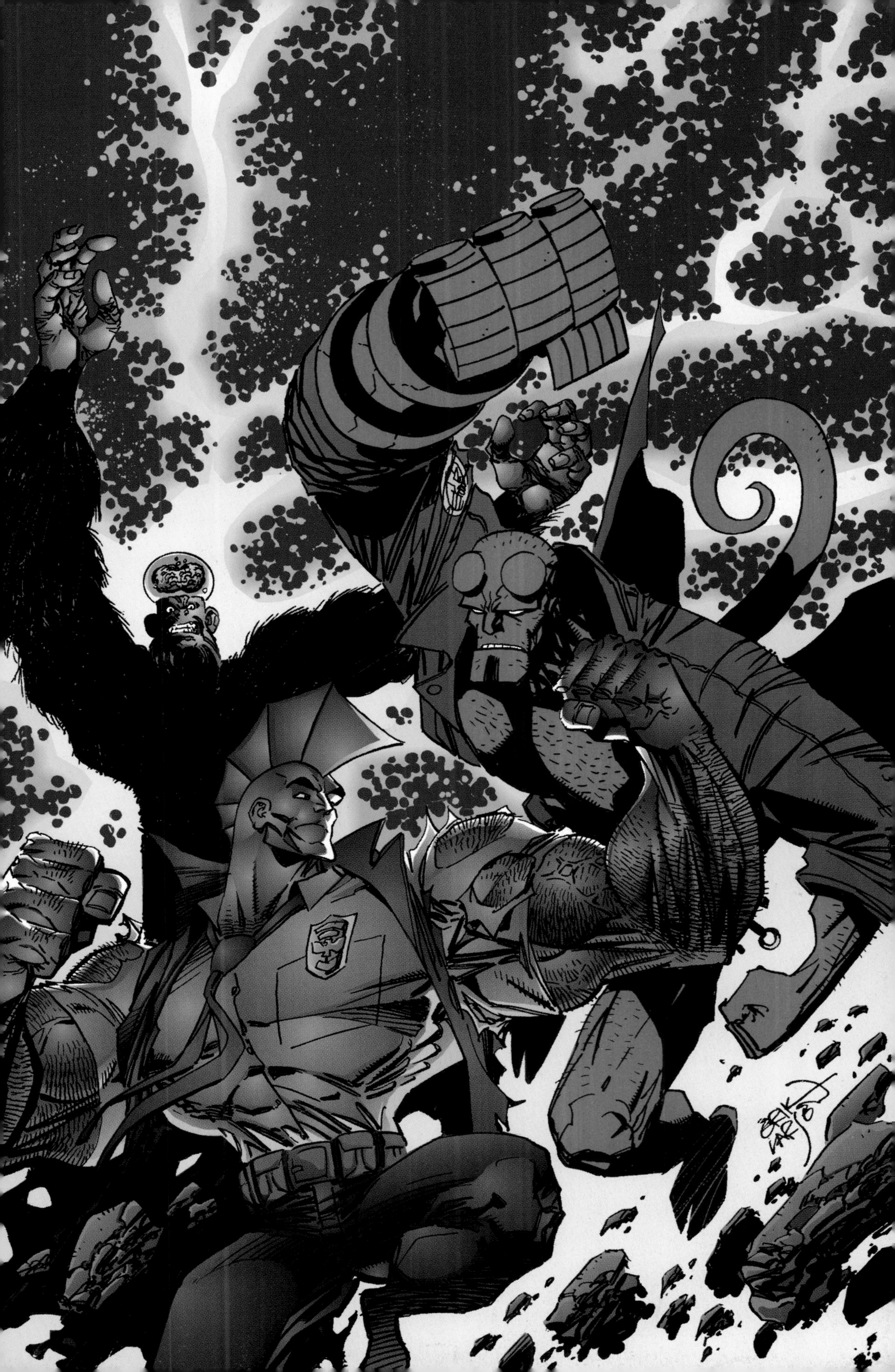

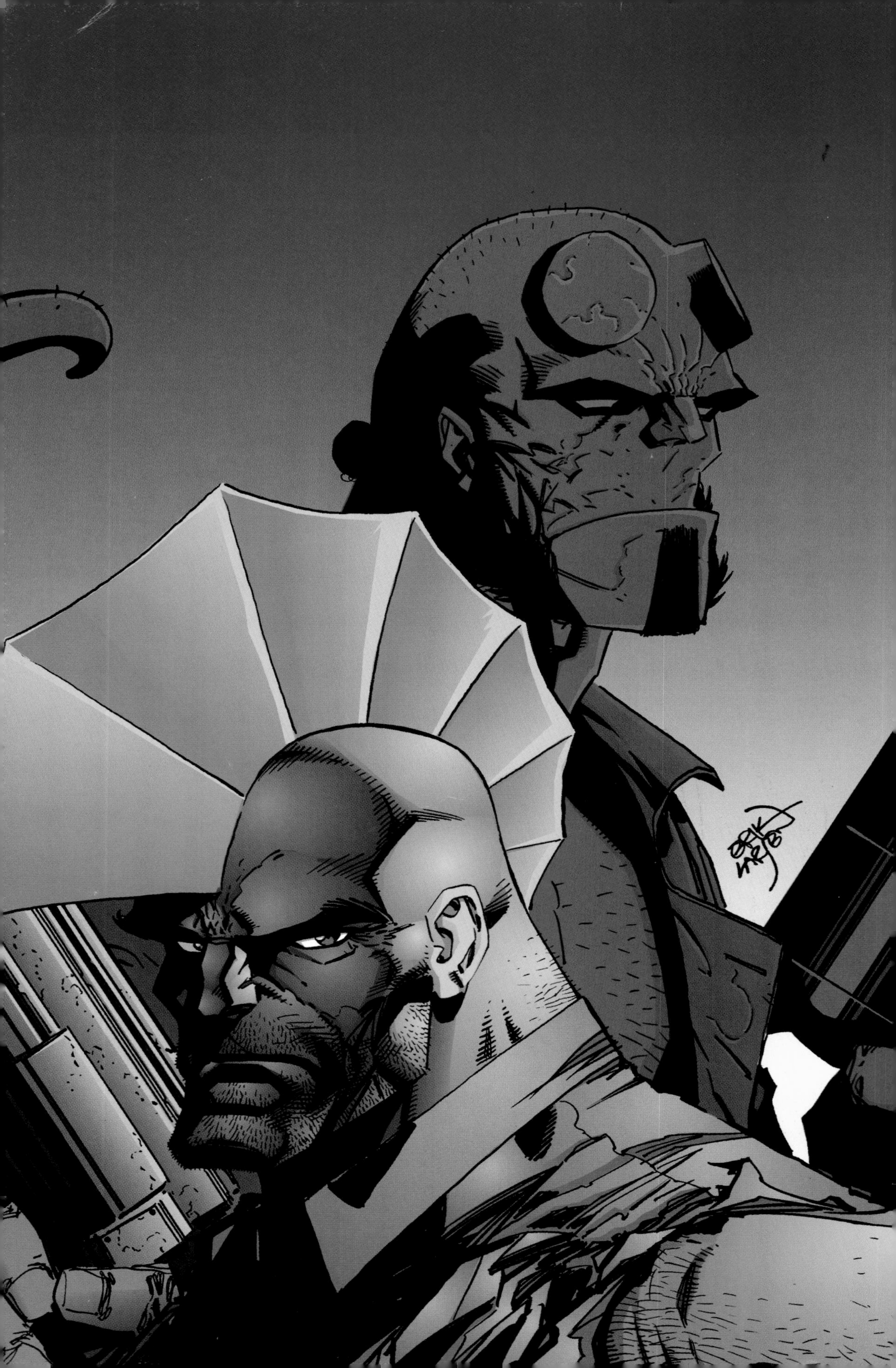

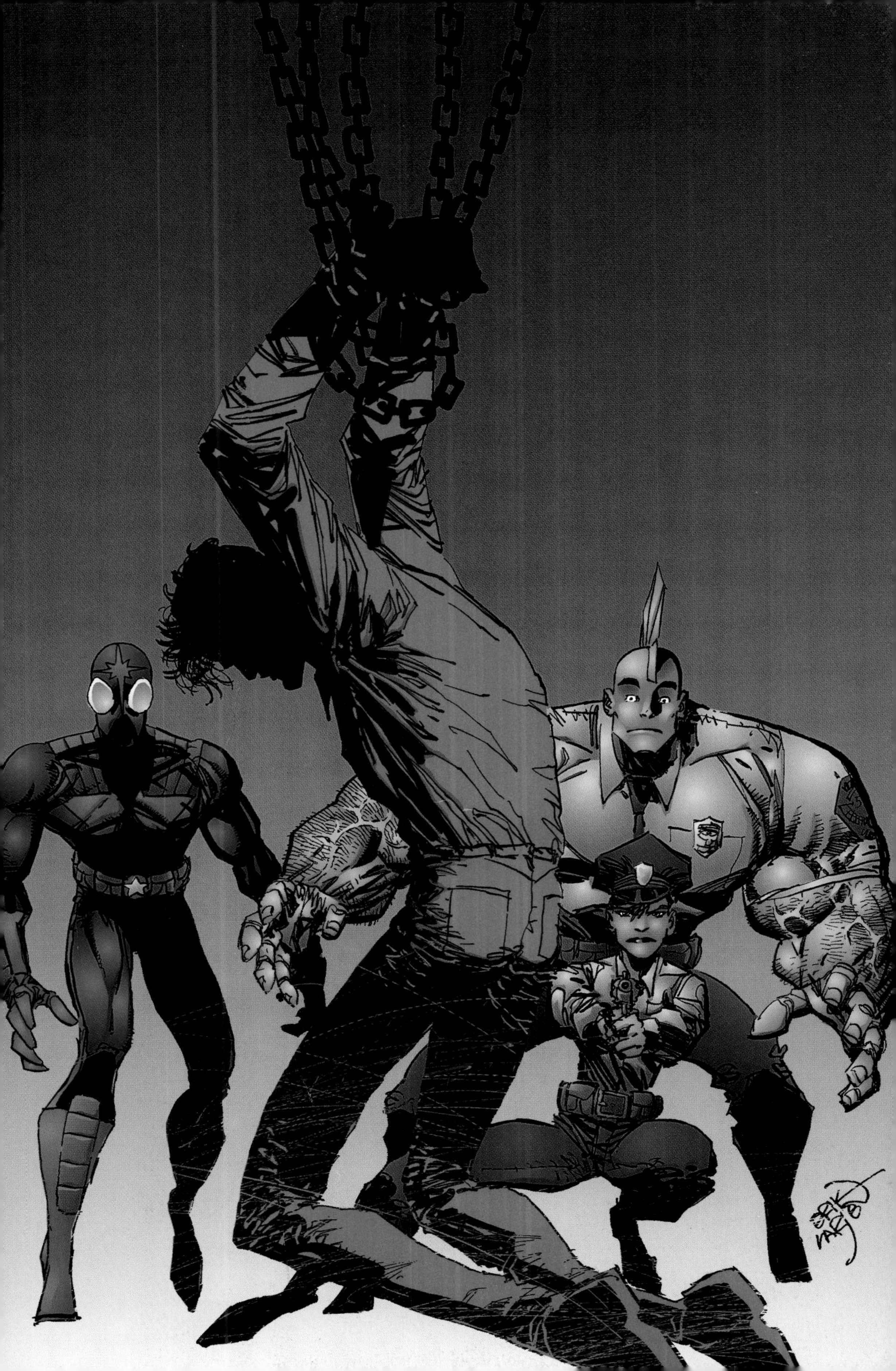

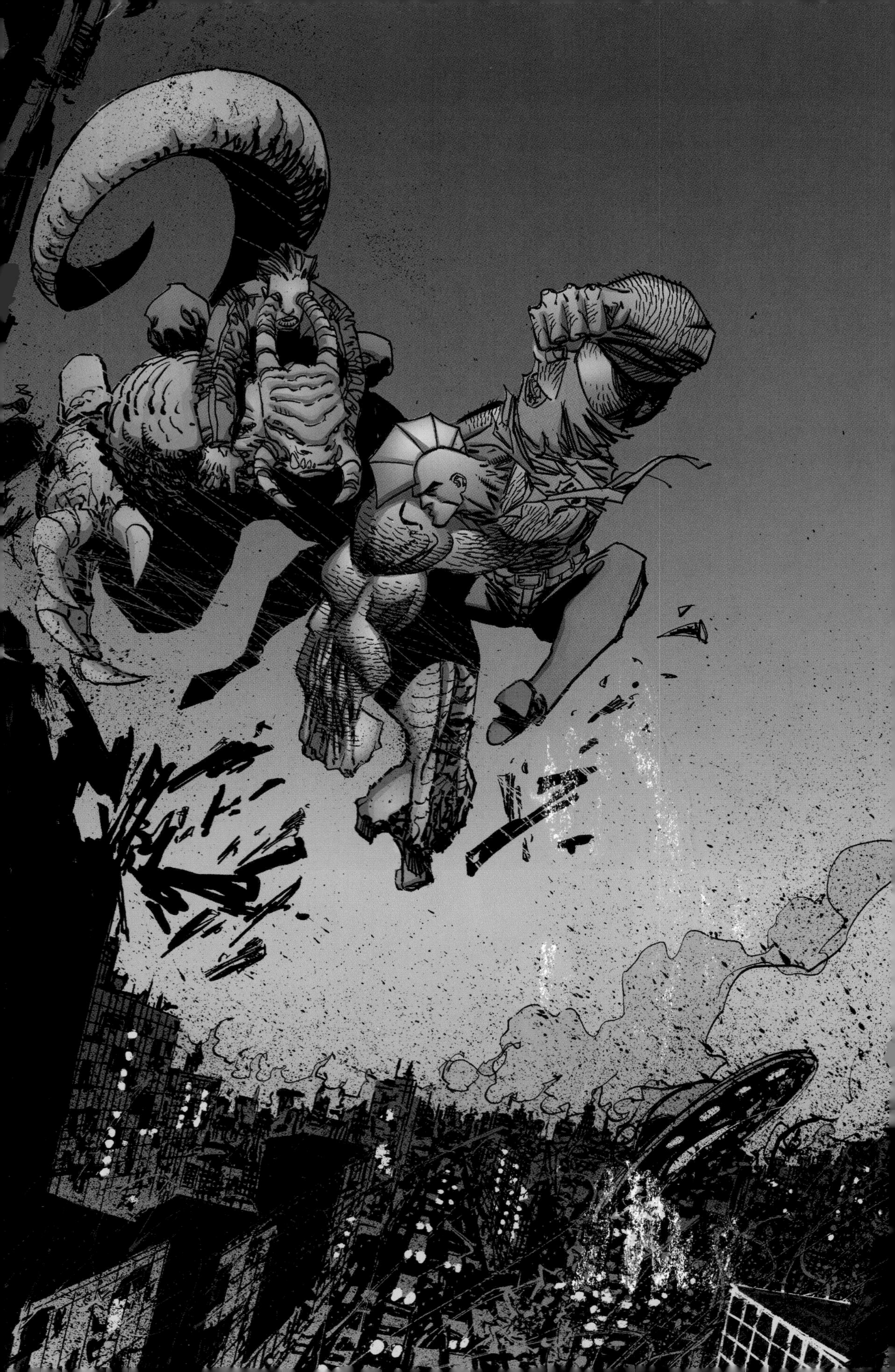

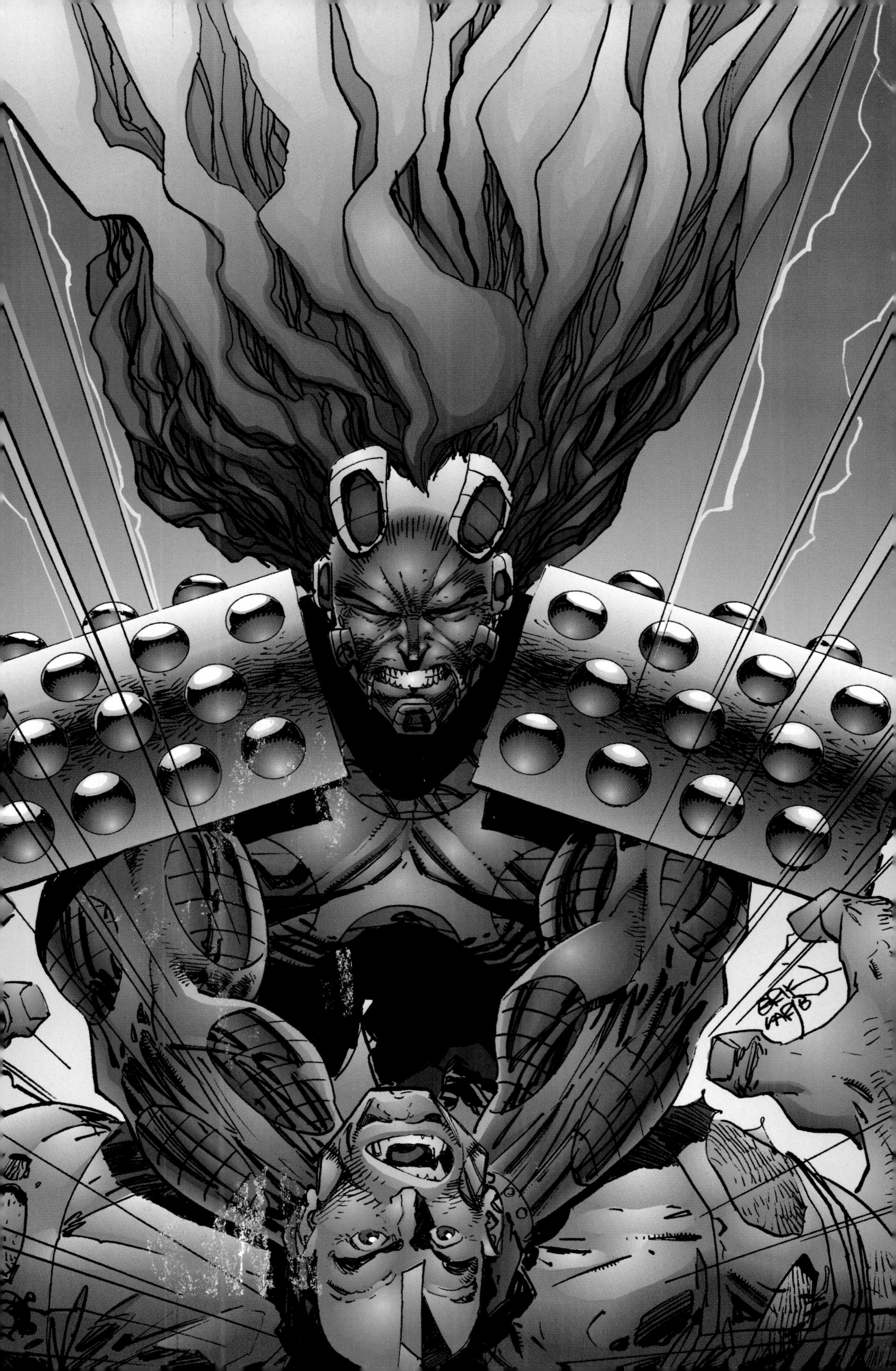

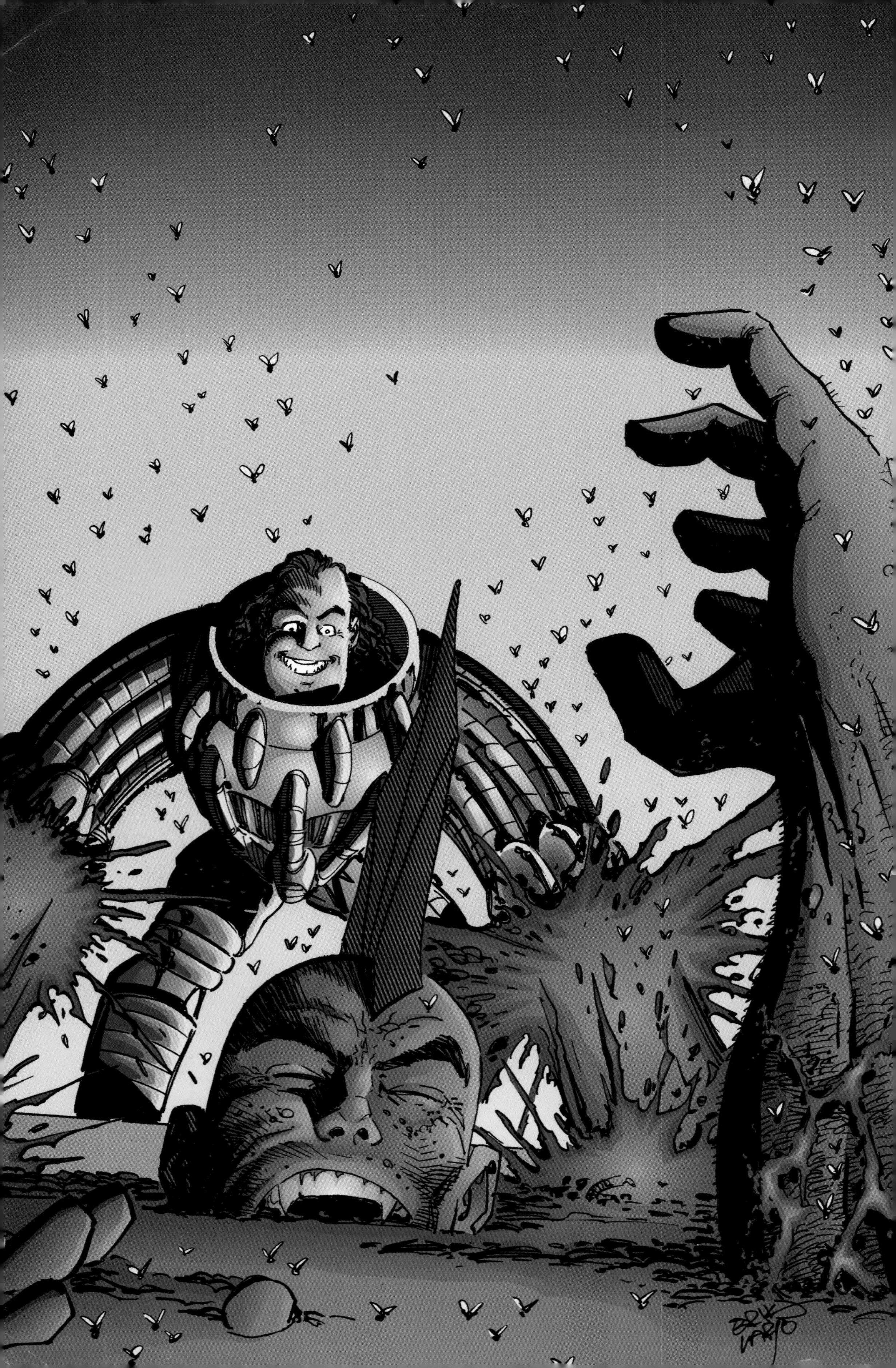

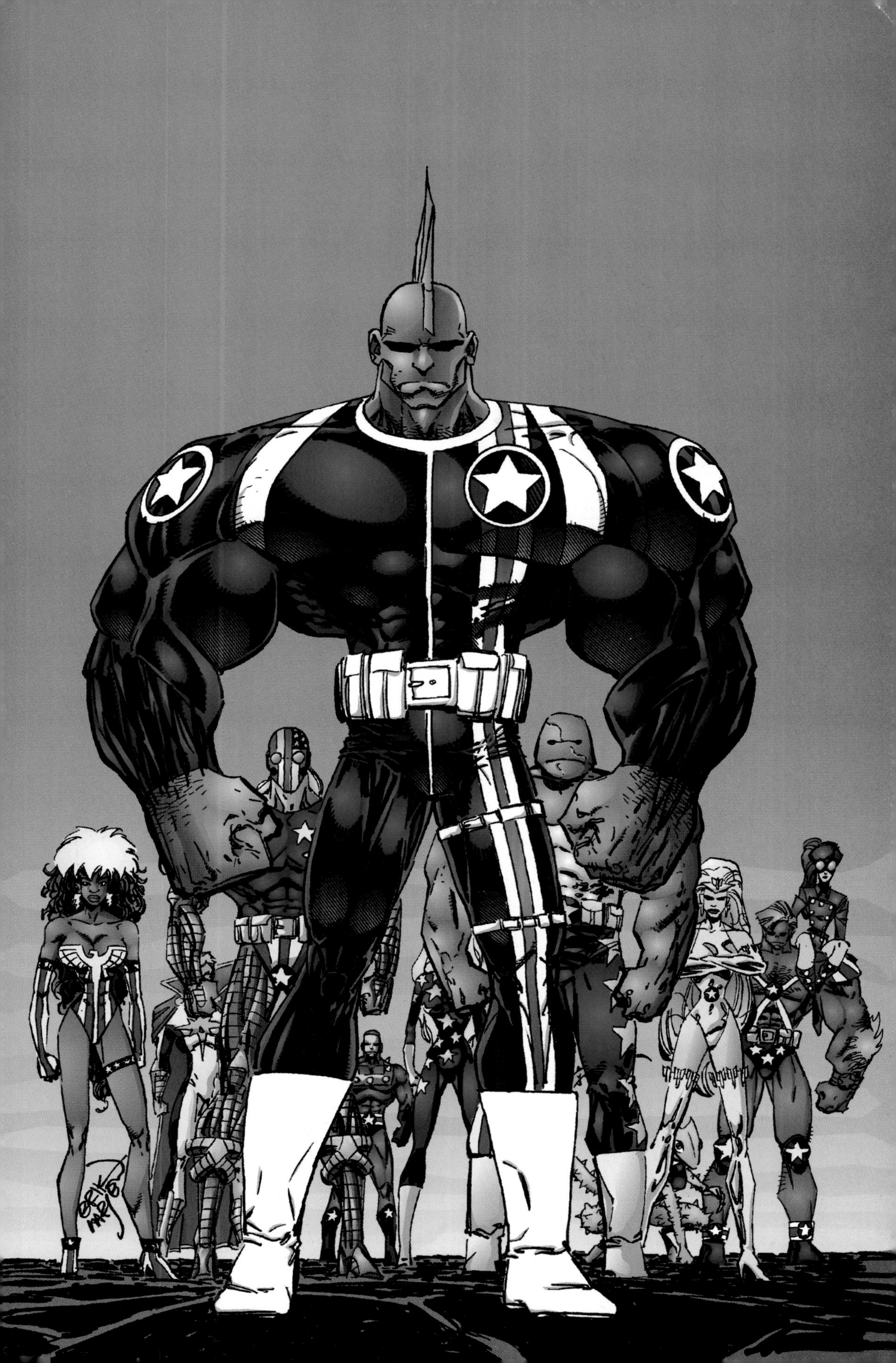

SAVAGE DRAGON® SKETCH BOOK

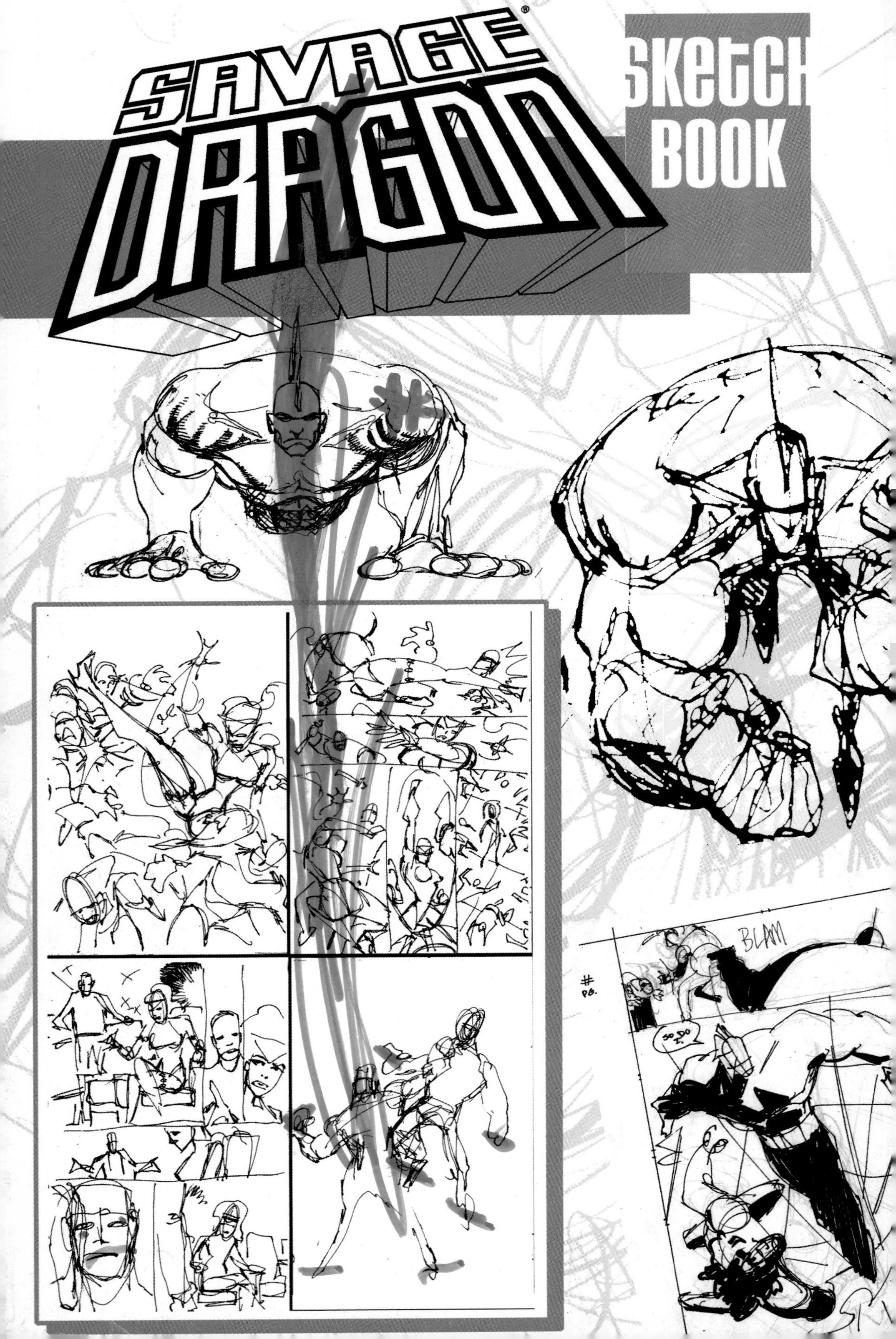
BLAM
SO DO I.
PG.

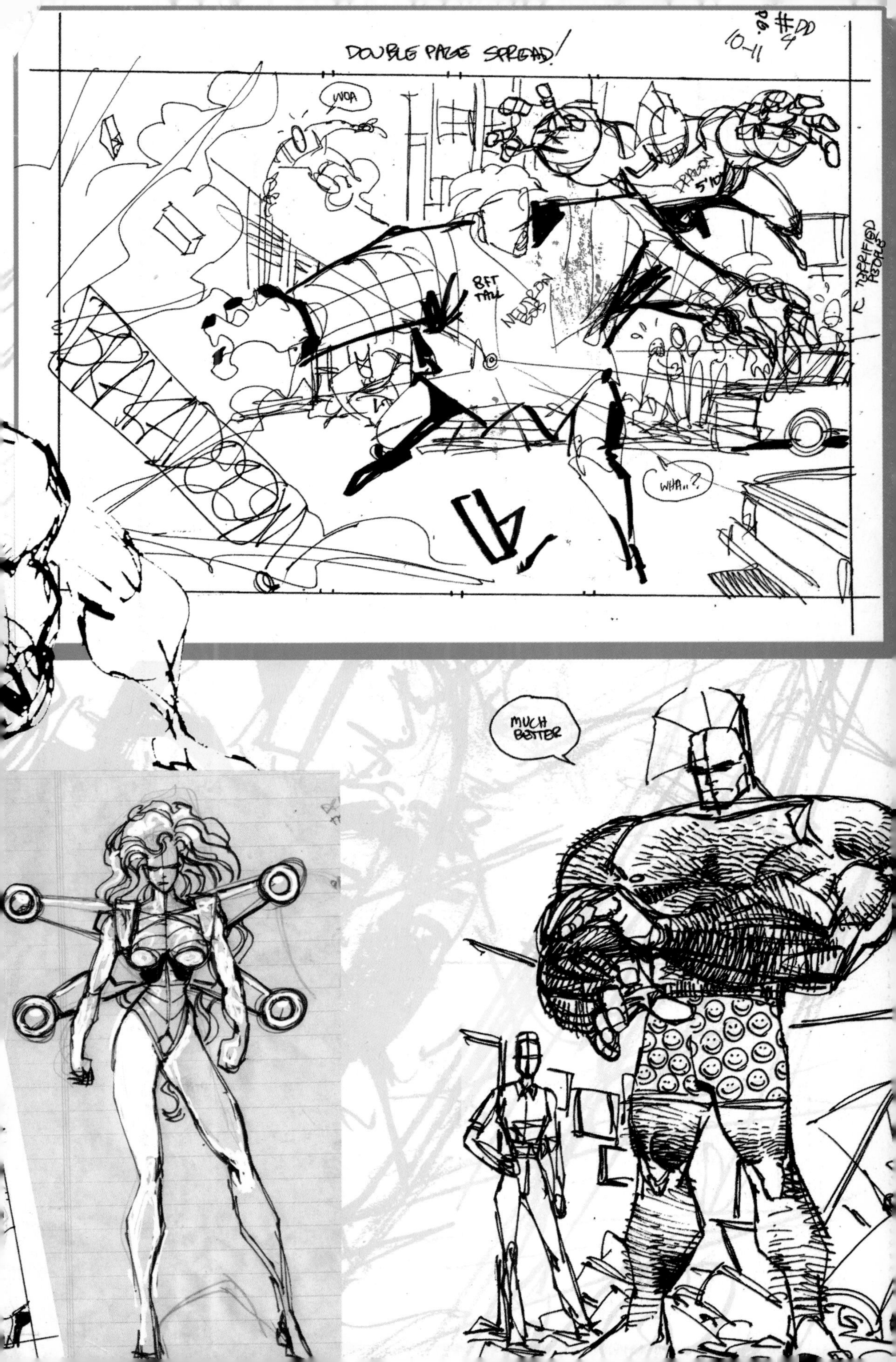
DOUBLE PAGE SPREAD!
PG. #DD 4
10–11
WOA
DRAGON 5'10
8FT TALL
NEUTRON BOB
TERRIFIED PEOPLE
WHA..?
MUCH BETTER

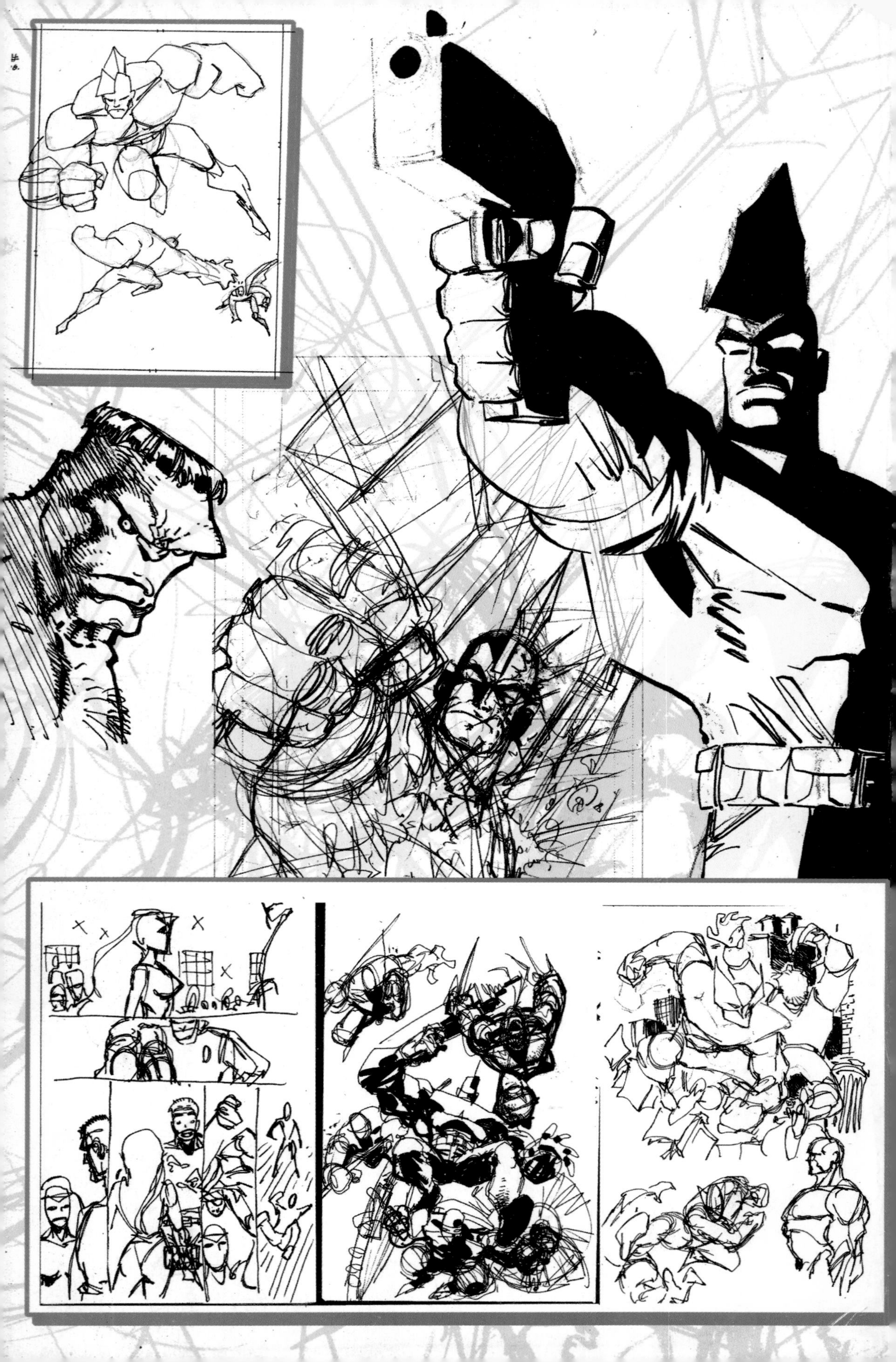